The Spear, the Sword, and the Pebble

Also available from Bloomsbury

Corinth in Late Antiquity by Amelia R. Brown
Greek Warfare by Hans van Wees
Parody, Politics and the Populace in Greek Old Comedy by Donald Sells
Periclean Athens by P. J. Rhodes

The Spear, the Scroll, and the Pebble

*How the Greek City-State Developed as a
Male Warrior-Citizen Collective*

Richard A. Billows

BLOOMSBURY ACADEMIC
LONDON • NEW YORK • OXFORD • NEW DELHI • SYDNEY

BLOOMSBURY ACADEMIC

Bloomsbury Publishing Plc

50 Bedford Square, London, WC1B 3DP, UK
1385 Broadway, New York, NY 10018, USA
29 Earlsfort Terrace, Dublin 2, Ireland

BLOOMSBURY, BLOOMSBURY ACADEMIC and the Diana logo are trademarks of
Bloomsbury Publishing Plc

First published in Great Britain 2023

Copyright © Richard A. Billows, 2023

Richard A. Billows has asserted his right under the Copyright, Designs and Patents Act, 1988, to be identified as Author of this work.

For legal purposes the Acknowledgments on p. xiii constitute an extension of this copyright page.

Cover design: Terry Woodley
Cover image © KHM-Museumsverband

All rights reserved. No part of this publication may be reproduced or transmitted in any form or by any means, electronic or mechanical, including photocopying, recording, or any information storage or retrieval system, without prior permission in writing from the publishers.

Bloomsbury Publishing Plc does not have any control over, or responsibility for, any third-party websites referred to or in this book. All internet addresses given in this book were correct at the time of going to press. The author and publisher regret any inconvenience caused if addresses have changed or sites have ceased to exist, but can accept no responsibility for any such changes.

A catalogue record for this book is available from the British Library.

Library of Congress Cataloging-in-Publication Data
Names: Billows, Richard A., author. Title: The spear, the scroll, and the pebble : how the Greek city-state developed as a male warrior-citizen collective / by Richard A. Billows. Description: London; New York: Bloomsbury Academic, [2023] | Includes bibliographical references. Identifiers: LCCN 2022030733 | ISBN 9781350289192 (paperback) | ISBN 9781350289208 (hardback) | ISBN 9781350289215 (ebook) | ISBN 9781350289222 (epub) | ISBN 9781350289239 Subjects: LCSH: City-states–Greece—History—To 1500. | Greece—Politics and government--To 146 B.C. | Greece—Civilization—To 146 B.C. Classification: LCC DF82 .B55 2023 | DDC 938—dc23/eng/20220629 LC record available at https://lccn.loc.gov/2022030733

ISBN:	HB:	978-1-3502-8920-8
	PB:	978-1-3502-8919-2
	ePDF:	978-1-3502-8921-5
	eBook:	978-1-3502-8922-2

Typeset by RefineCatch Limited, Bungay, Suffolk
Printed and bound in Great Britain

To find out more about our authors and books visit www.bloomsbury.com and sign up for our newsletters.

*This book is dedicated to the memory of
Princess, Thomas, Ophelia, and Ty
and to
Ursula, Kalli, Myfanwy, and Finn
may they live long and prosper*

Contents

List of Illustrations	ix
Abbreviations	xi
Acknowledgments	xiii
Map of Southern Greek City-States	xv

	Introduction	1
	What is a *Polis*?	2
	What is a City-State?	4
1	The Origin and Early Development of the City-State	15
	Early Iron Age Communities	15
	Overseas Settlements and City-State Development	26
	The Ethnos Model: Phokis	29
	The Centrifugal Polis Model: Boiotia and the Argolid	31
	The Centripetal Polis Model 1: Sparta and the Perioikic System	37
	The Centripetal Polis Model 2: Athens and the Deme System	39
	Conclusion: The Development of the City-State	45
2	Economic Development and the City-State	47
	Preconditions: Geography, Climate, and Demography	50
	The Early Greek Economy	55
	The Developed Greek Economy	59
	Making a Living in the Greek Economy	69
	Conclusion: The Greek City as Center of Economic Specialization and Exchange	76
3	The Spear: Warfare and the City-State	81
	Early Greek Warfare	82
	Hoplite Warfare	87
	The Hoplite Revolution	93
	Fleets in the Greek World: The Role of the Poor in Warfare	102

	Conclusion: The City-State as a Warrior Collective	105
4	The Pebble: Collective Decision Making and the City-State	107
	From Oligarchy to Democracy: The Varieties of Collective Decision Making	108
	The Political Theory of Collective Decision Making	116
	Public Information and Political Participation	128
	Conclusion: The City-State as a Collective of Informed Citizens	136
5	The Scroll: Literacy and the City-State	139
	The Origin and Spread of the Greek Alphabet	141
	Schools and the Spread of Literacy	146
	The Evidence for Reading and Writing	161
	Conclusion: The Literate Citizen	173

Conclusion: Literate Citizen-Warriors and City-State Culture 175

Appendix 1: A Note on the Sources 183
Appendix 2: Aristotle's *Politeiai* 185
Appendix 3: Overseas Settlements and *Metropoleis* 191
Notes 193
Bibliography 239
Index 259

Illustrations

1 Detail from the Chigi vase (mid seventh century) showing Greek hoplite warriors advancing in neat lines to confront each other in battle. (The Chigi vase is in the National Etruscan Museum, Villa Giulia, Rome, inv. no. 22697.) Public domain image retrieved from Wikimedia Creative Commons, Szilas/Gallery 2016
2 Athenian fifth-century public inscription concerning cultic matters, now in the Museum of Cycladic Art, Athens. Photo credit: Gary Lee Todd (2016) retrieved from Creative Commons under CCO 1.0 Universal Public Domain Dedication license (CCO 1.0)
3 School scene showing boys learning to read and play the lyre, from a red-figure Attic drinking cup painted by Douris *c.* 485 BCE. Antikensammlung, Staatliche Museen zu Berlin—Stiftung Preussischer Kulturbesitz. Foto: Johannes Laurentius, F 2285
4 Athenian *ostraka* (pot sherds) used to vote in an ostracism, one showing the name Kallias son of Kratias (ostracized in 485) and three with the name Megakles son of Hippokrates (ostracized in 486), now in the Cycladic Art Museum, Athens. Photo credit: Tilemahos Efthimiadis (2009) retrieved from Creative Commons under Attribution 2.0 Generic license (CC BY 2.0)

Abbreviations

ABSA	Annual of the British School at Athens
AJA	American Journal of Archaeology
AJAH	American Journal of Ancient History
AJP	American Journal of Philology
AR	Archaeological Reports
ASNSP	Annali della Scuole Normale Superiore di Pisa
AW	Ancient World
BABesch	Bulletin Antieke Beschaving (Annual Papers on Mediterranean Archaeology)
BICS	Bulletin of the Institute of Classical Studies
BNJ	Brill's New Jacoby
BSA	British School at Athens
CA	Classical Antiquity
CAH	Cambridge Ancient History
CJ	Classical Journal
CP/CPh	Classical Philology
CQ	Classical Quarterly
CR	Classical Review
EA	Epigraphica Anatolica
EJAS	European Journal of American Studies
G&R	Greece and Rome
GHI	Greek Historical Inscriptions

GRBS	Greek, Roman, and Byzantine Studies
HSCPh	Harvard Studies in Classical Philology
IG	Inscriptiones Graecae
JFA	Journal of Field Archaeology
JHS	Journal of Hellenic Studies
JITE	Journal of Institutional and Theoretical Economics
LSJ	Liddel, Scott, and Jones (eds.) *Greek-English Lexicon* (9th ed.)
MMJ	Metropolitan Museum Journal
OGIS	Orientis Graecae Inscriptiones Selectae (ed. W. Dittenberger)
PAPS	Proceedings of the American Philosophical Society
PCPS	Proceedings of the Cambridge Philological Society
RevArch	Revue Archaeologique
REG	Revue des Études Grecques
SEG	Supplementum Epigraphicum Graecum
SIG/Syll	Sylloge Inscriptionum Graecarum (3rd ed., W. Dittenberger)
TAPhA	Transactions and Proceedings of the American Philological Association
WJA	Würzburger Jahrbücher für die Altertumswissenschaft
ZPE	Zeitschrift für Papyrologie und Epigraphik

Acknowledgments

The idea of writing a book about the development of the Greek city-states first occurred to me many years ago now, around 1990. After doing a good bit of background reading and some preliminary writing, however, I reached the conclusion that a book on the Greek city-states would quite possibly be made instantly obsolete by the work of the Copenhagen *polis* project directed by Mogens Hansen, and I laid my work aside until that project had have been completed. In the intervening years, I became distracted by various other projects of my own—editing and commenting on the Hellenika Oxyrhynchia for *Brill's New Jacoby*, and writing books on Julius Caesar, the battle of Marathon, and Philip and Alexander of Macedonia, for example—but my interest in the Greek city-states continued to develop in my mind. It became clear to me that the Copenhagen project would not interfere with the kind of book I wanted to write at all, but my idea about what sort of book I wanted to write had changed drastically, partly due to my growing interest in the role of literacy in the city-states, so that the present work bears little resemblance to what I had in mind *c.* 1990, which is, I think, very much for the good.

It is a pleasure to acknowledge the help of Kurt Raaflaub, who read a very early draft of Chapter 1 and helped me improve it significantly and likewise of Alan Shapiro who kindly read my pages on Athens. Tal Ish Shalom read Chapters 4 and 5 and had some interesting comments to contribute, and for Chapter 5 in particular I have benefited from many conversations (and disagreements) over the years with William Harris. Even though I continue to disagree strongly with his views on Greek literacy, he has certainly saved me from various errors, and contributed to the relative sophistication of my ideas on the topics of education and literacy. Some readers for the Press have also had very useful comments, for which I thank them. Needless to say, none of the above are to blame for any errors or misconceptions that remain: I can be a stubborn thinker.

Finally, and above all, I must thank my family—Clare, Madeline, and Colette—who have lived with my frequent distractions while pursuing this project for far too many years now, and have done so on the whole with great patience and forbearance. I am truly lucky to have them in my life; and I thank them and anyone else who has put up with me and/or been helpful over the years: students, friends, family, you are the best.

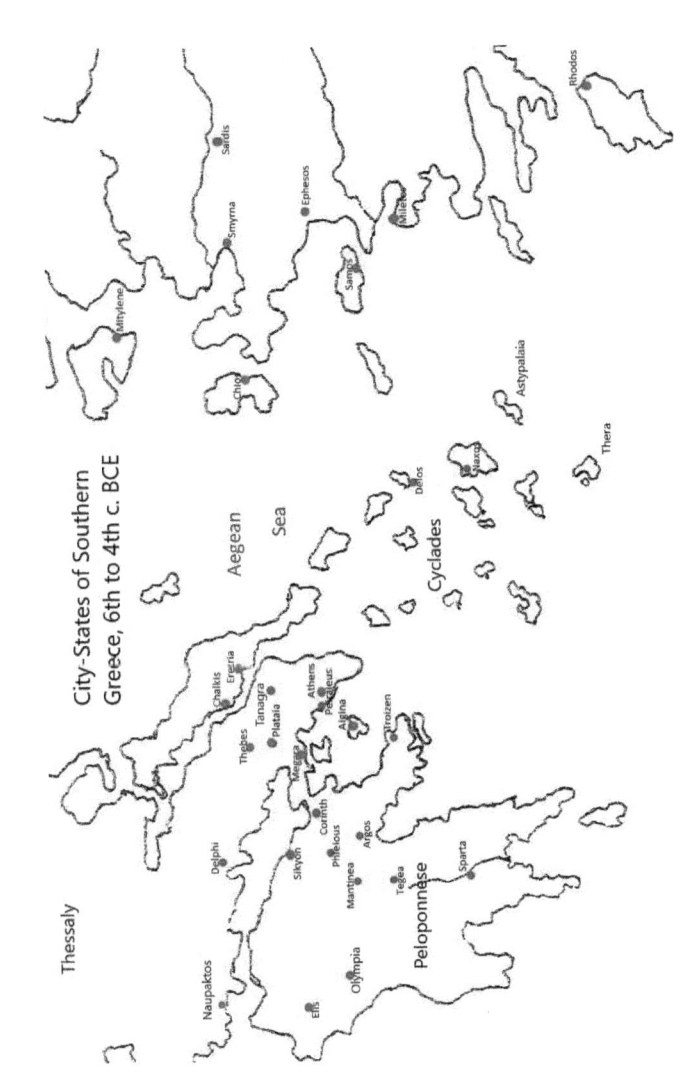

City-States of Southern Greece, sixth to fourth c. BCE

Plate 1 Detail from the Chigi vase (mid seventh century) showing Greek hoplite warriors advancing in neat lines to confront each other in battle. (The Chigi vase is in the National Etruscan Museum, Villa Giulia, Rome, inv. no.22697.) Public domain image retrieved from Wikimedia Creative Commons, Szilas/Gallery 2016 {{PD-US-expired}} (relates to chap. 3).

Plate 2 Athenian fifth-century public inscription concerning cultic matters, now in the Museum of Cycladic Art, Athens. Photo credit: Gary Lee Todd (2016) retrieved from Creative Commons under CC0 1.0 Universal Public Domain Dedication license (CC0 1.0) (relates to chap. 4).

Plate 3 School scene showing boys learning to read and play the lyre, from a red-figure Attic drinking cup painted by Douris (c. 485 BCE), ARV 43148, c. Antikensammlung, Staatliche Museen zu Berlin—Stiftung Preussischer Kulturbesitz. Foto: Johannes Laurentius, F 2285.

Plate 4 Athenian *ostraka* (pot sherds) used to vote in an ostracism, one showing the name Kallias son of Kratias (ostracized in 485) and three with the name Megakles son of Hippokrates (ostracized in 486), now in the Cycladic Art Museum, Athens. Photo credit: Tilemahos Efthimiadis (2009) retrieved from Creative Commons under Attribution 2.0 Generic license (CC BY 2.0) (relates to chap. 5).

Introduction

The ancient Greek city-state was the birth-place of classical Greek civilization, a civilization which arose uniquely in the classical Greek city-states and was a product of the city-state society and way of life. These city-states were small, politically autonomous communities. Each had a highly developed urban center; they had political systems that favored communal deliberation and collective decision making; they shared a military system that was based on self-equipped and self-motivated citizen militias within which each citizen-soldier was of roughly equal importance; and their cultural and religious activities were likewise collective, non-hierarchical, and often open air. It was living in such communities—which flourished between about 700 and 300 BCE—that enabled the classical Greeks to develop their rational outlook, the high importance they granted to the individual and his rights, their democratic political systems based on popular sovereignty, and such crucial cultural-literary forms as drama, philosophy, and rational historical and scientific inquiry. These political and cultural systems and forms continue to infuse western civilization to this day and make the ancient Greeks such a fascinating people. Without the particular socio-political form of the city-state, none of those crucial Greek inventions and achievements would have occurred in the forms that we know them and in which they have influenced us. Many, in fact, might not have occurred at all.

The Greek city-state, therefore, lies at the root of western history and civilization. This was not inevitable: Greek culture might have disappeared in large part after the end of the ancient world and the rise of Christianity and Islam. That did not happen thanks to the engagement with the classical Greek past of Muslim intellectuals of the medieval era (e.g., Al Farabi, Ibn Sina, Ibn Rushd), and western cultural leaders during the so-called "renaissance" (e.g., Erasmus, Giordano Bruno, Johann Reuchlin, Castiglione), "enlightenment" (e.g., Voltaire, Diderot, Kant, Lessing), and "romantic" (e.g., Byron, Goethe) phases of western history (fifteenth to twentieth centuries). As a result of that engagement, classical Greek culture retains a crucial influence in contemporary western civilization, and the Greek city-state in which it arose is therefore an important topic of historical inquiry.

What is a *Polis*?

A book dealing with the nature of the Greek city-state must necessarily begin by defining what a city-state was, and what it arose from. The term "city-state" is a translation, only partly satisfactory, of the Greek word *polis*, which appears to have embodied—at least in developed Attic and *koine* Greek[1]—both the concepts "city" and "state." In early Greek, however, the term *polis* did not carry the meaning of state, but rather referred to a town/city, or more especially to the fortified center of a town, a fact well known to scholars.[2] Indeed, at Athens it continued to be customary down to the end of the fifth century to refer to what we call the "Acropolis" simply as "the *polis*."[3] In Homeric usage the *polis* "was most often the seat of the ruler, the cult center, in a high place, and strongly connected with descriptive adjectives."[4] Even in the early sixth century we still find *polis* being used with the meaning "stronghold" or "fort" in an inscription from Ionia.[5] In general, then, one may say that in Homeric and other early Greek a *polis* is typically a fort or a fortified urban settlement, often more specifically the fortified citadel at the heart of an urban settlement, in which case it may be contrasted with the otherwise synonymous *astu*, which also means "urban settlement."[6]

It was during the sixth century that the term *polis* gradually changed its meaning and came to carry the sense of "state." We may begin with a famous and several times repeated gnomic utterance, first attested in a poem of Alkaios (*c.* 600–580), which asserted that it was not fortified city-walls which made a *polis*, but rather good men.[7] The starting point for this pronouncement is clearly the expectation that most of people did equate the *polis* with its fortifications. The force of the utterance, and its fame, rests on the rejection of this common view and the discovery of a new piece of wisdom: that it is the fighting men who defend the community, not its surrounding walls.[8] But the identification of *polis* and fighting men carries a greater implication: *polis* can no longer mean primarily the physical fortified settlement; instead its identification with the (male) warrior community leads to understanding *polis* as the commonality of the male inhabitants (and their dependents) in their politico-military capacity, i.e., roughly what we call the state. Clearly, therefore, we see here a development from an early "*polis* = fortified settlement" to "*polis* = defenders of the community" as the key stage in the transition to "*polis* = state." We shall see later (Chapters 3 and 4) that this insight has profound implications for the way the Greek city-state came to be organized militarily and politically, and consequently is key to understanding the classical Greek concepts of state (*polis*) and citizenship (*politeia*). The significance of the origin of the concept of the state from that which defends the community—at first the fortifications, later the fighting men—cannot be too heavily underscored.

Since I am using the term "state" freely here in reference to the Greek city-states, it will be useful no doubt to say something about the sense in which the term "state" is used in this work. Let it be noted, then, that I use the word "state" in no special technical sense, but purely in its standard usage as defined, for example, in *The Concise Oxford Dictionary* s.v. State: "2. organized political community with government recognized by the people." It is not the aim of this work to determine whether the classical Greek city-state was, by the standards of modern political theory, a true "state"; instead, the aim is to show what sort of socio-political and cultural entity the classical city-state was. With respect to calling the classical Greek city-states "states," I think any historian or other scholar of classical Greece knows and will freely acknowledge that city-states such as Athens, Sparta, Argos, Corinth, and the like were, by the fifth century if not earlier, "organized political communities with governments recognized by the people." As such, I consider the term "state" to be applicable to them and leave it to political scientists to decide whether their special technical sense of the term "state" also applies or not. That is no doubt a matter of considerable interest in its own right, but it is a matter for a different kind of work than the present one.[9] The classical city-states were both cities and states within the generally accepted meanings of those terms and will be examined here as such.

We can see, then, that the use of *polis* to mean something more than "city," something akin to "state," is found already in embryonic form in the sixth-century poets Solon and Theognis;[10] but it was more strongly advanced during the fifth century and reached its full expression in the works of the fourth-century political philosophers Plato and Aristotle. These two men made it their business to analyze thoroughly the nature and working of the *polis*, and to fix its ideal form. It is worth noting here the emphasis that both men placed on that element of the community responsible for defense. Plato, in his *Republic* (or rather *Politeia*, to give the book its Greek title), devotes by far the greatest part of his analysis to the Guardian/Auxiliary class, that is to the military/intellectual elite which defends and rules the community, and by it essentially equates the *polis* with and hands it over to them. Aristotle, in a rather neglected passage of his *Politika*, makes the *politeia* (constitution/citizenship rights) of the *polis* dependent upon the element primarily responsible for defense: a *polis* which relies chiefly on cavalry will be an oligarchy (that is, a state ruled by some sort of elite class or group) with full citizenship limited to the rich who own horses; a *polis* which relies on heavy infantry will be a broad oligarchy or moderate democracy with citizenship shared among the well-to-do middle class who serve as hoplites (heavily armed infantrymen); a *polis* reliant upon light infantry or sea-power will be a radical democracy with the indigent masses who fight lightly armed and/or row the warships sharing in the citizenship.[11]

The development of the concept of the state from identification of the *polis* with those who defend the community also accounts for another well-known feature of Greek political language: the failure to reify the abstract concept of the state. Modern historians speak and write of "Athens" or "Corinth" doing this or that. The ancient Greeks never did so: they always referred to "the Athenians" and "the Corinthians." Athens was a city, a physical place pure and simple, and as such it could not do or plan anything; whenever one wanted to describe some action or policy of the Athenian state, that state was referred to as *hoi Athenaioi*—the male Athenians. The *Athenaioi*, the *Korinthioi*, the *Sikyonioi*, etc., that is the male citizens who made up the state as a political entity, were of course—as Aristotle rightly emphasized—essentially the actual or potential fighting men available to represent the state in war. Clearly it is the development of "*polis* = state" from "*polis* = fighting men" which is, in part at least, behind the usage "*Athenaioi* (male Athenians) = Athenian state" rather than "*Athenai* (Athens) = Athenian state": the male citizens, in a certain sense, were the *polis*. Of course, there was much more to the *polis* than just the male citizens: women and children, resident foreigners contributing economically, socially, and culturally to the community, and the enslaved underpinning much of the community's economic production, were all important too. But the male warrior-citizens were seen by the ancient Greeks as the core of the *polis* community.[12]

What is a City-State?

Analysis of the term *polis*, then, reveals that it could have more than one meaning, and that its extension of meaning developed over time. The English term "city-state" aims to translate one particular meaning of *polis*, perhaps the most important meaning—at least in classical Attic and in *koine* Greek. It remains necessary to define just what is meant by "city-state," for this is a matter on which modern scholars are by no means unanimous; in fact, all too often modern scholars writing about the city-state are lamentably unclear or even downright confused about what they are discussing. The words *polis* and city-state (and German *Stadtstaat*, French *cité* and *cité-état*, Italian *città*, etc.) are frequently used interchangeably and without discussion of exact meaning, as if that were self-evident. This is far from being the case, however, as even the brief preceding discussion of the meaning of *polis* should have made clear. For present purposes, I prefer to stick to the term city-state for the socio-political entity whose basic nature this book discusses, while leaving the word *polis* as a wider term whose meaning includes but is not limited to what I mean by city-state.[13]

To begin with, the city-state must be understood from two different perspectives. It existed, firstly, as a physical entity: a certain defined geographic space with known borders and an urban center with a variety of public buildings, which ought to include city walls, a theater, one or more gymnasia, an *agora*, stoas and/or other buildings used for public business, temples, and water works.[14] In addition, the city-state had a political or cultural existence: it was a community of citizens who shared, in at least some basic way, a set of moral, political, religious, social, and cultural beliefs and values. As a physical entity, the key factor that concerned the citizens and made the city-state what it was, was the determination of what was included in the city-state and in what way, and what was excluded—i.e., where its boundaries lay and how those boundaries were established. As a political/cultural entity it was crucial to establish and understand who was part of the community and in what way, and who was excluded in whole or in part from sharing in the community, and how and why.

As a physical entity, it needs always to be remembered that the city-state was not just a city that was an autonomous state: it was an autonomous state made up of a city surrounded by a more or less expansive territory (*chora*). This *chora* was usually mostly countryside, though it often contained a number of subsidiary towns and villages, and that countryside was generally varied in its make-up: some mountain and some plain; some coast and some inland; some agricultural land, some pastoral land, and some waste land; some grain-bearing land, some vine-bearing land, some orchard land, some grove and wood land.[15] The urban area itself can be divided into the city proper—within the city walls—and suburbs, and within the city proper one must distinguish between public space and buildings, and private homes. This makes for a complex set of relationships between the various elements making up the totality of the physical city-state, and to these must be added the relationships between the city-state and its neighbors, which relationships defined its external boundaries.

As a political or cultural entity, one must distinguish between those who did and did not belong to the community, and between different degrees of belonging. The most fundamental distinction, of course, is between the full politically active citizens—those most completely in and of the community—and foreigners living in separate states—those most completely excluded from the community. However, there were many people who were in some sense in or part of most Greek city-states besides the full citizens: citizens without full political rights;[16] women of the citizen group, who were fully in the community but in a political sense not of it, possessing only the ability to pass on active citizen rights to the next generation, but not to exercise those rights themselves;[17] male children of the citizen group, who had potential citizenship, to be actualized only on reaching adulthood; in many states, members of *perioikic* settlements, who were only in a partial sense in the community, and who belonged fully only to their own sub-communities;[18] resident foreigners, who were in but not of the community, but who in some cases—as the *metoikoi* (metics) of classical Athens—played a vital role in the community's life;[19] sub-citizens of serf-like status, such as the *Helots* in Lakedaimon, the *Penestai* in Thessaly, the *Gymnetes* in Argos, and so on;[20] and finally the outright "chattel slaves" (*andrapoda*), who were in some places quite an important part of the community numerically and in terms of the functions they fulfilled, but who enjoyed few legal rights at best.[21] All these distinctions formed much of the substance of the *politeia*, the set of public, constitutional laws and norms which laid down how the community was structured, how it was to function and be governed, and what were the rights and duties of the various elements in the community. Even among foreigners there are some important distinctions to be made from the point of view of the individual Greek city-state: between members of friendly or allied communities and members of hostile communities; and between Greeks and *barbaroi* (i.e., non-Greek-speaking foreigners).

A city-state, therefore, was a very complex, multi-layered structure, both physically and in terms of its human component, both of which were vital to its make-up. When analyzing the city-state, it must always be borne in mind that the city-state was not in fact the only type of socio-political organization—or "state" if you will—in ancient (that is to say, in the present context, in archaic and classical) Greece. Much of Greece was instead given over to a different form of "state" generally referred to by the Greek term *ethnos*. Classical Greek commentators like Thucydides and Aristotle discerned a difference between regions of Greece given over to the city-state, and regions which were to their mind backward and primitive where there was a more diffuse, regionally or "tribally" based state form, and they appear to have assumed that at some early date all of Greece shared in this more backward form of socio-political entity.[22] Modern scholars have, until quite recently, paid scant attention to the *ethnos* state type, despite its wide diffusion and long history in ancient Greece. This is perhaps due in part to the fact that the nature, structure, and functioning of the *ethnos* are very difficult to determine, since Greek historical and politico-philosophical writings—indeed classical Greek culture in general—were the product almost exclusively of the city-states, and city-state writers were barely or not at all interested in the *ethnos*.[23] It is nevertheless clear that in mainland Greece virtually the whole of the northern and central regions (Macedonia, Epeiros, Thessaly, Akarnania, Aitolia, Lokris, Phokis, and even to some extent Boiotia) and much of the Peloponnesos (Achaia, most of Arkadia, and after a fashion Elis) were given over to the *ethnos* type of "state" throughout the archaic and into the classical periods.[24] The city-state developed in these regions, if at all, only late and generally only partially: that is to say, frequently not until the fourth century or later, and often only in a modified form or only in some areas.[25]

Unfortunately, the difference between *polis* and *ethnos* is too often ignored by modern scholars. To illustrate this one may point to some recent attempts to characterize the city-state by analyzing all known city-states. For example, the German scholar Ruschenbusch identified up to 750 Greek city-states and based on this posited a tiny "Normalpolis" with typically a territory of 50–100 square kilometers, an adult male citizen body of only 400–1,200, and a total population of c. 2,000 to 6,000.[26] Based on this, he came to some very conservative conclusions about politics and political structures in the "average" Greek city-state. However, Ruschenbusch simply brushed aside the difference between "Polis und Stammstaat" (city-state and *ethnos*) as irrelevant to his purpose, counting many towns and villages of *ethne* as city-states and thereby making his conclusions highly suspect.[27] More recently, the Copenhagen *Polis* Center of Mogens Hansen aimed to undertake a thorough and detailed analysis of the occurrences of the term *polis* in all our sources, beginning with a clear awareness of the range of meanings of that problematic Greek word.[28] Based on preliminary results of this analysis, Hansen proposed a "*Lex Hafniensis de civitate*" according to which, though the word *polis* has two common meanings—town and state—it in fact almost invariably refers, when used of named Hellenic *poleis* in the sense of "towns," to towns that were actually the urban centers of city-states.[29] The problem with this approach is that, quite simply, the determination of whether a *polis* referred to as such in the sources is or is not the urban center of a city-state is itself a judgment call, involving the very question at issue, and the judgments made are often questionable to my mind.[30] In sum, Hansen's "*Lex Hafniensis*" seems to be based on question-begging assumptions about the status of communities called *poleis* in our sources. The inventory of Greek *poleis* is unquestionably an immensely valuable and useful work, but it is not an inventory of city-states, since some of places called *polis* in our sources were city-states, while others were merely towns with some other status.

There is in fact an important body of ancient evidence that can be made the basis of an estimation of how widespread the Greek city-state was: I mean the corpus of Aristotelian *Politeiai*, or constitutions, for these at any rate clearly dealt with places that were autonomous states (in that they had their own constitutional arrangements worth analyzing), and not mere dependent towns. As is well known, Aristotle and his school carried out a research project into the constitutional arrangements of a huge range of states, culminating in the publication of a very large number of treatises on known constitutions, of which that on Athens actually survives.[31] According to Diogenes Laertios 5.27, the collected set of *Politeiai* filled 158 book scrolls, while late antique commentators on Aristotle report some 250 or 255 individual treatises.[32] Though they are all lost other than that on Athens, we have a certain amount of information about them which has been excellently assembled, analyzed and commented on by Olof Gigon.[33] The names of forty-four of the states for which an Aristotelian *Politeia* existed are definitely attested in various sources, a further thirty-one can be inferred from a collection of excerpts preserved under the name of one Herakleides, and another fifty-nine can be deduced from mentions in Aristotle's *Politika*, making a total of 134 states, a little over half of the original collection.[34] A number of these states are not city-states, however: e.g., the Achaians, the Aitolians, the Akarnanians, the Arkadians, the Athamanians, the Bottiaians, the Epeirotes, the Thessalians, the Kretans, the Cypriots, the Lokrians, and so on; others are not Greek: e.g., the Lucanians, the Lykians, the Thracians, the Etruscans, the Phrygians, etc. Of the 134 states whose constitution is known to have been examined by the Aristotelian research project, sixteen were *ethne* or confederations of some other type, and twenty-two were foreign peoples, leaving ninety-six city-states, or about 72 percent of the total of known treatises (full details on all this in App. 2 below).

If this proportion is roughly representative of the whole original set, and there is no obvious reason I can think of why it should not be, it would appear that Aristotle's research project identified something like 186 Greek city-states whose constitution seemed worth analyzing (i.e., 72 percent of 250: see App. 2). Since many of the city-states known to have been treated were very small and insignificant places—e.g., such places as Argilos, Aphyta, Kythnos, Lepreon, Kios, Peparethos, Tenedos—it seems reasonable to suggest that Aristotle and his pupils as far as possible treated every city-state they could identify and obtain information about. Even allowing that they overlooked or left out some city-states, therefore, it is very probable that the number of Greek communities that had developed into autonomous city-states by the middle of the fourth century was about 200 or so.

It is also clear from the preserved names of Aristotelian *Politeiai* that the majority of the Greek city-states were in the region of east Greece—that is the Aegean islands and the coast of Asia Minor—or else were new settlements founded in the eighth centuries or later, mostly in Italy and Sicily or around the Black Sea and its approaches.[35] Most of mainland Greece continued to be organized as *ethne* into the fourth century, the city-state developing only in parts of the Peloponnesos and south-central Greece. The size of the city-states varied greatly, ranging from the acknowledged giants Sparta and Athens to quite small places like those listed in the previous paragraph. I would guess though—and it is admittedly only a guess—that if one wants to get an impression of the average city-state the place to look is at states like Megara, Phleious, Sikyon, Tegea, and others like them (Teos in Ionia for instance): communities with moderately large though restricted territories and, with hoplite levies on the order of 2,000 to 3,000 men, probably having populations in the range of 20,000 to 30,000 people.[36] However, if one is looking for city-states whose political institutions and social and economic development established and/or illustrate norms for the development of city-states generally, one must actually avoid the average city-states and examine precisely the handful of "*megapoleis*" like Argos, Corinth, Miletos, Sparta, and above all Athens.

What needs to be recognized is that when we examine the development of the city-state, it is primarily the development of states of the size and importance of the latter group, and especially of Athens, that should be the object of our research, because it is these states which provided the models adopted and adapted by lesser communities in the course of their own development. The medium sized and smaller Greek city-states did not simply develop independently but were heavily influenced by the examples of the leading, which is to say by and large the biggest, city-states, and above all Athens. What we are undertaking to explain in an account of the nature of the city-state is the socio-political units which formed the ambiance of classical Greek culture. It is the astonishing and lastingly important achievements of classical Greek culture which make the development of the city-states in which it was created still an interesting and important subject of inquiry, and it is the overwhelming centrality of the largest Greek city-states, and especially of Athens, in the creation of classical Greek culture which establishes the largest city-states and Athens above all, both as the primary models for other Greek city-states, and as the primary focus for modern analysis of the nature of the city-state.

Athens' uniqueness in size, power, varied though ultimately radically democratic socio-political development, and cultural achievement, have obscured the centrality of her role in developing the model of the city-state. Plato's *Republic* and Aristotle's *Politika* do, it is true, react strongly against the Athenian model, but Athens is central to their discussions for precisely that reason, and Aristotle in fact ultimately endorses many features of the Athenian political system, though without admitting it.[37] More important, however, is the fact that Athens' socio-political invention—democracy—came in the later fourth and third centuries BCE to be seen as the defining characteristic of an autonomous Greek city-state, however much watered down the actual practice of "democracy" might be in individual city-states.[38] By the third century it was virtually universally accepted, as we can tell from abundant literary and epigraphic testimony, that a city-state should be ruled by a sovereign assembly (*ekklesia*) of the adult male citizens, though restricted in their decision-making by an established code of laws (*nomoi*); that day-to-day oversight of the governance of the state should be in the hands of a council (*boule*) representing and responsible to the assembly; that executive authority should be in the hands of defined boards or colleges of magistrates duly appointed on an annual basis by election and/or allotment, and accountable for their actions to the assembly; and that the rich had a duty from time to time, and as necessity demanded, to place a portion of their wealth at the disposal of the state to meet religious, military, or social needs.[39] This is essentially, in broad outlines, the model of the city-state developed by and at Athens.

A city-state, then, is essentially a community whose socio-political institutions corresponded—even if at times not very closely—to the above model, and an account of the nature of the city-state is properly an account of that model. This definition further enables us to settle a related question: when did the city-state arise? Clearly the city-state reached something approaching full development only in the fifth century BCE, with the establishment of the Athenian democratic system by Kleisthenes and his associates in the years around 508, and its development by his early and mid-fifth-century successors like Ephialtes and Perikles; and the peak of city-state culture, the so-called classical period, ran from about 470 to 320 or so. Equally clearly, whatever religious, social, and technological continuities there may have been from Mycenaean Greece, through the early Iron Age, to early Archaic Greece—and in my opinion such continuities will have been minimal to non-existent except perhaps in religion—it is nevertheless with the beginning of Greece's emergence from its long period of post-Mycenaean decline (i.e., what used to be called the "Dark Age," c. 1100–800 BCE) that one should begin the story of the rise of the city-state. Victor Ehrenberg already long ago established c. 800 as the appropriate starting point for city-state development, and it is a pity that this date should have been challenged in some subsequent works.[40] The chronological parameters for the study of the city-state proper here are, consequently, roughly 800 to 300 BCE, but with a concentration on the sixth and fifth centuries.

This work is primarily focused on the city-state as a military, political and cultural entity, and as such it focuses on the male collective of citizen warriors who were at the core of the Greek understanding of the city-state, as I have indicated. It can be seen, therefore, as a contribution to the study of Greek notions of masculinity, and to the ideology of the male warrior citizen that underpinned the conception of masculinity. That means that some important aspects of the history of the Greek city-states will not be treated: the history of women for example, and of those who were enslaved. Simply put, women and the enslaved did not take a stand in the *phalanx*, the military formation in which Greek citizen warriors most characteristically lined up to give battle in defense of the city-state and furtherance of its interests, nor did they take a seat at an oar bench in the fleet (Chapter 3). They did not (were not permitted to) attend, debate, and vote in council meetings and citizen assemblies, where the laws and policies of the city-state were discussed and decided (Chapter 4). And there is no evidence of women and the enslaved attending schools and learning to read and write there, the crucial attainment for full participation in the political and cultural life of the city-state (Chapter 5).[41] As a result, women and the enslaved do not receive significant attention in the core chapters of this book.

That is not to say that women and the enslaved were not important. They played a significant economic role (as noticed in Chapter 2 below) and women certainly played an important role in religion, for example.[42] As such, women and the enslaved are important topics, which have deservedly been the subject of much scholarly attention in recent decades,[43] but the aim here is to understand the politico-military core of the city-state, and the culture the citizen warriors created, from which women and the enslaved were largely excluded. The ancient Greeks themselves were aware of and provided justifications, of a sort, for the marginalization of women. Hesiod for example, insisted on the myth of Pandora, the first woman and the source of all the troubles that afflict mankind via her infamous box (really a *pithos* or storage jar): it is the only myth he recounted in both of his surviving epics, the *Theogony* 560–612 and the *Works and Days* 60–105. One of only a very few songs to survive for us complete from the era between Hesiod and Pindar (i.e., roughly 700–500), and the longest, is the de-humanizing song on women by Semonides of Amorgos. In it he compared women to a variety of animals and concluded that "women are the biggest single bad thing Zeus has made for us." Less obnoxious, but even more dismissive, is the infamous treatment of women in the funeral oration Thucydides attributed to the Athenian statesman Perikles (at 2.46), essentially telling women to be invisible. Then there is Xenophon's treatise on household/estate management, the *Oikonomika*, in which he advises a man of thirty or so to marry a girl half his age, so that he can "groom" her into being the perfect wife. Finally, Aristotle in the opening section of his *Politika* declared women to be deficient in reason and so needing to be under the control of men. The aim of these and other works was evidently, in part at least, to explain and justify the subordination of women and their exclusion from the active life of the citizen community.

The same was done, in even more extreme form, with the enslaved population. Greeks often used a particularly dehumanizing term for the enslaved: *andrapoda* meaning literally "man-footed." This term was based on the word *tetrapoda* (four-footed) referring to animals, and it reduced the enslaved to the status of "livestock": one had four-footed livestock (sheep, goats, oxen) and "man-footed" livestock, the enslaved. The enslaved were thus viewed as beasts who went on two feet, and obviously such "beasts" could not participate actively in the citizen community, any more than women could. It is not that women and the enslaved did not form enormously important parts of the community: it is that the ideology of the *polis* as a citizen community was built around the free male warrior-citizens, and there was thus a perceived need for women and the enslaved to be firmly pushed to the margins. In seeking to understand the formation and nature of this male warrior-citizen community, therefore, women and the enslaved will come in for only minimal attention in this book, at any rate in the core chapters (3, 4, and 5).

Also excluded from detailed discussion here is the event history of warfare, of alliance building, of exploitation of smaller cities by larger ones, and so on that occupy most of the attention of our major historical sources, like Herodotos, Thucydides, and Xenophon. After an examination of the origin of the city-state as a socio-political structure, how and what it emerged from, and a study of the economic growth that underpinned city-state development, we will see how the city-state was shaped as a citizen collective around three key foundations: military participation as citizen militia soldiers and rowers (symbolized here by the spear, the key weapon of the Greek warrior); political participation as debaters and voters in councils and assemblies (symbolized by the pebble—Greeks citizens often voted with pebbles); and participation in reading and writing so as to understand and engage thoughtfully in the core life of the city-state (symbolized by the scroll, the form of the ancient Greek book). Examining these foundations each in detail, we will find that the city-state was, at its core, a community of warriors and citizens who fought together and debated and voted together, and who wrote and read in order to be able to debate and vote effectively. Understanding this illuminates how and why the Greeks produced for themselves the remarkable and innovative culture that set them apart from all other ancient peoples and has sustained interest in them to the present day: the culture based in critical inquiry, in rational analysis, in relativism, and in individualism that produced the drama, the historiography, the philosophy, and the oratory that are still—for better or worse—read and admired today.

1

The Origin and Early Development of the City-State

If we are to deal adequately with the city-state's origins and early development, we must be clear about what it developed from, in other words what form of socio-political organizations were characteristic of Greece in the early Iron Age (roughly the tenth, ninth and early eighth centuries), the period sometimes also called the Geometric Age from the characteristic style of pottery decoration then in vogue.[1] Given our general poverty of information, whether literary or archaeological, about this period of Greek history, that is easier said than done. But there is a fallacy which must be but is not always avoided: to describe the development of the city-state in such a way that the appearance is created that the city-state—the entity whose development is to be analyzed—already existed at the start of the process, and/or that its development was somehow predetermined and inevitable. The archaeological record, scanty as it is, does not at all encourage the notion that there were numerous or substantial cities, let alone city-states, in Greece before 800; and there was nothing predetermined about the development of the classical city-states, as we shall see.[2]

Early Iron Age Communities

It is a truism to state that we are not well informed about the structure and political geography of the communities of Greece in the early Iron Age. As a starting point in seeking to get some notion of what they were like, consider the statements made about early Greece in Thucydides' so-called "Archaeology": in earlier times piracy was rife along the coasts and among the islands; brigandage was similarly rife on the mainland, due to a lack of walled *poleis* and a life lived *kata komas* (in villages). This style of life still continued in much of Hellas, for example among the Ozolian Lokrians, the Aitolians, the Akarnanians, and just as these peoples still went armed about their everyday life, so had all Hellenes in earlier times.[3] According to Thucydides, then, political communities in early Greece were more like the Aitolians and the Akarnanians of the fifth century than like the city-states of that time; they were organized as groups of villages, rather than being centered on walled cities, and conditions were very unsettled.[4]

We might ask what exactly Thucydides meant by all this. The Aitolians, Akarnanians, and Ozolian Lokrians did not in Thucydides' day, or at any time for that matter, form city-states: they were regionally and/or tribally organized communities of a type most often referred to as *ethne* (sing. *ethnos*). This term was frequently used by Herodotos to refer to various "tribes" or "peoples," and Thucydides used it specifically in reference to the Aitolians: "for the *ethnos* of the Aitolians is a large one" (3.94.4), and he further specified that the Aitolians dwelt in un-walled villages—*oikoun de kata komas ateichistous* (3.94.4). Although in general Thucydides, like other Greek writers, used the term *ethnos* quite loosely to refer to any group or (often foreign) people, it can be argued that here we have an early example of the special technical sense of the word meaning roughly "tribal state" as opposed to "city-state."[5] Shortly after Thucydides, the author of the *Hellenika Oxyrrhynchia*—in my view almost certainly Theopompos—referred to the Boiotian confederacy of the late fifth and early fourth centuries as an *ethnos*, and also called the Ozolian Lokrians and the Phokians *ethne*.[6] Another crucial passage is in the *Anabasis* of Xenophon (7.1.33), where he mentions a certain Koiratadas of Thebes who was going up and down Hellas everywhere offering his services as *strategos* to any community, whether *polis* or *ethnos*, that needed one. Evidently, the technical sense of *ethnos* as "tribal state," widely attested in the late fourth and third centuries, had developed by the end of the fifth and/or beginning of the fourth centuries, these three near contemporary historians being the first clear exponents of this usage.[7]

Such an *ethnos* was made up of a people acknowledging some form of (often fictive) kinship—a "tribe" if you will—inhabiting a recognized geographic region, and dwelling in scattered, often unwalled, villages and small towns, as we can see from Thucydides. These villages and small towns were only loosely tied together, and the governing functions of the *ethnos* were most probably concerned in the main with what one might call "foreign policy," especially warfare; but in so far as we can tell the basic governing structure of the *ethnos* was much the same as in the city-states: that is to say, one had some form of primary assembly of "citizens" (however defined), a council, and elected magistrates.[8] Not very much is known about the structure and institutions of early *ethne* (pre fourth century), but it cannot be automatically assumed that later *ethne* borrowed their institutions from the city-states, rather than sharing a common development to a certain degree. Unfortunately, the early *ethne* have been very little studied, but according to Thucydides early Greece was made up of such *ethne*, and it was from them—as trade and a more settled way of life developed and led to urbanization—that the city-states arose.[9] It can be argued that Aristotle took the same view.

In the opening sections of his *Politika*, Aristotle discussed the origins of the *polis* or state. He saw communities as originating in marriage, which gave rise to the family, the basic social unit. When a number of families banded together, they formed a *kome* or village, and when a number of villages came together, they formed a *polis* (*Pol.* 1252a–1253a). Political authority had its origins in the father of the family, and then in the senior male in the extended family or village. This type of authority is naturally akin to monarchical authority, and consequently the primitive village communities were ruled by monarchs. It is for this reason, too, that *poleis* in their beginnings were ruled by kings—as having developed from monarchical village communities—and that *ethne* were still so ruled in Aristotle's own day (*Pol.* 1252b). We see here, then, the same distinction that Thucydides made between more advanced city-states, and more primitive *ethne*—the latter still organized in villages and consequently often still ruled by kings—with the idea that the city-states evolved from the primitive, village-structured tribal state.[10]

In the rest of the *Politika*, Aristotle for the most part ignored the *ethnos*, concentrating his analysis exclusively on the city-state, one of the major shortcomings of this treatise. But that he was nevertheless well aware of the organization of large parts of Greece as *ethne*, and of the nature of their political structures and practices, is clear from the vast research project which underlay his ideas about politics: the huge corpus of *Politeiai* of individual states.[11] Of the 134 known *Politeiai* (see below App. 2 for details), forty-two dealt with communities of metropolitan Greece—i.e. mainland Greece up to and including Macedonia, and the immediate offshore islands of Ithaka, Kephallenia, Aigina, and Euboia. No fewer than sixteen of these forty-two were *ethne*—or perhaps rather thirteen if one eliminates some duplication[12]—covering a substantial portion of mainland Greece: Arkadia and Achaia in the Peloponnesos; in central and northern Greece Boiotia, Akarnania, Aitolia, Opuntian Lokris, Malis, Athamania, Epeiros, Thessaly, Perrhaibia, Macedonia, and Bottiaia. It seems very likely that the full corpus will have included also Ozolian Lokris, Phokis, Doris, Phthia, and the Magnetes. At any rate, Aristotle clearly saw that a large part of mainland Greece was organized as *ethne* rather than *poleis* down to his own day,[13] and presumably derived some of his ideas about the primitive structure and development of Greek communities from what he knew of these regions: his generalization about monarchy, for example, was no doubt based on the monarchical systems still surviving in his day in Macedonia, Epeiros, Athamania, and Thessaly.[14]

So, Thucydides and Aristotle thought that in early times—before the rise of the city-state—Greece was made up of tribal/regional communities (*ethne*) comprising loosely associated villages (*komai*). I believe that they both had in mind the period we would call the "Dark" or Geometric Age and the early Archaic Age. For Thucydides, this is specifically shown by the fact that, immediately after his assertion that the style of life of the *ethne* of his day was primitive and had been universal throughout Hellas in earlier times, he went on to state that it was the Athenians who first changed from this mode of life, taking up peaceful life and luxurious fashions until very recently adopting simple styles and the custom of exercising nude from the Lakedaimonians (Thuc. 1.6.1–5). That is to say that Thucydides drew a direct line of development from the primitive, unsettled life of the *ethnos* to the emergence of archaic and contemporary (to him) Athenian (and Greek) life and customs. In general, it is clear that, in so far as both Thucydides and Aristotle saw the *ethnos/kome* mode of life as a direct precursor of the *polis* of their own time, and as still surviving in backward regions, they regarded this mode of life as belonging to the period only a little before their own time—a few centuries earlier in modern terms.

Should we, then, accept this view of Thucydides and Aristotle as valid, and understand the Greek communities of the Geometric Age to have been akin in political structure and style of life to the *ethne* of the fifth and fourth centuries? Thucydides and Aristotle, after all, lived in a culture that was a direct outgrowth and continuation of Geometric Age Greek culture, and they had at their disposal a vast mass of evidence—early epic and lyric poetry, records in the form of lists of priests and magistrates and early laws, a plethora of legendary and semi-legendary stories, the writings of sixth- and early-fifth-century rationalizing philosophers and logographers, etc.—which may have provided them with some evidence and insights on which they based their view. This evidence, which is almost all lost to us, put them in a much stronger position, in many respects, than we can ever hope to be to understand early Greece. After all, what would modern students of early Greece not give to be able to read and make use of the lost archaic epics, the complete works of the seventh- and sixth-century lyric, iambic and elegiac poets, the proto-historical writings of men like Hekataios of Miletos, the lists of priests and magistrates and other early records collected by the likes of Hippias of Elis and Hellanikos of Lesbos?

Further, the assumption of Thucydides and Aristotle that "primitive" or "backward" societies of their own times could provide clues as to the conditions in Greece before city-state development is not obviously wrong. Modern scholars too try to shed light on early Greece by comparison with contemporary "primitive" societies and cultures such as those of Nuristan, Papua/New Guinea, the Melanesian Islands, and the like.[15] Modern scholarly methods are different, more sophisticated, than those of Aristotle or Thucydides; but the basic impulse is similar. It's also clear that Thucydides, at least, relied on analysis of Homer. Since the publication of Moses Finley's groundbreaking book *The World of Odysseus* in 1957, the study of "Homeric society" has been integral to almost every modern work on early Greece.[16] Though our grounds for regarding Homer as providing good evidence for early Greece—that is Greece in the period between about 850 and 650 BCE—are very different from those assumed by Thucydides, it is interesting that Thucydides did, like us, use Homer as a source of information about early Greece.[17]

There is, then, to say the least, some reason to take seriously the notion put forward by Thucydides and Aristotle that early Greece was made up of communities similar in many respects to the fifth-century *ethne* of central and northern Greece. Can we find good arguments to bolster this view? Here, as just noted, the evidence of Homer is obviously crucial. It is now generally agreed by the great majority of scholars that the society depicted in the Homeric epics is essentially that of the poet's own day—or perhaps a little earlier (see n. 16 above). This is the result of the recognition by Parry and Lord *et al.* that these epics were oral compositions, the product of a long-standing and deep-rooted oral bardic tradition that found its culmination in the poems of Homer and Hesiod, and that in oral bardic traditions of this sort the tales told are constantly—and essentially unconsciously—re-framed and re-interpreted to reflect the manner of life and preoccupations of any given bard's own society and time.[18] We can, therefore, very rightly and appropriately look to Homer for some idea of early Iron Age Greek society, political structures, and communities. The question is, then, what kind of communities with what kind of political structures does Homer depict?

The most notable description of political units in Homer is found in the so-called "Catalogue of Ships" in *Iliad* 2.493–762, which despite its (modern!) name is not so much a "Catalogue of Ships" as it is an account of the regions and communities of Greece that contributed men and ships to the expedition against Troy, and who their leaders were. One thing that is immediately clear about this description of regions and communities is that the political/geographic units depicted in the "Catalogue" do not at all correspond to those of late Archaic and Classical Greece, with only a few exceptions.[19] Rather than the classical city-states, what we see in the "Catalogue" is a Greece divided up into a relatively small number of large regional politico-geographic entities, which show little or no sign of any extensive centralization, being made up of a number of towns and villages all presented in the same way as if of equal status. Many of these "states" (using that word merely as a convenient short-hand) are characterized by tribal rather than local names;[20] and some of them have a number of leaders—sometimes but not always related to each other—who together rule over their region/people, presumably each having their own local power bases within the region, as certainly seems to be the case with the Epeians of Elis and the Boiotians.[21] The question of whether the political geography depicted in the Catalogue is historical or fictional, and if historical what period of history it reflects, has been much discussed.[22]

To begin with, it has often been noted that the "Catalogue," in terms of structure and style, fits very oddly in the *Iliad* as an account of the leaders and forces who fought at Troy. Indeed, it has been suggested that the "Catalogue" was in origin a discrete composition, adopted and adapted by Homer for his purposes in the *Iliad*. A geographic excursus specially produced for the *Iliad* would surely have begun with an account of the paramount leaders Agamemnon and Menelaos and their realms, rather than beginning with the (in terms of the story of the *Iliad*) unimportant realms and leaders of Phokis, Boiotia, Euboia, and Athens. Instead, the important leaders of the Troy story—Achilles, Agamemnon, Menelaos, Nestor, Diomedes, Odysseus—seem to be uncomfortably fitted into a geographical depiction of Greece created originally to serve some very different function than accounting for the forces and heroes at Troy. What could this purpose have been? Though there are some elements of the "Catalogue" that look Mycenean or purely mythical, it is my conviction that overall the "Catalogue" does not look Mycenean, yet is too detailed an account of known and real Greek places and regions to be anything other than a geographical treatise representing in at least an approximate form the genuine political geography of Greece at some period.[23]

The correct interpretation, it seems to me, was proposed by Giovannini and more cautiously endorsed by Kirk and Anderson: that the "Catalogue" essentially reflects the political geography of Greece in Homer's own time, that is to say roughly in the eighth century BCE. Key to this understanding is Giovannini's brilliant observation that the internal structure of the "Catalogue" closely resembles an itinerary, and specifically an itinerary starting in central Greece and proceeding around the Greek world from there.[24] This observation makes sense of the most puzzling aspect of the "Catalogue": the unexpected order in which the "states" are listed. The itinerary starts with the central Greek regions of Boiotia and Phokis and progresses from there in a great southward arc through mainland Greece via Euboia, Attica, the Peloponnesian regions, and the Ionian Islands, to Aitolia. Then comes a subsidiary itinerary starting in the same region and proceeding northwards, rather than southwards, through Lokris and Phthia to Thessaly and its periphery. Other than the transposition at the start of Boiotia and Phokis for unknown reasons, this is the world as seen from Delphi, and it surely indicates that the "Catalogue" was created after the rise of Delphi to pan-Hellenic prominence in the second half of the eighth century.[25] In other words, the structure of the "Catalogue" resembles the route laid out for the *theorodokoi* (sacred representatives) sent out by the great Panhellenic sanctuary at Delphi to announce the great Pythian festival at Delphi. Such *theorodokoi* were sent out from at least the early sixth century, and probably since the rise of Delphi as a Panhellenic sanctuary in the second half of the eighth century.[26] The "Catalogue" began its life, then, most likely as a kind of route instruction manual for the Delphic *theorodokoi*, before being elaborated with mythic data (especially the various regional "heroes") by Homer for its use in the *Iliad*. It is for these reasons that I am convinced that the "Catalogue" in the main reflects the political geography of Homer's own time, that is to say the very beginning of the Archaic Age.

I believe, then, that the Homeric "Catalogue" depicts primitive tribally and/or regionally based states of the late Geometric and early Archaic Ages—*ethne* in short—and that this provides strong support for the contention of Thucydides and Aristotle that this type of political unit was characteristic of early Greece. We do not, unfortunately, get a very clear idea from the "Catalogue" what these political communities were like, partly because the oral tradition required the insertion of various fictional and anachronistic elements, most notably the mythic leaders. Granted, however, that the structure of some realms has been distorted in this way, it is surely those regions which are relatively unimportant to the Troy-tale—such as Boiotia, Phokis, Euboia, Arkadia, the region of Elis, Aitolia—which are likely to reflect in the most unadulterated way the conditions of Homer's own day.

It is noteworthy that each of these communities is referred to in the "Catalogue" by a "tribal" name, which in the case of two of them—the *Abantes* of Euboia and the *Epeioi* of Elis—are unrelated to the regional name and so firmly fix the primarily "tribal" nature of the political communities. In the case of other communities, it might be supposed that the people took its name from the region, and that they were hence primarily regionally based. That seems definitely not to have been the case with the *Boiotoi*, however, a people who according to Greek tradition arrived quite late in central Greece and gave their name to the region they occupied—and the same is maintained, incidentally, about the *Thessaloi*.[27] One might also point to Odysseus' realm in the "Catalogue," made up of three islands—Ithaka, Same, Zakynthos—collectively inhabited by a people called *Kephallenes*, while in classical times the largest of these islands, Same, had come to be called Kephallenia, obviously after the people.[28] Most likely, then, in all these cases the "tribal" name is primary, and it is the peoples who gave their names to the regions: *Arkades* to Arkadia, *Phokees* to Phokis, *Lokroi* to Lokris, and so on. These peoples are not just regarded as inhabitants of a region, whether or not named after themselves; they are also seen as inhabitants of towns and villages which make up the principal settlements of each region. Thus, for each political community the "Catalogue" lists a number of settlements of which it is made up, generally with no distinction of status or importance.[29]

Notwithstanding the lack of a tribal name, such political communities as the realms of Agamemnon, Diomedes, Menelaos, Nestor, and the rest are also to be seen as *ethne*. For example, though Menelaos' realm in Lakedaimon could be seen as the core of the later city-state of the Lakedaimonians—and in a strictly geographical sense was indeed just that—it differed from the classical city-state in a fundamentally important respect: Menelaos' realm was made up of several towns, none of which is presented as of greater importance than the others—Pharis, Sparte, Messe, Bryseiai, Augeiai, Amyklai, Helos, Laas, and Oitylos, to list them in the same order as Homer—whereas the classical city-state of the Lakedaimonians was more properly the city-state of the Spartans, Sparta being the center and predominant town of the city-state while all other towns were subordinate, and only the Spartans holding full citizenship in the Lakedaimonian city-state.[30] Thus, Menelaos' realm is an entirely different political community than the classical city-state of the Lakedaimonians: it is a regional political unit made up of associated towns under a great leader; we cannot tell whether the inhabitants of the region formed a people called *Lakedaimonioi* who gave their name to the region, or whether in this case the name of the region is primary, but we certainly have here no city-state of the Lakedaimonians.[31] The same is true of all the other realms which lack a "tribal" name for their inhabitants: they are all presented as political communities made up of the towns and localities of a particular region under a particular leader or leaders—that is to say, as *ethne*.[32]

The Homeric "Catalogue," then, depicts Geometric Greece as made up of a number of tribal/regional political units, each of which was made up of a people inhabiting various towns and villages and associated together under one or several leaders called *basileis*, and which show a marked similarity to the primitive *ethne* made up of associated towns and villages, and sometimes monarchically ruled, posited for early Greece by Thucydides and Aristotle. The one political community depicted at length in the *Odyssey*, the realm of Odysseus in the Ionian isles, agrees very well with this picture.

It is very clear in the *Odyssey* that Homer describes, not a city-state of Ithaka as some scholars imagine,[33] but the realm of the *Kephallenes* more or less as it appears in the Iliadic "Catalogue," though now apparently including Doulichion (= Leukas), which was a separate realm in the "Catalogue." This is evident from the fact that the suitors, who sought not merely to marry Penelope but to succeed via that marriage to Odysseus' position as ruler, came not just from Ithaka but from Doulichion, Same (= Kephallenia), and Zakynthos as well; and from the facts that they are represented as all attending the assembly in Ithaka, and indeed as all having houses in Ithaka.[34] No Greek city-state would ever willingly accept an outsider as ruler; no Greek city-state would permit outsiders to attend and participate in assemblies; Greek city-states did not permit outsiders to own land or houses in their territory except as a special privilege granted as a result of notable benefactions; *ergo* Ithaka in the Odyssey is not a city-state but simply a part of the larger *ethnos* of the *Kephallenes*, rendered the most important of the islands making up this *ethnos*—though the smallest—by the fact of its being the home of the ruling family.[35]

It is noteworthy how well this picture of Homeric *ethne* agrees with the analysis of the early *ethne* by Adalberto Giovannini—by far the most important study of the *ethne* of ancient Greece.[36] Giovannini clearly showed that the many scholars who thought of Greek *ethne* as arising essentially in the fourth century and later by the pulling together into federal states of groups of cities and towns which had previously been independent *poleis* only loosely associated together by traditional religious or kinship ties, were wrong.[37] He demonstrated that our sources show such peoples as the Phokians, the Aitolians, the Thessalians, the Boiotians, and others functioned as *ethne* from the earliest times—for him from the sixth century, since he made no use of Homer. The Homeric "Catalogue," by pushing the *ethnos* type of political community back into the early Iron Age, confirms and rounds out Giovannini's argument, and makes it clear that, far from *ethne* developing from *poleis*, as many modern scholars have believed, it is the other way around: *poleis*—at least in mainland Greece—developed from primitive *ethne*, as Thucydides already saw, though to be sure not from all *ethne* and not always to the same degree or at the same time, as we shall see below.

It should be noted that the Homeric evidence so far discussed all concerns what one may call metropolitan Greece—that is, mainland Greece and its immediate offshore islands: Euboia, Aigina, the Ionian Islands. Mainland Greece is, of course, also that part of the Greek world in which *ethne* continued to flourish through the Archaic and Classical periods and into the Hellenistic era. In recent times, a number of scholars have noted the existence in Homer of what look very like early city-states, or at any rate of communities that have a number of city-state-like features: Troy and the Achaian camp in the *Iliad*; the two communities depicted on the Shield of Achilles; and Scheria of the Phaeacians.[38] As a caution, one should note that some features thought of as characteristic of city-states—assemblies, councils, massed infantry formations in warfare, temples, limited urban infrastructure—are also found in *ethne* and in their constituent towns, and so cannot demonstrate the presence of city-states.[39] However, the communities just referred to do display the true city-state characteristics of high degrees of urbanization and centralization, so that it does appear that the city-state had begun to develop in Homer's day. In this, as in other respects, the Homeric epics depict a world and society in transition, although one should recall also the likelihood of later interpolations or other alterations of the original Homeric poems.

However, it's worth bearing in mind that, in so far as there were early city-states developing in Homer's day, these lay for the most part outside of metropolitan Greece (Troy, the Achaean camp, the Phaeacians). In other words, the early stages of city-state development likely occurred primarily and most early in the eastern Aegean islands and coast, and in the new overseas settlements that were being founded in the second half of the eighth century. It has long been noted, in fact, that one of the most fully developed city-states in Homer, Scheria of the Phaiakians with its monumental city walls, its temples of the gods, and its allotments of land, is clearly based on the "colonial" foundations of the later eighth century, and the Achaian expeditionary force in the *Iliad*—in so far as it resembles a city-state—also resembles a "colonial" foundation.[40] As to Troy, with its monumental city walls, its *agora*, its palaces, and its temples on the citadel, it has been compared to eighth-century near-eastern cities by some scholars, though others see a Greek *polis*.[41] In so far as Troy does resemble a Greek city-state, perhaps Old Smyrna—one of the candidates for Homer's place of origin—should be considered as a possible model: it certainly had the massive walls and the *agora* at this time (mid to late eighth century), and at least one major temple dedicated to Athena, though not situated on the citadel.[42] The appearance in Homer that city-states were developing first in the east Greek and colonial regions does accord with the evidence of the Aristotelian *Politeiai* which suggests that the majority of Greek city-states were in precisely those regions (see App. 2 below).

What this amounts to is that for Homer, Greece was a land of regional or tribal "states," clearly akin to the primitive *ethne* that Thucydides believed existed in early Greece, and that Homer primarily depicted early city-states as existing on the edges of the Greek world. This makes excellent sense in light of the views of Thucydides and Aristotle about early Greece, seeming in fact to confirm them, and in light of the fact that *ethne* remained prominent in mainland Greece down to the time of the Roman conquest. We can confidently conclude from this that in mainland Greece the city-states developed—where they did develop, that is in parts of the Peloponnesos, south central Greece (Attica and after a fashion Boiotia), and the offshore islands—from more loosely organized regional/tribal communities akin to *ethne*, and that the earliest development of the city-state in fact occurred on the edges of the Greek world—the west coast of Asia Minor and the colonial areas. The one resource available to modern scholars that Thucydides and Aristotle lacked, namely archaeological investigation, seems to me to have a tendency to confirm this, in so far as it is capable of shedding light on this matter.[43]

The picture of early Iron Age Greece that emerges from the archaeological excavations and surveys conducted and published to date is of a distinctly impoverished society—at any rate relative to Mycenaean and late archaic and classical Greece—with relatively few settlements and those mostly small and unimpressive. Even the more notable mainland early Iron Age settlements that were to develop into major city-states—Athens and Argos, for example—are distinctly unimpressive, and there is little or no sign of the kind of urbanization and physical infrastructure that characterize the city-state, at any rate before about 750.[44] In fact, several of the most archaeologically imposing Dark Age sites were destined not to become city-states at all, but to wither away in the course of the eighth century: the Lefkandi/Xeropolis settlement on Euboia, Zagora on Andros, Koukounaries on Paros.[45] It seems not unlikely that these sites stand out among Dark Age settlements precisely because they were abandoned at the beginning of the Archaic Age, that is that the Dark Age settlements at more enduring sites were so completely overshadowed by their archaic and classical successors as to have been rendered virtually archaeologically invisible. As far as the archaeological evidence goes, it is not at all clear that Athens was a very much more impressive settlement in the late tenth to early eighth centuries than others in Attica, such as Eleusis, Marathon, and Thorikos; that Sparta was much more important in Lakedaimon at this time than Geronthrai, or Helos, or Prasiai; or that Argos was destined to be a city-state of which Mycenai, Tiryns, Asine, and Nauplion would be mere perioikic communities.[46] The places where we do see archaeological remains suggestive of the kind of urbanization and centralized communal life and effort that characterize the city-state are, as one would expect from the above analysis, mostly outside of mainland Greece: Smyrna in Ionia above all, though some of the other east Greek settlements like Ephesos, Samos, Miletos, and Melie may also be mentioned.[47]

Overseas Settlements and City-State Development

An important aspect of city-state formation that we must now consider is the process of establishing the boundaries of the various city-states, and so the political geography of the city-state world. An aspect of this process that has been emphasized by some recent scholars is the development of the notion of territoriality. In early Iron Age Greece, with its few and small settlements scattered in a largely empty countryside, there are unlikely to have been worries and conflicts over control of territory and boundaries with neighbors. The process of city-state formation was in part—an important part—a process of establishing control over defined territory as against, and often at the expense of, one's neighbors.[48]

For much of the Greek world, the process was a relatively simple one. On the vast majority of Greek islands the city-state simply became coterminous with the island it occupied: other than the three great islands of Krete, Cyprus, and Euboia, which are special cases, there are only a handful of exceptions.[49] In east Greece—that is, the coast of Asia Minor—the settlements were highly nucleated from early times, as we have seen, and their mutual independence was mostly secure: there was a certain amount of inevitable bickering over borders, and a few cases of absorption of smaller communities are known—the Meliac War in the eighth century led to the destruction of Melie and the division of its lands among its neighbors, and Myous was absorbed by Miletos at an early date[50]—but by and large the various east Greek settlements developed into city-states controlling their surrounding lands in a fairly straight-forward way. The process was largely similar for the new overseas settlements of the mid eighth century and later: there were struggles to incorporate as much native land as possible, and later rivalries between neighboring colonies, but by and large each new settlement was founded as, or became in due course, a full-fledged city-state. Just how remarkable this was has often been overlooked, however. After all, the *polis* as city-state was only beginning to develop in metropolitan Greece at the time when the earlier western settlements were being founded (second half of the eighth century), and some of the founding communities were themselves not city-states at all but *ethne*: the Achaians founded Sybaris, Kroton, and Metopontion in south Italy, and Skione in the Khalkidike; the Lokrians founded Lokroi in south Italy.[51] There was evidently something about the physical process of founding new settlements in the circumstances of the early Archaic Era that caused all such settlements to be founded as—or at any rate rapidly to become—city-states, even when the founding communities themselves were pre- or non-city-states.

The reasons for this are in fact not far to seek. They are to be found in the circumstances in which the migrants found themselves. Attempting to establish a new settlement in the face of actually or potentially hostile native inhabitants, the settlers naturally felt the need for a very centralized, well-defended settlement. Hence, these settlements were founded as towns that in due course grew into small or large cities, rather than as scattered villages or farmsteads; and these "colonial" towns were normally quickly provided with defensive fortification.[52] The new settlements, for the same reason, could not afford internal disunity during the early stages of establishing the settlement: hence the division of land, both of housing allotments in the towns and of farming allotments in the *chora*, was distinctly egalitarian.[53] There was, during the first few generations of the settlement, no fixed system of government or established aristocracy or upper class. It seems that during his lifetime, the *oikistes* or leader of the "colonial" expedition governed the new settlement, and the settlements frequently copied magistracies and other such institutions from their *metropoleis*,[54] but the socio-economic egalitarianism of the founding period, and the stresses and dangers the new community faced, naturally encouraged the development of collective decision-making structures—i.e., state councils and assemblies—again to maintain the needed unity.

One of the factors potentially operating against unity and making it imperative to do everything possible to maintain it, was that many *apoikiai* (the term the Greeks used for these new settlements) comprised settlers from two or more Greek communities. In the west, for example, the Khalkidian *apoikia* of Naxos in Sicily also had settlers from the Cycladic island that gave the colony its name, the Khalkidian *apoikia* at Rhegion in Italy had also some Messenian settlers, and the *apoikia* of Gela on the south coast of Sicily had migrants from both Rhodes and Krete. In the Black Sea region, the sheer number of Milesian *apoikiai* makes it clear that the settlers in them must have been of mixed origin, and in a number of cases we know where some of the non-Milesian settlers came from: the Milesian *apoikia* of Kardia included Klazomenian settlers, Amisos included migrants from Phokaia, and Parion had settlers from Paros and Erythrai.[55] Further, the Megarian *apoikia* of Herakleia included settlers from Boiotia.[56] Other examples could be cited, but the point is that in many cases the inhabitants of *apoikiai* did not all share the same legal, political, and religious traditions. In light of this it should come as no surprise that the earliest law-givers of whom Greek tradition preserved memory were active in the western settlements in the second half of the seventh century, that is a generation or two after the original foundations: Zaleukos of Lokroi in Italy and Charondas of Katane in Sicily.[57] These men are reported to have been active as lawgivers widely in the western "colonial" region, not just in their own cities, clearly fulfilling a need for agreed upon, written laws that arose from the mixed origins of the settlers, their desire for unity, and their lack of clear and accepted guidance in these matters once the *oikistes* was dead. Similarly, it will be no accident that many of the newly founded cities were among the leaders in archaic Greek temple building: the need to establish communal cults and festivals in a highly visible manner will have made itself strongly felt in the circumstances outlined above.[58]

All these are phenomena that put the *apoikiai*, especially the western *apoikiai*, very much at the forefront of city-state development, and one can add that, in their need for communal defense against the native peoples, the new settlements must have developed and relied upon a greater degree of fairly equal participation in warfare than will have been common in the metropolitan communities, perhaps even to some extent pioneering the development of hoplite warfare (see further Chapter 3 below). In sum, it is very likely that some of the crucial stages of city-state development happened earliest and most fully in the *apoikiai*, and that to some extent the older Greek communities that developed into city-states were learning from the *apoikiai* in the later eighth and seventh centuries. Although this has often been acknowledged by scholars,[59] in practice the western settlements still tend to be left to one side in studies of early Greece, as belonging to a more or less marginal region to be dealt with primarily in specialized studies, an attitude no doubt due in part to the strong attraction for modern scholars of the Ionian cities in the Archaic Era, and in greater part to the overwhelming centrality in Greek politics and culture achieved by Athens and Sparta from the late sixth century onwards. But it is clear that during the Archaic Age the western *apoikiai* were a vital part of the Greek world interacting with metropolitan Greece in numerous and important ways, and very much a part of all the political, social, and cultural developments going on in Greece in this period: it was not for nothing that the western "colonial" region came to be known during this period as *he megale Hellas*—Great Greece!

In mainland Greece, by contrast with the situation on the islands, along the coast of Asia Minor, and in the "colonial" region, the process of establishing the territories and boundaries of the classical city-states was extremely complex, involving the determination of which regions would remain *ethne* and which develop city-states, and in the latter regions which settlements would become urban nuclei of independent city-states, and which would either disappear or become dependent demes or perioikic communities of a more successful neighbor. For much of mainland Greece, evidence of this process is insufficient to examine it in any detail, or even totally lacking, but there are a number of cases where enough is known to establish at least the outlines of the process, and they illustrate some clearly variant models of early Greek state formation.

The Ethnos Model: Phokis

The main reason, without doubt, why so much is known about Phokis is that the great international oracle of Apollo at Delphi lay in this region, and there can, likewise, be no doubt that the history of Phokis was mightily affected, one might even say deformed, by the presence of this formidable entity. The rise of the Delphic Oracle to Panhellenic importance occurred in the second half of the eighth century, the very period which also saw the beginning of city-state development in mainland Greece.[60] The oracle was already known to Homer, though not—apparently—the name Delphi: he twice refers to the oracle of Apollo, on one occasion emphasizing its wealth (*Iliad* 9.404–5; cf. *Od.* 8.80), but he always calls the place Pytho, with the very appropriate epithets "rocky" (*Iliad* 2.519 and 9.405) and "sacred" (*Od.* 8.80; see also 11.581). The Homeric "Catalogue" (*Iliad* 2.517–26) lists eight settlements of the *Phokees*—Kyparissos, Pytho, Krisa, Daulis, Panopeus, Anemoreia, Hyampolis, and Lilaia—and two leaders: Schedios and Epistrophos, the sons of Iphitos. Four of the settlements known to Homer were also important towns in archaic and classical times—Daulis, Panopeus, Hyampolis, and Lilaia—and Pytho is of course Delphi under another name. Krisa, sometimes called Kirrha, was an important town in the early archaic period,[61] and if the ancient tradition which identified Kyparissos as an early name for the classical town of Antikyra is correct (Paus. 10.36.10), then all but one of the eight places listed by Homer were known as significant towns of Phokis in later times also, and even Anemoreia was known to later writers—Strabo mentions it as the border between Delphi and Phokis after the former had been made independent (9.423)—though it was apparently insignificant in classical times and later.

The number of significant settlements in Phokis increased in the classical period—Herodotos listed fifteen towns destroyed by the Persians in 480 (8.33-5), Demosthenes spoke of twenty-two towns (*poleis*) in Phokis (19.123), and Pausanias listed twenty towns destroyed at the end of the Third Sacred War in 347/6 (10.3.1-2)—but none were of great size or distinction, only Elateia being sufficiently important to make it a surprising omission from Homer's "Catalogue" (assuming that Kyparissos was indeed Antikyra).[62] The one town which might, in the archaic period, have grown large and strong enough to develop into a city-state controlling much or all of Phokis was Krisa/Kirrha, to the south of Delphi overlooking the Krisaian Bay of the Corinthian Gulf. In the seventh century, Krisa controlled Delphi and apparently sought control over the rest of Phokis: at any rate, when the growing international importance of Delphi led a powerful coalition of states to declare war on Krisa in order to end its control of Delphi—the so-called First Sacred War fought in the 590s—most of the other Phokians apparently fought against Krisa.[63] The war ended in the destruction of Krisa, and thereafter there was no town in Phokis that stood out in size and power, capable of unifying the region into a city-state.

In all sources that we have concerning Phokis in the sixth, fifth, and fourth centuries, the region is uniformly presented as one political unit lacking any urban center, that is as an *ethnos*.[64] The Phokians fought several wars in the sixth century against the Thessalians and Boiotians, took part on the Greek side in the Persian War, allied themselves alternately with Athens and Sparta in the fifth century, fought the Thebans and others in the Third Sacred War.[65] From the late sixth century they occasionally minted coins with the legend ΦΩ or ΦΩΚΙ.[66] Through all of this it is absolutely clear that the Phokians were a united political community (see n. 64). Although sources like Herodotos, Demosthenes, and Pausanias speak of *poleis* in Phokis, it is certain that the word in this context means "towns," for the simple reason that none of these *poleis* ever acted as an independent political community but always as part of the political community called "the Phokeis." The one exception to the absence of city-states in Phokis is, after a fashion, Delphi. From the mid fifth century on Delphi was separated from the rest of Phokis and formed, with the Krisaian plain, a more or less independent quasi-city-state.⁶⁷ This was essentially due to the importance of the oracle, and the interest of all Greek powers in ensuring that no one state (i.e., the Phokians) should control it too closely; and in fact the oracle, and through it Delphi as a whole, was always supervised by—and to a considerable extent under the thumb of—the leading powers in the Amphiktyonic League.⁶⁸

The Centrifugal Polis Model: Boiotia and the Argolid

In Boiotia we have a region in which one community—Thebes—became so much larger and stronger than the others as to be clearly predominant and able to aspire to uniting the whole region under its control as a city-state of the Thebans, but without ever quite being able to bring this to pass. This is perhaps a controversial view of the matter: so far as I am aware, scholars to date have generally interpreted the history of Boiotia as a struggle between attempts by the Thebans to bring all communities into a Boiotian "League" or "Confederation" which they expected to dominate, and the desire of a number of Boiotian communities to be fully autonomous and independent city-states.⁶⁹ In fact, as Giovannini has pointed out, and as the evidence of the Homeric "Catalogue" analyzed above seems to confirm, the Boiotians had formed an *ethnos* from Geometric Age times, and the struggle was over the transformation of that primitive *ethnos* into something else, with the late-fifth- and fourth-century Boiotian "Leagues" emerging essentially as a compromise.⁷⁰ That is to say, I argue that the preferred outcome from the Theban perspective was absorption of all of Boiotia into the Theban city-state; the preferred outcome in the view of other Boiotian towns like Orchomenos, Thespiai, and Plataia would have been their total independence as free and untrammeled city-states; and the gradual consolidation of the *ethnos* structure into the Theban-led confederation (*koinon*) of Classical times was the compromise that came to be settled on.

Historical sources for Boiotian history begin only in the sixth century, when we hear of a war against the Phokians usually dated to *c.* 560, of participation in the founding of Herakleia Pontika about the same time, of a war against the Thessalians *c.* 540, and of a Theban attempt to subject the other Boiotians—and especially the Plataians—around 519.⁷¹ Also in the late sixth century the Boiotians began to mint coins with as obverse type the so-called Boiotian shield: such coins were minted at Thebes, Haliartos, Akraiphia, Koroneia, Mykalessos, Pharai, and Tanagra, the various mint sites being distinguished by the initial letter of the name of the town (or perhaps rather people) in question, usually placed in the center of the reverse.[72] It is interesting to note that just as in the Homeric "Catalogue" Orchomenos was listed separately, as not belonging to Boiotia, so the late-sixth-century coins of Orchomenos were not ethnic issues with the Boiotian shield, but bore another device—an ear of grain—showing that Orchomenos was not part of the Boiotian *ethnos* in the Archaic period.[73]

In terms of city-state formation, the most significant piece of information is that from Herodotos (6.108) about Thebes and Plataia. Herodotos specifically states that it was the Thebans who were pressuring the Plataians, and adds a bit later that the Corinthians, arbitrating the dispute between Thebes and Plataia, urged the Thebans to leave in peace those of the Boiotians who chose not to be reckoned among the Boiotians: *ean Thebaious Boioton tous me boulemenous es Boiotous teleein*. In other words, the Boiotians were seen as a single political community in Homer, and were presented as such in politico-military activities of the mid sixth century, but in the late sixth century the Thebans were trying to bring about some change in the political structure of Boiotia that caused the Plataians—and conceivably, from Herodotos' report of the Corinthian arbitrators' words, some other Boiotian towns—to wish to opt out of Boiotian unity. This change must clearly be seen in the context of city-state formation: I believe we must conclude that the Thebans sought to incorporate all of Boiotia into their city-state, as the Spartans had done in Lakedaimon and the Athenians in Attica, and that some of the communities resisted this and sought instead to become independent city-states. It is revealing that a number of the communities listed in the Homeric "Catalogue" were in fact absorbed by Thebes and had become mere *komai* of Thebes in the Classical era—Peteon (Strabo 9.2.26), Hyrie (Strabo 9.12.1), and Schoinos (Strabo 9.2.22)—and that Akraiphia, which in the late sixth century minted coins as a separate Boiotian town (see n. 72), was also absorbed by the Thebans (Pausanias 9.23.5). Further, we know that during the Peloponnesian War, the Thebans absorbed Plataia and its territory (Thuc. 3.68.3–4; *Hell. Oxy.* 16.3), and that by the mid fourth century they had absorbed Thespiai and Orchomenos too.[74] One might note that the ancient sources frequently simply equate the Thebans and the Boiotians, so great was Thebes' dominance most of the time.

The resistance of Boiotian towns to incorporation by Thebes, their desire to become independent city-states, and the ultimate failure of Thebes to turn Boiotia into a Theban city-state, can be attributed to three factors. In the first place, there is the centrifugal tendency, the local patriotism and desire for local autonomy, that is such a strong feature of Greek history. In the second place, there is the intervention of outside powers—primarily the Athenians, but in the fourth century also the Spartans—who supported the centrifugal tendencies of Boiotian towns like Plataia and Thespiai in order to weaken the power of their rival Thebes. Thirdly, and perhaps most importantly, in trying to bring the other Boiotian towns under their control the Thebans were evidently not offering them full Theban citizenship, but at best some form of perioikic status: when Thebes in fact succeeded in absorbing Plataia, Thespiai, and Orchomenos, they killed, drove away, and/or enslaved their populations and repopulated the communities with Theban settlers (see above n. 74 for sources). However, though Thebes was never quite strong enough to fully unify and centralize Boiotia, its power was too great to allow the other Boiotian towns to become fully independent city-states, except Plataia for a time, thanks to Athenian protection. Hence the anomalous half-way position in which Boiotia remained: part *ethnos* and part region of city-states.

The prominence of Argos had its origins in the early Iron Age, as a result of a shift of the main focus of settlement and power in the Argive plain southward and westward away from Mycenai and Tiryns, the two dominant settlements in the region during the Bronze Age. The history of Argos is that of a Greek superpower *manqué*: it never succeeded in matching Sparta and Athens, or even Thebes for that matter, as an aspirant to dominant power in the Greek world. For all that, Argos was throughout archaic and classical times one of the most important and powerful city-states in Greece—it was, for example, the only Peloponnesian community which successfully resisted incorporation in Sparta's sixth- and fifth-century Peloponnesian League—and the roots both of its success and of its failure lie in its early Iron Age and Archaic Age development. It is very clear that it was the main aim of Argos in this period to bring under its control all the north-east Peloponnesos and the Argolid peninsula, just as Sparta unified the southern Peloponnesos under its control and Athens unified Attica. Had Argos succeeded in its aim, it would have been an equal if not superior rival to Sparta and Athens, and the course of classical Greek history would have been very different than it was.

The archaeological evidence shows that Argos was one of the most significant settlements in Greece during the early Iron Age.[75] During the eighth century, Argos consolidated its control over the Argive plain and its environs by founding the Heraion at the eastern edge of the plain—opposite Argos at the western edge—and by destroying/absorbing Asine and—in the early seventh century—Nauplion, both on the coast at the southern extremity of the plain. The process of securing control over Mycenai and Tiryns was more difficult: Tiryns seems to be attested as an autonomous community by inscribed laws of the late seventh century, and both Mycenai and Tiryns asserted their independence after Argos' disastrous defeat by Sparta at the battle of Sepeia c. 494, remaining independent for about a generation until attacked and destroyed by a resurgent Argos in the early 460s.[76] In the end, Argos successfully established full control over the entire Argive plain and its environs, but it was essentially by means of strong-arm tactics.

That Argos' ambitions were not limited to incorporating the Argive plain is made clear by a range of evidence concerning its relations with such neighboring communities as Corinth, Kleonai, Sikyon, Phleious, and the towns of the Argolid peninsula, as well as by testimony concerning the so-called "Lot of Temenos"— by which is meant Argive control of the whole north-east Peloponnesos. The myth of the "return of the Heraklidai"—that is the conquest of much of the Peloponnesos by Herakles' descendants—had the three leaders of the Heraklidai divide their conquered territory into three parcels: the north-east (around Argos and the Argolid), the south-east (essentially Lakedaimon), and the south-west (Messenia). They then cast lots to see who would rule which portion, and Temenos was the hero who gained control of the north-east portion of the Peloponnesos. The "Lot of Temenos" represents, thus, essentially an alternative mythic political geography to that found in the Homeric "Catalogue," in which— it will be recalled—the north-east Peloponnesos was split into two realms: a northern realm under Agamemnon including Mycenai, Corinth, Sikyon and Achaia, and a southern realm under Diomedes, Sthenelos, and Euryalos including Argos, Tiryns, Asine, the whole Argolid peninsula, and Aigina (*Iliad* 2.559–80).

The "Lot of Temenos" tradition saw the north-east Peloponnesos as one political entity, including Sikyon, Phleious, Corinth, the Argolid peninsula, and Aigina, and centered at Argos. It has been strongly, and I believe rightly, argued that this "Lot of Temenos" tradition is late, and that Argos never controlled these regions during the Early Iron Age.[77] It seems clear, in fact, that this tradition represents mythic propaganda embodying an Argive desire or aim to control the entire north-east Peloponnesos. The interest of Argos in controlling this region is fairly well attested, though most of the relevant sources are—when taken in isolation—of doubtful reliability. As a result, scholars have often attacked the source tradition about early Argive expansionism piece by piece, showing each individual piece to be unreliable and thus—by espousing a kind of scholarly divide and rule—demolished it.[78] This technique—of taking sources one by one in isolation and, by showing that each individual source is dubious, purporting to disprove the entire tradition—is inappropriate: one must also consider the pattern that the sources as a whole establish (if, that is, such a pattern is discernible), and bear in mind that the plausibility of the general tendency, if not always the specific details, of individual dubious sources may be strengthened or outright confirmed by the pattern or network of source information of which they are a part. In the present case, though the reliability of many sources attesting early Argive interest in or control over places like Aigina, Corinth, Sikyon, Epidauros, the Thyreatis, and the Kynouria[79] may justly be doubted, they do collectively add up to a strong tradition of Argive expansionism in the northeast Peloponnesos which should be taken seriously and is, in fact, quite plausible.

The question of the date at which the "Lot of Temenos" tradition was invented must surely be looked at in light of its aim, bearing in mind that the tradition was presented in the history of Ephoros—writing in the mid fourth century—as already a venerable mythic tradition (above n. 77). It seems likely, first of all, that the Argives cannot have extended their ambitions eastward to the Argolid peninsula or northward to the Corinthia and Sikyon before they had consolidated their control over the Argive plain, that is to say, before construction of the Heraion in the mid eighth century and the destruction of Asine at the end of that century.[80] The earliest date for wider Argive ambitions, of the sort suggested by the "Lot of Temenos" myth, would seem to be the seventh century, then. It is immediately interesting to note that the early seventh century is one of the more widely accepted dates for the career of that mysterious and controversial figure, the tyrant Pheidon of Argos.[81] Pheidon was clearly a man of wide ambitions: ancient sources connect him unequivocally with places as far apart as Olympia in the west, Aigina in the east, and Corinth in the north; and in fact Ephoros directly links him with Argive so-called "recovery of the Lot of Temenos."[82] The period of Pheidon, then, would seem to be a very plausible candidate for the time at which the notion of a "Lot of Temenos" was invented, especially as Pheidon was supposedly a descendant of Temenos.

Unfortunately, the date of Pheidon is very much in dispute: the ancient sources disagree on this point, and modern scholars likewise have situated Pheidon variously in the mid eighth, the early seventh, and the early sixth centuries. It seems to me, however, that the best evidence does suggest an early-seventh-century date, at the very beginning of the great age of archaic tyrannies which covered much of the seventh and sixth centuries (see n. 81). This would mean that Argos was seeking control of the Argive plain and then of the northeast Peloponnesos generally at roughly the same time as Sparta was winning control over Lacedaimon and Messenia, and as Athens was unifying all of Attica, which makes good historical sense. The development would then be from the two regional, *ethnos*-like political entities attested by Homer, to the beginning of city-state development at Argos in the mid eighth century and a consequent Argive claim to and attempt to gain supremacy over the whole north-east Peloponnesos. Pheidon is attested to have died seeking to win control over Corinth; Corinthian fear of Argos is a likely explanation for Corinth's exceptionally loyal adhesion to the Spartan alliance system in the sixth and fifth centuries, and in the early fourth century Argos actually succeeded for a brief time in absorbing Corinth.[83] Fear of Argive domination at Sikyon is prominent in the activity of the tyrant Kleisthenes of Sikyon.[84] Argos actually won control for long periods of time over Kleonai, and over Nemea and its important pan-Hellenic festival.[85] Argive interventions at Epidauros and in the rest of the Argolid peninsula, and on the island of Aigina, are well attested.[86] By the mid sixth century, Argive influence had long extended over the Thyreatis and further down the east coast of Cape Malea, according to Herodotos.[87]

Ultimately, however, Argive power over the Argive plain remained fragile into the fifth century, and its influence beyond the Argive plain was never more than transitory. Three reasons can be given for this. In the first place it seems that Argos' policy with respect to the communities to be incorporated was not a generous one, that is that the Argives were not offering their inhabitants equal status as Argive citizens in the manner of the Athenians in Attica: the record of Argive treatment of communities like Asine, Nauplion, and Mycenai is clear enough in this regard (above n. 76). This in itself need not have prevented Argive success: the Spartans were highly successful in Lakedaimon and Messenia with a policy that was certainly not more generous. In the second place, however, some of the communities Argos was trying to incorporate were themselves quite large and populous, especially Corinth. The Corinthians probably began as early as the Argives to develop a city-state structure of their own and emerged from successful early conflicts with the Argives and Megarians, via extensive trading and colonizing activity and the centralizing and strengthening work of the Kypselid tyranny, as one of the largest and most important city-states of Greece in their own right.[88] Very likely, Corinthian resistance and rivalry was a major factor in scotching Argive plans to incorporate the northeast Peloponnesos in their city-state. One might add that Sikyon, Phleious, and Epidauros also grew to be quite substantial cities, contributing significant hoplite forces to the battle of Plataia in 479 for example, and their resistance to Argive domination will also have been a factor.[89] Thirdly, and perhaps most importantly, there is the rivalry of the Spartans. As we shall see below, the Spartans had consolidated their control over Lakedaimon and were extending their power into Messenia at a time—the mid to late eighth century—when the Argives were still only establishing their control over the communities surrounding the Argive plain. Though the seventh century was a difficult period for the Spartans, they emerged from it immensely strengthened, and in the course of the sixth and early fifth centuries established and consolidated their hegemony over the entire Peloponnesos, several times defeating Argos in the process, and making alliances with cities such as Phleious, Sikyon, Corinth, etc. which precluded Argos from incorporating those cities.[90] Consequently, Argive ambitions remained perpetually unfulfilled, and Argos' borders never for long extended far beyond the immediate environs of the Argive plain, with the rest of the north-east Peloponnesos home to a number of smaller independent city-states.

The Centripetal Polis Model 1: Sparta and the Perioikic System

The realm of Menelaos depicted in the Homeric "Catalogue" did not extend beyond the Eurotas valley, as we have seen above, and the settlement called Sparta is not given any special prominence in it, though it seems elsewhere in Homer to be viewed as the actual home of Menelaos. There is some reason to doubt that the Homeric Sparta was even the same place as classical Sparta: it was probably located three miles away, on the other bank of the Eurotas River (i.e., the east bank), at the site of the classical cult complex called—perhaps significantly—the Menelaion.[91] The early history of archaic and classical Sparta seems to me to confirm this hypothesis, for we know that Sparta was formed by the synoikism of four previously autonomous villages—Pitana, Limnai, Mesoa, and Kynosoura—at a date not precisely determinable but possibly to be placed in the early eighth century, with the later addition of a fifth village—Amyklai—around 750.[92] This means that at the very time the original document underlying the Homeric "Catalogue" was being created, the development of Sparta was radically changing the political landscape of Lakedaimon. Obviously, if the four villages that collectively made up the "town of Sparta"—according to Thucydides 1.10.2 Sparta remained physically an agglomeration of these four villages through the fifth century—were originally separate, they cannot have been called "Sparta" before uniting, and they presumably in fact adopted that name when or soon after they synoikized, borrowing it from the mythical home of Menelaos and Helen which lay within their collective territory.

Once the community of Sparta had been created by this synoikism, it began the process of city-state development. It was very favorably situated to gain predominant power in Lakedaimon: in the center of the Eurotas valley which forms the agricultural and demographic heart of Lakedaimon, and controlling the so-called "Spartan basin"—22 kilometers long and 8 to 12 kilometers wide—the most important and fertile agricultural plain of Lakedaimon, since the Helos plain at the mouth of the Eurotas river was in antiquity significantly smaller than it is today and much of it was marshy.[93] The process whereby Sparta established control over the entire Eurotas valley and its mountainous hinterlands of the Parnon range to the east and the Taygetos range to the west is shrouded in legend.[94] The crucial fact concerning this process for present purposes is that, although the Spartans called their developed *polis* "the Lakedaimonians," they did not offer to the other towns and villages of Lakedaimon full citizenship of the city-state, with the already noted exception of Amyklai that was incorporated as a fifth village of Sparta. Instead, the Spartans created two subordinate statuses for the inhabitants of Lakedaimon outside the five villages of Sparta: perioikic status and helot status.

The Helots, whose name seems to be derived from the town of Helos at the mouth of the Eurotas, formed a substantial portion of the Lakedaimonian population who were reduced to a serf-like status. There is an extensive literature about this, and I will not go into much detail here.[95] Suffice it to say, in the first place, that ancient traditions connecting the origins of the Helot population with the conquest of Helos, and unequivocal evidence that the Spartans continued to have a Helot population after the loss of Messenia, make it clear that there were many Helots in Lakedaimon.[96] In the second place, the condition of Helots was similar to that of slaves elsewhere in Greece but with certain differences: on the one hand, the Helots enjoyed a fairly normal family and community life within the limits of their subjection, being tied to the land on which they lived and worked and ineligible for treatment as simple chattels; on the other, the Spartans formally declared war on them each year and in accordance with their formal status as enemies often harassed them mercilessly.[97] Thirdly, the status of the Helots, though an extreme case, was not unique in ancient Greece, being paralleled by less well-known populations in regions like Thessaly (the *Penestai*), the Argive plain (the *Gumnetes*), Krete (the *Klarotai*), Sikyon (the *Katonakophoroi*), and so on.[98]

The *Perioikoi* were in effect placed in a half-way position between the Spartans and the Helots. The *Perioikoi* were the inhabitants of towns and villages around Lakedaimon—and to a much more limited extend also in Messenia after its incorporation into the Spartan state—which, while incorporated into the Spartan state, were neither granted Spartan citizenship nor reduced to servile status. The perioikic towns retained a limited local autonomy and their inhabitants enjoyed personal freedom, but the *Perioikoi* had no political rights or privileges in the Spartan state—or as the Spartans misleadingly called it, the *polis* of the Lakedaimonians—to which they belonged. All political rights and privileges were retained by the Spartiates, the full citizens of Sparta itself, and all important decisions within the "Lakedaimonian" city-state were taken by the Spartiates.[99]

Spartan control of Lakedaimon was secure enough by the last quarter of the eighth century for the Spartans to undertake the conquest and incorporation of the neighboring region to the west, Messenia. The initial conquest in the closing decades of the eighth century had to be repeated in the mid seventh century after a major revolt. Like the inhabitants of Lakedaimon, the Messenians were reduced to perioikic and helot status, with the latter status certainly much predominating. The land of Messenia, other than that of the few perioikic communities, was divided among the Spartiates.[100] The Spartans also seized some border regions to the north of Lakedaimon from the Arkadians—the Belminatis, the Skiritis—and extended their control across the Parnon range to the east coast of the Peloponnesos, incorporating communities like Prasiai and Epidauros Limera, and in the mid sixth century driving the Argives out of the Thyreatis and incorporating that region too into the Spartan state.[101] The end result was that by the middle of the sixth century the city-state formally called "the Lakedaimonians," but actually being the city-state of the Spartans, controlled the southern two-fifths or so of the Peloponnesos, making it geographically far the largest of the Greek city-states, but in many respects also the most precarious, requiring a constant policing effort by the Spartans to maintain it.[102]

The Centripetal Polis Model 2: Athens and the Deme System

Thucydides tells us that Attica was synoikized into the Athenian *polis*—i.e., made one city-state of the Athenians—by the hero-king Theseus, and that the festival of the *synoikeia* was still annually held to celebrate the event (Thuc. 2.15.1–2). This statement is sometimes taken seriously by modern scholars, despite the fact that they know full well (as Thucydides clearly did not) that Theseus was a figure of myth, not history: they interpret Thucydides' statement to mean that Attica was synoikized by Athens in the Bronze Age already.[103] As a matter of fact it may well have been the case that Attica was a single political unit run from a palace/fort on the Athenian akropolis during part of the Bronze Age, but I don't see how

Thucydides could have known about this, nor what relevance it could conceivably have for Archaic and Classical Athens, given the intervening so-called "Dark Age" during the early phase of which (*c.* 1100–950) most of Attica seems on present evidence to have been deserted.[104] All that we can really take from Thucydides' statement is that in his view the synoikism of Attica occurred in the distant past, and that standard belief in his day credited Theseus—the great pan-Athenian hero—with bringing it about.

There is in fact very clear evidence demonstrating that Attica in its entirety was not yet incorporated into the nascent Athenian city-state as late as the mid seventh century. During the Classical period, the Athenian deme of Marathon sent its own, separate *theoroi* (sacred representatives) to the quadrennial Pythian festival at Delphi. The practice of sending such sacred representatives can only have arisen after the Delphic Oracle had gained international fame and standing in the second half of the eighth century. The clear implication is that Marathon was an independent community as late as the third quarter of the eighth century, otherwise the Athenian *theoroi* would certainly have counted for Marathon too.[105] In the Homeric *Hymn to Demeter*, most likely composed in the mid seventh century, the Attic towns of Thorikos and Eleusis are mentioned with not only no hint or suggestion that they were part of the Athenian city-state, but no mention of or allusion to Athens at all.[106] The apparent implication that they were still independent at some period within the memory of the hymn's composer is confirmed, as far as Eleusis is concerned, by evidence from Herodotos. Herodotos reports that the early-sixth-century Athenian statesman Solon, during his visit to the court of the Lydian king Kroisos, told the story of Tellos of Athens, the happiest man he had ever known (Herod. 1.30). Tellos died in victorious battle against the men of Eleusis. While the historicity of both Solon's visit to Lydia and of Tellos are doubtful at best, the significance of this story is that Herodotos' Athenian informants around the middle of the fifth century thought of Eleusis as having been independent—indeed hostile to Athens—during the lifetime of Solon. For if he had known Tellos as the story states, Solon must have been already alive and aware of things (i.e. at least about ten years old) at the time of Tellos' supposed battle against the Eleusinians.[107] If, for the sake of argument, we suppose that Solon was about fifty at the time of his archonship in 594, he would have been born around 644; he is certainly unlikely to have been born much earlier. This is to say, in modern terms, that mid-fifth-century Athenians thought of Eleusis as having been still independent of Athens as late as the third quarter of the seventh century.

I see no reason to doubt this Athenian tradition: it is not the sort of thing the Athenians invented, their myths about the unification of Attica being aimed rather at pushing it back into the remotest possible past. The idea that the synoikism of Attica was still an ongoing process during the eighth and seventh centuries seems to be confirmed by three other facts: Thucydides' contemporaries still preserved the memory of the time when the various towns of Attica had their own *prytaneia* and *archontes* (town halls and magistrates) and each ran their own affairs (Thuc. 2.15.1); the Attic towns of Pallene and Hagnous had no intermarriage in classical and later times, according to Plutarch, which suggests their independence and mutual hostility at some date surely much later than the end of the Bronze Age (Plut. *Theseus* 13.3); even during the sixth century it is clear from our sources that Athenian political life was plagued by factional strife originating in a regionalist disunity that surely presupposes that the synoikism of Attica was still only a recently completed process.[108]

Archaeological evidence cannot alter this conclusion, as some scholars believe. Whatever the archaeological remains may teach us about the similarities of material culture among the towns of Attica, and of the predominance of Athens in this respect, they cannot—by their very nature—inform us about the political relationships between Athens and the towns of Attica, and among the towns of Attica besides Athens.[109] There remains the evidence of Homer in the "Catalogue" (*Iliad* 2.546–56). Here, Attica is treated as a unity belonging to "the Athenians," and a certain amount of cultic information is attached in lieu of the normal enumeration of other settlements besides Athens. It might at first sight appear, therefore, that Homer represents Athens as already a city-state comprising all of Attica. Against this, however, is the very singularity of this "Catalogue" entry: Attica is the only region of Greece for which no list of settlements is given, and the omission of places like Eleusis, Marathon, and Thorikos seems simply inexplicable except on one hypothesis, which has to do with the process of establishing the canonical text of Homer. As is well known, Peisistratid Athens played a pivotal role in refining the "true" text of Homer, and it has long been suspected that this was not done without a certain amount of tinkering with the text to suit Athenian interests.[110] As early as the sixth century Megarians characterized the explicit positioning of Ajax's Salaminian contingent next to the Athenians as an Athenian interpolation, and Hellenistic scholars cast suspicion on a number of other passages, with a considerable degree of plausibility in several cases.[111] It seems very likely that the Attic entry in the "Catalogue" was altered under Peisistratid influence to depict an anachronistic Athenian city-state, in conformity with other known Peisistratid initiatives aimed at promoting the as yet fragile unity of Attica as the Athenian city-state: heavy promotion of the Panathenaic festival, building up of the Eleusinian

Mysteries and bringing of them under central Athenian control, sending out from Athens of traveling deme dikasts, and so on.[112]

The main argument used to preserve the antiquity and hence genuineness of the Athenian "Catalogue" entry is that it lists Menestheus son of Peteos as leader of the Athenians, rather than the sons of Theseus: the assumption is that the obscure Menestheus would not hold this position if the "Catalogue" entry had been altered/interpolated as late as the time of the Peisistratids. As a matter of fact, Theseus seems to have been entirely unknown to Homer, assuming that the mention of Theseus and Peirithoos in Hades at *Od.* 11.631 is an interpolation, as seems very likely (above n. 111). However, Boardman has argued that in Peisistratid Athens Theseus was a significantly more obscure hero than he became in the fifth century, and though more recent work by Shapiro, Walker, and Mills has significantly nuanced Boardman's too extreme position, it remains clear that it was under and after Kleisthenes' reforms that Theseus became recognized as the national Athenian hero *par excellence*, unifier of Attica and even proto-founder of Athenian democracy.[113] Much of the developed Theseus myth, as known from the fifth century and later sources, is demonstrably of late invention: the heroic journey from Troizen to Athens was created to parallel the "Labors of Herakles" and so make Theseus an Athenian counterweight to the Dorian Herakles, and also to cement Athenian links with and/or claims to northern Attica (Eleusis) and the Megarid. That Theseus was added late to the lists of heroes involved in the great mythic tales of the Kalydonian boar, the voyage of the Argo, and the battle of the Lapiths and Centaurs, seems indicated by the fact that he plays no significant role in any of these stories.[114] Theseus' role in the tales of Oedipus and of the "Seven against Thebes" and the "Return of the Heraklidai," as depicted in Athenian tragedies, obviously reflects fifteenth-century Athenian self-image and propaganda, and is no doubt an invention of that same era.[115] It is very likely that Theseus the unifier of Attica was an invention of Kleisthenic Athens, just as Theseus the inventor of democracy was a creation of fourth-century political pamphleteers.[116] The authentically ancient (pre-sixth century) Theseus myths seem not to have been much more than the Kretan Minotaur, the Marathonian bull, and perhaps the Amazonomachy—though even here there are suspicious parallels with Herakles.[117] The role of Menestheus as Athenian leader in the "Catalogue" entry is, therefore, no evidence against a sixth-century date for that text in its current state.

This discussion of Theseus brings us back to our starting point, for Thucydides' ascription of the synoikism of Attica to Theseus is in fact one of the surest signs that in this instance Thucydides has, whether knowingly or unknowingly, let himself be misled by early-fifth-century Athenian propaganda as enshrined in the accepted traditions and festivals of Thucydides' own day. It seems very likely that there was some form of tribal/regional association of the towns and villages of Attica—and perhaps of the Megarid too—in late Dark Age times, but the deformation of the entry in the Homeric "Catalogue" prevents us from knowing anything of its structure or limits. At any rate, such an Attic *ethnos* would comfortably explain the archaeological evidence regarding material culture that led such scholars as Snodgrass and Whitley to argue for an early synoikism of Attica (above n. 109). What needs to be strongly emphasized, however, is that Attica as the Athenian city-state is the product of developments of the eighth to the sixth centuries, and that it is very conceivable that the process of city-state formation in Attica in these centuries could have turned out very differently, producing for instance several independent or would-be independent city-states as in Boiotia: e.g., Eleusis, Marathon, and Thorikos as separate city-states besides Athens.

The extraordinary feature of the Athenian unification of Attica was not, then, its early date—for it was in fact achieved quite late—nor the size of the city-state thus created—for Sparta created one far larger, and Argos was not so very far behind Athens in size. What was truly remarkable about the Athenian unification of Attica, and what laid the basis for all of Athens' later political and military achievements—including the invention of democracy—was the way in which Athens incorporated the other towns and villages of Attica into the Athenian city-state. For unlike Sparta, Thebes, and Argos, the Athenians did not try to create subordinate or "perioikic" communities in Attica with lesser rights as compared to the inhabitants of Athens itself. Instead, the Athenians granted to all of the free, native inhabitants of Attica equal status in the Athenian *polis*, making them *Athenaioi* in the fullest sense and so, as the concept and precise rights and duties of citizenship developed, made them full Athenian citizens.[118] As a result, the Athenians never faced the kind of centri-fugalism among the smaller towns of Attike that the Thebans faced in Boiotia and the Argives in the Argolid, for example, as we have seen. The Athenians were able to make their city-state coterminous with Attica in this way, and the only significant issues they faced in terms of political geography after the unification of Attica concerned their north-eastern and north-western borders.

The limit of Attica in the north is set by the Parnes mountain, and the course of the border there in classical times is established by a string of frontier forts such as Panakton and Phyle.[119] Towards the coasts on either side, however—the Euboian Channel in the east and the Saronic Gulf in the west—the Parnes range ceases to be an effective barrier and hence frontier, and there was consequently frequent trouble and strife over Athens' borders in these regions, concerning Oropos in the north-east and Salamis and Megara to the north-west. The history of Oropos is complex. The dialect spoken by the Oropians seems to point to connections with the Eretrians; there is some evidence of Theban control in the mid sixth century, and the Athenians appear to have seized control before the end of the sixth century.[120] The Oropians rebelled against Athenian control with Eretrian support in 411 (Thuc. 8.60), and there followed over 350 years of alternate autonomy, Theban control, Eretrian control, and Athenian control, until the town was definitively incorporated into the Athenian state in the second half of the first century BCE (so Wiesner in *RE* s.v. Oropos with full sources). What is clear, at any rate, is that from at least the late sixth century on Athens was determined to bring Oropos under its control and if possible to incorporate the town into Attica.

Equally problematic was Athens' border to the north-west. Conflict with Megara, over control of Eleusis, over control of Salamis, and over the border between Eleusis and Megara—i.e., over the border between Attica and the Megarid—is attested from about the mid seventh century onwards, once the Athenians had incorporated Eleusis.[121] The early status of Megara itself is obscure, especially as it is not mentioned in the Homeric "Catalogue," at any rate in the existing form of that text. On the one hand, though lying outside the Peloponnesos, Megara's inhabitants spoke the Doric dialect of Greek and were divided into the standard three Doric tribes Hylleis, Dymaines, and Pamphylloi; on the other hand, there are strong mythic connections with Athens, and the geography of the Megarid links it rather to Attica than to the Peloponnesos, or even to Boiotia for that matter.[122] From the late eighth through to the early sixth centuries, Megara developed into an important independent city-state, sending out a substantial number of colonies (most notably to the Black Sea region), undergoing the tyranny of Theagenes, contesting control of Salamis with Athens, and producing in Theognis one of the most important archaic poets.[123] In the early sixth century, however, Megara had to fight on two fronts against Corinth to the west and Athens to the east, losing substantial territory in both directions— Perachora and Krommyon to Corinth, Salamis to Athens—though ultimately maintaining itself as an independent city-state. There can be little doubt that Athens would have liked to have incorporated Megara: the mythic tradition of Theseus' slaying of the Megarian sow, and especially of his placing of a boundary marker at the Isthmos between the Peloponnesos and "Ionia" (i.e. Attic territory), is a clear pointer to such a desire; and one should note further Peisistratos' seizure—temporary though it proved—of Megara's harbor Nisaia, and the well-known Athenian diplomatic, economic, and military pressure on Megara in the fifth century.[124] Ultimately, though, Athens had to content itself in this direction with holding Eleusis and Salamis: Megara remained permanently beyond its grasp.

Conclusion: The Development of the City-State

What emerges from this brief review of the formative process in some key Greek communities is a number of crucial conclusions that in some respects are well known to scholars of ancient Greece, but several of which are in practice too often ignored. In the first place one must stress that there was absolutely nothing predetermined about the political geography of classical Greece. The various communities I have looked at—and there is no reason to suppose that things were significantly different for other Greek communities—could perfectly well have had different histories and developments, leading to quite different results. Nothing about the geography of these regions, or about their demography and social structure prior to 800 BCE, predetermined the classical outcome: Phokis could perfectly well have become a city-state centered at Krisa, or Boiotia have been fully incorporated into the Theban city-state; alternatively, Attica might very well have developed more along *ethnos* lines in a way similar to Phokis or Boiotia. The city-states that arose could well have been larger or smaller than they actually became and there could have been more or fewer in a given region: Attica could well have been home to two, three, four, or even more city-states rather than the one city-state of the Athenians; the north-east Peloponnesos might have developed into the one city-state of the Argives; the southern Peloponnesos would certainly more naturally have comprised at least two city-states—as it did after the liberation of Messenia in 368—or even more; and so on.

Several key facts should be born in mind. There were two processes of state development going on in early Iron Age and Archaic Age Greece, that of the *ethnos* as well as that of the city-state, and to all appearances the *ethnos* actually had deeper historical roots than the city-state. Even within the process of city-state development there was no uniformity, at least two major variants being discernible, one of which comprised two important sub-variants, making therefore three alternative models of city-state development. The main division is between centripetal and centrifugal development. The latter was a process leading to larger numbers of smaller city-states, as in the efforts of communities like Plataia, Thespiai, and Orchomenos in Boiotia to become autonomous city-states, or of Phleious, Sikyon, Kleonai, Epidauros, Troizen, and the rest of the north-east Peloponnesos. The former, centripetal, process was that which saw Athens and Sparta unifying large regions, and on a lesser scale the unification of the Argive plain area by Argos. Within this centripetal development, however, one can see two clear sub-models, which may be called—after the terminology used by their most important and influential exponents—the perioikic model and the deme model. The former model, used most notably by Sparta but also espoused with lesser success by Thebes and Argos among others, incorporated towns and villages into the nascent city-state with a subordinate status vis-à-vis the urban center and its inhabitants; the latter model, made famous by Athens but also found in a basically similar way at Corinth, Megara, Chalkis, Eretria, and other places, gave to the inhabitants of the incorporated towns and villages a political status more or less equal to that of the people of the urban center.[125]

What all this means is that, far from following some predetermined path of development laid down by the facts of geography, demography, or whatever, the communities of Greece developed as they did as a result of a series of conscious choices and deliberate actions and policies, both by those within the community and by those without it, which sent each given community down one of a set of alternative available paths of development to produce the ultimate outcome we see in classical Greece. For example, the decision of several Greek powers to attack and destroy Krisa in the First Sacred War had a major impact on the way Phokis developed as an *ethnos*. The choice made by the Athenians to offer equal status to the other inhabitants of Attica, and the choice of the peoples of the Attic towns and villages to accept this offer and struggle within an Athenian city-state to make it a reality, had a crucial impact on the development of the Athenian city-state: without it the emergence of Athenian democracy, and everything that went with that political system in social and cultural terms, would scarcely have been feasible. The same can be said of the strange, twisted Spartan social, cultural, and political system, so clearly a result of the Spartans' determined pursuit of an extreme form of perioikic city-state development, and of the fierce though mostly futile resistance of many of those thus "incorporated" by the Spartans. In sum, it was choices made on crucial issues at crucial moments by the inhabitants of the various Greek communities that determined whether they were to become *ethne*, large or small city-states, or demes or perioikic communities of city-states. Those conscious choices and deliberate actions and interactions to a large degree determined the ultimate nature, size, and shape of the various Greek communities, and so shaped their history, their political structure and practices, their sociology, economy, and culture.

2

Economic Development and the City-State

In trying to understand the rise and nature of the ancient Greek city (and city-state), historians have posited several basic analytical models of what the city was for and about. Mid- to late-nineteenth-century historians tended to view the Greek cities, akin to early modern cities, as centers of production, and not a few twentieth-century historians followed that view in a more or less nuanced way.[1] According to this view, based especially on what is known of fifth-century Athens and Corinth, a host of specialized manufactured or imported goods were produced by urban craftsmen and traders for sale to a rural population of food producers. In the late nineteenth and early twentieth centuries, many historians protested against the anachronism of understanding the ancient Greek city according to economic structures and practices of a much later age: they argued that the ancient Greek cities were in fact cities of consumers, living essentially by exploiting a rural population of food producers, most of whom were little more than subsistence farmers, and offering little in exchange for that exploitation.[2] It is fair to say, I think, that this latter view takes Sparta, with its economically unproductive warrior-citizen class exploiting rural Helots, to be the more typical model of the ancient Greek city, rather than Athens. This "primitivist" model of the Greek city-states and their economy was for decades the dominant one among historians of classical Greece. More recently, however, Donald Engels has proposed a third model, that of the service city: the urban dwellers provided various services—organizational, cultural, religious—in return for the surplus food produced by the rural population.[3] In this model, cities like Athens and Corinth are again taken to be more typical, rather than Sparta. All three models have their virtues and also drawbacks: I would note, for example, that the sharp distinction between urban and rural populations each seems to assume in fact misrepresents the situation of ancient Greece, when most families engaged in farming lived in the cities and walked or rode out to their farms—which usually consisted of many scattered plots of land in different parts of the *chora*—as needed according to the seasons and the farming cycle.[4] Thus the urban population and the land-working, food-producing population were to a great degree one and the same, both producers and consumers.

Each of these three models seeks to understand the city-state in terms of its economic structure, and it is certainly true that the nature of the economy, and the question of economic development, is critical to understanding the city-state and its emergence. A crucial element of every city-state, after all, was its highly urbanized core, the actual city (*astu*) of the city-state *(polis)*, and the process of urbanization that created these urban centers must certainly have had an economic underpinning, including a considerable degree of economic specialization. This is no new discovery: already in the early fourth century BCE, Plato and Xenophon pointed to economic specialization as crucial to the development of the city. When Plato considered the origin and function of the *polis* in the second book of his *Republic*, his explanation was in terms of economic specialization:

> I think a city comes to be ... because not one of us is self-sufficient, but needs many things ... As they need many things, people make use of one another for various purposes. They gather many associates and helpers to live in one place, and to this settlement we give the name of city ... And they share with one another, both giving and taking, in so far as they do, because they think this better for themselves ... One man obviously must be a farmer, another a builder, and another a weaver. And should we add a shoe-maker and some other craftsmen to look after our physical needs?
>
> *Republic* 369b–d

So, it was to facilitate and regulate this form of economic specialization and exchange that humans came together and formed cities *(poleis)*, according to Plato.[5]

Xenophon similarly emphasized the importance of economic specialization and exchange in the developed Greek city, noting that in small towns there was little scope for economic specialization, but that in the larger cities it had advanced so far that men in the shoe-making business no longer made shoes entire, but broke shoe-making down into constituent parts with each worker specializing in just one part of the shoe-making task:

> For in small towns the same workman makes chairs and doors and plows and tables, and often this same artisan builds houses, and even so he is thankful if he can only find employment enough to support him. And it is, of course, impossible for a man of many trades to be proficient in all of them. In large cities, on the other hand, inasmuch as many people have demands to make upon each branch

of industry, one trade alone, and very often even less than a whole trade, is enough to support a man: one man, for instance, makes shoes for men, and another for women; and there are places even where one man earns a living by only stitching shoes, another by cutting them out, another by sewing the uppers together, while there is another who performs none of these operations but only assembles the parts. It follows, therefore, as a matter of course, that he who devotes himself to a very highly specialized line of work is bound to do it in the best possible manner.

Cyropaedia 8.2.5

Thus, while it has often been pointed out that Greek thinkers were very keen on the principle of self-sufficiency (*autarkeia*), meaning ideally the ability to produce in one's own home and estate(s) everything that one's own family and retainers needed to consume, even writers who praised *autarkeia* also noted the impossibility of achieving it in real world conditions.[6]

When we consider the ancient Greek economy, there can be no doubt that farming of various sorts was the predominant form of economic activity. But the ancient Greeks developed a fundamentally urban culture, and it would have been impossible for significant cities to have grown and "high culture" to have developed in Greece without the aid of a diversified economy in which cash-cropping, manufacturing, and trading played important roles, as not only Plato and Xenophon but plenty of other ancient Greek writers made clear.[7] Simply put, subsistence farmers do not create cities with sophisticated and expensive infrastructure and cultural activities: they lack the necessary interest, communal spirit, and disposable wealth to do so. Subsistence farming is not in general a lifestyle productive of significant surplus wealth, and that goes particularly in the context of the Greek ecology. Anyone who travels extensively around Greece cannot help but be struck by the mountainous nature of the terrain, the rockiness and aridity of the soil, the poverty of the landscape: it must on reflection strike the observer as remarkable that a thriving, abundant, wealthy, and urbanized people, and culture could have arisen on such terrain and soil at all. Areas of Greece that remained limited to subsistence farming in antiquity are known: regions like Aitolia, Akarnania, Lokris. Such regions neither developed cities nor participated in an active way in the creation of classical Greek culture. Generating the surplus wealth to engage in urban development and the creation and consumption of "high culture," and particularly to evolve the kind of communal spirit and communally shared surplus wealth necessary for city-building and dwelling, required diversified and specialized economic activities and roles, as Plato saw.[8] Our evidence for ancient economic behavior is admittedly scrappy and incomplete, dispersed, and unfortunately non-quantifiable; but such as it is, a review and analysis of this evidence is crucial to understanding the conditions of city-state development.

Preconditions: Geography, Climate, and Demography

Geographically, Greece is a poor country. The ancient Greeks themselves were aware of the fact, and attributed what they saw as their tough, manly, freedom-loving nature to the poverty of their land and the toil required to wrest a living from its soil and climate.[9] Modern scholars have not been slow to make the same observations. Greece is a mountainous country, with few substantial agricultural plains. The most favored regions of Greece, as far as farming is concerned, are the western Peloponnesos—Messenia and Elis—which have relatively large and fertile plains and a higher annual rainfall than most of the rest of Greece, since the rain in Greece comes mostly from the west; and Thessaly and Macedonia in the north, which combine very large (for Greece) agricultural plains with a plentiful year round supply of water from rivers—the Peneios and its tributaries in Thessaly, in Macedonia the Haliakmon and Axios—fed by the run-off from the Pindos mountains and their northern Balkan extensions.[10] North-western Greece—Epeiros, Akarnania, Aitolia, west Lokris, etc.—is mostly mountainous, with relatively little in the way of plains suited to agriculture.[11] East-central and south-eastern Greece—Phokis, Boiotia, Euboia, Attica, the eastern Peloponnesos—have no perennial rivers and receive relatively little rainfall annually, making successful agriculture heavily dependent on the winter and spring rains: a below average rainfall spelled a difficult year for farmers, and several below average years in a row could spell disaster.[12] The Aegean islands were in the same case as south-eastern Greece: a meager annual rainfall occurring predominantly in winter and early spring made for a heavy reliance on average or above average rain years for successful agriculture. The Greek cities on the coast of Asia Minor were in a different case, in that they lay at or around the mouths of large, perennial rivers—the Maiandros, the Kaustros, the Hermos, the Kaikos—which provided them with fertile plains and generally plentiful water.

In most of Greece and in the Aegean islands the top soil is rather thin, stony, and of relatively poor quality—again the same regions pointed out above as relatively favored in rainfall are the most favored in this respect also. In practical terms this means that wheat—the most nutritious cereal crop—could only be grown in the best and most favored areas; throughout most of Greece the predominant cereal crop grown was barley. Basically, wheat requires a fairly rich soil and relatively abundant watering, so that although almost all Greek communities were able to produce wheat in some parts of their terrain, most of the agricultural territory of regions like Aitolia, the Argolid, Attica, the islands, etc. was more suited to the less demanding but also less nutritious barley.[13] These were the staple crops of ancient Greece; in addition, a variety of beans and pulses, and of vegetables like cabbages, leeks, onions, and garlic were grown in market garden plots.[14] Fruit and nut trees were also cultivated, above all the olive and the vine: olives and olive oil were of course an indispensable part of the Greek diet, and olive trees were cultivated throughout southern and central Greece wherever they would grow, and the same goes for the vine and its product, wine. Other fruit trees cultivated were the fig and the apple, for example. It was common for fruits and cereal to be grown together by intercropping: that is, cereals were planted between the rows of olive trees, fig trees, or whatever.[15]

Much of the Greek terrain, despite the extensive practice of terracing the hillsides, is simply unsuited to any kind of agriculture, so that animal husbandry has always played a significant role in the farming economy. Many farmers would keep a few pigs for occasional meat; chickens, introduced into Greece from India via Persia by the late seventh century, were widely kept for their eggs and any who could afford it would own some oxen as draft animals, but through most of Greece's history animal husbandry has been predominantly focused on sheep and goats, in that order. Cattle require flat terrain and rich grazing, and in Greece can only be raised in substantial numbers at the expense of agriculture: that is to say, one can only find room in Greece for cattle ranching by taking land out of agricultural use. Since agriculture produces several times more food value per acre of land, this would not normally be considered a reasonable choice, as long as the climate made agriculture viable. Sheep and goats, on the other hand, can thrive on grasses and scrub that would not well sustain cattle, and are able to negotiate steep hillsides. They are thus well suited to the Greek terrain, where they are pastured in the hills and mountains during the long dry summer, and on marginal and fallow lands in the plains during winter. This pattern has often involved moving the flocks of sheep and goats very long distances on a seasonal basis, so that so-called transhumant pastoralism has often been a major feature of Greek farming life.[16] It should be emphasized that sheep and goats were kept not for their meat—although they were eaten on special occasions such as weddings or religious festivals—but for their wool and milk, from which cheeses were made that formed an important source of protein in the Greek diet. Another form of animal husbandry much practiced in Greece was beekeeping: it is widely attested in many parts of the Greek world—Attic honey was particularly famed—and in the absence of cane or beet sugar, honey was the chief sweetener available to the Greeks.[17]

One cannot discuss the geography of Greece without mentioning the sea. Mainland Greece is a peninsula, the southernmost extension of the great Balkan peninsula. Furthermore, southern Greece is made up of peninsulas projecting from the mainland: Attica in the east, then the Argolid and the rest of the Peloponnesos, linked to the mainland only by the narrow isthmus of Corinth, and today, in fact, made an island by the Corinth Canal. Most of the more historically important mainland communities were situated at, or in easy reach of, the coast: Athens, Megara, Corinth, Argos, Sikyon, etc. Much of Greece too is made up of islands, ranging from the giants—Krete, Cyprus, Euboia—through the medium sized islands such as Rhodos, Samos, Chios, and Lesbos off the coast of Asia Minor and the Ionian Islands off Greece's western coast, to such small—though not always unimportant—islands as Aigina, the Cyclades, the Sporades, and so on. Finally, there are the Greek cities on the coast of Asia Minor, port cities barring a few exceptions (though now many more of them lie some way inland due to extension of the coast by silting), and oriented very much toward the Aegean where their fellow Greeks lived, rather than toward the inland regions of Anatolia.

Consequently, the sea played a major role in the lives of the great majority of Greeks. It was an important source of food, to place the most obvious matter first: seafood has always been a significant part of the Greek diet, and in ancient Greece even for those too far from the coast to obtain fresh seafood regularly, there were dried, salted, and pickled fish, and the famous Greek fish sauce (γαρον or *garum*).[18] In a negative sense, the sea was often a source of danger: piracy was rife in early Greece, as we can tell from Homer and the early historians.[19] In a positive sense, it was a source of additional income through going on raiding expeditions and/or on trading voyages, and/or by trading with foreigners who visited Greece, like the Phoenicians whom Homer depicts as so ubiquitously plying their wares in the eastern Mediterranean region.[20] In the course of the eighth and seventh centuries the sea also increasingly represented a means of escape from impoverishment or difficulties in one's home community, by joining one of the numerous overseas migrations which created a string of new Greek communities along the coasts of Italy and Sicily, and around the Black Sea and its approaches.

The climate is not the same everywhere in Greece, but it does in most regions fall into a broadly similar pattern: rainfall is scanty and seasonal; most of Greece is dry most of the year with rainfall occurring during a few months of winter and early spring; and few Greek rivers are substantial enough to maintain a significant flow of water year-round. Beyond this it is rather dangerous to generalize about Greece, for it is a land of micro-climates, with conditions varying quite significantly from region to region: thus, for example, the more abundant rainfall in western Greece, and the more continental climate of northern Greece. All the same, the variance falls within the overall pattern of relatively small plains and valleys suitable to agriculture, long, hot, dry summers and relatively mild winters, seasonal rainfall occurring in winter and early spring, all contributing to a distinct precariousness in the agricultural economy.[21] One can add to this pattern the predominance of northerly winds across the Aegean during summer, the so-called Etesian wind, today called the *meltemi*.

In the system of dry farming used in Greece, due to the absence of perennial rivers for irrigation, the quantity of the seasonal rainfall is crucial to the success or failure of agricultural crops: as Theophrastos put it (*Hist. Plant.* 8.7.6) "it is the year which bears, and not the field," i.e., it is the given year's weather, and above all the rainfall, that determines the success or failure of the crop, even more so than the nature of the field's soil.[22] Any change for the better in the mean annual rainfall, however small, could consequently have the effect of making agriculture a more feasible and attractive proposition in many of the marginal territories of Greece, and so have an effect on Greek economic—and hence social and ultimately political and cultural—life totally out of proportion to its strictly climatic significance. And any positive developments in agriculture would have an impact on population growth.

This brings us to the matter of demography, which is strongly bound up with the question of land use. Although our picture of early Iron Age Greece has changed substantially over the past few decades, as the period has come in for much more intense study by numerous archaeologists, one thing that has not changed and is not likely to change is the perception that Greece was relatively underpopulated in this era, as compared to the preceding Bronze Age and the subsequent Archaic and Classical periods. The number and size of settlements in Greece in the period between about 1100 and 800 was demonstrably less, by a considerable margin, than before and after.[23] On the other hand, the population of Greece was clearly increasing quite dramatically during the eighth, seventh, and sixth centuries. The evidence for this is varied and irrefutable, as even the more skeptical historians of demography like Walter Scheidel now acknowledge.[24] First and foremost, there is the archaeological record of resettlement of the Greek countryside, resulting in a vastly greater number of settlements throughout

Greece, while at the same time the size (and hence clearly the population) of settlements was also growing apace.[25] Concomitant with this, and clearly indicative of demographic growth, we find a sharp increase generation by generation in the numbers of burials found by archaeologists.[26] Finally, happening at the very same time as the number and size of settlements in Greece proper was expanding rapidly, there was the extraordinary expansion of the Greek world via the so-called colonizing movement, involving the migration from Greece to new settlements around the Mediterranean and Black Sea coasts of tens of thousands of Greeks (see App. 3), which would have been simply inconceivable without very significant demographic growth to fuel it.

This pattern of high demographic growth sustained over a period of centuries obviously must have had an economic underpinning, and must in turn have had economic effects.[27] Long term, sustained demographic growth on a significant scale must be fueled by at least a certain amount of economic growth and development: otherwise the population would soon outgrow the ability of the economy to sustain it, and demographic growth would hence be quickly slowed and halted, if not actually reversed.[28] Simply put, once the population surpasses the carrying capacity of the land—that is, the land can no longer produce enough food to feed everyone—food must be imported otherwise the population must decrease to match the carrying capacity. And of course food imports have to be paid for by exports of surplus goods. The kind of economic growth necessary to fuel Greece's demographic growth is not possible—given the geographic and climatic factors outlined above, and the level of agricultural technology and technique we know the ancient Greeks to have possessed—with a significant predominance of subsistence farming. It might perhaps be objected that the Greeks sustained their demographic growth by the practice of extensive emigration (the migrations of the archaic and early Hellenistic eras), but that is not true of the period from the middle of the sixth to the latter part of the fourth centuries, and even at the height of Archaic migration, the archaeological record makes it clear that the number and size of settlements in mainland Greece were growing apace, that urbanization was also proceeding rapidly, and hence that Greece's demographic growth in this period far outstripped the level of migration from Greece.[29] We must, therefore, look for evidence of advanced and productive economic practices as the engine of sustained demographic growth: specialized farming of salable crops, significant manufacturing activity, and associated with—indeed necessary to—both of them, the extensive practice of both local and long distance trading.

The Early Greek Economy

As we have seen, there are very good reasons for believing that the farming economy of Greece in the early Iron Age was characterized by a predominance of pastoralism, that is of animal husbandry rather than agriculture (see above at n. 16). Certainly, the growing of cereal crops was well known to Homer, as were cultivation of the olive and the vine, and these are represented as significant parts of the productive activity in the *oikoi* (households, including lands in use) of the leaders.[30] However, wealth in the Homeric world was not characterized by land ownership, as in most historical societies and certainly in those that had agricultural economies, but by two other measures: treasure (*keimelia*), meaning primarily metal goods such as bronze tripods and cauldrons, weaponry, lumps of iron, in addition to items fashioned of so-called precious metals; and, more importantly, domesticated animals—cattle above all, but also flocks of sheep and goats and herds of swine.[31] Clear indications of this latter point, frequently cited, are the use of the ox as the standard measure of value—as when Diomedes exchanged his armor worth 9 oxen for Glaukos' armor worth 100 oxen, or as when Achilles at the funeral games for Patroklos presented as prizes for the wrestling competition a tripod worth twelve oxen and a skilled slave woman worth four oxen—and the description of Odysseus' wealth given by the swineherd Eumaios to the disguised Odysseus himself: twelve herds of cattle, twelve flocks of sheep, twelve herds of swine, and twelve herds of goats on the mainland, and eleven herds of goats on the island of Ithaka in addition to the 600 sows and 360 boars in Eumaios' charge. The use of the ox as the standard of value and the description of wealth purely in terms of herds and flocks owned (rather than land) are clear indications of a society with a predominantly pastoral farming economy.[32]

The depiction in Homer of a predominantly pastoral economy is confirmed by other evidence. Snodgrass has pointed to the frequency of animal figurines as dedications at Greek sanctuaries in the ninth and eighth centuries, gradually declining in numbers in the later eighth and seventh centuries when we start to find dedications of vessels and even model granaries, and has interpreted this—surely rightly—as a sign of an early pastoral economy gradually giving way in the later eighth and seventh centuries to predominant agriculture.[33] The scarcity of archaeologically detectable settlements in early Iron Age Greece which, given the phenomenal demographic growth we see in the eighth century (above at pp. 53–4), must to some degree be misleading—that is, there has to have been an early Iron Age population base from which the eighth-century population "explosion" could take off—has led some scholars to posit a significant degree of transhumant pastoralism during the early Iron Age.[34] The tent villages and temporary huts often used by transhumant pastoralists are extremely difficult if not impossible to detect archaeologically, and we know that from late antiquity right up to the late 1950s Greece was home to several major groups of transhumant pastoralists: most notably the Vlachs and the Sarakatsani.[35] As we have seen above (pp. 51–52), and as the history of peoples like the Vlachs and the Sarakatsani confirm, much of Greece is well-suited to the practice of transhumant pastoralism.

It is worth noting that some of the social practices and attitudes attested for Classical Greek peoples bear a striking resemblance to practices and attitudes attested among the Sarakatsani in J.K. Campbell's excellent study *Honor, Family, and Patronage*. Sarakatsan marriage, for example, took the form of a pseudo-abduction, a form of marriage also attested in classical Lakedaimon, and reflected ubiquitously in Greek mythology with its many well-known tales of marriage by abduction.[36] Sarakatsan society was strongly rooted in kinship groups—families, extended families, "clans"—of a type also widely attested in ancient Greece.[37] Sarakatsani marked important occasions and meetings by the eating of what was virtually a "ritual meal" of meat, a practice extensively attested in Homer and found in Classical Greece in the form of the sacrificial meal at festivals.[38] The blood feud and guest-friendship are well-marked features of both Sarakatsan and Archaic Greek society. It could be suggested that some or all these parallels are due to the survival in Archaic and Classical Greece of customs and attitudes rooted in a transhumant pastoralist past.

There are also specific cases to be made: Megara in the late seventh and sixth centuries is an interesting example, for instance. Aristotle informs us that to suppress the power of the wealthy and gain the support of the people, the tyrant Theagenes (c. 650 to 630) slaughtered the flocks/herds (*ktene*) of the wealthy as they were being pastured along a river (*Politika* 1305a 24). The land along the banks of a river would, of course, likely be prime land for agriculture, and the point here surely is that—having freed the land from its pastoral use in this brutal way—Theagenes must have made this land available to his non-wealthy supporters for agricultural use.[39] The mid-sixth-century poet Theognis lamented the fact that in his day the *polis* of Megara had been taken over and run by new men, men who in previous times dwelt outside the city like deer in the fields, knowing neither justice nor laws, clad in goatskins (*Theognidea* 53–56). Is it unreasonable to see here former pastoralists—compare the goatskin cloaks favored by the pastoralist Sarakatsani—in the service of the aristocrats, now become settled agriculturalists with citizen rights in the emerging city-state of Megara?[40] In the context of the other evidence adduced above, this conjecture seems reasonable. Overall, we do see an array of evidence pointing to a predominance of pastoralism in early Greece, giving way gradually—and at an uneven pace in different regions of Greece—to a predominance of agriculture.

Such a change from pastoralism, including much transhumant pastoralism, to agriculture would have wide-ranging social, economic, and demographic effects, some of which are clearly visible in the archaeological record. The resettlement of the Greek countryside, visible in the much greater number of Archaic as opposed to early Iron Age settlements found by archaeological surveys, may in part have been the result of people moving out from early Iron Age centers of settlement like Athens and Argos, but the small scale of those settlements themselves renders this an inadequate explanation.[41] The settling down into permanent villages, centers of agricultural activity in the Greek countryside, of populations previously engaged in transhumant pastoralism seems likely to have been at least as important. Agricultural farming being more productive, in terms of calories of foodstuffs per acre, than pastoral, this switch would make it possible for the land to sustain a larger population. As the population rose, the input of more person-hours of labor into the agricultural process would in turn make the agriculture more productive, and so permit a further increase in population.[42] Again, this is exactly the pattern that the archaeological record attests to, as we have seen, and that the literary evidence also suggests. For the next major literary figure of ancient Greece whose works survive, the Boiotian composer of didactic epics Hesiod, active—by general consent—about a generation later than Homer, reveals a very different economic landscape than that found in Homer.

The socio-cultural milieu of Hesiod is unquestionably that of the peasant agriculturalist—meaning here by "peasant" nothing more than one who farms the land on a relatively small scale on his own account, as opposed to a tenant or sharecropper—and this is true whether or not one accepts the self-revealing remarks in the *Theogony* and, more importantly, the *Erga* as genuine autobiography. To some extent this may be no more than the result of compositional context, that is to say, the world of Homer and that of Hesiod might, up to a point, have co-existed side by side as different levels of society. Indeed, they certainly did so, for we have seen above that agriculture was well known to Homer, and we possess in the *Iliad* what looks very much like a portrait of a proto-Hesiod: Thersites in *Iliad* 2.211–23. Just as Hesiod reviled the "gift-devouring lords" with their arrogance and their crooked judgments, so too was

Thersites wont to rail against greed, arrogance, and unfairness of the *basileis*.[43] And in the physical description of Thersites—the ugliest of all who came to Troy, as Homer avows (*Iliad* 2.216)—we surely see the *autourgos*, the peasant farmer, from the perspective of the wealthy lord: his bandy legs and lame foot, his stooped shoulders and balding, misshapen head, what are these but the effects of a life of toil in the fields under the fierce Aegean sun, as seen through the lens of aristocratic prejudice.[44] However, although the peasant agriculturalist was already present in the Homeric world, and may—in the persons of men like Thersites—already have been protesting against the rule and ways of the *basileis*, there is a crucial difference between Homeric and Hesiodic society. In Homeric society Thersites was a fringe figure, a minor irritant to the lords, easily suppressed—though no doubt Homer exaggerates the degree of unpopularity of a Thersites. However, Hesiod found so much of an audience for his views, including his criticisms of the *basileis* and their ways, that he became the pre-eminent literary voice of his generation: he is the only post-Homeric composer of epic hexameter verse whose works survive intact, and was universally regarded as second only to Homer as a hexameter poet and teacher among later Greeks.

This suggests a profound change in social attitudes between the mid eighth and the mid seventh centuries, such as would indeed have accompanied a shift from a pastoral economy dominated by wealthy owners of large herds and flocks to an agricultural economy of predominantly small-holding peasant farmers. Naturally, such a shift could only have occurred gradually over a long period of time; it was by no means complete in Hesiod's time but was still in process as late as the sixth century: see, for example, the evidence regarding early sixth-century Megara cited above. When we are finally able to get a clear contemporary picture of Greek life—in the later fifth and fourth centuries—we certainly see that the farming economy is predominantly agricultural rather than pastoral, and that in city-states like Athens, Megara, Corinth, Argos, and the like, at least, land-ownership was not concentrated in the hands of a wealthy few, but quite widely dispersed among the citizen population.[45] As regards the pattern of land-holding, some ancient evidence and analogy from modern Greek farming suggest that land was usually owned in small scattered parcels.[46] Major causes of this were the system of inheritance, with all the sons of a marriage taking a share of the parents' land-holdings, and the dowry system, whereby a woman at marriage would bring with her to her new family a portion (her share as one of the children) of her parents' land holdings. This scattered land holding system had—and has—economic advantages in a country with Greece's diversity of (generally rather poor) farming land and micro-climates: one's pieces of land in one area might fail to bear well in a given year while parcels of land in other areas produced adequately or even abundantly, so that the scattered land owning was a hedge against disaster.[47]

The Developed Greek Economy

Already in the late eighth and early seventh centuries, then, we find a Greek economy clearly in transition. The transformation of the Greek economy certainly did not stop at the stage of subsistence agriculture: the evidence regarding ancient Greek economic behavior is scanty at best, but such as it is it clearly favors a more developed economy, one in which there was production of crops intended for sale rather than immediate consumption by the farmer's family and dependents; in which specialized craftsmen and artisans formed a significant part of the population and played an important role in the economy; one in which economic exchange between specialized producers and consumers of various sorts was vital, including—to facilitate such exchange—the growth of markets and of local and long distance trade.[48] It's obvious, to begin with, that many of the inhabitants of the larger cities from at least the sixth century on—Miletos, Athens, Corinth, Argos, Samos, and so on—lived primarily not on food that they or their immediate family and dependents had produced themselves, but on food they had purchased. These were the people who practiced trades other than farming: potters, carpenters, smiths, masons, cobblers, builders, shopkeepers, doctors, seers, bakers, traders, sailors, prostitutes, launderers, and so on, and so forth.[49] For these people to be able to exist, and as we shall see it is clear that by the fifth century they existed in large numbers throughout the Greek world, it was obviously necessary for those engaged in farming to produce a surplus of salable foodstuffs above and beyond their families' subsistence requirements.

They clearly did so from very early times: note for example that Hesiod already regarded it as quite natural for a farmer in his day to have a salable surplus of produce, and even to decide to take that surplus on board ship to trade it for profit (*Erga* 618–94). It is also noteworthy that Hesiod imagines his farmer taking his ease during the "dog days" of summer, when there is little to be done on the farm, and drinking "wine of Biblis," that is, wine imported from Phoenicia, which must have been paid for by the sale of surplus produce (*Erga* 585–94). Of course, this does not as yet imply the deliberate production of salable crops: one might simply farm for subsistence and sell whatever one chanced to grow over and above one's subsistence needs. Consider, however, that other archetype of the sturdy independent farmer imagined by the late-fifth-century Athenian comic playwright Aristophanes in his play *The Acharnians*: I mean Dikaiopolis. In this play, written in the early 420s when the Athenians were annually penned into their city by Spartan incursions, Dikaiopolis complains about the nuisances of city life and yearns to be able to return to his farm in the countryside, to take up his round of peaceful farming pursuits. Yet when he makes his separate peace with the Spartans and returns to his farm, one of the first things he does is to announce an *agora* (an open market) and engage in trade with Megarians and Boiotians:

> These are the confines of my market place. All Peloponnesians, Megarians, Boeotians, have the right to come and trade here, provided they sell their wares to me and not to Lamachos.
>
> 719–25

It turns out that one of the joys of a peaceful agrarian life is being able to acquire the specialized products of neighboring communities in exchange for one's own products. A joy felt by Athens' neighbors too, according to the Megarian who comes to trade with Dikaipolis with the words:

> Hail! Market of Athens, beloved of Megarians. Let Zeus, the patron of friendship, witness, I have regretted you as a mother mourns her son.
>
> 726–40

The upshot of the matter is that Dikaiopolis, as the chorus says at line 836–40, becomes a man truly happy because: "peacefully seated in his market he will earn his living."

As uninterested as our sources are in the matter of economic production and exchange, it is nevertheless possible to find here and there references to trade by given states or regions of characteristic crops and products. For example, there are numerous references to the extensive production of olive oil in Attica, to the export of olive oil from Attica, and to the widespread reputation for excellence enjoyed by Attic olive oil around the Greek world.[50] All of this presupposes the production of olive oil as a cash crop by a large number of Attic farmers; unless this were the case there could have been no such extensive olive cultivation as we hear of, for the production of olive oil for subsistence purposes would only have been carried out on a much smaller scale: a handful of trees would produce sufficient olives to meet a single family's consumption. The export and wide reputation of Attic olive oil are, of course, the result of the sale of deliberately produced surplus olive oil by Attic farmers to exporting merchants. Our evidence does not by any means allow us to quantify the number of Athenians engaged in production of olive oil as a cash crop; all we can say is that the practice was widespread and on a considerable scale. In addition, the numerous Athenian state owned olive trees scattered throughout Attica, the produce of which was used for various public purposes—provision of oil for the gymnasia and the prizes of olive oil awarded to victors at the Panathenaic Games, for example— but some of which was certainly sold and exported to provide cash revenue for the state. Further, in the sixth and fifth centuries the Athenian potters famously dominated the trade in luxury decorated ceramics, exporting their products to consumers all around the Mediterranean.[51]

Athens might, of course, be considered exceptional, but the evidence of trade and exchange throughout the Mediterranean is in fact now plentiful and clear.[52] The Megarians, for example, were particularly noted for the production for export of cheap garments—tunics and cloaks—of wool from sheep which were pastured in the large part of the Megarid that was too rough for agriculture: sheep herding was such a notable practice in the Megarid that people joked that Megarians treated their sheep better than their children. In the early fourth century, Xenophon was even able to claim that "most Megarians" (*Megareon d'hoi pleistoi*) made a living by making garments.[53] One could proliferate examples of specialized goods produced for trade *ad nauseam*: wine from Mende, Samos, Chios, Thasos, and other places; tuna and mackerel from the Propontis and Black Sea, so that the characteristic badge of the Propontic city of Kyzikos, on its coins, was a tuna; grain from Thessaly, Kyrene, the Greek cities of southern Italy and Sicily, and those around the Crimea; timber from Macedonia and the southern Black Sea coastal region; fine wool from Sybaris and Miletos; bronze work from Corinth and Argos; pottery also from Corinth as well as Athens; and so on and so forth. Not to labor the point, there is a great deal of evidence for various regions of the Greek world specializing in particular products, with an eye to having a tradeable surplus which could pay for necessary imports.[54] As already mentioned, ancient Greek writers were well aware of the need to engage in surplus production and trade: Herodotos emphasized, for example, that no region can ever hope to be truly self-sufficient, but instead all lack some necessities of life and produce a surplus of others (above n. 6); and Plato, in his *Laws*, emphasized that, as regretful as is the necessity for trading contact with the outside world, it *was* a necessity and must be carefully arranged for and regulated in the ideal *polis*.

In assessing the scale and importance of trade in ancient Greece, the factors underlying the Archaic migration movement play a crucial role. A generation or so ago, most scholars would probably have agreed that overpopulation and land hunger were the two great motivations for the migration movement, with trade playing only a minimal role, if any;[55] but properly evaluating this movement requires us to observe some crucial distinctions. In the first place, in terms of motivation, one must distinguish between individual settlers and organizing metropolis: the motives causing the former to decide or agree to participate in establishing a new overseas settlement were likely in many if not most cases quite different from the motivation of the founding community in deciding to organize such a settlement. This is crucial, because it is at the individual level that one of the key motivations for migration frequently put forward by modern scholars, must have operated: land hunger. Simply put, the "colonizing" community generally did not gain new land by founding a new settlement; the individual migrants who went on the expedition did. It is very probable that the desire and expectation of gaining a nice allotment of farm land to form the basis of a new and prosperous life was a vital motivating factor for the majority of the men who joined new settlements, both those who went in the first wave and those who joined the settlement subsequent to its establishment; these latter must have been very numerous, as the astonishingly rapid growth of many of these settlements demonstrates.[56] In itself, this says nothing about the motives of the mother community in deciding to establish a "colony," though to be sure there may often have been a link between the two sets of motivations.

Another crucial distinction is between different types of "colonizing" communities. The Greek overseas settlements whose founding community, or communities, is/are known can be divided into two groups (see App. 3 below on this). About half of the known settlements were founded by numerous communities which established one or two each, almost always at locations whose most obvious asset was access to good farmland. The other half, however, were founded by a small handful of communities which each established a substantial number of settlements—over thirty in the case of Miletos—many of which were clearly founded as *emporia* or to create friendly ports of call at crucial points along major trade routes.[57] Clearly there is good reason to suspect a fundamental difference in motivation between communities that founded just one or two settlements—like Thera or Paros or Kolophon—and a community such as Miletos which founded more than thirty. In the former case, the relieving of overpopulation, whether caused by demographic growth or—as in the case of Thera's founding of Kyrene (see Herodotus 4.150–58)—by contracting food production brought about by drought or the like, is a very plausible motivation. It should be noted that, since we know the sending of migrants to an *apoikia* (lit.

"away home") was an ongoing process, the initial migrants being just a first wave, one or two settlements founded in sites that had access to good and plentiful land could relieve demographic stress in the mother community for several generations. However, no conceivable demographic stress could account for settlement activity on the scale of Miletos, Corinth, Khalkis, Eretria, Megara, Phokaia and Samos (details in App. 3 below). In these cases, it is clear that some motivation other than population pressure must be sought.

The most important motivating factor for this latter group of "colonizing" communities must have been an interest in trade. Miletos, for example, blanketed the coasts of the Black Sea, and the approaches to the Black Sea (Hellespont and Propontis), with an extraordinary host of settlements, for the vast majority of which the greater part of the population must have come from cities other than Miletos.[58] The Black Sea region was notorious in antiquity for its wealth of products desired by the Greeks: wheat from the Crimea and the great river valleys debouching into the Black Sea from the north; hides for leather from the nomadic or semi-nomadic Scythian peoples; fish, especially tuna, from the Black Sea itself as well as from the Propontis; slaves from the native peoples to the north and west of the Black Sea, Thracians and Scythians especially; metals–iron and gold above all–from various regions around the Black Sea; and timber from the southern coastlands of the Black Sea.[59] In the seventh and sixth centuries, Miletos was one of the largest and wealthiest cities in the Greek world, if not the largest and wealthiest, with a known interest in overseas trade: note, for example, Miletos' role in the Greek trading *entrepot* Naukratis in Egypt, the Milesians' good relations—reputedly connected with trade in wool—with Sybaris in Italy, and the name of *Aeinautai* ("perpetual sailors") given to an upper class group in Miletos.[60] It is obvious that the Milesian interest in "colonizing" the Black Sea and its approaches was aimed at creating valuable ports of call for Milesians engaged in the Black Sea trade, that in effect the Milesian settlement activity around the Black Sea had to do with creating a Milesian trading sphere of influence guaranteeing Milesian domination of the immensely profitable trade with this resource-rich region.

The same case can be made with regard to Corinth, which founded half a dozen settlements at the approach to and along the eastern shore of the Adriatic Sea, as well as Syracuse in Sicily and Potidaia in the north-west Aegean; to Chalkis and Eretria which between them founded more than twenty settlements in two regions—Sicily and Italy in the west, and the Chalkidike peninsula in the northwest Aegean area; and to Megara, which founded seven settlements: one in Sicily, and six bracketing the entrance to the Black Sea at the Bosporos—Selymbria,

Byzantion, and Mesembria on the north shore; Astakos, Chalkedon, and Herakleia on the south shore—thus ensuring Megarian access to the Black Sea and its resources. As for Phokaia and Samos, they founded fewer settlements, but at sites that were clearly chosen with an eye to long distance trade. All of this makes it clear that an interest in trade routes and in access to areas rich in important resources was a key motivating factor in the activity of a number of "colonizing" communities which between them founded almost half of the known Greek *apoikiai* or overseas settlements (see below App. 3).

Another, related distinction is between the trading settlement—sometimes called an *emporion*—and the settlement not founded primarily with an eye to trade.[61] The term *emporion* can be a hindrance to a clear understanding of this distinction, as it is often taken to refer to a site that was a trading station pure and simple rather than a permanent settlement with full city-state institutions and status. In reality, this latter distinction is largely a false one: there is no clear-cut difference between *emporia* and *apoikiai* that were full *poleis*; rather, there is a good deal of subtle shading and overlap. For example, Naukratis in Egypt was unquestionably founded as an *emporion*, yet from an early stage in its history—if not from its very beginning—it was a full-fledged city-state in every important respect.[62] The Greek settlement of Emporiai in northern Spain, at modern Ampurias, was—as its name clearly indicates—founded as a port of trade, yet it was a full-fledged city-state in the classical era.[63] The distinction that needs to be made is not between overseas settlements with or without city-state status, for all Greek settlements overseas that lasted acquired that status; it is between settlements founded in order to facilitate trade and those founded for other reasons. A key example will be instructive.

The Euboian settlement of Pithekoussai, on the island today called Ischia in the Bay of Naples, was the first permanent Greek settlement in the western Mediterranean founded around 770 BCE. A number of influential scholars have argued that it was founded as an independent farming *apoikia*, not at all as a trading settlement.[64] This claim disregards the most basic geographic facts about Ischia in a truly remarkable way. Ischia is a rocky islet with very little agricultural land. While it is true that, thanks to the fact that Ischia is a volcanic island, the little agricultural land that is available is very fertile, there is simply not enough of it to have attracted settlers looking primarily for agricultural lands to farm. In fact, the evidence suggests that much of the available land on Ischia was planted as vineyards, producing wine for export rather than being used for subsistence crops.[65] It must be pointed out that no ancient settlement would be founded at a site where it had to import all of its food: under ancient conditions of transport that simply was not a viable policy. All colonial settlements thus had access to some land and farmed it to produce at least a reasonable amount of the inhabitants' subsistence requirements. That is not to say that all ancient colonial settlements were founded as purely farming communities. In the case of Pithekoussai, no search for available agricultural land would have brought the Euboian founders all the way to Ischia, by-passing such favorable settlement sites, with abundant land where major colonies were later founded, as Kerkyra, Tarentum, Metapontion, Sybaris, Kroton, and others. And even had these settlers for some reason turned up their noses at all these sites, why having reached the Strait of Messina would they turn north to the rocky islet of Ischia, ignoring the rich coastal plains of eastern Sicily to the south?

It is clear how patently absurd this notion is. The real advantage of the site at Ischia is in fact obvious: it was adjacent to the Etruscans, who at that time dominated western Italy from Liguria in the north through Campania in the south, and to the Phoenician trade routes in the western Mediterranean. It was to trade with the Etruscans and Phoenicians that Euboians founded their colony at Pithekoussai, followed not long after by the colony of Kyme (Cumae) on the mainland near Ischia. The Etruscans controlled important sources of iron, notably on the island of Elba in the northern Tyrrhenian Sea, and they also had access to tin via an overland route through Gaul from Cornwall in southern Britain; the Phoenicians had access to silver and gold from Sardinia and Spain. Recent thorough archaeological excavation of Pithekoussai has confirmed what should always have been clear from the geographical facts outlined above: the discovery of numerous ore smelting plants and metal workshops have shown beyond doubt that the colonists of Pithekoussai traded for metals from the Etruscans and Phoenicians for export back to metropolitan Greece.[66]

Further, not enough attention is paid to Greek settlements strung out along trade routes in their role as ports of call. Ancient Greek mariners, lacking modern navigational aids—the compass, the sextant, the chronometer, accurate maps—and sailing in vessels very vulnerable to adverse weather conditions, always coasted whenever they could: they navigated by landmarks, and needed to be able to put into friendly ports of call for supplies, especially fresh water, to seek shelter from bad weather or to wait for a following wind (since they could not tack into the wind), or simply to spend the night comfortably and safely ashore.[67] One should in this context consider the Euboian colonies of Zankle (Messina) and Rhegion, on either side of the Strait of Messina, and the two Megarian colonies Chalkedon and Byzantion on opposite sides of the Bosporos, the crucial bottleneck in the trade route from Greece to the Black Sea. It would be absurd to doubt that access to—indeed even some control over access to—the trade routes to Etruria and to the Black Sea were important considerations in founding these cities. Properly understood, therefore, the Archaic migration movement is evidence for the growth of long-distance trade, in raw materials and foodstuffs among other things, as a major feature in the economic life of at least a number of the more prominent and advanced of the developing Greek city-states.

Another case is worth making to drive the point home: the island of Aigina. With a surface area of about 86 square kilometers, Aigina is one of the smaller Greek islands, roughly equal in size to such islands as Keos, Mykonos, or Salamis. Unlike those small and unimportant islands, however, Aigina played a role in late archaic Greek history out of all proportion to its size, and that role is undoubtedly due to the part the Aiginetans played in the development of Greek long-distance trade. Along with Miletos and Samos, Aigina was one of the three major founding communities of the Greek trading colony of Naukratis at the mouth of the Nile in Egypt.[68] Aiginetans are also attested trading with the Etruscans in the west, notably by a dedication to Zeus of Aigina found at the Etruscan port of Graviscae. Herodotos (4.152) tells of one Sostratos of Aigina who was beyond compare for the wealth he had derived from trading; and scholars have long connected a series of Attic vases found in Italy and bearing the letters *SO* or *SOS* painted on them—evidently a merchant's mark—with this Sostratos of Aigina and his family. In effect, it is thought that Sostratos made a business of trading Attic products to Italy, among other things no doubt.[69] We also hear of a class of small tradewares—minor bits of pottery and metalwork, knick-knacks, in effect—called *Aiginetika* from their typical manufacture on or trade via the island of Aigina.

So far, we are dealing only with piecemeal, anecdotal, or even speculative bits of information that could be dismissed as unimportant. But certain statistical data indicate that the Aiginetans must have been involved in trade in a big way. The small size of the island, its aridity, and the fact that a third or more of its landmass is rocky—comprising a great extinct volcano—mean that, based on its natural carrying capacity, Aigina should have a population only in the range of 4,000 to 6,000 people.[70] Even with the economic benefit of modern tourism and use of the island as a weekend/dormitory community for the modern metropolis of Athens, the population was only just over 11,000 in 1981, rising to 13,500 by 2001, according to the census data. We know that the population was far greater in the late sixth and early fifth centuries BCE thanks to the evidence of Aiginetan fleets. Shortly before the Persian invasion leading to the battle of Marathon in 490, the Aiginetans were able to man seventy warships to do battle against the Athenians, as Herodotos informs us (4.92). In the campaign of Salamis in 480, the Aiginetans contributed their thirty best warships, while others—surely at least equal in number—were detailed to guard their home island (Herod. 8.46). We again hear of seventy warships manned by the Aiginetans in their war against the Athenians in the early 450s (Thucydides 1.105). The number seventy for Aigina's fleet is consistent here; in the campaign of Salamis and the war against Athens *c.* 458 at least, these ships must have been predominantly if not exclusively triremes. The total crews for seventy triremes, at 200 men per ship, would amount to 14,000 men, and even if we allow that a number of the ships may have been *pentekonters*, with about fifty-five men per ship, the total manpower involved would still likely be some 10,000. These 10,000 to 14,000 men aged *c.* eighteen to forty-five will have had families: allotting a standard, conservative one woman and two children per man, we arrive at a free population of around 40,000 to 56,000 people for the island in the first half of the fifth century. In fact, adding slaves and allowing for the fact that the men mobilized can hardly have represented the total male population, since the older and infirm men would not have been called up for such service, it is evident that the overall population most likely will have been in the range of 50,000 to 70,000.[71] How could such a population have been sustained?

Even if we accept the much smaller population estimates of Figueira and others, it is clear that Aigina's population exceeded the carrying capacity of the land by several orders of magnitude. Aigina had no mines or other natural resources whose exploitation could have provided these people with a livelihood, and apart from the minor products lumped together as *Aiginetika* we hear of no significant manufacturing on the island. It is clear, from the naval power of this tiny island and its role in trade with Egypt and Italy, that the majority of the Aiginetans must in fact have lived from overseas trade, middleman trade at that.[72] As the early-fourth-century historian Ephoros put it: "owing to the poor quality of the land Aigina became a centre for trade, with its inhabitants plying the sea as merchants."[73] Since the Athenians at this time had no real harbor—as they did not develop the Peiraieus until after 494—we can conclude that the Aiginetans controlled/carried the trade of the Athenians in the sixth and early fifth centuries; close Aiginetan links with Argos and the towns of the Argolid peninsula suggest that Aigina likely played the same role for them.

In line with the above assessment of Aiginetan manpower and the conclusions about Aiginetan trade drawn from it, is the evidence we have about Aigina's wealth in the late sixth and fifth centuries. We may begin by noting that the Aiginetan tribute paid annually to the Athenian led alliance system—the so-called Delian League—amounted in the mid fifth century to thirty talents, higher than all other payers except Thasos. However, Thasos was a much larger island than Aigina (four times as large, in fact), and owned significant silver mines, which enabled it to pay thirty talents. Whence came Aigina's thirty talents? Not from any natural resources the islanders controlled, as pointed out above. We can note that another Aegean island that was more than twice as large as Aigina and controlled a wealth-producing natural resource, Paros with its famed marble quarrying, paid only eighteen talents, not much more than half the tribute paid by Aigina. This Aiginetan wealth was not new in the mid fifth century: going back one hundred years to the mid sixth century, Aigina was one of the first Greek states to mint silver coins, beginning *c.* 570. More than that, the Aiginetan silver coinage, with its distinctive badge of a turtle on the obverse, became something of an international coinage, anticipating the role that Athenian silver coinage was to play from the mid fifth century onwards. Aiginetan silver coins are found in hoards from all over Greece: Krete, all over the Peloponnesos, the Cycladic islands, and also much further afield in the wider Mediterranean and near eastern world.[74] Since the island of Aigina has no silver mines, the silver for this abundant coinage had to be imported, much of it likely from the silver-wealthy island of Siphnos; which is to say, the silver had to be paid for. Given Aigina's lack of all other resources, there can be no doubt that the wealth to pay tribute to Athens and mint abundant coinage came from Aigina's middleman role in international trade.

Obviously, an entire city-state could only develop a dependence on middleman trade, and grow to such a large size in population, wealth, and power based on middleman trade, if there were an extensive overseas trading network in existence to be exploited. We know that there was such a network by the early sixth century, extending from Olbia, Pantikapaion, and Kolchis on the northern and eastern shores of the Black Sea, to Poseideion in Syria, the cities of Cyprus, Naukratis in Egypt, and Kyrene in Libya in the southern and eastern Mediterranean, and across the western Mediterranean via numerous Greek ports in Italy and Sicily, all the way to Massilia and its sub-colonies (Nikaia, Antipolis) in southern France and Emporiai (Ampurias) on the Mediterranean coast of Spain. We know the multitude of agricultural products, raw materials, and manufactured goods that were traded: staple foods like grains, olive oil (and other oils: linseed oil, flax oil), and wine made up the bulk, along with key raw materials like metals (copper, tin, iron, bronze, steel, lead, silver) and timber, and also many other more specialized foodstuffs, like fish in preserved form (pickled, salted, sun-dried), fruits, nuts and legumes of various sorts, and honey, and manufactured products like cloth and clothing, leather goods, ceramic wares of all sorts, metal weapons, tools, and decorative items, and wooden furniture and the like.[75] Obviously too, large scale long distance trade involving these items required that there be a large cash-cropping sector in the agricultural economy, to generate the tradeable surpluses and pay for imported goods, and a large scale manufacturing economy to consume and work with the raw materials (timber, metals, leather hides, and so on) and to pay for their import.

The notion that this trade was never much more than a small adjunct to a basically subsistence economy, carried on by an unimportant and numerically tiny "class" of shippers and merchants, as was long ago suggested by scholars like Hasebroek and Finley, is no longer sustainable. In recent decades, scholarly opinion on ancient Greek economic life has moved decisively towards the view that such trade was much more significant in volume and range, so as to play a very important part in the economic life of the ancient Greek cities and produce a class of men engaged or at least interested in trade who were wealthy and sociopolitically important, in great part thanks to what has been learned from intensive archaeological explorations, not least underwater archaeology and what we have learned from it of ancient shipping.[76] That is to say that by 600, and increasingly thereafter, the Greek economy was a relatively sophisticated and varied economy, based not primarily on subsistence farming but to a great extent on cash-cropping, manufacturing, and associated markets and short and long distance trade networks. This economy generated a very considerable amount of surplus wealth that both permitted the Greek population to grow substantially generation by generation, and enabled Greek communities to be distinctly prosperous.

Making a Living in the Greek Economy

How then did all of this economic growth affect the lives and livelihoods of the Greek citizens who helped to bring it about? What level of prosperity could an average Greek inhabitant of a city-state expect to attain? These are crucial questions that will affect our understanding of how city-states functioned at the micro-level of the citizen and his family. Because, of course, a successful economy generating surplus wealth does not necessarily mean that the surplus wealth will be reasonably fairly distributed, such that many or even a majority of the inhabitants can thrive and lead comfortable lives. Needless to say, we are starved of good data for understanding economic life in ancient Greece: we have no GDP or GNP figures, no mean income or income distribution figures, none of the quantifiable data that modern economic historians are able to use to get a good picture of modern economic life. But that does not mean that we are helpless: a variety of literary and epigraphic sources reveal glimpses of lifestyles, wages, and prices that can enable us to get at least an outline picture of how the economy worked for ordinary Greek citizens.

It should be noted, as a preliminary point, that by the fifth century the economy of the advanced Greek city-states was extensively monetized. The Greeks used silver and bronze coins as money for everyday transactions in the market place, to pay for goods and services, to finance larger scale and longer distance trading activities, to fund and pay for public services and activities of all sorts, and so on.[77] The standard silver coin of the Greek cities (which varied slightly from city to city in exact weight and value) was called a *drachma*, which amounted to a good day's wage for a craftsman. The drachma was divided into six smaller silver coins called *oboloi*; and each obol was in turn divided into eight bronze coins called *chalkoi*. Larger value silver coins were the *stater*, worth 2 drachmas; the *tetradrachma*, worth 4 drachmas, and rarely even larger denominations worth 8 or 10 drachmas. For accounting purposes when dealing with large amounts of money, the word *mna* signified 100 drachmas, and the word *talanton* (talent) denoted 60 mnas or 6,000 drachmas, but these were of course not coins. Shopping in the market place would be done with *chalkoi* and obols; payment for services would tend to be in obols and drachmas; large scale trade would likely be done with tetradrachmas, which are found throughout the Mediterranean in hoards; public finances would be reckoned in mnas and talents.

Having established the monetary system, we can begin by considering the evidence for the pay given to rowers in Athenian and other Greek fleets in the fifth century, and the pay for jury service in fifth-century Athens. In both cases, though the pay varied slightly over time with changing circumstances, a daily rate of 3 obols, or half a drachma, was fairly standard.[78] This clearly indicates that half a drachma per day was understood to be a sufficient income to enable a man to feed himself and his family. We may note here Aristophanes' stereotypical juryman Philokleon in his play *The Wasps*, who describes the receipt of his 3 obols at the close of the day as one of the main delights of jury service, recounting with relish the flattery he receives from his household because he now has money to spend.[79] The point of the 3 obol pay in both cases, rowing the fleet or staffing the juries, was to compensate for income lost on other activities: without it the poorer citizens would not have been able to afford to serve in these capacities. Evidently, therefore, an ordinary day laborer in the fifth-century Aegean world—note that rowers in the Athenian and other fleets came from all over the Aegean region[80]—could normally expect to make at least 3 obols per day at whatever work he found to do, and could survive quite well on this income.[81] It should be borne in mind that for all but the very poorest these wages were not the only income: many relatively poor Greek citizens would nevertheless own some land at least, even if only a small garden plot where they could grow some vegetables, perhaps a row or two of vines and a few olive trees, hiring themselves out to supplement what they could produce for themselves.[82] This was the case with Aristophanes' juror Philokleon, to whom his 3 obols were a welcome extra, giving him cash to spend on luxuries, as noted above.

We also have evidence of wages paid to construction workers, from the surviving inscriptions preserving the accounts of the building of the Erechtheion at Athens in the late fifth century, and of building work at Eleusis in the mid fourth century. In both cases we see that it was fairly standard for workmen—stonemasons, carpenters, haulage workers, ceramic workers, and so on—to be paid at least a drachma per day, or double the 3 obols paid for rowing or jury service; in the case of Eleusis in the mid fourth century, in fact, wages were on the whole rather higher, in some cases double those attested for the Erechtheion.[83] Since a family could clearly survive on slightly less than 3 obols per day, it's obvious that those receiving a drachma or more per day did quite well and had disposable income after providing the necessities. These two kinds of workers, rowers in the fleet providing simple physical labor, and semi-skilled workers performing various tasks in building construction, represent the lower to lower-middling elements of the population, and indicate that it was normal for poorer Greeks outside the elite or even well-to-do segments of society to have cash incomes in the range of 3 to 6 obols per day, or (allowing for days off for festivals and such) some 15 to 25 drachmas per month.[84] It should be borne in mind that, as mentioned above, such cash incomes were by no means the only income a family would have, in many cases. Besides the reality that many families owned larger or smaller plots of land and drew some of their food needs from them, there is the reality that other members of the family besides the male "head of household" might likely work.

Although the ideal expressed in such aristocratically produced writings as Xenophon's *Oikonomika* was for women of the family to stay in the home and out of sight of men, it's clear from a variety of evidence that such behavior was not in fact typical for non-elite women, and that many women worked and contributed to the family income.[85] For example, Aristophanes many times alleged that Euripides' mother ran a vegetable stall in the market of Athens, and we hear of another female vegetable stall holder in his play *Wasps*, and in addition, the play's protagonist Philokleon upsets the stall of a baker's wife, ruining her loaves of bread.[86] In Aristophanes' *Frogs* we meet with two female inn-keepers, and in the *Thesmophoriazousai* a woman who makes a living weaving garlands for sale in the market.[87] Such activities by women are not just comedic fantasy, either: in Demosthenes' speech *Against Euboulides* the plaintiff Euxitheos recounts how, out of poverty due to the family's losses during the Peloponnesian War, his mother supplemented the family's income by making and selling ribbons in the market place.[88] In Xenophon's *Memorabilia*, Sokrates advises an elite friend who has taken in the womenfolk of deceased relatives, to have the women earn their keep by weaving cloth and selling what they make: we can be confident that such advice would have been unnecessary outside elite circles, where men and women would have been doing this as a matter of course.[89] Poorer women were also known to hire themselves out as wet-nurses: the same Euxitheos referenced above told how, during the extreme poverty induced by the disastrous closing phase of the Peloponnesian War, his mother hired herself out as a wet nurse. He goes on to add that many Athenian citizen women served as wet nurses, and that he is prepared to name some of them.[90] It is clear, in fact, that women outside of the elite class quite normally contributed by their work in the "feminine" crafts like weaving and garland-making, and in retail, to the incomes of their families. It's also clear that sons of the family, at least those older than eleven or twelve years, will have begun to work and add to the family income. The point being that the 15 to 25 drachmas that a working man could expect to earn in a month may have made up the bulk of a poor family's income, but they were by no means the whole of it: a family income of 30 drachmas or more must have been common among the poor.

Now figures like 30 drachmas don't in and of themselves mean very much, although we can tell that even Greeks earning no more than that could feed themselves and their families, but the information we have regarding prices of basic foodstuffs and other necessities provides us with a context for understanding these incomes: it is the cost of living, after all, that gives context and meaning to incomes. As is widely known, the ancient Greeks subsisted primarily on a diet based on the so-called "Mediterranean triad": grain, olives (primarily in the form of olive oil), and grapes (primarily in the form of wine). The most important of these, making up as much as 75 percent of the poorer people's caloric intake, was grain: wheat (especially emmer and einkorn wheats which are native to the eastern Mediterranean region and can thrive on poor soil and in dry climates) and barley being the staple grains in the Greek diet.[91] Wheat is the more nutritious and tasty of the two, and was thus more highly prized, being typically sold at double the price (by volume) of barley; the latter, barley, tended to be the staple grain of the poorer segment of the population. Wheat typically sold at 6 drachmas per *medimnos*; barley was typically hulled before sale and bought in the form of barley meal (*alphita*) at a typical price of 4 drachmas per *medimnos*. The widely used Attic *medimnos* contained 48 *choinikes*, with one *choinix* of wheat being considered a good day's ration for a man engaged in strenuous activity (soldiering or physical labor);[92] women and children were assumed to be able to get by on half a *choinix* per day. Though Greeks greatly preferred wheat if they could afford it, considering barley less appealing and nutritious, the reality is that 1.2 *choinikes* of barley meal have the same caloric value as a *choinix* of wheat (*c.* 2,600–2,700 calories). A family of four (man, woman, and two children) thus would require 2.5 *choinikes* of wheat per day, or 3 *choinikes* of barley meal. For one thirty day month, thus, the family of four would need 75 *choinikes* of wheat or a little over 1.5 *medimnoi*, costing in normal times some 9 drachmas; or 90 *choinikes* of barley (just under two *medimnoi*), at a normal cost of 8 drachmas.

A poor family subsisting on barley could thus provide itself with its basic grain requirement at a cost no more than 8 drachmas per month in normal times. The barley could be consumed in the form of bread (though barley loaves are rather coarse) or as a kind of porridge or stew with other foodstuffs and flavorings added. Quite poor families often had small plots of land where they could grow vegetables to add to their barley stew, but even the completely landless poor would not necessarily have to buy vegetables. Edible wild greens (*chorta*) grow abundantly throughout Greece and are widely gathered and consumed in modern times (even seen as something of a delicacy in these vegetarian-friendly times) and were certainly also gathered and consumed in antiquity too, as were wild-growing herbs for flavor. A barley stew mixed with wild greens and herbs would require only one other ingredient to be considered complete, in a poor family: olive oil. This was considered a staple and necessary part of the diet in ancient (as in modern) Greece; the price of a standard *metretes* (just under 40 liters), the amount contained by a typical trade amphora, of olive oil was about 72 drachmas. The *metretes* was made up of 144 *kotylai*, and the daily ration of olive oil for an active man was set at one quarter of a *kotyle*, or for a less active man (or a woman or child) at one eighth. A family of four would thus need five-eighths of a *kotyle* per day, or some 16 *kotylai* per month at a cost of 8 drachmas. The other required part of the diet, wine, could be bought at between three and four drs. for an amphora, and four *kotylai* (about 0.8 of a liter) of wine was considered a good ration for an active man.[93] At 3 drachmas the amphora, four *kotylai* would cost half an obol, the cost being thus 15 obols (2.5 drachmas) per month. Whether or to what degree women and children were given wine to drink (remember that Greeks drank their wine heavily watered down) is unclear, but we can certainly take it that a poor family would spend no more than 4 drachmas per month on wine. The total monthly cost for grain, olive oil, and wine would thus be less than 20 drachmas, assuming that the family produced no grain, olives, or wine for their own consumption, which is likely to have been rare.

As an old saying has it, "man does not live on bread alone." Meaning that people generally want and need more than their bare food requirements to live well. To begin with, people tend to want a little variety in their diet. Various extras were available to the poorer citizens at little expense. Olives and dried figs, for example, could be purchased for only 2 drachmas the *medimnos* (which would likely have lasted a few months); honey could be bought at 3 obols for a *kotyle*, which would have been about a week's supply. Sheep and goat cheeses were widely and cheaply available: at Athens, for example, there was a special cheese market at the end of each month. We also hear frequently of people buying fish in the market place; for the poorer people, that would be small fish like anchovies and sardines, or salted or pickled fish. Other standard necessities were similarly cheaply available: a basic cheap *chiton* (tunic, the standard garb of the ancient Greek) cost just 3.5 obols; a pair of shoes could be had for 6 drachmas; and such garments and shoes were expected to last for two years.[94] A cloak for the cold weather season cost more of course: a basic woolen cloak could be had for some 10 to 11 drachmas. The point is that a poor family having an income of some 30 drachmas per month (allowing for days off for festivals and such) would have an annual income of around 360 drachmas, so that after spending perhaps 240 on basic food necessities, they would still have some 120 drachmas available for extra foods, clothing, and other wants. There is, of course, the question of housing: some scholars assume that poor Greeks would be renters and calculate substantial sums for rent as part of their annual expenditure.[95] That seems most unlikely, however: even most poor Greek citizens will have had a family home that belonged to them. An inscription from 414 reveals the sale of seven houses at Athens for a median price of 410 drachmas: the cheapest cost 105, the most expensive well over 1,000. That is to say that the value of a small, cheap house was around 200 to 300 drachmas. The Athenian law on poor relief granted public assistance of 2 obols per day for food to any poor citizen too disabled to work who owned property valued at less than 300 drachmas.[96] In other words, even the poorest Athenian citizens nevertheless were likely to own property worth several hundred drachmas, and that property was undoubtedly the house that they lived in, albeit a very small and cheap house.

The evidence is clear therefore that in the classical Greek economy, even the poorer segment of the citizen population was able to make enough income of various sorts to live reasonably well, with some disposable income for extras over and above the necessities. Undoubtedly, the institution of slavery helped in this: it was the majority of the enslaved who took the place of the very poorest sections of modern societies, living in many cases a bare subsistence life with hardly any or no luxuries at all. Within the citizen "class," if one may call it that, the gap between rich and poor was in fact relatively narrow—compared to other historical societies, including many modern societies, that is—and as Aristotle emphasized in his *Politika*, there was a substantial middling element who were neither rich nor poor. This middling element corresponded more or less to those who could afford to serve as hoplites, what we may call the "hoplite class," and in most city-states they made up a significant percentage of the population. In Athens, *c.* 435, Thucydides informs us that there were 13,000 citizens available for active service as hoplites, and a further 16,000 reserve hoplites who could be called upon for more limited service, as frontier garrisons or to man the city walls for example. These latter were made up of the oldest age classes—that is those over forty or forty-five, at a guess—and the very youngest, youths in their late teens that is, and in addition metics—men from other city-states permanently domiciled and making their livings in Athens.[97] Unfortunately, we are not told how many of these 16,000 were citizens as opposed to metics, but it is surely unlikely that the very youngest and oldest age classes were close to being equal in number to the men in the prime of life, so we may guess that perhaps 6,000 or 7,000 of these reservists were citizens, with the remaining 9,000 or so being metics.[98] That would mean that about 20,000 Athenians were sufficiently well-to-do to serve as hoplites, and that number is consistent with the number of 21,000 Athenians who were eligible to pay the *eisphora*, the occasional property tax assessed to meet fiscal emergencies: the minimum property requirement for this tax was set at 2,500 drachmas, which we can thus take to be the hoplite "census." This means that, out of a total male citizen body of between 40,000 and 50,000 by most estimates, something like 45 percent to 50 percent were well-to-do enough to qualify to pay property tax when called upon, and to serve as hoplites.

It has been estimated that, for a Greek man to qualify as a hoplite based on land ownership and farming, he would need to own about 5 hectares of farmland. One of the richest men in Athens in the late fifth century, Alkibiades, is reported to have owned, as the foundation of his wealth, an estate of 29 hectares, not quite six times the amount owned by an ordinary not too well off hoplite. Another very wealthy Athenian, the father of the orator Demosthenes, owned (early fourth century) two manufacturing workshops worth a total of some 7 talents or 42,000 drachmas, not quite twenty times the wealth of the ordinary hoplite.[99] That is not a large gap between rich and middling: by contrast, in the USA today, a person is quite well-to-do if they have property worth about 500,000, while the richest people have wealth of tens of billions of dollars. In America, that is, the very rich have wealth several thousand times greater than the middle class, a powerful indication of how narrow the gap between rich and middling was in ancient Greece. The same rather narrow gap between rich and middling is indicated by the Solonian property classes at Athens: the richest were designated as having incomes exceeding 500 *medimnoi*, while the middling *zeugitai*— apparently meaning those who could equip themselves as hoplites—had incomes of between 200 and 300 *medimnoi*. Leaving aside the exact significance of such incomes counted in *medimnoi*, the point here is that to qualify as rich citizens needed incomes only two to three times the incomes of the middling citizens. The social structure of the classical Greek city-states, that is to say, was such as to ensure that the economy, productive and wealth-generating as it was, worked reasonably fairly for the citizen class at least. The cost of living was so low and wages so relatively high that all but the poorest citizens by and large had disposable income, middling citizens had considerable disposable income and lived very well, and though the rich were only moderately wealthy by modern standards, the vast bulk of their incomes was disposable and could be saved, invested, spent on luxuries or—as was essentially required by the Greek cities in lieu of direct taxation of the wealthy—spent more or less voluntarily on public service.

Conclusion: The Greek City as Center of Economic Specialization and Exchange

When we think back to the three models of the ancient Greek city referenced at the beginning of this chapter, we can now see that each of them is flawed and incomplete. The correct model that can allow us to understand the intrinsic nature of the Greek city is that described by Plato and also referred to at the start of this chapter: the ancient Greek city existed for the sake of making possible economic specialization and the exchange of products and services. As Plato noted, for one man to spend his time producing all the many goods and services he and his family would need, is inefficient in a variety of ways. To have to spend a few hours farming, an hour at carpentry, an hour on building repair and extension, an hour or two at pottery and smithcraft, and so on and so forth, would exhaust the time, energy, and ingenuity of even the most active and versatile of men. Focusing on a particular activity, specializing in it, increases one's expertise in that activity, improving both the quality and the speed of one's work.[100] It is, therefore, far more efficient in every way for one man to be a smith, another a potter, a third a farmer, and so on. But for specialization of this sort to be truly efficient, a large number of people must live close together in communities where a critical mass of population is reached, at which there are enough persons to take up the production of a group of families concentrating all their productive energies on potting, another on carpentering, and so on, and there must be sufficient families engaged in farming, producing a large enough surplus of foodstuffs available for exchange, that the food needs of the families engaged in specialized crafts of various sorts can be met. As Plato went on to notice, humans are not content merely to exist at a basic subsistence level: they desire luxuries, entertainments, a richer and more varied lifestyle than mere satisfaction of the most basic needs. This requires further expansion of the community, to include more highly specialized workers providing a wider variety of goods and services, and therefore also a larger number of more productive farmers to feed these specialized workers of various sorts. It also requires the development of trade between communities, as no one community can produce the full array of desirable goods and services: goods and services must be exchanged not only within a community between its members, but also between communities, so that specialists in retail trade and long-distance trade are required, as well as shippers, sailors, and financiers.

All of this is what the ancient Greek city was all about, in the view of a highly intelligent and observant ancient Greek commentator who was by no means inclined to over emphasize the importance of economic activities. And all of this makes perfect sense in terms of what we know of Greek city-state life. The farmer sold his surplus and cash crops in the *agora*, either at a market stall run by a member of his family, or to a retail trader (*kapelos*) who ran a market stall selling such produce as a way of making a living. The *agora* was on most days filled with market stalls selling a wide variety of farm produce, fish, and manufactured goods.[101] Around the *agora* were long buildings called stoas, with shops run by the more prosperous producers and merchants. Writers like the author of the *Constitution of the Athenians* attributed to Xenophon boasted complacently of the wide range of goods regularly bought and sold in the *agorai* of the Athenians, thanks to Athens' command of the sea and the central role in Aegean trade it gave her.[102] Plato filled his Socratic dialogues with examples and metaphors drawn from all sorts of crafts and professions, aware that his audience would know such crafts and professions and the activities involved in practicing them as matters of everyday experience. Inscriptions and dedications attest to the activities and prosperity of practitioners of all sorts of trades and crafts.[103] The evidence is scattershot, anecdotal, inferential, and anything but quantifiable, but seen properly it reveals a picture of an urban society in which economic specialization and exchange were indeed at the core of communal life, just as Plato states. The Greek citizen, that is to say, was not a drone living by exploiting an oppressed class of rural "serfs," except in a few unusual communities like Sparta. He was a man who farmed the land himself, owned and worked in a manufacturing workshop making a specialized product, owned and operated a fishing vessel, or provided some desirable service for which his fellow citizens were prepared to pay. And, notwithstanding some snobbish statements by members of the wealthy elite about "*banausic* activities," he was a man who took some pride in his trade or business.

It is of course true that the Greeks kept slaves, and that the Greek economy was in part a slave economy. The rich in the Greek city-states often owned numerous slaves: we hear of as many as a thousand, in the case of the rich Athenian Nikias who hired them out for an obol a day each to work in the silver mines of Laureion, and owning a dozen or more slaves engaged in productive crafts does not seem to have been very unusual among the wealthy.[104] The impression is sometimes given, in works on the Greek economy, that almost all productive work in ancient Greece was done by slaves; but this was not the case. For the numerous Greek citizens who belonged to the middle or hoplite "class," owning a slave or two, as they often did, was not a matter of having someone who could work in one's place, but someone who could work beside one.[105] That is, the typical reasonably prosperous Greek craftsman would own a slave, or a few slaves, to perform some of the rougher or more physically demanding tasks in his workshop, but he would work alongside them, supervising and training them as he went. Slavery certainly played an important role in the economies of the larger and more highly developed Greek city-states, such as Athens, Corinth, Chios, Syracuse, or Byzantion, but slaves did not displace or replace the free working crafstman or farmer or fisher, they worked under and alongside them.[106]

To motivate their slaves to be as productive as possible, Greek masters permitted them to keep a percentage of the profits they generated, so that an active and saving slave could look forward to eventually purchasing his freedom and setting up as a free craftsman.[107] Many such ex-slaves eventually became middle class members of the community themselves, with the status of *metoikoi*: registered resident aliens. They typically paid a poll tax for the right to live and work in a city-state and contributed thus to the city's public finances as well as its economic life, and if sufficiently prosperous they might even be called upon for hoplite service in war. Of course, most *metoikoi* living in Greek city-states were free-born immigrants; we hear of them predominantly in our Athenian sources, where the fact that they numbered in excess of 10,000 in the later fifth century, as many as 9,000 of them prosperous enough to serve as hoplites, illustrates in yet another way the varied and specialized nature of the economy, as they could not own land and came to Athens exclusively to make a living from a craft of some sort or from trade.[108]

A key factor in the life of the city-state is that, though our surviving literary sources are dominated by the distorting viewpoint of the wealthy elite who overwhelmingly produced them, the city-states themselves were not so dominated. As Aristotle was at pains to demonstrate carefully in his deservedly famous analysis of the city-state, the *Politika*, it was the *mesoi*—literally the "middlemen," but as we would say the "middle class"—who were the most important part of the city-state community: numerous, crucial in warfare as they formed the "hoplite class," economically vital, politically tone-setting. Without a large and prosperous "middle class," a middling element that was well-to-do enough to afford such luxuries as a set of hoplite armor, leisure time to engage in warfare, politics, and cultural activities such as theater going, the most crucial inventions of Greek civilization could not have come about: the hoplite warfare that kept the Greeks free of Persian domination, the long distance sea-faring, trading, and migration that opened up the near east and the wider Mediterranean world to the Greeks, and the democratic political system that became the constitutional norm in Greek city-states after the mid fourth century.[109] That large and prosperous "middle class" was made possible by the relatively highly developed and specialized economy of the late archaic and classical city-states.

And it was of course also that economy that made feasible the expenditure of large surplus resources on the physical infrastructure that was highly characteristic of the city-states of Greece: monumental temples, city walls, public water supplies, public granaries, theaters, gymnasia, stoas, and so on. The major Greek temples, like the Heraion at Samos, the temples of Apollo at Didyma (Miletos) and of Artemis at Ephesos, the temple of Zeus at Olympia, or the Parthenon (temple of Athena) at Athens, cost hundreds of talents to build: Plutarch alleges that Perikles' opponents spoke of "1,000 talent temples," though this is no doubt an exaggeration.[110] Even the maintenance of city-walls was a huge expense, frequently requiring public subscriptions and gifts from wealthy benefactors.[111] Beginning with the theater of Dionysos at Athens in the mid fifth century, it became standard for every Greek city to have a well constructed stone theater: more or less well preserved examples are known from all around the Greek world.[112] Water was crucial to the life of a city and its citizens, and we know of some extraordinary and expensive public works projects aimed at establishing a plentiful water supply: the famed tunnel of Eupalinos at Samos, built in the late sixth century, for example, or the *Enneakrounos* (nine source) fountain built in Athens during the Peisistratid tyranny.[113] In general, during the course of the sixth, fifth, and fourth centuries, the Greek cities developed an array of expensive public infrastructure expectations that were met by a mixture of public resources and private benefactions.[114] It would simply have been inconceivable for the Greeks to have created such urban infrastructure, which was aimed at providing services to the general citizen population be it noted, without a highly productive economy that generated a significant surplus which the citizens were prepared to devote to public purposes.

The Greek city, center of the Greek city-state, was therefore both a producer city and a consumer city—after all, as Adam Smith noted, all production is ultimately for the purpose of consumption, the two go hand in hand—and it was a service city too. The production of specialized goods, the consumption of goods of all sorts, the provision of desirable services: without all these factors operating smoothly together, the Greeks could not have evolved the sophisticated urban culture that has made them so admired and influential in subsequent history. When we read the plays of Aristophanes, the dialogues of Plato, the treatises of Ps-Xenophon and Xenophon himself, and of Aineias Taktikos, or the political and ethical treatises of Aristotle, and of course the histories and biographies of the likes of Herodotos, Thucydides, Xenophon, and Plutarch, we see reflected in their anecdotes, assumptions, metaphors, and casual asides a society with a great economic diversity, a society founded on the generation of surplus wealth through economic specialization and exchange, a society in which surplus wealth was generated not just by the rich but by a large and self-confident "middle class" too, and a society in which the expenditure of one's surplus wealth not just on private satisfactions but also on public services—military, political, religious, and cultural—was taken for granted. Admittedly, our evidence for all of this is overwhelmingly Athenian and/or Atheno-centric, but as the famous Athenian statesman Perikles noted, at least in the words attributed to him by Thucydides (2.37 and 40), Athens was a model to other Greek cities and an education to Greece. Biased words no doubt, uttered in a highly patriotic context, but words carrying a great deal of truth all the same, as Athenian institutions and culture did indeed come to be widely admired and imitated throughout the Greek world in the fourth and subsequent centuries.

3

The Spear: Warfare and the City-State

Aristotle pointed out in his *Politika* that there is a close relationship between the nature of a state's armed forces and the nature of its socio-political structure and arrangements, one of the most acute and important of his political insights though not always accorded the recognition it deserves.[1] Aristotle is no doubt somewhat over-schematic, relating a reliance on cavalry (drawn from the wealthy horse-owning elites) to extreme oligarchy, a reliance on heavy infantry (that is, a citizen-militia of hoplites drawn from the well-to-do middling element) to moderate oligarchy, and a reliance on light infantry and naval forces (in each case the manpower in question would be drawn chiefly from the lower/poorer classes) to democracy. Yet it is a readily observable phenomenon that the military system and arrangements of a society have a considerable effect on the political system and arrangements, and vice versa. As an illustrative example of this principle, we might consider the French Revolution and its aftermath.

The political and social revolution in France in the closing decades of the eighteenth century called forth an entirely new type of warfare, that of the *levée en masse*—the mobilization of national manpower and national resources on an unprecedented scale—made possible by the extension of political rights and social improvement to the middle and (to a limited extent) even lower classes of society and the concomitant rise of nationalism. The old eighteenth-century system of "Cabinet warfare" fought by essentially mercenary armies officered by an international aristocracy was rendered obsolete: to compete with the huge and highly motivated French armies the other states of Europe had to attempt to introduce similar "national" armies, and in doing so they had to confront powerful forces of liberalism and nationalism that threatened and eventually drastically altered the socio-political structures of the "*ancien regime*."[2]

Examples of this phenomenon from the ancient world can also readily be cited: the creation of a national and imperial Macedonian state in the mid fourth century BCE went hand in hand with the creation of a national Macedonian army of heavy pike infantry and cavalry.[3] The collapse of the aristocratic governing structure of Republican Rome and its replacement by military autocracy in the course of the first century BCE was clearly greatly influenced by the contemporaneous demise of the citizen-militia military system and its replacement by a professional, long-service, standing army.[4] There are reasons to see the emergence of the city-state as another such case, since it appears that the development of the *polis* as a city-state was influenced by the equation of the *polis* with its fighting men, which in turn can be taken to result from the development of hoplite warfare; and the growth of radical democracy within the city-states can be related to the development of large scale naval warfare, with fleets rowed and crewed by the lower classes. Since this chapter focuses on the hoplite warrior in the phalanx, and the rower on the oar bench of the trireme, examining their relationship to the development of the warrior citizen ideology, there will be no discussion of women or the enslaved. Though they did have roles to play in Greek warfare (be it often as victims),[5] they did not take a stand in the phalanx or a seat at the oar bench, and so are not relevant to the discussion here.[6]

Early Greek Warfare

A few decades ago, a broad scholarly consensus agreed that an Homeric age of rather primitive warfare, dominated by aristocratic champions fighting individual duels backed by a group of well-armed *hetairoi* (companions) and a much less well-equipped mass of ordinary soldiers who shouted encouragement and insults but did little real fighting, gave way in the early seventh century to a very different style of more advanced and highly disciplined mass infantry warfare: the so-called "hoplite revolution." This notion is particularly associated with such British scholars as Anthony Andrewes and H.L Lorimer;[7] in recent decades it has come under attack from a group of scholars who have cast into question the traditional view of Homeric warfare and argued for an early form of hoplite warfare in Homer.

The genesis of the notion that the *Iliad* depicts hoplite or "proto-hoplite" warfare is quite straightforward: Joachim Latacz, and others after him, pointed out that Homer depicts massed infantry as forming the armies on both sides in the Trojan War, an observation already in fact clearly apparent to any careful reader of the *Iliad*, and familiar even to ancient readers (see e.g., Polybios 18.28.6; Diodoros 16.3.2).[8] In some passages these masses of soldiers are even described as forming *phalanges* (lines) and/or *stichas* (files), terms highly suggestive of the classical Greek hoplite phalanx which was indeed a disciplined formation of lines and files, as we shall see below.[9] It is argued that the aristocratic duels, and the predominance of the aristocratic leaders and their small bands of *hetairoi*, as well as certain other prominent features of Homeric battle description, are poetic elaboration of the mythic tradition, and are essentially fictional, disguising rather than describing the true nature of early Greek warfare of Homer's day. If correct, this view has very important implications for the development of the city-state, which was in an important sense a band of roughly equal male warriors, as I have pointed out above (pp. 2–4). A careful review of Homeric and hoplite warfare is in order. We should start by analyzing Homer's depiction of battle as it stands, to see whether it forms a coherent and plausible system of warfare. In doing so, there are a number of crucial issues that need to be addressed: battle formations and tactics; the nature of the fighting; the nature and cost of the equipment used; the nature and importance of the use of horses and chariots in Homeric warfare, and their cost; and the socio-political implications of all of the above.

As Homer describes it, eighth-century Greek warfare was characterized by a high degree of looseness and indiscipline: formations were unorganized and fluid; men advanced to fight, retreated, and advanced again as they saw fit, paying little or no attention to cohesion, communal discipline, or orders. Often men would move from one part of the battlefield to another because a more interesting fight seemed to be going on there, or for some other reason. The major concern of the Homeric warrior seems to have been to defeat an enemy champion in a personal duel, and then to despoil his corpse of arms and armor to carry off as trophies and, if possible, to maltreat the corpse, while the defeated warrior's companions would do all they could to rescue his corpse and preserve his armor. Many of the fiercest massed fights in Homer were indeed over the body and arms of some defeated warrior, the contest over the corpse of Patroklos being the most notable.[10] The basic fighting unit described by Homer is a small band of *hetairoi* around a leading champion, with common soldiers providing ill-defined but clearly undisciplined backing. The best known such unit is perhaps that of Telamonian Aias, consisting of the great Aias himself as the central champion, providing a bulwark of physical leadership and protection with his massive strength and huge ox-hide shield; Aias' half-brother Teukros, a noted archer who fired his arrows from behind Aias' shield; the lesser or Lokrian Aias, a mobile, lightly armored javelineer; lesser *hetairoi* such as Mekisteus and Alastor (*Iliad* 8.329–34); and "many people and brave ones followed as companions, and took over the great shield from him whenever the sweat and weariness came over his body" (*Iliad* 13.709–11). These champions and *hetairoi* fronted the enemy warriors and fought in hand-to-hand combat, picking out enemy champions with whom to duel. Meanwhile, as the above cited passage from the *Iliad* continues (13.716–22), lightly equipped troops sheltered behind them and showered the enemy ranks with arrows, slingshots, and other projectiles. We have here then, a coherent and persuasive account of an aristocratic form of warfare, in which massed groups of common soldiers are present, but their role is relatively insignificant.[11]

The basic reason why the common people held back from physical confrontation and were ineffective in the hand-to-hand fighting, was their lack of equipment. As *Iliad* 13.713–15 puts it, speaking specifically of the Lokrians but in words that fit the common soldiers generally: "the heart was not in them to endure close-standing combat, for they did not have the brazen helmets crested with horse-hair, they did not have the strong-circled shields and the ash spears." This is the nub of the matter: to engage in close combat, defensive armor was required, and most soldiers did not have it. The reason they did not is most likely to be found in their poverty—which is supported by the archaeological record—and in the expense of the equipment. Another well known passage from the *Iliad* is informative here: in bk. 6 the Lykian hero Glaukos and the Achaian champion Diomedes come together and challenge each other to a duel, but realizing that they are ancestral guest-friends, they hold off and instead exchange their armor as a symbol of their relationship (6.119–236). Of this exchange, Homer has the following to say: "but Zeus the son of Kronos stole away the wits of Glaukos who exchanged with Diomedes the son of Tydeus armor of gold for bronze, for nine oxen's worth the worth of a hundred" (6.234–6). Glaukos' golden armor worth 100 oxen is no doubt epic exaggeration, but Diomedes' plain, workmanlike set of bronze armor is clearly intended to sound real, and the value of nine oxen can be taken as representing the true cost/value of a basic set of armor in Homer's own day: otherwise, his audience would not take the point he was making. Armor worth nine oxen might be cheap compared to the fancy equipment of a rich foreign ruler of myth, but what does such a cost mean in real terms? Oxen were highly valued beasts, the essential beasts of burden for ploughing, hauling and carting in the ancient world. We know that in later times (sixth century and later) to own a yoke of oxen was the mark of a well-to-do and independent farmer: it was pretty certainly owning a yoke of oxen that marked Solon's middle property class the *zeugitai*, for example.[12] If owning two oxen marked a man as well-to-do in the sixth century and later, we may be sure that a pair of oxen marked at least an equivalent degree of prosperity in Homer's day.

To be able to dispose of the value of nine oxen on goods that were not economically productive, such as a suit of armor, was clearly something that only a wealthy man could do at that time. Homer's story tells us, then, that the basic equipment of the warrior champion—helmet, cuirass, and greaves of bronze, plus large ox-hide shield and stout ash spears—was beyond the means of any but the rich in eighth-century society. The poorer soldiers, equipped with little or no defensive armor, and using cheap projectile weapons like arrows, slingshots, and stones, simply could not confront a well-armed champion and his *hetairoi* with any prospect of success.

The role of the chariot in Homeric warfare exacerbated this disparity between champion and common soldier. The great champions in Homer rode to battle in chariots pulled by teams of (usually) four horses. These chariots were two-man carriages, a charioteer and a warrior: the warrior was of course the great aristocratic champion, while the role of charioteer would be played by one of his *hetairoi*, usually a younger man. The use of chariots in Homeric battle is one of the most contentious aspects of Homeric warfare, as Homer has been accused of betraying a complete ignorance of how chariots are used in battle: Homer's chariots are essentially platforms to convey the warrior to the scene of battle, or around the battlefield, and are used in a thoroughly individual way. Champions might, arriving at the field of battle, ride in their chariots to and fro in "no man's land" between the armies, hurling throwing spears at the enemy and/or taunting them. Or they might "park" the chariot near their own lines, dismount, and fight on foot, the charioteer remaining with the chariot ready to drive off the moment the warrior should remount. The chariot has thus been likened to little more than a "taxi," ferrying the warrior to and from battle. This role is considered unhistorical: by contrast, the massed chariot warfare of the Assyrians is pointed to, in which dozens or hundreds of chariots were drawn up in formation to execute fearful charges at enemy formations.[13] The assumption is that genuine Greek chariot fighting must also have been of this type: massed formations of chariots operating together. The unsuitability of the Greek terrain to such warfare is overlooked, and Homer is charged with an utter unfamiliarity with chariot warfare.

However, the near eastern style of massed chariot warfare is not the only example of chariot fighting known from the ancient world. Consider a passage from Caesar's *De Bello Gallico*, for example:

> This is the method of fighting from chariots. First they [the Britons] ride all over the place hurling javelins, and they oftentimes disturb the [enemy] ranks by mere fear of the horses and the noise of the wheels; then they draw up among the

squadrons of cavalry, dismount from their chariots, and fight on foot. The charioteers, meanwhile, move a little away from the battle and draw up the chariots in such a way that, if they [the warriors] are pressed by enemy numbers, they have a quick means of retreat to their own ranks.

4.33.1–2[14]

It is remarkable how closely this use of chariots by Caesar's British antagonists resembles the use of chariots described by Homer, and we can conclude from this that there is in fact nothing militarily implausible in Homer's description of chariot fighting. Given the nature of the Greek terrain, in fact—small plains divided from each other by mountain ranges and cut by numerous stream beds—a style of warfare involving massing large numbers of chariots is hardly feasible, and only the type of chariot fighting described by Homer and Caesar seems plausible at all. To this observation we can add the abundant testimony to the presence and use of chariots in eighth- and seventh-century Greece: numerous depictions of chariots on painted vases, for example; archaeological evidence in the form of remains of actual chariots; and the popularity of chariot racing at Greek festivals.[15] In sum, Homer's depiction of the use of chariots in warfare must be taken seriously as an accurate account of how his contemporary aristocrats rode to battle and moved about the battlefield. Now, keeping horses, was at all times, an exceedingly expensive proposition in ancient Greece, and only wealthy aristocrats could afford to do so. Horses fulfilled no economic function, but required extensive and high quality pasture land, as well as other food (hay, oats, etc.). One needed to enjoy access to considerable surplus land and income, therefore, to raise horses. Homeric war chariots were typically drawn by teams of four horses, and the chariots themselves were an additional expense, made as they were of wood with an extensive bronze reinforcement.[16] The key role played by chariots in Homeric battle is, therefore, another testimony to the primarily aristocratic nature of Homeric warfare.

The socio-political implications of this style of warfare are fairly obvious. Only a society dominated socially and economically by a wealthy elite would develop a warfare built around aristocratic leaders and their retainers; and in such a society the aristocratic leaders would naturally hold political power. That is of course exactly the type of society depicted by Homer, and taken by virtually all scholars since the publication of Finley's ground-breaking book *The World of Odysseus*, to be a more-or-less true portrait of the society of Homer's day, or a little earlier.[17] It should be noted that the socio-political order, and the style of warfare, go together: scholars who accept an aristocratic Homeric society are inconsistent if they nevertheless argue against accepting Homer's aristocratic style of warfare. Finley's crucial insight (derived from the work of Parry and Lord)[18] was that orally-composing bards like "Homer" inevitably portray their stories and characters in terms of the ideas, outlooks, and ways of doing things they and their audiences are familiar with; that is to say, that the social, political, and military behaviors and outlooks portrayed in the Homeric epics are those of the bard's own day. Again, if one accepts that Homeric society can be understood as eighth-century society (as I believe one should), then one must accept that Homeric warfare is also eighth-century warfare: the two go together, methodologically and in terms of the necessary connection between social order and system of warfare.

Hoplite Warfare

Now let us consider the nature of hoplite warfare as it emerges from depictions and sources of the late seventh century and later.[19] Hoplites fought, as is known, in massed formations of thousands of men who were all equipped and armed with essentially the same kind of arms and armor. In the first place, the hoplite carried a crucial piece of defensive equipment which, above and before all else, characterized this type of warrior: the hoplite or Argive shield. This type of shield—circular, highly concave, usually about one meter in diameter—was made of a solid wooden core with extensive bronze reinforcement on the outside: at least a bronze rim and central boss, often a complete outer shell of bronze.[20] The hoplite shield was, as shields go, unusually heavy and cumbersome. It was possible to use it effectively for two reasons: it had a double grip—a central strap or cuff that one slid one's lower left arm through up to the elbow (*porpax*), and a rim strap held in the hand (*antilabe*)—which meant that much of its weight depended from the shoulder and torso, rather than being supported only by the left arm as in the case of shields with just a central grip; and its high degree of concavity enabled one to rest the rim on one's left shoulder for long carriage, and to lean one's whole body weight into it when it was pressed against the shield of an enemy.[21] This shield, with its weight and size, was cumbersome and limited one's mobility, but in return it gave outstanding protection to the left half or more of one's torso, and since about half of it projected out to one's left, it was possible for a comrade standing to one's left to come close and shelter his exposed right side behind the projecting part of one's shield. A consequence of these two facts—the cumbersomeness and its effect on mobility, and the shelter afforded to a comrade standing close to one's left—was that this was a shield truly effective only when used by many men drawn up in neat lines, each man standing close to and hence being partly protected by the shield of the man to his right.[22]

The other defensive equipment worn by the hoplite—helmet, cuirass, greaves—was not unique to this type of heavy infantryman, but certainly did increase his lack of mobility: especially the "Corinthian" helmet favored by most hoplites, which covered the whole head from the neck up except the chin, mouth, and eyes, and which—besides being heavy—limited the wearer's vision to what was straight ahead and severely impeded his hearing.[23] Thus armored, the hoplite was carrying up to 50 lbs of wood and metal on his body and was consequently rather slow, clumsy, and easily tired: with little visual range and hearing, heavy equipment limiting his speed and movements, and the weight wearing on his muscles, a lone hoplite—or even a smallish band of hoplites—was easy prey to more lightly armed and hence more mobile troops, including especially cavalry, who could maneuver to attack from the flank and/or rear, where hoplites were extremely vulnerable as they could not see the attackers coming and could not quickly shift around to ward off the attack.[24]

The hoplite panoply, therefore, is a panoply that comes into its own only in a formation, and indeed, the most crucial element of hoplite warfare is the formation in which hoplites fought—the phalanx.[25] The hoplite phalanx was not simply a mass of heavy infantry: it was a complex and ordered formation of lines and files, requiring considerable discipline to establish and maintain. Lengthwise, the phalanx consisted of eight or more lines of men, the men in each line stationed close together for mutual support and to enjoy the protection of the overlapping portions of each other's shields (see above n. 22): this overlapping of shields was called *sunaspismos*, which literally means "shields together."[26] Depth-wise, the phalanx consisted of numerous files—the number determined by the total number of troops available—each eight or more men deep, with each man standing directly and closely behind the man in front and ready to step forward into his place and line should the front man in the file fall, the crucial point being to keep the front line intact.[27] Thus a hoplite army of 8,000 men would typically be drawn up to form, lengthwise, eight lines of 1,000 men each and, depth-wise, 1,000 files of eight men each. Fighting in this formation required of one, not heroic feats of arms or the more dashing type of courage, but steadfast discipline and doggedness, since the vitally important thing was to maintain the integrity of the formation, and especially to keep the front line intact, which meant that every man had to maintain his place in his line and file, except when it became necessary for him to step forward into the next line if and when the front man of his file should be killed or otherwise incapacitated. So long as the integrity of the formation, and especially of the front line, was maintained, a hoplite phalanx was extraordinarily hard to defeat: effectively, only another hoplite phalanx of roughly equal or greater strength could hope to do so, and the art of leadership in a hoplite army was hence reduced to seeing that the formation was properly dressed and making sure to give battle on ground where one's flanks could not be turned. The more heroic and/or brilliant forms of leadership played little or no role in hoplite warfare, and the general was reduced to being little higher in status than the hoplite warriors of rank and file.[28]

The course of hoplite battle was, consequently, at least as ideally imagined, rather simple and in conformity with a standard pattern. A suitable battleground was chosen, usually by the defending general taking up position on his ground of choice: a flat plain broad enough to deploy the force available to him in a proper phalanx, but with natural or man-made obstacles on either side forcing the enemy to approach from in front only. The two armies armed themselves, assumed their formations, and moved toward each other at a steady, normally rather sedate pace, to maintain formation. Usually, musicians of some sort marched between the lines playing a simple rhythmic tune to help the soldiers keep in step,[29] and as the armies approached each other they would begin to sing or chant a simple hymn, called the *Paian*, to invoke the aid of the gods, increase the sense of unity, and maintain their courage. The aim was for the armies to meet in a straight, frontal confrontation, but there was often a tendency for the right wing of each army to overlap the enemy's left wing, as each man tended to edge slightly to the right as they advanced, seeking the protection of the shield to his right, giving rise to the *sunaspismos* described above. When the two armies were close, they would generally shout battle cries and increase their speed to a quick jog so as to crash together, each side hoping to bowl over the enemy's front line and so to win a clear advantage, if not outright victory, at once.[30] Usually, the opposing front lines, backed as they were by seven or more other lines of men, would hold in this initial confrontation, and a period of hand-to-hand fighting would ensue, each man trying to stab with his spear over or under the rim of his opponent's shield, so as to hit him in vulnerable areas such as the neck or thigh/groin.

The crucial phase of the battle is connected to another term: *othismos*, which literally means pushing or shoving.[31] Though the idea accepted at one time of rugby scrum-like organized shoving has been shown to be overstated, it is nevertheless clear that in the critical stage of the battle a more or less concerted pushing and heaving forward began, the aim being to physically drive the enemy ranks backward, lift them off their feet, disrupt and break up their formation, and so put them to flight and win the battle.[32] The main reason, incidentally, for the Spartans' long invincibility in hoplite battles was not so much their skill with weapons or their indomitable courage—important as these were—but their extraordinary concerted discipline during the *othismos*, the fruit of their constant training for hoplite battle, which invariably enabled them to drive back the troops opposed to them and break up their formation. The only strange thing about this is that it took the usually so intelligent and inventive Greeks several centuries to come up with a solution to the Spartan superiority in this respect: the Theban Epaminondas' decision to greatly increase the depth of that part of his phalanx which opposed the Spartans at Leuktra in 371 so as to resist their concerted shoving, while cavalry were ordered to harass the Spartan flank and disrupt their formation from the outside in.[33] At any rate, the *othismos* generally decided the battle: often one side drove the other back and won a clear victory; at times the battle ended inconclusively as neither side managed to drive back the enemy, or each drove back part of the other's formation—usually the two right wings driving back the two left wings.[34]

Flight began from the rear of the phalanx, as troops stationed there felt by the backward pressure on them that their front ranks were giving ground and saw that the lines in front of them were becoming disrupted. Men would begin to peel away, singly or in groups, and head rearwards to a place of safety, not infrequently dropping their heavy, cumbersome shields so as to facilitate a quick getaway: so much was this so, that to retain one's shield in battle became a sign of victory and/or courage, and to lose it a sign not only of defeat but also often of cowardice.[35] During the course of the fighting and its immediate aftermath of flight and pursuit, no attention was paid to the dead, whether to secure their corpses or their armor and weaponry, but once the battle was clearly over heralds from the two sides would arrange a truce enabling both sides to recover their dead for proper burial. If one side had won a clear victory, they would strip the enemy dead before handing them over for burial and use some of the captured armor and weapons to construct a *tropaion* (trophy) at the spot on the battlefield where the enemy first began to give way. Occasionally, if both sides retained control of different parts of the battlefield, both would set up a *tropaion*.[36] Casualties on the winning side were usually quite slight, thanks to the excellence of the defensive equipment and of the phalanx formation, and not much more numerous on the losing side, thanks to the advantage in mobility dropping one's shield gave one, facilitating a safe escape for all but those in the front rank.

That, then, in brief outline, is hoplite warfare, the crucial elements being: the large, double-grip shield; the complex, disciplined phalanx formation with its *sunaspismos*; the *othismos*; the neglect of the dead until the truce after the conclusion of the battle; and the *tropaion* at the battle's turning point. Now admittedly this is an account of how hoplite battle was ideally supposed to work, and real-life practice never corresponds exactly with the ideal. There was undoubtedly a good deal of variance in how exactly things were done, how exactly fighting was conducted and a battle proceeded: no two hoplite battles are likely to have been exactly alike, and very likely no actual hoplite battle went exactly according to the ideal system. Despite recent attempts to critique the received ideas regarding hoplite warfare,[37] its basic organizing principles and features are well attested, and not one of these crucial features is to be found in Homer. The *tropaion* was unknown to Homer. A keen interest in securing the bodies of the dead and/or of stripping them of their armor as booty is one of the most prominent and important features of Homeric battle, many of the most fiercely contested and largest scale engagements beginning as a struggle over the body and/or armor of some slain warrior.[38] This is something that simply could not occur in hoplite warfare, as such behavior would totally disrupt the all important phalanx formation. The *sunaspismos* and *othismos* do not occur in the fighting in the *Iliad*, the few scenes of mass struggle that have been interpreted as examples of these maneuvers actually being simply denser massing together of troops brought about by other causes: a burst of enthusiasm for battle (*Iliad* 16.210–17), a coming together of dispersed troops to make a stand (*Iliad* 13.83–135), the gradual massing of troops as men rushed in to support their comrades in the struggle over the corpse of some fallen champion (*Iliad* 17.212 318), and the like.[39] Though the *Iliad* does occasionally mention the drawing up of troops in a regular sounding order (e.g., at 2.361–66) and often refers to ranks and files of troops (*phalanges* and *stichas*), there is in fact nothing remotely resembling the hoplite phalanx: the armies do battle in no particular formation, grouping together and dispersing again at will, warriors or groups of warriors advancing forward or retreating or moving from one wing to the other as it occurs to them to do so, and the armies moving to and fro fighting, pursuing, retreating, regrouping in a very fluid and undisciplined fashion.[40] The shields described in Homer, finally, are certainly not of the hoplite type, being fashioned of ox-hides rather than wood and bronze, and carried with the help of a neck-strap (*telamon*) rather than the double grip of the hoplite shield.[41]

Hoplite warfare is, in fact, clearly the warfare of an entirely different sort of society, with a different economy, than the society and economy depicted by Homer and reflected in Homeric warfare. In contrast to the ill-equipped masses who play little part in Homeric battle, in hoplite battle we have thousands of very well and relatively expensively equipped warriors who each play a roughly equal part in the fighting. There were no outstanding aristocrats, no retainers clustering around aristocratic champions: instead, there was the ordered discipline of the phalanx formation which imposed the fundamental equality of role just mentioned. Though individual dueling did occur during the hand-to-hand combat phase of hoplite battle, it necessarily occurred within the limitations of the phalanx formation, not in the free-wheeling way depicted in Homer, with champions leaving the formation to move about "no man's land" between the two armies seeking a worthy foe. Again, in the hoplite system the needs of the formation dictate that every man hold his place and not expose the men beside or behind him by creating a gap in the line. Thus, too, the warrior who became tired or demoralized must nevertheless hold his place in the formation: there was no possibility of stepping out of formation to take a breather, or to stage a temporary retreat to regroup. And should retreat and flight become inevitable, there were no chariots to ferry the tired and/or defeated aristocrat to safety: he must take his chances in flight on foot like every other warrior, trusting to his own agility and foot speed, to luck, and to whatever measures he was willing to make to lighten himself for greater mobility, to make good his escape, just as the "common" soldiers did.

In sum, hoplite warfare is a fundamentally egalitarian style of warfare, at least among all those—and for the system to work these must number several hundreds if not thousands—who could afford to equip themselves in the panoply and take their place in the phalanx: this is why it was extensively idealized in our sources which derive from moderately oligarchic or democratic city-states which prized the idea of a certain equality of status among the middling citizens. It is a style of warfare that is radically ill suited to an aristocratic order of society, in that it affords the aristocrat no special place or role in defending the community. It is a style of warfare that requires hundreds or thousands of ordinary members of the community to be well-to-do enough to equip themselves with arms and armor. For that to happen, there must be an economic system that allows for a substantial and well-to-do "middle class" to arise, and that is able to provide plentiful enough supplies of metals—bronze and steel—and sufficient numbers of smiths and manufacturers, to make arms and armor readily available in sufficient quantity and at affordable prices.

On the face of it, then, there is indeed no significant similarity or overlap between Homeric warfare and hoplite warfare. To find some sort of "proto-hoplite" warfare, or some influential precursor elements to hoplite warfare, in the Homeric depictions of battle, it becomes necessary to dismiss by far the greater part of Homeric descriptions of battle and fighting as poetic elaboration, as fictional. Why not rather accept the aristocratic style of warfare described in Homer as true, and regard the occasional hints of disciplined mass warfare as misleading, perhaps the result of anachronistic revision or interpolation of the Homeric original? It is the socio-economic side of things that tells us we must in fact do so: Homeric society was, by its description in the epics and by universal scholarly assent, based not just on Homer but on the archaeological record too, an aristocratic society with a primitive and highly unsophisticated economy. It must have had an aristocratic form of warfare, a form of warfare not based around "middle class" participation or a developed metal-importing and metal-working economy. The form of warfare depicted by Homer is thus suited to the type of society depicted in Homer, while hoplite warfare is not. It is surely right, therefore, to speak of a revolution in Greek warfare from Homeric times to the hoplite warfare of the late archaic and classical city-states, a "revolution" that must have had an economic underpinning and profound social and political effects. It remains to examine these economic, social, and political backgrounds and effects of the "hoplite revolution."

The Hoplite Revolution

When we come to consider how such a "revolutionary" transformation in the nature of warfare, from the Homeric warfare of aristocratic lords and their *hetairoi* to the hoplite warfare of the city-state, could have come about, there are at least four essential prerequisites without which it could not have happened. First, there had to have taken place economic development such as to make metals and metal products widely available at an affordable price, and such as to create a large enough and prosperous enough "middle class" with disposable wealth sufficient to acquire expensive metal goods. Second, the particular equipment of the hoplite warrior—the helmet, greaves, cuirass, and above all the indispensable shield—had to have been invented and become widely known and available. Third, it was necessary that there be, not just a "middle class" able to afford hoplite equipment and service, but a "middle class" that felt committed enough to the community and its interests, a "middle class" that felt it had enough of a stake in society, to have the social discipline and cohesion to undertake *en masse* the highly demanding role of being hoplite warriors. Fourth and finally, the rigid, disciplined, structured phalanx formation in which hoplites fought was not a natural formation that could evolve organically: it was an extremely artificial structure that had to have had an inventor, an organizer who first envisaged it and somehow persuaded or cajoled hundreds if not thousands of men in his community to agree to undergo the unnatural training and discipline required for the formation to work. We must examine each of these prerequisites in detail.

As to economic development, it has been extensively discussed in Chapter 2 above, and therefore can be dealt with here relatively briefly. The crucial point is the availability and cost of metals, specifically bronze and steel. So long as metals were so scarce that a simple workaday panoply cost the equivalent of nine oxen, as Homer reports at *Iliad* 6.234–36 (cf. p. 84 above), so long being well armed would necessarily remain the privilege of a wealthy elite few. There are two ways in which a warrior's panoply could become more generally affordable: the cost of metal goods could decrease and/or more and more people could come to have significant disposable wealth. The likelihood is that both of these factors operated together to make massed hoplite warfare possible, as the discussion of economic development in Chapter 2 has shown, and both factors were in their ways equally important.

Regarding the cost of metal goods, since Adam Smith explained the principles of supply and demand in his epochal book *The Wealth of Nations*, we have known that the surest way to lower the cost of a product or good is to increase its supply: increased supply tends to drive down price. Metals are naturally scarce in Greece. Though a few favored localities did have iron or copper mines, their output was never sufficient to satisfy any extensive demand in Greece, and there is no source of tin—vital to alloy with copper in order to make bronze—in Greece at all. Consequently, it required the development of extensive overseas trade networks for metals to become more widely, and hence cheaply available to the ancient Greeks. By the late seventh century, thousands of Greeks were arming themselves in hoplite panoplies, as Herodotos' story of the "bronze men from the sea"—that is, Ionian and Karian hoplites—employed as mercenaries by the Egyptian rulers of the Saite dynasty shows.[42] By the middle of the sixth century, the larger Greek city-states—such as Sparta, Argos, and Tegea, for example—were fielding substantial hoplite phalanxes, as Herodotos' accounts of wars fought between them show.[43] For such numbers of heavily armed men to have been possible, large quantities of metals must have been imported into Greece by the mid to late seventh century, and much more still by the middle of the sixth century. We know that metals were imported from Cyprus, Anatolia, and Italy, and tin from as far away as Cornwall. The technology of alloying tin with copper to make bronze had been known for over a millennium by our period, but another crucial and necessary technological advance was the ability to turn iron—in its natural state an inconveniently brittle metal—into steel. In the late eighth and early seventh centuries, the Chalkidians of Euboia in particular learned the technique of filtering the smoke from their charcoal furnaces through the molten iron to produce carbonated steel.[44] Alkaios attests to the consequent high reputation of Chalkidian swords in the early sixth century.

The relative abundance and consequent cheaper price of metals and metal goods tells only part of the story, however. A warrior's panoply still remained an expensive item, as we can tell from later evidence of the fifth and fourth centuries: the purchase of a panoply remained beyond the means of much of the citizen body of the developed Greek city-states, even in the most "advanced" and prosperous city-states. At Athens in the third quarter of the fifth century, for example, we learn from Thucydides that rather more than 20,000 out of a probable total of about 50,000 adult male citizens were of "hoplite status," that is could afford to own a hoplite panoply.[45] This means that a little over half of the citizen body could not afford hoplite armor, which will certainly have been less costly then than in the seventh or sixth centuries, if for no other reason than that the expensive bronze cuirass had been replaced by the cheaper linen *thorax* (see below). Granted that, even after a substantial increase in the supply of metals had brought costs down, the panoply remained an expensive item, it is clear that for hundreds, and eventually thousands of men in the various city-states to be able to equip themselves as hoplites, a considerable rise in the prosperity of many non-elite inhabitants of nascent city-states had to have taken place. That rise in prosperity was made possible by the economic development discussed in the previous chapter: increasing use of the land for agriculture rather than pastoralism; the development of specialized cash crops suited to the land being cultivated, and hence making the land more productive; the growth of exchange and trade networks, both local and long distance, based on the agricultural surpluses and cash crops; and the associated development of specialized manufacturing of various sorts. It is the growing, economically prospering "middle class" that was able to find the surplus wealth needed both to equip themselves with hoplite panoplies, and to find the time to engage in unpaid military activities. I note too that the increasing number of Greeks making a living from manufacture is crucial: all those hoplite panoplies had to be manufactured by someone after all.

That brings us to the second prerequisite: the development and wide availability of the hoplite panoply. Archaeological evidence, in the shape of finds of ancient military equipment deposited as grave goods or dedications, has been crucial in helping to determine how, when, and where the various parts of the hoplite panoply were developed, and the key work in this field was done by Anthony Snodgrass in his classic 1967 book *Arms and Armour of the Greeks* (now to be consulted in the 2nd edition of 1999). A good deal of new evidence has been discovered since then, but his basic conclusions seem not to have been disturbed. In essence, the basic panoply—bronze greaves for the lower legs, bronze bell cuirass covering the torso front and back, Corinthian helmet for the head—had all come into being by about 700, as had the heavy thrusting spear, about 8 ft. long with a bronze or steel head and a bronze butt spike. The type of sword used varied somewhat: a short stabbing sword (*xiphos*) was widely used, though the single-edged slashing short-sword called the *machaira* was common by late Archaic times. By far the most crucial piece of equipment, however, as we have already seen, was the characteristic shield of the hoplite warrior, sometimes generically called the *hoplon*, but more properly the Argive *aspis* (shield). As has already been pointed out, the defensive armor worn by the hoplite warrior was deemed to be for his own protection, but the shield was for the sake of the formation: hence the shame in discarding one's shield in defeat.

The typical hoplite cuirass in the Archaic period was the bronze so-called "bell" cuirass, so named after its distinctively bell-like shape. It was fashioned from two large sheets of bronze, hammered into rounded, very roughly torso shaped forms for front and back. The two pieces were joined by hinges at the shoulders, and fastened together by flanges at the sides once on the wearer; cut-outs made way for the head and arms, and a distinctive up-curve of the metal around the waist prevented painful friction against the hips.[46] Such a cuirass required considerable metal working skill to produce, and the same was true to an even greater degree of the Corinthian helmet, which was also beaten out of a single sheet of bronze. The shield, by contrast, was made mostly of wood, a solid wooden core, though it did have extensive bronze reinforcing at the center and around the rim, and often a complete facing of bronze. Highly concave, it too required considerable skill to make. The double grip enabled it to be held and wielded effectively, aided by the high degree of concavity that meant one could rest the rim on one's left shoulder so as to rest the arm carrying it. All of the equipment making up the standard hoplite panoply was available to Greeks able to purchase it by the second quarter of the seventh century, at the latest. Wearing it, a man was carrying a good fifty or more pounds of equipment, as we have noted above, and the effect of it all was to render him both relatively invulnerable, but also slow and clumsy. The helmet and shield, in particular, produced this effect. The Corinthian helmet, covering the entire head with cut outs for the eyes and mouth, limited visibility to what was directly in front, and muffled the hearing considerably too. The Argive shield was so large and unwieldy that, though it provided excellent protection from attack in front, it impeded mobility to the point of being the first thing to be discarded in flight. A man wearing such a helmet and carrying such a shield, in addition to the stiff and necessarily awkward bell cuirass and the greaves, was slow in movement, ponderous, and though extremely well protected against frontal attack, was correspondingly vulnerable to outmaneuvering by a more lightly equipped and mobile soldier. Hoplite equipment, therefore, though it could be effective in face-to-face duels between comparably equipped individual warriors, in a skirmish or battle required the presence of masses of supporting troops to prevent the hoplite being attacked from his vulnerable flank or rear. The equipment may likely have been developed to be used in aristocratic one-on-one duels, but it was a type of panoply uniquely suited to mass formation fighting, if enough men could be thus equipped and someone could organize them into a cohesive unit.

An obvious prerequisite to getting masses of men to fight together in a disciplined formation, is some motivating factor making them ready and willing to be mobilized and organized. In a hierarchical society, or in a highly centralized and bureaucratic one, in which military equipment is mass produced by/for the elites or the government and issued by them to commoners recruited and trained to fight under their direction, warfare requiring thousands of men fighting in highly organized and disciplined formations need not have any socially or politically democratizing effect.[47] The communities of early Iron Age/early Archaic Age Greece, however, were not highly centralized and bureaucratic as we have seen—and though rather hierarchical, they were too loosely structured and the wealth of the elites was insufficient to permit the creation of highly structured and organized military forces in this sort of top-down manner. Individual Greeks procured economic prosperity for themselves, through a spirit of hard work and fierce competition, as emphasized for example in Hesiod's epic *Works and Days* at lines 29–42. Having procured sufficient prosperity, be it as farmers, potters, smiths, traders, or whatever, they acquired the defensive armor and offensive weapons needed to play an effective role in their communities' battles on their own initiative and at their own expense, so far as we can tell. Certainly, that was the case in the late sixth and fifth centuries, with some special exceptions.[48] How exactly it came about that the emerging middle "class" of reasonably prosperous farmers, artisans, and traders acquired enough sense of communal cohesion and shared interests to agree to put themselves under the extreme discipline of the hoplite phalanx, is not known and probably cannot be known. But one may conjecture based on the limited evidence we have, and my conjecture is that the migration process played a role in starting the move towards more organized and collective warfare, and the phase of tyrannies around Greece in the second half of the seventh century and first half of the sixth was key in bringing it to full fruition.

If one brings to mind the circumstances of the initial wave of migrations: in each case several hundred men, commanded by an *oikistes* (founder) who would govern the new settlement during its initial phase, would sail to a pre-identified settlement site—or perhaps rather row since it seems likely they generally traveled in the early galleys called *pentekonters* (fifty-oared vessels). When they arrived, they would certainly face considerable hardships, among which might very likely be the hostile actions of native peoples trying to drive them away. Consequently, two crucial elements were pretty certainly observed: other than the commanding role of the *oikistes*, care was taken to ensure, for the sake of unity and cohesion, as much equality among the colonists as possible, and they must all have been well-armed and ready to fight. In terms of equality, we know that each colonist received an equal housing plot in the core settlement, and an equal allotment of farm land in the surrounding territory: thus they each felt equally committed to a venture in which all were stakeholders.[49]

In terms of weaponry, since it was highly likely that they would have to fight for their nascent settlement, all migrants must have been able-bodied and well-armed men. It is not at all unlikely, though it cannot be proved, that the men who went out on these "colonizing" ventures will have equipped themselves with, or in some cases maybe been equipped by the community or the (usually aristocratic) *oikistes* or his relatives/associates, with the best and most up to date arms and armor. And when they were obliged to fight off natives seeking to drive them out, the fostering of cohesion, of communal military action—rather than any individual heroics—will surely have occurred naturally as offering the best hope for success. In this way, the communal spirit, egalitarianism, and collective discipline required for hoplite phalanx warfare may very well have had its beginnings in the overseas settlements and been gradually adopted in metropolitan Greece from reports of successful warfare engaged in by these settlers. As men in metropolitan Greece, still dominated by aristocratic elites and plagued by the communal disunity fostered by rival aristocratic *oikoi*, learned of the successful experiments in some of the overseas settlements in communal living and collective action in a much more egalitarian spirit, it is easy to understand how the emerging "middle class" would have sought the same kind of social and ultimately political way of life. But the aristocracies were not likely to surrender their privileged positions without a fight. Force would be needed to displace them, and leadership to organize that force. That leadership was provided by the men who were thrust forward as tyrants in the developing cities, and the organization of force took the form of hoplite phalanx warfare.[50]

This brings us to the fourth of our prerequisites: an organizing figure. It must be emphasized again that, though the phalanx may have developed fully and been adopted widely over a long span of time, quite likely centuries, it was all the same a deeply unnatural formation that could not have come about organically but must in its original form have been invented and imposed by a "founding" organizer. Large numbers of men do not spontaneously arrange themselves into lines and files; they do not naturally impose upon themselves, *en masse*, organized structures and collective discipline. Every such highly organized military innovation for which we have clear evidence has been imposed by an organizer. Thus, the Macedonian pike (*sarissa*) phalanx was invented and imposed by king Philip II, for example, and in early modern Europe the establishment of the ordered regimental system, organizing and modernizing European armies, was pioneered by Maurice of Nassau and furthered by military leaders like Gustavus Adolphus of Sweden.[51] The question is, who was it who first put together in his mind the potentialities aroused by the panoply of armor and especially the large Argive shield, and the emerging "middle class," to come up with hoplite warfare? The answer is that we do not know, and probably never will. But there are some things we do know that may point us towards a possibility. The most crucial part of the hoplite panoply, the part that made the phalanx formation desirable, effective, and perhaps even necessary, was the shield. About one meter in diameter and held by a central arm grip and a hand grip at the right edge, the shield had an inbuilt tendency to project out to the left of the wielder, while leaving part of his right side somewhat exposed. If a large number of men wielding such shields formed a neat line, however, each man could use the projecting left part of the shield of the man to his right, to cover his own relatively exposed right side: hence the well-known dictum that the shield was carried for the sake of the formation, not just for the individual (above n. 22). The fact that this type of shield was called the "Argive *aspis*" apparently points to Argos as its place of origin, and a strong tradition found in Herodotos and elsewhere paints Argos as the strongest state in early Greece, before the rise of Sparta to dominance in the sixth century.[52] It seems at least possible that the hoplite phalanx was pioneered precisely at Argos, by the Argives.

It is widely thought that the hoplite phalanx came into being a little earlier than the middle of the seventh century, since it appears to be depicted in two scenes on Greek painted vases of that time: the so-called "Chigi vase" and

"Macmillan *aryballos*."⁵³ The phase of early Greek history characterized by tyrannies in the nascent city-states also began by the mid-seventh century, perhaps a few decades earlier in fact. It is surely no unwarranted speculation to connect these two contemporary developments, as for example Anthony Andrewes did in his justly well-known book *The Greek Tyrants* (1956). However, Andrewes, I believe, put the cart before the horse somewhat: he argued that it was the hoplites of seventh-century Greece, militarily important and seeking equivalent social and political importance, who backed the early tyrants and put them into power. That leaves still open the question of how hundreds or thousands of "commoners," in community after community, organized themselves—in spite of their often disparate backgrounds and interests as farmers, artisans, traders—into cohesive hoplite phalanxes imbued with collective discipline and common purpose.⁵⁴ Is it not more convincing to suggest that it was in fact those leaders who sought to achieve political primacy in their communities, who recognized the potential military strength of the emerging "middle classes," and organized them into hoplite phalanxes in order to overthrow the traditional socio-political order of competing aristocratic *oikoi*? That is to say, it was likely by means of organizing the rising "middle class" to fight in disciplined phalanx formations that the early tyrants, or at least some of them, were able to use this new power to rise to political dominance in their respective communities. Though his date has been widely disputed, a strong case can be made that it was the Argive tyrant Pheidon who was the first of the archaic tyrants, holding power in the second quarter of the seventh century: the very period when the hoplite phalanx was apparently being invented.⁵⁵ I think it makes excellent sense to put all of this together, and see in Pheidon a plausible candidate for the role of inventor of the hoplite phalanx: that would certainly explain how the Argives were able to defeat the Spartans at the battle of Hysiai in 669, and how Pheidon was able to wield enough power to take control of the Olympic games in an uncertain Olympiad, but probably that of 668.⁵⁶

Whether or not Pheidon and the Argives invented and pioneered the hoplite phalanx, it was most likely in being by about 650, and it was the Spartans who eventually perfected the system, in the early to mid sixth century. The spread of hoplite warfare was uneven, as it was adopted quickly in some regions, more slowly or not at all in others. As late as the fifth and fourth centuries, in fact, there were regions of Greece where the predominant style of fighting remained as mobile light infantry (Aitolia, Lokris, Akarnania), cavalry (Thessaly, Macedonia), or archers (Krete).⁵⁷ But by the middle of the sixth century the hoplite phalanx had undoubtedly become the dominant force in Greek warfare and on Greek battlefields. The social and political effects of the switch to hoplite warfare were profound, and indeed such in my view as to justify speaking of a hoplite "revolution."

The first effect to notice will have been an exacerbation of a tendency already noticeable in the poetry of Hesiod: a decline in the prestige of the aristocrats, indeed the growth even of a certain disdain for them. Hesiod famously takes the *basileis* to task for their injustice and inverts the aristocratic institution of gift exchange to become bribery: in calling the *basileis*, literally, gift devourers (*dorophageis*) in a clearly critical sense—as revealed both by context and by the fact that the verb *phagein* characteristically carries a sense not just of eating but of greedy eating—he is the first Greek we know of to turn the neutral word *doron* (gift) towards the pejorative meaning of "bribe" that it has in such compound words as *dorodokein*: to take bribes.[58] We see this disdain of the elites and their outlook carried into the military sphere in the next generation, in the poetry of Archilochos: he expressed his dislike of military leaders who affected the aristocratic notion of looks as a measure of worth—expressed in the term *kaloi k'agathoi*, the handsome and good (i.e., the aristocrats), with looks and worth inextricably bound together—in his poem calling for a more down to earth and less "pretty" general, who cared more for his soldiers than his looks.[59] This decline in the prestige of the aristocrats went hand-in-hand with a decline in their political position: the *leitmotif* of the "age of tyranny" was the exiling (or often killing) and expropriation of aristocrats by the tyrants and their supporters, leading to a rather different Greece in which, though the aristocracy and its values certainly survived and remained influential, the hoplite "class" had replaced it as the dominant element socially and politically, as well as militarily, in the Greek city-states—as opposed to the *ethne* which, like Thessaly for example, often remained dominated by the aristocracy. Perhaps the most telling example of this, among many, is Thucydides' comment on the regime of the "Five Thousand," which he explicitly glosses as meaning those able to equip themselves as hoplites, that was installed as an interim regime between the fall of the "400" and the restoration of full democracy in 411. He states, without providing any factual basis for his assessment, that under the regime of the Five Thousand "the Athenians seem to have had a better government than ever before, during my time at least" (Thuc. 8.97). What accounts for this judgment, surely, is simply an ideological conviction that the hoplite class ought to be the dominant and governing element in a properly ordered city-state.

What characterized hoplite warfare, and by extension the "middle class" citizens who made up the hoplite phalanx, was a powerful sense of communal identity and community of interest, steadfast discipline, and a very strong sense of self-worth. Acquiring and demonstrating these qualities by and through service in the hoplite phalanx made the hoplite warriors ready for, and indeed caused them to demand, a corresponding role in the political life and decision-making process of their communities. This is what turned the pre-state communities described in Chapter 1 above, into the city-states of the classical era. For a city-state is not just a city, it is also a state. The communities described by Homer, and analyzed historically so well by Finley and others, could hardly be called states.[60] Power lay in the heads of the aristocratic families, the *basileis*, and their *oikoi* (households, comprising companions, hangers on, and dependents as well as family members), who often behaved with scant regard for communal decision making or interests. Individual *basileis* or small groups of allied *basileis* often went on trading or raiding ventures on their own cognizance, like Mentes the Taphian and Odysseus' character in his many tales in the *Odyssey*, or pursued internal dissensions and feuds. Public opinion, as expressed through occasional *agorai* (public meetings of the people), had little or no power to control events, or at times even influence them. It has been argued, indeed, that traces of such independent aristocratic decision making and activity continued well into the sixth century, even in communities as prominent as Athens.[61]

We can first start to talk about Greek states, rather than mere communities, I believe, when hoplite phalanxes form the military of the communities, and the hoplite warriors consequently begin to assert collective control of decision making in the field of what we call foreign policy. Tyrants, as I have suggested above, seem to have played an important role in facilitating this transition, by providing crucial leadership and focus, but the hoplite "middle class" is the key component in the process of city-state formation. Before the advent of hoplite warfare, there is nothing sufficiently centralized and organized in Greece to be called a state; once the hoplites have taken the community's military activities and hence military and foreign policy into their hands, we have a community that is sufficiently unified, centralized, and organized to be called a state.[62] It is for this reason that the state was always perceived by the ancient Greeks themselves as a male collective—*hoi Athenaioi, hoi Korinthioi, hoi Milesioi*: the hoplites were in origin the state, and the developing city-state thus came to be closely identified with the hoplite class who formed its backbone. This is the "hoplite revolution."

Fleets in the Greek World: The Role of the Poor in Warfare

Our sources for the ancient Greek world were overwhelmingly produced by persons belonging to the more well-to-do segment of society, as is well known, and tend to reflect as a result the outlook, interests, and attitudes of the upper class. With respect to warfare, that means that the interest of the sources is primarily focused on the hoplites, who came from the well-to-do sector of society, often to the degree that an impression is created that only hoplites were involved in land warfare. That is a false impression: enough scattered information can be found to show that the poor played a significant, though often overlooked, role in land warfare as light-armed infantry—archers, slingers, and javelineers—used for scouting, skirmishing, flank protection, and other support roles before, on the fringes of, and after the hoplite battle.[63] Further, in some areas of Greece, such as Aitolia, Akarnania, Lokris, and Krete, light-armed infantry—javelineers and archers—continued to be the predominant military force throughout the classical era. All the same, the poorer members of Greek society really became crucial to warfare as a result of developments in sea warfare. It's widely known, of course, that warfare at sea in the ancient Mediterranean was conducted with warships that were oared galleys, and the rowers in these galleys were recruited mostly from among the poorer part of the population. But before the late sixth century, warfare at sea was intermittent and on a small scale, and the primary warship was the *pentekonter* or fifty-oared galley: it was the development in the late sixth century of the much larger and more heavily manned *trieres* or trireme warship, and of large fleets of these warships engaged in much more extensive sea warfare, that changed the balance of ancient Greek warfare and gave to the poor a vastly expanded role with consequent socio-political effects.

The trireme was a remarkable feat of naval engineering: we know quite a bit about it thanks to "the trireme project," a joint undertaking by British and American scholars and the Greek navy to design and build a full scale working replica of a fifth-century Athenian trireme.[64] Long and narrow—about 37 meters (*c.* 120 feet) by about 5 meters (*c.* 16 feet)—and with an overall height of some 4 meters (*c.* 13 feet—3 meters of superstructure and a draft of 1 meter),[65] the trireme held three banks of oarsmen on each side with an overall number of some 150 to 170 rowers, each pulling on his own oar. In addition to the rowers, each ship had a crew of about thirty expert sailors—steersman, lookout, quartermaster, and so on—and marines, many of them equipped with missile weapons for obvious reasons.[66] The overall crew of a trireme was thus some 200 men, meaning that fleets of 100 or more triremes, well attested in fifth-century naval warfare, would involve the mobilization of at least 20,000 men each. The vast majority of these crews were drawn from the poorer segment of society, and the crews of warships were paid for their service: standard pay for rowers in the fifth-century fleets was 3 or 4 obols a day, depending on circumstances (finances and so on). The rowers on the uppermost level of oars, needing the most skill and stamina, were often paid at a slightly higher rate, as were the expert crewmen and marines. The overall cost of running a trireme was, therefore, in excess of 100 drachmas a day in pay alone, and a fleet of sixty triremes (by no means a large fleet) would cost one talent per day, meaning that a three-month campaign with such a fleet would cost over 90 talents in pay to the crews alone. Naval warfare with fleets of triremes was, then, an extremely expensive undertaking, both in manpower and in money.

Though there are various legendary or semi-legendary traditions suggesting that triremes originated in the early seventh century, the first well attested use of triremes in significant numbers was in the fleet of the tyrant Polykrates of Samos in the 520s BCE.[67] By 500, the Greek cities of the eastern Aegean had substantial fleets of triremes—as many as sixty to one hundred for the larger cities like Samos, Chios and Miletos—as we know from Herodotos' account of naval fighting in the Ionian Revolt of the 490s.[68] The great trading city of Aigina seems to have had up to seventy triremes at this time too, but the Athenians made a great leap forward in the late 480s when they constructed a fleet of 200 new triremes using the money they made from a rich new vein of silver in their mines at Laureion in southern Attica.[69] These 200 triremes were fully mobilized for the campaign of Salamis in 480, requiring about 40,000 men to crew them, which means that essentially every able-bodied Athenian citizen served in the fleet in the campaign and battle of Salamis. In the aftermath of Salamis, the Athenians continued warfare by sea against the Persians, using their naval strength to cajole and organize the communities of the Aegean islands and coasts into their great naval hegemony, the Delian League (often called "the Athenian Empire"). It was the readiness of poorer Athenians to serve in these great naval campaigns which led to the general recognition that the power and wealth of the Athenian city-state depended on her middling and poorer citizens, who manned her fleet, not on the well-to-do and wealthy citizens who served as hoplites and cavalry.[70] That widely recognized fact had major political and social consequences.

The key is that the role of the less well off segment of the population in manning and rowing the fleet gave them the self-confidence and socio-political standing to demand and obtain a full and active role in the running of the city-state: that is it led to the establishment of radical democracy at Athens (and elsewhere, e.g., at Syracuse) in the middle and second half of the fifth century. That is widely known and acknowledged, and was so already in the fifth century BCE: our first surviving source making this connection is the anonymous treatise on the *politeia* (governing system, constitution) of the Athenians, found among

Xenophon's writings and so referred to as Ps-Xenophon (or at times as "the Old Oligarch"), written fairly certainly in the early 420s. Rowing in the fleet required great commitment and discipline; it brought together many thousands of citizens, the bulk of them not well off but including some better off citizens, from every walk of life and region of the community, in a collective undertaking in which they collaborated closely, spent weeks or months in very close proximity to each other sharing hardship and danger, and so got to know each other fairly well and learned to rely on each other.[71] The poor were able to undertake this role in part because of the pay, which compensated for loss of other income, but also because the equipment required of the rowing citizen was minimal: the *polis* issued each man his oar, and besides that all he needed was a cushion, waxed on the bottom to allow him to slide backward and forward while rowing, and a leather loop to fasten his oar to the oar-port through which he rowed. The community had to rely on the poorer citizens to undertake this role simply because of the huge numbers of men required: as noted, 200 per ship and therefore many thousands for any substantial fleet. Democracy was the price the community paid for naval power, looking at it from the upper class perspective adopted (ostensibly at least) by the Ps-Xenophon treatise, or the prize the *demos* (common people) won for manning the fleet, looking at it from the common man's perspective. As Aristotle noted, in the quote with which I opened this chapter, military system and political system went hand in hand, and the segment of the population chiefly responsible for the state's power, in this case the middling and poorer citizens, held predominant power in governance.

Conclusion: The City-State as a Warrior Collective

The key takeaway from this review of classical Greek warfare, is that it was a thoroughly collective system of warfare, requiring self-reliant and self-motivated citizens to be ready and willing to put themselves at the service of the community for its military endeavors, risking their lives in doing so, and undergoing shared dangers and hardships for the perceived good of the community. Whether it was in the close-order lines and files of the hoplite phalanx on land, or in the densely packed rowing benches of the warships at sea, thousands of adult male citizens co-operated in disciplined co-ordination to attain the shared goal of safety for the community and/or expansion of the community's power and status in the Greek world. These citizens were not recruited by a remote ruler or a government in which they had little or no part, nor were they trained and disciplined under the lash by elite officers who felt a natural sense of superiority to them. They agreed willingly to take on the roles of hoplites and rowers as part of the community on whose behalf they served, and as sharers in the benefits or costs of success or failure.

In performing this service, whether as hoplites in the phalanx or as rowers in the triremes, they shared a basic equality of status and experience: every hoplite and every rower had essentially the same equipment, the same role, and the same status as every other hoplite or rower. The general commanding the hoplite phalanx, and the various officers under him, were just citizens of the community too, selected to take on for a time leadership roles, but wearing the same hoplite panoply and fighting in the phalanx in the same way as other hoplites once the battle started. Though the roles of the officers in the fleet—general, ship commander (*trierarch*), steersman (*kybernetes*), and so on—were different than that of the rowers, these officers too were citizens selected by the community for temporary leadership roles, and as the author known as Ps-Xenophon stated "of necessity a man who is often at sea takes up an oar," that is even the generals and ship commanders knew what it was to pull an oar.[72]

It was in great part the collective and distinctively voluntary and egalitarian nature of the citizen-militia style of warfare, on land and at sea, of the Greek city-states that made those city-states what they were: warrior-citizen communities in which military participation and political participation went hand-in-hand. The Greeks themselves referred to these communities as male collectives—*hoi Athenaioi, hoi Argeioi, hoi Milesioi, hoi Ephesioi*, and so on—because in a very important sense that is what they were: the men who were willing and able to take up arms or an oar to fight for the community were the crucial part of the community. Their readiness and willingness to take on this role gave them the collective standing, discipline, and sense of shared belonging to demand and take on the role of active citizens. It was, that is to say, serving in the hoplite phalanx and the trireme's rowing benches that made these men participating citizens, and made the Greek city-states communities with collective governing systems. Let us, then, turn to considering the collective governing systems of the city-states in the next chapter.

4

The Pebble: Collective Decision Making and the City-State

The citizen militia style of warfare practiced by the city-state Greeks, with its dependence on thousands of citizens being ready, willing, and able to undertake to act as the state's army and/or fleet when the situation called for it, necessarily required that in each city-state thousands of inhabitants were classed as and regarded themselves as citizens. That raises the question what it meant to be a citizen of a Greek city-state: what requirements had to be met to hold citizenship, what rights and privileges and duties went with that role, what form of governing system did these citizens form part of and act under.[1] I suggested in the previous chapter that the highly collective and egalitarian nature of the Greek citizen militia system encouraged the men who manned the phalanxes and fleets of the city-states to view citizenship in a very expansive way, demanding and regarding it as their right to play as active a role in politics as they did in warfare. We must examine, then, how exactly the governing systems of the Greek city-states functioned, and how active the role of the citizens was. Did the Greek city-state form the same sort of collective politically as it did militarily?

Greek philosophers in their ordering and categorizing way pointed out that any society could be governed in one of three ways: either one man could hold paramount power and rule, a system they called monarchy (one man rule); or some sort of elite group could dominate and rule, a system they called oligarchy (rule by a few); or power and governance could be in the hands of the majority, which they called democracy (power to the people). Each system had its advantages and drawbacks, as laid out in a well-known account presented by Herodotos (3.80–82). However, from at the latest 500 BCE onward, Greeks came to insist that monarchy was a political form inconsistent with the proper nature and functioning of the city-state. Many Greek cities had gone through a phase of monarchical rule during the prior two centuries—between about 680 and 510 BCE—but they regarded this kind of rule, which they called *tyranneia* (origin of the English word tyranny), as no longer acceptable. With monarchy ruled out as being incompatible with the proper Greek way of life, that left oligarchy and democracy as the only possible options for how a Greek city-state might be organized and governed. Much of the history of the classical city-states is presented as a struggle between oligarchically ruled and democratically ruled cities, and between pro-oligarchy and pro-democracy factions within the cities. Oligarchy and democracy are thus presented as radically different and opposed governing systems, but were they really? It can be argued in fact that, as practiced in the classical Greek city-states, oligarchy and democracy had much more in common than is usually thought, representing merely different ends of a shared political system: that of collective deliberation and decision making.[2]

From Oligarchy to Democracy: The Varieties of Collective Decision Making

It is generally accepted that in early so-called Homeric times, that is as depicted in the Homeric epics (roughly in the eighth century BCE), Greek communities were dominated and ruled by powerful aristocratic leaders who were called *basileis* (lords), each of whom stood at the head of a great *oikos* (family, household, estate) with relatives, companions (*hetairoi*), and a network of retainers, tenants, workers, servants and other subordinates supporting their power.[3] In some ways these *basileis* with their *oikoi* functioned as semi-autonomous socio-political entities, but they were also part of the larger communities and there were communal institutions that somewhat limited the independence of the *basileis*. The most important of these were the *boule*, a council in which the lords met to discuss communal issues and try to decide on communal policies, and the *agora*, a public meeting or assembly in which members of the community came together to hear the lords discuss communal issues and to express, by booing or cheering, their views about the issues and policies under discussion.[4] These two institutions, the council and the assembly, found in Homer only in embryonic form, were to have crucial roles in the developing Greek city-states and their governing systems.

The power and predominance of the *basileis* and their *oikoi* was broken in many Greek communities, and particularly in the ones that developed into city-states, by a wave of tyrannies that occurred in the seventh and sixth centuries. The tyrants of early Greece were very disparate men, with varied backgrounds and aims, but wherever they took power they did so at the expense of the local *basileis* and against their opposition. Inevitably, therefore, it was a part of their policies to break the power of the *basileis*: many were exiled or killed, many were expropriated and thus permanently weakened.[5] Often tyrants only managed to hold power for a few years before being killed or driven out. Some tyrants lasted longer, but even the most successful tyrants rarely managed to pass their power on to their sons; and even when that did happen the tyranny rarely lasted through the second generation.[6] However successful a tyranny was, and however short or long it lasted, certain features were typical. The tyrants tended to promote the development of hoplite warfare, and thus the importance of the middling hoplite "class" in Greek society, as argued in Chapter 3 above. They tended to promote the process of urbanization and unification of the developing city-state.[7] And when a tyranny ended, some sort of council and assembly emerged still existing as crucial features of governance, but invariably in a much adapted and strengthened form compared to their Homeric antecedents.

The council of state was a crucial feature of the governing system in essentially all Greek city-states we have knowledge of: some well-known examples are the Areopagos Council at Athens, and the democratic Council of the 500 which took over many of the Areopagos Council's powers and functions after 508; the *Gerousia* (Council of Elders) at Sparta; the *Bola* (merely the Doric Greek form of the word *boule*) at Argos; the *Aisymnetai* with their council house the *Aisymneton* at Megara; and the local civic councils in Boiotia as well as the federal council on the Kadmeia in Thebes attested by the *Hellenika Oxyrhynchia*, whose author was almost certainly the early-fourth-century historian Theopompos of Chios.[8] The exact roles and powers of state councils in the Greek world varied considerably from place to place, and from time to time, but certain functions appear to be typical. Virtually all councils would seem to have had a deliberative role, discussing public policy and making proposals to executive magistrates and/or to popular assemblies. Very common seems to have been an oversight role, for example making sure that magistrates functioned properly within their designated powers and carried out duly set public policy, and often including some oversight of religious matters. Councils are attested as playing a judicial role, effectively acting as juries for certain kinds of trials, as the Areopagos council at Athens famously did for murder trials. In some cases, as apparently with Sparta's *Gerousia* and arguably the Areopagos council in early Athens, the state council may effectively have been the governing body, setting policy as well as overseeing its execution.

How state councils were selected or appointed varied widely, and unfortunately, as so often with the ancient world, our sources are completely inadequate. We do, however, have reasonably good information about the state councils of Sparta and Athens, and these may serve as models for the variety of Greek state councils since they represent very different locations on the political spectrum. Sparta was a relatively extreme oligarchy, and its council the *Gerousia* was small (only thirty members including the two kings *ex officio*), the councilors were elected by the Spartiate citizens from among eligible Spartiates over sixty years old who belonged to a restricted group of (aristocratic?) Spartiate families, and once elected the councilors served for life. Athens in the sixth century was a relatively moderate oligarchy: its Council of the Areopagos had an indeterminate number of councilors (but probably well over 100),[9] these councilors were ex-magistrates (the so-called "nine archons") who served on the council for life after completing their year of office, and they were drawn from the wealthy elite, since one had to belong to one of the top two property classes of the Solonian system to become one of the "nine archons." Athens in the fifth and fourth centuries, finally, was a relatively extreme democracy: its Council of the 500 had a large membership as the name itself clearly indicates (i.e., it had 500 councilors), members of the council were selected by lot from among eligible and willing Athenians over the age of thirty regardless of socio-economic status, council slots were allotted to the various demes (local communities) of the Athenian state proportionate to their population to ensure that every part of the Athenian state was fairly represented, and councilors served for only one year, with repeat terms on the council possible but only after an interval of some years (perhaps ten years), making such repeat terms seemingly rare.

The functioning of state councils is even more obscure: we really only have good evidence for how the Athenian Council of the 500 worked, thanks mostly to the Aristotelian *Athenaion Politeia*. We can see that the Spartan *Gerousia* functioned for the most part behind closed doors, secrecy being a major part of the Spartan system as Thucydides tells.[10] The *Gerousia* offered yes or no proposals to the Spartiate assembly; and apparently had the power to veto assembly decisions it deemed "crooked," that is not a simple affirmation or negation of the proposal presented by the *Gerousia*. We know too that the *Gerousia* functioned as the jury court for major public trials; that it worked closely with the magistrates, especially the five *Ephoroi*, likely exercising oversight of them; and that its deliberations guided Spartan policy.[11] As to the Athenian Areopagos Council, it certainly acted as a jury for some kinds of important public trials, including famously murder trials; it certainly exercised oversight of the state's religious festivals, conducting inquiries into any wrongdoing with respect to the state cults; it certainly offered advice to the magistrates, and exercised oversight of them at least in the sense of scrutinizing their qualifications before they took office, and investigating their conduct in office when they stepped down—powers of which the council was stripped in about 462 by the reforms of Ephialtes.

This is not the place to go into the functioning of the Athenian Council of the 500 in detail, a topic on which an entire book could be and has been written.[12] Suffice it to say that many (most?) meetings of the *boule* were held with the council house doors open, so that interested citizens could listen in; that the council had a rotating executive committee of fifty men, the councilors from each of the ten *phylai* holding this responsibility in turn for one tenth of the year; that the council was officially in session every day of the year except festivals and days of ill omen; and that the council functioned essentially as a standing committee of the assembly, preparing the agenda for assembly meetings, presiding at them, and offering proposals called *probouleumata* to the assembly on issues it had deliberated and reached consensus about. A final point worth making has to do with participation: since Athenian councilors served only for a year, Athens had to find 500 new councilors each year. Over the course of twenty-five to thirty years this means that, even allowing for some citizens serving a second term on the council, well over 10,000 Athenians in any generation must have served a term on the state *boule*, an extremely high rate of participation showing the very high degree of civic engagement in democratic Athens.

This creates a picture of considerable variety: councils could be large or small; councilors could be elected, allotted, or appointed *ex officio*; membership could be for life or for a limited term, and it could be restricted by age in different ways; membership could also be restricted by socio-economic status or open to all (at least in principle); and the powers, functions, procedures, and exact public roles could differ quite widely. But behind all this variety there were some fundamental similarities that must be observed. All these councils of state were selected for appointment in some way by the citizens, they acted with and were in some sense beholden to the citizens, they were drawn from among the citizens (even if only from some designated sub-set of citizens), they advised and guided but were bound by the decisions of the citizens, and thus they served, as we might say, "at the pleasure of" the citizens. All this by way of contrast with the Homeric councils made up of the *basileis* as a matter of right, neither appointed by nor from among the citizen body, nor beholden to them in any way; or indeed with the fourth-century royal council (*synedrion*) of Argead Macedonia, whose members were appointed by the king, served at his pleasure as his advisers, and might be native Macedonians or men drawn to the king's service from elsewhere in Greece. The classical city-state councils, whether oligarchic or democratic, were populated by citizens selected from and acting on behalf of the community, reaching decisions that normally had to be confirmed by the community at large.

That brings us to consideration of the civic assemblies, the public meetings of the citizens at large. In Homer the assemblies (*agorai*) were a place for the lords to debate each other in public and gauge public opinion; the assemblies did not vote or make decisions of any sort. In classical city-states, assemblies of citizens were the ultimate sovereign element of the city-state, whose decisions must be implemented by the council and magistrates. Such assemblies might be referred to by various names: *apellai* at Sparta, *aliaia* at Argos, *heliaia* in Solonian Athens, and finally *ekklesia* in democratic Athens in the fifth century and later, the term which increasingly came to be the standard word for a citizen assembly around the Greek world after the fifth century. By whatever name, the presence of a decision-making primary assembly of adult male citizens, meeting at regular intervals and making final decisions about communal issues, is standard for the classical Greek city-state. This goes for both oligarchic and democratic city-states: the difference between the two is not whether there should be a primary decision-making assembly, but how it should function and who should get to participate in it. That is to say, it is the definition of active citizen status that is at issue: in oligarchic states active citizenship was defined relatively narrowly, in democracies it was defined relatively broadly. A narrow definition of citizenship would typically impose some sort of socio-economic limit on citizenship, most often a property requirement, and it might also limit the power of the citizens and their assembly in some way(s). A broad definition would do the opposite: opening citizenship to native adult males regardless of socio-economic status and giving the assembly of citizens wide powers. Common to both was the principle that the assembly of citizens should be the sovereign element in the state, expressing its will by voting.

As usual we are poorly informed about the details of how assemblies of citizens were limited in make-up and power except at democratic Athens, though we do have some interesting insights. Membership of the assembly at Sparta, for example, was limited to native inhabitants of Sparta itself from Spartiate families, who successfully completed the harsh Spartan training system (the *agoge*), were selected into dining groups (*syssitia* or *phiditia*) and possessed sufficient landed wealth to be able to sustain the monthly contributions of food to their dining group. Spartan citizens had to maintain throughout their lives the standards of behavior, especially of dauntless courage in warfare, expected of the Spartiate: failure to do so could entail loss of the active citizen right to attend and vote at assemblies. As already indicated, Spartan assemblies had the power only to affirm or reject proposals put to them by the *Gerousia* via the assembly meeting's presiding officer, often one of the Ephors (one of the board of five "Overseers," the most important magistrates at Sparta). Voting was by acclamation, with the presiding officer deciding by the noise made whether the "ayes" or the "nays" were more numerous; in special cases a formal division might be made and the votes actually counted.[13] Prior to the vote, the issue to be voted on was discussed in front of the assembly by leading Spartans—the kings, the Ephors, members of the *Gerousia*—so that the citizens could be informed of the pros and cons of the issue: ordinary Spartiates were apparently not permitted to speak, nor were amendments to the proposal permitted. The power of the citizen assembly at Sparta was thus quite limited, just as membership was severely restricted (no reduced-status Spartans, no *Perioikoi*, no Helots), but the assembly did have the final say on matters of public concern and importance, meaning that Sparta was a state in which the citizen class of Spartiates was sovereign.

At the other end of the political spectrum stands the *ekklesia* of democratic Athens, the one citizen assembly of which, as noted above, we are quite well informed.[14] This is not the context for a full discussion of the procedures and practices of the Athenian *ekklesia*, but it is clear that the reforms of Kleisthenes *c.* 508 established the assembly of citizens as the undisputed sovereign element in the nascent Athenian democracy, and further reforms over subsequent decades only strengthened that. The assembly of citizens, by public vote—either by a show of hands or, in some cases, by casting white or black pebbles to signify a yes or no vote[15] in which votes were carefully counted (unlike the acclamation system at Sparta), decided all matters of communal interest and concern. In principle, the assembly could take up and decide any issue it wanted to, and in practice a very wide range of business was taken up and discussed and decided by the assembly. Every free-born Athenian adult male had the right to attend and vote at assembly meetings, unless he had been specifically barred from doing so for cause (e.g., for being found guilty of immorality or impiety towards the gods). We know that assembly meetings were typically attended by thousands of citizens: for some special kinds of assembly meetings, in fact, a quorum of at least 6,000 citizens was set.

Considering that the Athenian citizen body in the mid-fifth century numbered in excess of 40,000 adult males, perhaps even as many as 50,000 at its peak, the number of 6,000 attending a given assembly does not sound all that many.[16] Was the Athenian "democracy" in fact run by only a smallish percentage of the citizens, who alone showed up for assembly meetings? That would be an inappropriate conclusion to draw, because there is no reason at all to suppose that it was more or less the same few thousand Athenians who attended every assembly meeting. There were, by the middle decades of the fifth century, a minimum of forty assembly meetings each year, and often more. The assemblies were spaced throughout the year, with at least four in each *prytany*, that is each thirty-six-day period presided over by one of the ten "tribes" (*phylai*). Whether any given citizen made the effort to attend any given assembly meeting must have depended on a variety of factors. One important factor will have been where in Attica a citizen lived: inhabitants of Athens itself and the nearby Peiraieus no doubt attended more assemblies than inhabitants of the remoter parts of Attica, since it was simply far more convenient for them to do so. The time of year will also have been a factor: at the harvest times of the major crops—grain, grapes, olives—citizens who farmed will not have had leisure to attend assemblies, while at low intensity times in the farming year they will have. Citizens on active service as rowers in the fleet or hoplites will not have been available to attend assemblies. The business to be conducted at any given assembly will have been of greater concern to some citizens than to others, giving such citizens a much stronger motivation to attend. Rural citizens who had business in Athens or the Peiraieus may well have taken the opportunity, while they were in the city, to attend an assembly meeting or two. And so on. Such considerations make it very likely that the group of citizens attending, and voting varied quite widely from assembly to assembly, and in my view make it very plausible that the great majority of Athenian citizens attended at least occasional assemblies in the course of the year, let alone in the course of their lives. The sources suggesting a high degree of political participation by Athenian citizens, that is to say, are most likely right,[17] and the situation is not likely to have been much different in other Greek city-states.

Every citizen of the Athenian state had the right to bring up business to the assembly, though such business normally had to be vetted by the *boule* first. In each *prytany*, one assembly was devoted primarily to religious business, and one primarily to private issues of citizens; in both cases quite average or even lower class citizens may not infrequently have had matters to raise. On the more public, political issues members of the elite who took a particular interest in policy and politics tended to be the proposers of laws and decrees, as we know from the many preserved inscriptions which record the names of proposers. All the same, all citizens also had the right to speak on any issue if they wished, and to propose amendments from the floor, though it took a considerable amount of self-confidence to get up and address an audience of thousands of Athenians.[18] The Athenian citizens in assembly could be quite rowdy and did not take kindly to having their time wasted: note for example the words of Sokrates in Plato's dialogue *Protagoras*, emphasizing that if the assembly felt their time was being wasted they might laugh the speaker out of countenance or shout him down, often resulting in the "archers" removing the failed speaker from the assembly.[19] For the most part then, speakers came from the educated elite, but we do know of occasions when very ordinary Athenians—a barber or a carpenter, for instance—addressed the assembly.[20] In sum, the Athenian assembly enjoyed very wide, almost untrammeled powers, and it had the widest membership of any citizen assembly we know of. A very great deal more can be said about the Athenian *ekklesia*, but that will suffice in the present context.

The other Greek state that we have substantial information about is Boiotia between 447 and 386, thanks to the description of the Boiotian constitutional arrangements in the *Hellenika Oxyrhynchia*. Boiotia was, it transpires, a moderate oligarchy in this period, with citizenship limited to those who had "a certain amount of wealth" (*plethos ti chrematon*), most likely the degree of wealth that enabled one to function as a hoplite warrior. Although Boiotia as a whole was a federal type state (or *ethnos*) under this constitution, the various Boiotian cities governed themselves to a considerable degree autonomously, so it is worth noting the arrangements with respect to city councils and assemblies. Each Boiotian city, we are told, set up four councils, with each council taking it in turn to make preliminary determinations about matters of common concern. The decision of the presiding council would then be referred to the other three councils, which had to ratify the preliminary decision for it to become binding (*kyrios*). Apparently, then, the active citizen body in each city was divided into four groups, each of which had the responsibility of acting as state council, in turn, for a quarter of the year; matters debated and voted on by the citizens acting as presiding council would then be voted on by a meeting of all four councils—that is, by an assembly of the citizens—to make the binding determination.[21] All active citizens, then, took turns on the state council; all active citizens voted on issues as councilors and/or as members of the citizen assembly, but only those with sufficient wealth (most likely the hoplite census) were active citizens. It is clear that active citizenship was in the Boiotian cities, as the term implies, very active: the privilege of holding active citizenship brought with it duties of serving on the council and participating in assembly meetings that citizens could not easily avoid. If we are right to understand that all those with the "hoplite census" were active citizens, that would mean that 35–40 percent of adult male Boiotians regularly participated in the political process in their cities.

Other Greek city-states, like Corinth or Argos or Elis or the hundreds of others, had assemblies of citizens which fell somewhere in the range indicated by the Spartan, Boiotian, and Athenian examples in terms of membership, procedures, and powers. The point is that every Greek city-state, so far as we know, whether oligarchic or democratic in governing system, had an assembly of citizens—however widely or narrowly active citizenship was defined—which met regularly and openly, and which enjoyed some degree of sovereign power, whether relatively limited or unlimited. That is to say, Greek city-states were socio-political entities structured around the notion of citizenship, in which citizens expressed their will through systems of collective debate and decision making, systems in which a state council and an assembly of citizens played key roles. No ancient Greek city was fully democratic in the modern sense: all denied active citizen rights to women, and all were distinctly "nativist," offering virtually no path to citizenship for non-native inhabitants (that is, slaves and metics).[22] Accepting these limitations, the range for active citizenship ran from close to 100 percent of adult native males in Athens, through perhaps 35 to 40 percent of adult native males in the Boiotian cities, to around 10 percent of adult native males in the Spartan city-state.[23] That is a substantial range, illustrating the very different levels of participation between the relative extremes of radical democracy and fairly restrictive oligarchy; yet in all cases thousands of active citizens governed in a collective way.

So, in sum, while it is certainly true that oligarchies and democracies differed from each other in a number of important ways besides the degree of active participation, we must not allow that to obscure their fundamental similarities. As already stated, but worth stating again, they were variations on a common system, that of groups of citizens discussing, debating, and voting collectively on matters of communal importance. That process of communal discussing and voting is what we call "politics," and it is no accident that the very word "politics" derives from the word *polis* in its meaning of "city-state." It was precisely in the Greek city-states, as the noted historian Christian Meier long ago argued in a deservedly famous book, that politics as such had its origins.[24] Not coincidentally, it was also in the Greek city-states that political theory had its birth.

The Political Theory of Collective Decision Making

In the third quarter of the fourth century BCE, the philosopher Aristotle and his pupils undertook one of the great research projects known to us into the nature and historical development of governing systems, or *politeiai* as the Greeks called them. The result of this project was the publication of some 250 treatises on known "states" and their governing systems, filling some 158 papyrus book scrolls.[25] This research project then provided the evidential basis for Aristotle's justly famed and still widely read and discussed analysis of government and governing systems in his treatise *Politika,* or *Politics* as it is generally named in English (the title more properly means "matters concerning the state"). The *Politeiai* and the *Politika* thus belong together, the former being—to use a modern term—the data base, and the latter the theoretical system based on that data base. Unfortunately, the *Politeiai* are now lost except for the treatise on the Athenian governing system (the *Athenaion Politeia*), which came to light in the late nineteenth century on an Egyptian papyrus, and brief fragments and synopses of the remainder (see App. 2 for details). Together the *Politeiai* and the *Politika* represent the full maturing of Greek political theory, that is the analytical theorizing of the governing system underpinning the Greek *polis*, a process of analysis and theorizing which had begun a hundred years or so earlier.

The earliest Greek rationalists—traditionally though to my mind dismissively and pejoratively known as "the Pre-Socratics"—showed little or no interest in reasoning about governing systems. From Thales in the early sixth century, through Anaximandros, Xenophanes, Pythagoras, Empedokles, and Herakleitos, to Parmenides and Zeno in the mid fifth century, their primary concerns appear—from the all too scanty fragments and references that are all that remain of their theorizing—to have focused on understanding the natural world, and on matters that we would characterize as ontology and epistemology: trying to understand the nature and meaning of existence and knowledge.[26] It is with the rise of what we call the "Sophistic movement" in the third quarter of the fifth century that an interest in understanding the nature of "politics," that is how and why city-states were governed as they were and what the best possible governing system would be, came to be a major part of Greek philosophizing. It was, that is to say, the great Sophists, beginning with Protagoras of Abdera and continuing with such notable younger contemporaries as Thrasymachos of Chalkedon and the Athenians Antiphon and Sokrates, who turned the full light of rational analysis on governing systems and "politics."[27] It is surely no coincidence that this sophistic analysis of "politics" and development of political theory occurred at around the same time as the full flowering of Athenian participatory democracy and the accompanying debates around the propriety and scope of popular participation in governance; just as it is no accident that the Sophists were drawn to Athens and conducted much of their theorizing, debating, and teaching there. That is to say, it was Athenian democracy which provided the spur or catalyst to engage in rational theorizing about governing systems.

Unfortunately, the writings of the Sophists are almost entirely lost, and the few original sophistic works that do survive do not deal with political theory.[28] Nevertheless, three surviving writings do offer us examples of early sophistic political analysis: in the first place there is the passage of Herodotos already referenced above (Herod. 3.80–2), in which the varieties of possible governing system are presented in turn with the merits and flaws of each; then there is Protagoras' great speech on *dike* (justice) and *aidos* (shame) in Plato's dialogue of that name (Plato *Protagoras* 320c–328d); finally there is the treatise known as Ps.-Xenophon *Constitution of the Athenians*, sometimes referred to as "the Old Oligarch." All three belong to roughly the same time period, between about 435 and 425.[29] Each is to some degree controversial as revealing sophistic ideas: Herodotos insisted that the political discussion he presented was conducted by Persian nobles, though no one (I think) believes that, and the ideas and analysis presented are palpably Greek and show strong signs of sophistic rational categorizing thought. One can in principle doubt whether the speech in Plato's dialogue in any way resembles an actual speech by Protagoras, or indeed represents Protagoras' thought at all. Such doubts seem to me excessively skeptical, however, and it seems far more likely that Plato offers here Protagoras' true ideas in something akin to the form that Protagoras presented them: the point of the dialogue, after all, is precisely to offer a critique of Protagoras' known views. The Ps-Xenophon treatise is not usually connected much to sophistic influences at all, being taken more or less at face value as a traditionalist upper class indictment of popular governance (hence the common reference to it as "the Old Oligarch"), but I believe that a strong case can be made that behind a masquerade of traditionalist attack it is in fact a sophistic defense of democracy as a valid governing system.

Though Herodotos placed his piece of political analysis in the context of the palace coup that led to the Persian grandee Darius becoming king of the Persian Empire, the situation is one that must in fact have been experienced in many Greek *poleis*: a monarchical ruler had been overthrown and/or assassinated, and there was a debate about what sort of governing arrangements should be instituted to replace his rule. That was the situation faced by the Athenians, for example, after the overthrow of the Peisistratid tyranny in 510.[30] The debate in Herodotos begins with a critique of the flaws of monarchical governance, emphasizing the arbitrariness and cruelty of one-man rule, or tyranny. Then the merits of majority rule are praised, emphasizing the equal protection of the law (*isonomia*) and the public accountability it offers, along with the fairness of distributing public office by lot.[31] There follows a critique of the ignorance of the majority of the people, the foolishness and violence of the mob; instead, the benefits of rule by the "best men" are lauded, because the best men offer the best counsels. This system is characterized as oligarchy or rule by the few and is finally unfavorably compared with monarchy. The unity of purpose and wisdom of governance when the best man is placed in charge is contrasted to the factional strife and violence that inevitably result when multiple leaders are vying with each other for pre-eminence, as inevitably happens in an oligarchy. One notes the rational categorizing: governance can be in the hands of one man, of an elite few, or of the majority; characteristic merits and flaws of each of these three options are laid out. This categorization remained at the root of all subsequent Greek political theory: it is found in Aristotle's *Politika*, and in subsequent third century and later political theory, down to the time of Polybios and Cicero.[32] Eventually, it gave rise to the idea of a recurring cycle of governing systems: primitive monarchy (good) would over time become corrupted into tyranny (bad), which would be overthrown and replaced by aristocratic governance (good). However, this in turn would become corrupted into oligarchy (bad) and be overthrown and replaced by sound and moderate majority rule or democracy (good). This would inevitably degenerate over time into arbitrary mob rule or *ochlocracy* (bad), leading to chaos and social breakdown that could only be resolved by the emergence of a strong leader able to impose order and make himself monarch, and so the cycle would start again.[33]

That sophistic political theorizing should begin with the basic work of rational categorizing is natural, but in the hands of Protagoras it quickly moved on. In Plato's dialogue the *Protagoras*, the eponymous sophist and Sokrates are depicted as debating the question whether *arete* (excellence or virtue) is teachable, with Protagoras arguing that it is. The basic claim made by Protagoras was (319a) that he could teach men *politike techne* (the art or craft of "politics") and how to be good citizens (*agathous politas*).[34] The subject matter taught by Protagoras is also termed *arete* (excellence or virtue: 320a), but this is later further refined as being specifically *politike arete* (excellence in political matters: 322e–323a). So, while ostensibly concerned with the question whether "virtue" (as it is usually translated) is teachable, the topic of Protagoras' speech is really *politike techne* or *arete*: the craft or form of excellence concerned with running the *polis*. It is, that is to say, a speech concerned with political theory. In this speech Protagoras states that the key qualities making up *politike techne* are *dike* (a sense of justice enabling us to discern right and wrong) and *aidos* (a sense of shame which pushes us to choose the right), and that all men have a share in these qualities and thus a share in *politike techne* (except a diseased few who should be rigidly excluded from the *polis*). It is for this reason that in *poleis* like Athens all men rightly have an equal share in deliberating and decision making in the council and assembly: because all men have a share in the basic qualities needed to engage in political debate (324d). Further, Protagoras insists that *politike arete* is not just teachable, but is actually taught to all members of the community from birth, by parents, relatives, friends of the family, teachers, priests, political leaders and so on, who tell children how to behave, what is right and wrong to do, what is proper to believe in, and so on: because all have a share in *politike techne*, all are also both pupils and teachers of this craft, through what we would call today the socialization process (see esp. *Protagoras* 325c–d and 327e). Of course, while all share the basic ability to acquire *politike arete*, not all have the same aptitude for it, just as everyone can learn to paint but not everyone can paint supremely well; and that aptitude is not necessarily hereditary, which is why sons of skilled political leaders do not often display the same skill as their fathers. Protagoras' claim, then, is to be a uniquely skilled teacher of *politike arete*, able to bring out the best in his pupils in regard to this valuable form of excellence.

Two things are notable about Protagoras' political theory as revealed in this speech: first, the relative sophistication of his analysis, showing that all men have the basic aptitude to learn what they need to know to participate in "politics," and that they learn this through the basic socialization process; and second, that through this analysis Protagoras established as proper and right a political system rooted in collective discussion, debate, and decision making. If *politike techne* were exceedingly rare, found only in very unusual men, it would be right and proper to make such men kings and let them rule; or if *politike techne* were the kind of craft that only dedicated specialists could master—like medicine or navigation—it would be right to put the select few specialists in charge and let them rule as an aristocracy (or as we might say, as technocrats); but since *politike techne* is found virtually universally in humans, it is right for all men to share in the political process. That is to say, Protagoras makes a case for democracy, but his analysis is open to placing some limitations on full citizenship on the basis of relative aptitude for or commitment to learning and exercising *politike techne*. In other words, a moderate form of oligarchy is not necessarily inconsistent with Protagoras' views on *politike arete*, but these views do necessarily require a governing system with a reasonably broad citizen base who reach political decisions through collective processes of debate and decision making. This of course is precisely the political system that had developed in the sixth and fifth centuries in Greece, and especially at Athens with its radical democracy; and what Protagoras did with his political analysis, then, is to provide a theoretical basis and justification for the collective governing system of the classical Greek city-state.

The Ps.-Xenophon treatise on the constitution of the Athenians takes this theoretical analysis further in a number of interesting and important ways. But before getting into that, we need to look at what sort of treatise it is, and how it suggests sophistic influence.[35] On the surface it presents itself as an aristocratic critique of Athenian democracy, but while it uses some standard aristocratic terminology, and employs the standard upper-class derogations of the people and popular power, such matters very visibly occupy only a small portion of the treatise's overall verbiage: the bulk of the treatise in fact consists of a skillful defense of Athenian democracy, showing point by point how the Athenians are in fact right to keep the governing system they have, and act very wisely and effectively in maintaining their governing system and their power.[36] The apparently aristocratic aim and viewpoint of the author seems thus to be no more than a pose to cover his real intent: to justify Athenian democracy to unsympathetic upper class listeners/readers. Such an assumption of a fake literary persona to present a persuasive case to a hostile audience in itself smacks strongly of the sophistic approach to argumentation, what critics of the sophists called "making the weaker case seem the stronger," and thus suggests that the author at a minimum had some sophistic training in the art of persuasion.[37] But one can go further: in justifying Athenian democracy the author employs clearly sophistic rational theorizing, of a type found also in the ideas of the likes of Thrasymachos of Chalkedon, for example, showing that the unknown author was indeed directly influenced by the sophists. Three clearly sophistic political principles emerge in the treatise's analysis of Athenian democracy: that the segment of a state's population chiefly responsible for its power and standing in the world deserves *ipso facto* to have the predominant say in politics and governance; that those of a particular socio-economic "class" are the ones best able to discover and most likely to pursue what is to the benefit of that "class," and that whoever is in power in a society will naturally make the laws and rules governing society such as to benefit themselves and exploit those not in power.

The first of these theoretical principles is presented right at the start of the treatise when the author states that, as much as one might disapprove of Athenian democracy, the Athenians were right to put power in the hands of the common people because the Athenians derived their power, standing, and wealth overwhelmingly from their fleet, and "it is the people who man the ships and bring about the power of the *polis* ... far more than the hoplites" (Ps-Xenophon *Const. Ath.* 1.2). Because of this, he adds "it seems just (*dikaios*) that everyone shares in the magistracies... and that whoever of the citizens wishes to may speak." Clearly implied here is the principle that those primarily responsible for a state's strength and defense should have the main say in governance, and that a state dependent on naval power—and thus on the common people's contributions in manning the ships—will naturally and rightly be a democracy, while a state depending on hoplites (heavily armed infantry) for its power will have a more narrowly based governing system, in which the men of sufficient wealth to own hoplite equipment predominate. Though this principle cannot be securely attributed to any specific sophistic philosopher, it became a well-known principle in Greek political theory: most famously through its presentation in Aristotle's *Politika* (6.6.1–3), as noted in Chapter 3 above. The Ps-Xenophon treatise reveals, thus, that this well-known principle of Aristotelian political theory was not original to Aristotle but was first put forward in sophistic circles in the fifth century.

The second principle addresses one of the basic criticisms of broadly based, popular governing systems: how could the uneducated common folk possibly know what was best for them? This criticism was not only voiced by traditionalist upper class or "aristocratic" critics of democracy: it was also put forward in sophistic circles, most famously by Sokrates, who disparaged the ability of the uneducated to understand "good" governance and argued that only those well-educated enough to know what is "good" should have a say in governance, just as only those knowledgeable about medicine or navigation should be doctors or navigators.[38] The author of the Ps-Xenophon treatise disagreed: he argued that while the uneducated common people may not know what is "good" or "best," they do know and understand what is to their own benefit and advantage. They understand, as the author put it at some length (Ps-Xenophon *Const. Ath.* 1.4–7), that they are better off following leaders characterized by poverty (*poneria*) and lack of education (*amathia*) but having good will (*eunoia*) towards the people and the democracy, than following an adviser who has virtue (*arete*) and wisdom (*sophia*) but is ill-disposed (*kakonoia*): "for when whoever wishes may get up and speak, the *poneros* (i.e., lower class) man discovers what is good (*to agathon*) for himself and those like him." Throughout this treatise the author uses the value judgment terms "good" (*agathos*) and "bad" (*kakos*), "fine" or "noble" (*kalos*) and "poor" (*penes*), "valuable" (*chrestos*) and "useless" (*poneros*) in the traditional aristocratic senses so well elucidated by Nietzsche in the first part of his *Genealogy of Morals*: as terms of approving self-reference by the upper class for the positive words, and of dismissive derogation of the lower classes for the negative words. That is to say, these words are not used with any moral significance, as they came to be by Plato and later philosophers, but rather as terms of social status, except when in the sentence just quoted the author states that the *poneros* can discover "the good" (*to agathon*) for those like him. By implication the traditional aristocratic terminology is criticized and undermined: if it is just (*dikaios*) for the "bad" man (*kakos*) to do better than the "good" man (*agathos*), then there is something wrong with the way the terms *agathos* and *kakos* are being used; and if there is a good (*agathon*) for the *poneroi* that is separate from and different than the *agathon* of the *chrestoi*, then the very concept of "good" is relative.

Finally, we come to the third principle: that those in power naturally establish rules and laws to benefit themselves and exploit those not in power. This is stated explicitly by the author in section 1.9 of the treatise: "if you seek 'good governance' (*eunomia*), first you will see that the *dexiotatoi* (most intelligent men) establish laws to benefit themselves; then the *chrestoi* will punish the *poneroi* and the *chrestoi* will take counsel for the *polis* and will not allow "madmen" (*mainomenous anthropous*) to take counsel or to speak or to attend the assembly; as a result then of these 'good' measures the *demos* will very quickly fall into slavery." As he goes on to note, the common people do not want to be slaves to the upper class, however "good" the upper class may judge that situation to be. Rather than that, the *demos* will choose "bad governance" (*kakonomia*) over "good governance" (*eunomia*) when it allows them, the common people, to grow strong and be free (section 1.8). In other words, the upper classes will establish a governing system that benefits themselves and exploits the common people, turning them into "slaves"; the common people, establishing democracy, create a system that benefits the common people themselves at the expense of the upper classes. And this is seen by the author as only natural and right: every socio-economic "class" of course seeks its own advantage. That this is sophistic thought is established by the well-known fact that this is precisely the principle put forward by the sophist Thrasymachos in bk. 1 of Plato's *Republic*: in every state the rules of justice are established by the "stronger" (i.e., the dominant ruling element) to benefit themselves; thus an oligarchic state will have laws establishing oligarchy as just, while a democratic state will have laws establishing democracy as just, and justice is thus simply what is to the advantage of the stronger element.

In sum, then, we see that in early sophistic political thought, the system of collective self-governance characteristic, in the somewhat different forms of democracy and oligarchy, of the Greek city-states was established as being rooted in basic human nature, which endows every man with the capacity to learn what is needed to play an active role in politics and which enables even relatively poorly educated men nevertheless to understand and pursue what is to their own advantage; in a military system which called on large segments of society to put their lives on the line for the community and thus gave them the strength and right to demand a say in governing the community, and in the natural principle that those who are strong enough to do so will take control of governance and make rules and laws that are to their own advantage. There was undoubtedly a good deal more to sophistic political theory: sophists like Thrasymachos and Antiphon and Sokrates certainly had a good deal to say about politics, the latter in particular reputedly as a vocal critic of democracy,[39] but as we lack writings on political theory by these sophists we cannot say much for sure about their theorizing. There is another text, however, written in the early 390s, which sheds a very interesting light on some aspects of sophistic political theory: Aristophanes' play *The Ekklesiazousai*.

In this play, Aristophanes presents a situation in which the women of Athens achieve political equality with the men. Once women are politically active like men, the traditional role of women as wives and mothers is seen as too restrictive, and so traditional marriage—and with it the traditional family unit—is abolished, and women attain the same sexual freedom as men. And then, since the traditional family unit existed in large part to secure property rights and the hereditary transmission of property, private property is also abolished, and the wealth of the Athenians is communalized. Aristophanes' interest in all this is comedic of course: he parodies these ideas relentlessly, but we know that these were very serious ideas being discussed in philosophical circles.[40] We know this because, some fifteen or twenty years after Aristophanes' play, none other than Plato proposed these very ideas—political equality for women and abolition of the family unit and of private property—in his most famous work, the *Republic*. In other words, as often with Plato's more interesting ideas, these notions were not original to Plato but arose in sophistic discussions in the late fifth century, thereby becoming fodder for Aristophanes' parodying in the early 390s. It is clear that these ideas build on the basic sophistic theorizing we have already discussed. If the necessary prerequisites for *politike arete*—the senses of justice and shame—exist naturally in all *anthropoi* (humans), as Protagoras argued, then are women not humans too? Should not political participation be extended to women? If the *polis* is a collective belonging to the citizens who make it up and govern it, then should not the landed property and other wealth of the *polis* likewise belong to all, be shared by all, and benefit all equally? And why should alternative focuses of loyalty and belonging, that is family units and lineages, be allowed to detract from focus on and loyalty to the *polis*? Of course, these ideas were, to the vast majority of classical Greeks, too extreme ever to be put into effect, but we can see how they naturally flowed from the sophistic rational theorizing discussed above.

After about 390, the sophistic political theory justifying collective governance, and thereby the collective governance system itself, came under strong attack from the noted philosopher Plato. Inspired perhaps to some degree by his mentor Sokrates, Plato declared that politics and governance are a *techne* (art or craft) requiring special expertise, similar to the practice of medicine or navigation, and that it is therefore absurd to permit crowds of ordinary and inadequately educated citizens to have a voice in political decisions. Instead, governance should be placed in the hands of an elite ruler or small committee of rulers: men (and potentially women) who have the intellectual capacity and high level of education to decide in a fully informed way what is best for the community and its members to do. Thanks in part, no doubt, to his frankly absurd notion that learning what is good and right is attained by a prolonged study of mathematics and music theory, Plato's ideas never had any practical effect so long as the Greek city-state lasted: even his greatest pupil Aristotle rejected Plato's political theory almost *in toto*. It was only after the demise of the Greek city-states and the advent of more authoritarian political systems, and of Christianity and Islam, that Plato's political ideas and his rather spiritual and rigid approach to morality came to seem appealing. In more modern times, however, Plato's philosophy has come under withering (and to my mind fully justified) criticism: Nietzsche in his work *Beyond Good and Evil* (1886) forcefully attacked Plato's idea of "the good in itself"; Karl Popper in *The Open Society and its Enemies* (1945) showed how Plato's political theory essentially provided a blueprint for totalitarian systems of governance, systems that have lost all appeal since the world's appalling experience of the brutality of such governments in the twentieth century; Eduard Jan Dijksterhuis pointed out, in his work *The Mechanization of the World Picture* (1969), the error of Plato's "over-estimation of what unaided thought, i.e., without recourse to experience, could achieve." The Platonic intervention in classical Greek political theory was, thus, at best a sidetrack, quickly superseded by Aristotle's more empirical approach.

This brings us back to Aristotle's *Politeiai* and *Politika*, which I have already suggested represent the full maturing of Greek political theory. The very fact that he orchestrated the research project culminating in the *Politeiai* shows that Aristotle had a very different approach to political theory than that of Plato: he wanted to root it in the actual history and practice of politics. The surviving treatise, on the constitution of the Athenians, demonstrates this, in that it has two parts: first a historical overview of the changes in the governing system of the Athenians, from earliest times to Aristotle's own day; then a detailed account of how the Athenian governing system was structured and how it functioned in

Aristotle's time, that is the mid fourth century. It's reasonable to assume that this was typical of the rest of the treatises, though in some cases the historical section may have been slender or lacking due to want of information. We can also tell by very clear indications that this research project informed the theorizing of the *Politika*, since references to historical and contemporary governing practices in a host of Greek city-states—and in a few cases non-city-state and even non-Greek societies—are peppered throughout the *Politika* as proofs and illustrations of the various points Aristotle makes. Aristotle's approach, that is to say, was fundamentally empirical. As a city-state Greek living in the great era of Greek city-state civilization, he took the collective decision making system of the Greek city-states to be the truest and best kind of governing system, and examined the various forms of this system to show how and why they worked well, and to try to show what the best possible form of this system would be.[41]

Famously, Aristotle started his *Politika* with an observation that formed the basis of all his theorizing: that the human is by nature a *politikon zoon*—a creature designed or intended to live in a *polis*, that is a state or community. Further, he insisted that the *polis* is a shared enterprise, designed to enable the citizens who share in it to attain to the fullest degree possible the goal (*telos*) of human life, namely happiness (*eudaimonia*). The *polis* achieves this by instilling in its citizens a common agreement on a governing system and set of laws which are rooted in the shared notions of *arete* (excellence or virtue) and *dike* (justice), concepts which had been fully discussed and explained in Aristotle's preceding treatise the *Nicomachean Ethics*.[42] An essential part of the partnership of the *polis*, for Aristotle, is that the citizens, in their necessary difference which enables them to share for mutual benefit their various qualities and abilities, have all the same a kind of "reciprocal equality" which guarantees their mutual freedom and is expressed in sharing in the rule of the *polis*, each holding one or other of the various offices of rule for a year at a time (or some other time period) in turn (1261a). It is thus crucially important to determine and define who exactly the citizens are, and he defines the citizens as follows: "the citizen in an unqualified sense is defined by no other thing so much as sharing in decision and office" (1275a). The citizens of a *polis* are therefor just those who are "entitled to participate in an office involving deliberation or decision," and it is the mass of such citizens who, above all, make up the *polis* (1275b). In participating in deliberation and decision making, the citizen must consider, in discussion with fellow citizens, what is good and just and advantageous for the community, and in doing so he naturally engages in reason and speech (*logos*) and thus fulfills his *telos* of attaining the virtuous and happy life. For Aristotle the goal or function (*telos*) of human life thus involves being an active citizen of a *polis* engaged in the governing process of that *polis* through debating and voting.

All of this is to say that in his political theory, Aristotle essentially endorsed and justified the collective deliberation and decision-making system that had come to characterize the Greek city-state. Given his principle that participating in governance was crucial to the citizen fulfilling his *telos*, it is obvious that monarchy was inconsistent with a properly functioning *polis*.[43] The basic issue of governance is thus the question of active citizenship: the more widely citizenship is shared, the more democratic the governing system; conversely, the more narrowly citizenship is restricted, the more oligarchic. The core of Aristotle's *Politika* (bks 4–6) is thus a lengthy discussion of the varieties of oligarchy and democracy, the various ways of restricting or opening up citizenship, of organizing participation in citizenship, the strengths and weaknesses of the various sub-forms of oligarchy and democracy. Further, Aristotle's ideal governing system, which he simply called *politeia* (governing system, or constitution), is essentially a somewhat restricted form of democracy, in which every member of the *polis* who has the basic reasoning capacity to participate virtuously in deliberation and decision making is *ipso facto* a full participating citizen, sharing in all the rights and duties of governance through the various stages of life—young men focusing on defense, mature men on governing, and old men on religion—and in a turn-and-turn-about fashion (bk. 7).

It is also important to notice that Aristotle basically built on sophistic political theorizing as described above. He accepted the classification of constitutions found in the Herodotos passage, and built on it, delineating more fully the six basic forms of governing system: good and bad monarchy; good and bad oligarchy; good and bad democracy (1279a to 1289a). He noted that the majority of men have the basic capacity to act as citizens, in terms of reason and virtue and the ability thus to discern and follow justice, thus essentially agreeing with Protagoras as we saw above, and he further argued that virtue is a habit acquired by practicing virtuous behavior, as set out by the laws and taught by parents and rulers, that is it is acquired by the socialization process as Protagoras had argued.[44] Like Ps-Xenophon, Aristotle noted a close and causal relationship between the type of governing system—democratic or oligarchic—and the segment of the population a *polis* chiefly relied upon in warfare (6.6.1). And like Ps-Xenophon and Thrasymachos too, Aristotle noted that different kinds of regimes establish different rules of justice intended to benefit themselves: an oligarchic conception of justice, arguing that wealth justifies greater power; and a democratic understanding of justice, arguing that justice demands fundamental equality of the citizens (bk. 3). In thus accepting and building on the key principles laid out in sophistic political theorizing, and adding a strong empirical support for these principles through his research project on *politeiai*, Aristotle presented the city-state governed by active citizens engaged in collective debate and decision-making as the only type of community compatible with a life of virtue in which people are free and enabled to pursue their *telos*. States governed by monarchs or very restricted oligarchies/aristocracies are states whose governing system is characterized by "mastery"; only states self-governed by participating citizens have proper "political" rule.[45]

Public Information and Political Participation

We see, then, that the Greek city-state was, as a matter of practical political reality, a collective of actively participating citizens sharing in political discussion and making decisions by voting, and that Greek political theory explained and justified this system as natural and right. However, accepting that all men have the natural and innate ability to share in political discussion and decision making, and that playing an active role in protecting the city-state and enhancing its power gives them the right to participate fully, does not mean that the citizens were naturally ready and able to participate in political debate and voting effectively. There is another criterion that needs to be met: the citizens need to be informed. To participate properly in a complex political system, one needs to know the laws and rules governing and organizing that system, so that one knows how to go about playing one's part. To participate usefully and effectively in discussions and votes on laws to be enacted, policies to be put into effect, agreements of various sorts to be reached by the community, one has to have knowledge of what these laws, policies, agreements and so on are. Ideally, in fact, one needs to have advance knowledge of them, so that one may consider them carefully and engage in advance discussion with relatives and associates. In other words, the collective political system of the Greek city-states required an effective way to disseminate information. We happen to know how the Greek city-states went about making the relevant information available: literary sources tell us of laws and policies and so on being written up and publicly displayed in the central areas of the cities, but more importantly many actual laws and decrees and other types of public notices set up by Greek cities still survive to be read and analyzed today, thanks to the Greek habit of inscribing notices of long term importance on stone.

Publicly displayed writing was, that is to say, very common in the Greek city-states, especially in the central town squares and in sanctuaries. Texts set up by the community for communal purposes such as laws and law "codes," public memorials, lists of public officials (magistrates, priests, and the like), treaties and records of arbitrations, communal dedications to gods, and other public pronouncements of various sorts, eventually including correspondence with other cities and rulers, decrees of honors accorded to benefactors, and much more, were to be found ubiquitously in the central town squares (*agorai*), including on the walls of public buildings around the square, and in neighboring sanctuaries. Many of these texts still survive to be studied by specialists in epigraphy, and analyzed by historians (see Plate 2 for an example). All these texts share the attributes of being publicly displayed and of seeking thereby the attention of anyone passing by and looking on, and in many cases the hope or even expectation that passersby will be willing and able to read what is written is made clear.

The evidence clearly suggests that the earliest kind of communal documentation to be committed to publicly displayed writing consisted of laws of various sorts. The writing down of laws in the Greek city-states appears to have begun in the early to mid seventh century, and to have originated in the western colonies in Italy and Sicily, being specifically associated with the names of two prominent early law-givers: Zaleukos of Lokroi and Charondas of Katane. While almost everything about these two semi-legendary figures is disputed—their exact period of activity, their purported biographical details, which laws attributed to them (if any) are genuine, and thus the nature of their law-giving activity—most scholars do recognize that there are genuine historical figures behind the accumulation of legend, that they were active at an early date (perhaps as early as about 675, not later than the early sixth century), and that the tradition seeing them as the first producers of written law in Greece must be taken seriously.[46] Key for present purposes is the clear implication in the (admittedly inadequate) evidence that the laws of early lawgivers like Zaleukos were not just written down, but publicly displayed and thus publicly accessible. This tradition, that Greek city-states began to seek to have written laws publicly displayed by the middle of the seventh century is confirmed by epigraphic evidence.

The earliest surviving inscribed laws, from Dreros on Krete, date from the middle or second half of the seventh century; contemporaneous with the earliest written laws of the literary record, that is to say.[47] The question confronting us is what the purpose of these publicly displayed written laws was: some scholars have argued that such displays were of symbolic significance only, that it was not at all expected that onlookers would actually read the texts.[48] That might seem counter-intuitive at first glance, but there are parallels: the so-called "law code of Hammurabi," for example, though publicly displayed throughout second millennium Mesopotamia in the cuneiform script, surely could not be read by the vast majority of viewers; the same can be said of the great rock inscription of the Persian king Darius the Great at Bisutun in Media. It is not inconceivable, then, that publicly displayed early Greek laws were meant as symbolic monuments of some sort, not as texts to be read by the citizens. Against this view, however, some scholars have noted the presence in early Greek inscriptions of elements that show a clear awareness of readers and a desire to aid them: the use of spaces or other dividers between sections of text, the use of a form of punctuation (usually vertical lines or rows of dots) to mark individual words or phrases, or using separate lines of text for distinct matters.[49] In the end, however, our judgment concerning the function of such publicly displayed texts must be decided by the evidence concerning their reception.

Among the very early public written laws were the laws written up by Drakon at Athens around the year 621. Drakon's laws, we are told, were inscribed on the sides of long blocks of wood or stone called *axones*; these were then placed on spits, so that the blocks could be turned allowing the different faces to be viewed in turn.[50] These *axones* were then publicly displayed in the town square of Athens, the *agora*, at the *Stoa Basileios*, and the very fact of the system of rotating spits permitting the viewing in turn of the various inscribed faces indicates the intention that these texts should be read, not just looked at as a monument. And the evidence is clear that they were read: Drakon's laws became a topic of public debate and controversy, with a widespread view developing that they were too harsh (giving us the phrase "Draconian measures"), and that they should be changed. This led, after only just over twenty-five years, to the appointment of Solon as specially empowered *nomothetes* (law establisher) to write new and "better" laws for the Athenians. The public debate on the laws of Drakon is an extreme case, in terms of the evidence we have, but it seems not to have been unusual: we know that the laws of Zaleukos and Charondas were discussed and debated through generations of Greeks, indicating that they were being read, and that seems to have been typical. We know the names of quite a number of "archaic" (that is, seventh and sixth century) lawgivers whose laws were debated both at the time and through subsequent generations—Pittakos of Mitylene, Philolaos of Corinth, Andromadas of Rhegion, Demonax of Mantinea, to name a few—and whose laws were clearly read, in order to become a topic of discussion.[51] In sum, it seems evident that these publicly displayed texts not only were meant to inform, rather than just impress visually, but that they succeeded in this intent, that is that they actually were read by at least some significant set of the citizens.[52]

We should also consider the circumstances in which these written laws were produced. Hammurabi's "code" was monumentalized as an expression of that great king's power and moral authority; the situation was very different with respect to the early Greek lawgivers. As has been noted, the setting up of inscribed laws in Greek cities was a social act.[53] In each case, the initiative for writing up and displaying the laws appears to have come from the citizenry, often in a context of civic dispute or disruption as a way to produce greater unity: that is what we explicitly hear in the cases of Zaleukos, Solon, Pittakos and others.[54] Why would the citizens have desired to see written laws publicly displayed, if they could not profit by reading those laws and so informing themselves? Every human community based on agriculture and property has laws of a sort, that is acknowledged and observed rules and regulations about such things as ownership and transference of property, inheritance, marriage, killing and harming, and so on; but not all have written laws. Before the middle of the seventh century, every Greek community had *nomoi*—which may be translated as laws, rules, customs, or norms—by which it was guided and its people were limited. These laws or customs were not written down as yet, but they were not conceived of as "unwritten laws," because that concept could only arise after laws had been written. They were simply the rules the community was guided by; and some communities—the Spartans most notoriously—continued to be guided by such traditional *nomoi* which were not written down through the classical era. Even communities which relied heavily on written law continued to observe some traditional *nomoi* that were not written down: at Athens, for example, Sophokles in his play *Antigone* (produced *c*. 442) referred at ll. 454-5 to "unwritten laws" (*agrapta nomima*) that all humans observe; and Thucydides had Perikles in his "Funeral Oration" mention habitual Athenian obedience to the laws (*nomoi*), especially to "those unwritten ones [*hosoi agraphoi ontes*] that bring recognized disgrace" (2.37.3).[55]

Since communities can function with unwritten rules that are remembered as tradition and passed on orally, what was the motivation and purpose among the developing Greek city-states from the mid seventh century on to produce and display written laws? This has been the topic of much debate,[56] but a few points seem clear: there was often a desire to change the traditional norms and introduce new laws that would in some way be better, and these new laws needed to be offered in a clear, fixed, and accessible way. It is this latter point that required the new laws to be written down, and publicly displayed, and it again seems clear that the goal was not to create a monument, but to enable the new laws and regulations to be known, indeed widely known. That aim or intention came to be expressed explicitly, by introducing language requiring the law to be publicly inscribed "so that all may know": note, for example, the regulations concerning the sanctuary of Kodros at Athens, which were inscribed "so that it may be possible for anyone who wishes to know them."[57] Obviously this aim of enabling "all to know" required citizens to read the published laws, and these public displays thus expressed a communal expectation that citizens, in substantial numbers at least, would take it upon themselves to do so.

The importance of written laws, and the effects of having laws written down and thus accessible to all, are noted in our surviving sources. A text frequently cited in this context is Euripides *Suppliants* 433–7: "when the laws are written the weak man and the wealthy man have equal justice (*dike*), and the weaker man if he is defamed may sue the better off, and the lesser man, should he be in the right, defeats the powerful man."[58] The point here obviously is that, by having the laws written down, obviously in a public place, the poor and weak gain access to the laws and can employ them against the wealthy and powerful and so gain justice. Written laws enable the poor to know what the laws say, and so to benefit from them; this clearly implies that they are reading the laws. Even more significant, I think, is a passage from Plato's *Protagoras*. In his famous speech on the universality of moral sense at 320c to 328d, Protagoras argued that all humans share the ability to acquire political excellence (*politike arete*) because all have the basic prerequisites: a sense of shame and an understanding of justice. However, aptitudes need to be nurtured and trained, and he points out that from birth a child's nurses and parents make it their business to instruct the child about what is right and wrong to do. Then they send their sons to school, where the teachers of various sorts continue this training in good behavior. Finally, Protagoras notes (326c–d): "when they have finished with teachers, the *polis* compels them to learn the laws, lest left to themselves they should drift aimlessly ... so indeed the *polis* writes out the laws, the inventions of good and ancient lawgivers, and compels the citizens to rule and be ruled according to them." Again, the point here is that the laws are written down and displayed so that the citizens can be compelled (*anangkazein*) to obey them. In other words, the citizens are expected to inform themselves concerning the laws and what they say, obviously by reading them: that is the point of setting them up publicly in written form.

There is no reason, then, to think that seventh, sixth, and fifth-century Greek communities did not understand how much literacy they could expect citizens to have attained, or how willing they would be to inform themselves. And the doubtless unexpected consequence of published written laws—that these laws became the subject of critical analysis and debate, often leading to further calls for changes to the law—shows that the laws were indeed read and discussed, that is they actually did succeed in their aim of informing the citizens. To be sure, not all publicly displayed texts were as obviously intended to be widely read as the law texts. Copies of treaties, for example, might have served simply as monumentalized records intended to be consulted, if at all, only by public officials; the same might be said of lists of priests and officials, records of arbitrations, copies of official correspondence, and the like. In each case, an intention to make it possible for passersby to read and be informed by the texts is clearly a possible motivation, but it cannot be established as an important or main motivation.

Other publicly displayed texts, however, very clearly were intended to be read and to inform. Among the most common publicly displayed texts in Greek cities were inscriptions recording honorific decrees for civic benefactors: it has been estimated, for example, that honorific decrees make up nearly three-quarters of all surviving Athenian public inscriptions between the end of the sixth and the end of the fourth century.[59] This has to do with the fact that ancient Greek city-states, always reluctant to impose direct taxes on the citizens—that is, on themselves, since it was groups of citizens who decided these matters—relied heavily on wealthy benefactors to fund various aspects of public business. Such benefactors were honored by the community in a variety of ways, and the honors bestowed on benefactors were granted in the form of official decrees of the citizens in assembly, and recorded as public acts by being inscribed on stone and displayed in a prominent public location. A very common feature of these honorific decrees was a so-called "hortatory formula," words that explicitly voiced the expectation that people would read the inscribed decree and be impressed by the way the city thanked its benefactors, perhaps even be motivated to benefit the city themselves in order to be similarly honored. The best way to illustrate this is no doubt to quote a few indicative examples.

An Athenian decree from the year 330/329, for example, honored a grain merchant named Herakleides of Salamis, and after decreeing appropriate honors it included the following statement:

> so that others may also behave in an honor-seeking way, knowing that the Council honors and crowns those who behave in an honor-seeking way.[60]

A decree of the Delians from the reign of the Macedonian king Demetrios II (239–229 BCE) honored as a benefactor one Aristoboulos of Thessalonika, and included the words: "so that all may know that the people knows how to honor good men."[61]

From Histiaia on Euboia we have a decree from about 225 honoring Athenodoros son of Pisagoras of Rhodes and expressing this aim:

> so that all may know that the people of Histiaia knows how to honor its benefactors and more people may compete to provide benefits to the city when they see worthy men being honored.[62]

A decree of the Samians from about 245 honored at length their fellow citizen Boulagoras and, after listing his many services, stated:

> so that we may be seen to be honoring good men and encouraging many citizens to follow the same course of action, be it resolved by the people to praise Boulagoras son of Alexis ... and the controllers shall inscribe this decree on a stone stele and dedicate it in the sanctuary of Hera.[63]

From Ephesos we have, dating to c. 300, a decree honoring a certain Agathokles of Rhodes for selling grain to the citizens at a reduced price. He was rewarded with Ephesian citizenship, and the decree concludes with these words:

> the temple administrators shall inscribe these honors in the sanctuary of Artemis, where the other grants of citizenship are inscribed, so that all may know that the people knows how to return thanks to its benefactors.[64]

The examples are drawn from a wide variety of cities, and it would be easy to continue with many more examples of this phenomenon, but I think the point is clear: decrees of honors, and the public display of those decrees in inscribed form, were intended to communicate the benefit-rewarding habits of the Greek cities and the hope that others, seeing this, would be inspired to provide benefits. That is, the inscriptions were intended to inform the onlooker, and thus to be read.[65] As Stephen Lambert in his crucial study of Athenian honorific decrees noted: "it seems reasonable to suppose that part of the intention of inscribing honorific decrees on the acropolis was so that the honour should be enhanced by being widely known about, and indeed that is arguably implicit in the language of hortatory intention clauses ... and in other types of decrees where provision is explicitly made that it should be inscribed 'so that everyone may know.'"[66] I would go further and say that the intention through public inscription of enhancing the honor by making it widely known is frequently explicit, rather than merely implicit, in hortatory intention clauses. It may be pointed out that the examples quoted above are all rather late in date, from the later fourth and third centuries, and indeed no examples of the "hortatory formula" are known before the mid fourth century. However, that should not be taken to suggest that the aim of influencing people by inscribing these decrees, and thus the expectation of the inscribed decrees being read, was new: it was the explicit hortatory formula that was new, but the hortatory intention of honorific decrees was clearly there from the beginning, and with it the expectation that such inscribed decrees would inform and inspire, that is would be read.[67]

Not all public information was of long term or permanent importance, and so suitable for inscription on stone. There was more ephemeral information that needed to be brought to the citizens' attention, and for this purpose ephemeral public notice boards were used: the best known example is the whitened boards which were displayed in the *agora* of Athens in front of the monument of the ten tribal heroes.[68] These boards were used to publicize notices regarding the activities of the council and assembly: texts of proposed decrees and laws, notifications of citizens called up for military or naval duty, *probouleumata* from the council—that is measures discussed and preliminarily agreed upon by the council—and a host of other notices regarding the business of the state council and citizen assembly were regularly displayed and, obviously, read by the citizens moving about the *agora* engaged in their own business. Whitened boards (*leukomata*) were not only used for state business at the monument of the Ten Heroes, however. For example, such whitened boards were used to record transactions of public and especially sacred monies.[69] A variety of public documents were written on whitened boards and stored in the public record office of Athens, the *Metroon*.[70] Such boards were not only in use at Athens: Adolf Wilhelm long ago pointed out attestation of their use for example at Delos and Amorgos to publicize and keep record of public matters in a less expensive way than inscription on stone.[71] A final example will, I think, suffice to make this point: an inscription records a decree of the *phratry* (lit. brotherhood, a socio-religious association of citizens sharing a fictive kinship) of the Demotionidai from the Attic deme of Dekelea. The decree includes provision for recording the decision on a stone stele (i.e., the inscription we have), but also that it be written up on whitened boards to be displayed both at Dekelea itself, and in the city of Athens at a place "where the Dekeleans frequent."[72] Here the intention that these whitened boards are to inform citizens, in this case fellow phratry-members and demesmen, by enabling them to read important information could hardly be more clearly expressed.

All in all, then, we see that the citizens of Athens, and of other Greek city-states, were well aware that, for their system of shared, collective debate and decision-making to function properly, it was necessary that the citizens be informed about all sorts of aspects of political and other communal business; and that the way they made information available to the citizenry was by displaying it publicly in inscribed form on stone (or more rarely bronze or wooden) surfaces, and/or writing it up on public notice boards—usually specially whitened to enable the writing to stand out clearly—placed in well frequented public areas. It will no doubt be noticed that this system of informing by publicly displayed written notices involves a basic assumption, not to say requirement: in order for it to function, the citizens, or at least the bulk of them, must be literate, able to read the public notices. Certainly to some degree literate citizens could have read the notices, and then shared the information contained and discussed it with citizens who had not and perhaps could not read the notices. We do know that orality, that is sharing information through oral transmission, remained an important feature of classical Greek culture.[73] But Greeks, growing up in a culture which prized competitiveness and self-sufficiency (*autarkeia*), hated to be in a subordinate, dependent role in society, a role which being illiterate would put them in. Further, the presence of literate informed citizens willing and able to share the necessary information with illiterate fellow citizens in a timely fashion could not always be counted on. And the clear expectation of the system, especially of the clauses in notices that virtually demanded that "all" should read and inform themselves, is that citizens for the most part were in fact able and willing to read and inform themselves. If the citizens were not in fact literate, the system simply could not work in the way clearly intended. In the next chapter, then, we shall investigate the evidence for widespread literacy in the Greek city-states.

Conclusion: The City-State as a Collective of Informed Citizens

The upshot of all this, then, is that the Greek city-state was very much a kind of collective. We saw in Chapter 3 that one aspect of this collective system was the citizen militia system of warfare the city-state Greeks practiced, which emphasized relatively egalitarian and collective modes of fighting both by land and sea. Their participation as warriors on behalf of the community gave Greek citizens both the power and status within the community, and the perceived right, to demand and attain a share in political decision making. This means that the city-state was, politically speaking, essentially a male collective in which those who did not play a full role in the military process—women, slaves, resident foreigners, in some places the poorer segment of society—were subordinated and unable to play an equal or, often, any role in politics. But for those of the citizen "class"—that is those who stood in the hoplite phalanx and/or, among naval powers, those who rowed and otherwise crewed the warships—political participation via the public assembly meetings and the representative state councils was an acknowledged and actively enjoyed right. Even in the more restrictive, "oligarchical" city-states like Sparta the citizen "class" numbered in the thousands, and in the more democratic city-states like Athens the politically entitled citizen body numbered in the tens of thousands, making up the vast majority of the indigenous free-born adult males. These collectives might still seem rather restricted in terms of modern "democracies" which rightly expect equal participation for women and the poor, and which reject slavery entirely (in law at least, if not always in reality); but the more proper comparison for the classical Greek city-states is earlier or contemporary societies, not modern ones. The point is that the Greek city-states were vastly more open and participatory societies, politically and as a result in most other ways, than any other societies of the Mediterranean and western Asian world that went before them or were contemporary with them. The informed participating citizen was a classical Greek invention, and an important one. Even if equal political participation, via public debate and voting by show of hands or the casting of pebbles, was still somewhat limited in the Greek city-states, the idea that equal participation was both desirable and possible was first mooted and put into practice in the classical Greek city-state, and that reality deserves acknowledgment.

5

The Scroll: Literacy and the City-State

Humans are by nature very visually oriented creatures, and the look of a city is thus crucial to how we feel about it, how we respond to it. In great part, of course, the look and feel of a city are determined by the nature of its public and private architecture, its layout, and its public spaces: and all these features of ancient Greek cities have received considerable attention from scholars of material culture and urban planning. There is another aspect to the look of the ancient Greek city, however, that deserves to be noted. When one visits the central parts of any major modern city, one of the things that most immediately strikes the eye and invests the city with its "feel," is the prevalence of advertising billboards and digital screens: brightly colored images of sleek and alluring consumer goods, or appealing foods and drinks, usually accompanied in some manner by extraordinarily beautiful and elegantly dressed models, are everywhere and give the city a feel of being prosperous, up to date, vibrant, and alive. No such images were, of course, on display in ancient Greek cities. There were statues and frescoes, to be sure, though not in the abundance of modern advertising. But there was another sort of public display that must have struck the eye and impressed the mind.

I drew attention in the previous chapter to the habit of the city-state Greeks of displaying public notices in written form in the central spaces of their cities, for the information of the citizens. As a result of this habit, it is clear that from at least the later fifth and fourth centuries on, throughout the center of any Greek city-state that was more than a small town (and often even in the small towns), one would see public documents prominently and monumentally displayed: on the walls of temples and other public buildings, on the sides of altars and memorials, on large rectangular slabs of stone (usually marble) called *stelae* set up around temples and in the town square (*agora*), and on more ephemeral notice boards with specially whitened surfaces, a host of laws, decrees, notices of dedication or of honors granted and thanks bestowed, letters from important rulers or friendly city-states, and so on would be incised in large and regular letters. The incised letters of these engraved documents were often filled in with bright paint, usually a vivid red, to make them more visually striking and easy to read. Thus, where the look of a modern city is to a great degree determined by images, the look of a Greek city was impacted by the written word publicly displayed.

The bright advertising images of the modern city tell us something important about the people who live and work there: that they are consumers, living in a consumer society with an economy based on conspicuous consumption. What do all those very visibly displayed texts tell us about the Greeks who lived surrounded by them, who paid (via their public funds) the money required to set them up, who saw them every day as they went about their business in the public areas of their cities? The message surely is that these were communities of readers, communities which were influenced and regulated by the written word, by public documents that provided them with a shared pool of information and rules to be guided by and to conform to. That conclusion might seem obvious and even inescapable. Yet it is far from being an accepted view of the Greek city-state communities. On the contrary, very able and influential scholars have argued that law codes and other texts prominently displayed in important public locations were just monuments, like statues or columns, meant to look impressive but not necessarily to be read and to inform; that most citizens and other inhabitants of the Greek city-states were in any case illiterate, or virtually so, and therefore incapable of reading these public texts; that the written word was, even, highly suspect to the average citizens of the city-states.[1]

I think we must take the ubiquity of the written word more at face value. The evidence for reading, writing, literacy generally, and education in ancient Greece is unfortunately insufficient to establish incontrovertible conclusions: as a recent scholar put it, "popular literacy (i.e., in classical Athens) ... although surmisable, cannot be substantiated."[2] This skeptical outlook, however, too often relies on a process of argument whereby each individual surviving piece of evidence is examined separately, found wanting or unreliable, and dismissed, leaving the scholar to conclude that there is no good evidence for widespread literacy in ancient Greece. This style of argument is in my view wrong: one must look at the evidence, inadequate as it is, as a whole altogether, and consider the underlying assumptions and outlook implied in it. When one does this, I argue here, what emerges is that the ancient Greek city-state really was a community of readers as one of its most basic and important features, and the fact that—as I shall argue—the citizen communities of the Greek city-states represented the world's first truly literate communities had an incalculable impact on every aspect of classical

Greek society, politics, and culture, because it affected the way the brains of Greek citizens received, digested, and processed information, and therefore the very architecture of their neural pathways. The classical Greeks, in fact, represented a new type of human: *homo lector*, one might say, man the reader, and it was the fact that he was *homo lector* that enabled him to be, as has been recognized since at least the time of Aristotle, *homo politicus*—political man.

The Origin and Spread of the Greek Alphabet

The first prerequisite for widespread literacy to be possible is a system of writing that is well established and relatively easy to master, and we know that was the case once the Greeks had acquired their alphabetic system of writing.[3] The "Greek" alphabet was not, in origin, Greek at all. The symbols (that is, letters) used, and the names by which they were referred to, were borrowed by the ancient Greeks from the Phoenicians, a fact of which classical Greeks themselves were well aware. This is evidenced by various bits of information. For a start, there are the Greek words *poinikazein* (to write) and *poinikastes* (writer, scribe): literally these words mean "to Phoenicianize" and "Phoenicianizer," and their use as alternatives for the more normal Greek words for "to write" and "scribe"— *graphein* and *grammateus*—are an indication of awareness that writing was a skill the Greeks had borrowed from the Phoenicians.[4] Then there is Herodotos' outright account of the Greeks, especially the Ionians, borrowing the alphabet from the Phoenicians and referring to the letters as "Phoenician letters" for that reason.[5] More important to the modern scholar, however, is the evidence of the Phoenician and Greek letters themselves found in ancient inscriptions: the earliest surviving Greek inscriptions are later than the early Phoenician ones, while the letter shapes are so similar as to clearly indicate borrowing; and the fact that the names of the letters are very similar in both languages, and are meaningless in Greek but significant in Phoenician, is a clear indication of their Phoenician origin. All of this is now well known and is generally accepted.[6] What is still subject to debate, however, is the date, location, and purpose of the Greek borrowing of writing from the Phoenicians.

As to the date, a broad scholarly consensus exists accepting *c.* 800 BCE as the time when Greeks first adapted Phoenician (or more properly western Semitic) letters to write down the Greek language.[7] This consensus is based on archaeological evidence: finds of examples of Greek writing on stone, clay, or other surfaces (lead tablets, for example) are abundant from the fifth century on, fairly common from the sixth century, much rarer for the seventh century, and only a handful exist for the eighth century, none of them earlier than *c.* 770 BCE. The pattern is clear and points to the beginning of the eighth century as the inception of alphabetic Greek writing.[8] Scholars seeking to date the Greek borrowing of the alphabet significantly earlier, are forced to posit a lengthy period during which the Greeks used the alphabet but never entrusted texts to durable materials like stone, clay, and metal, which seems inherently unlikely given the prevalence of writing on such materials from the later eighth century on.[9] In addition, they face the difficulty of explaining what alphabetic writing could have been used for in the very small, impoverished, and scattered Greek communities of the early Iron Age before 800. Writing for economic purposes—contracts, bills of lading, and such like—might often be done on perishable materials that would not have survived, but it is hard to imagine any economic purpose for writing in such tiny and otherwise culturally backward communities, or among the transhumant pastoralists who most likely made up the majority of the Greek population before about 850 (as argued in Chapter 2 above); nor does it seem at all likely that the Greeks of the early Iron Age were using writing for literary purposes, or administrative/political purposes, of which no trace has remained. The approximate date of 800 for the borrowing of Phoenician letters to create the Greek alphabet must be accepted unless new evidence—in the form of inscriptions or other pieces of writing predating 800—should be found.[10]

The question of the location of the borrowing is tied up with the matter of the purpose for which the Greek (or Greeks) who were responsible for that first borrowing (or rather, adaptation) intended or used alphabetic writing. Two theories have been proposed regarding the reason for the Greeks' adaptation of the western Semitic alphabet: that they initially used writing for essentially commercial purposes, to keep records of transactions, contracts, lists of goods, and such, and that writing was taken up for the purpose of permanently recording literary compositions, in particular the Homeric epics. The latter theory, which would locate the first "creation" of Greek alphabetic writing on the west coast of Asia Minor, the region that was home to "Homer"—whether one means by that name an individual poet who composed the two great epics that survive under his name, or merely uses it as a short-hand for the bardic tradition the two epics represent—faces significant chronological difficulties, however. As we have seen, the archaeological evidence indicates *c.* 800 (or perhaps rather earlier) as the date of the adaptation of the "Phoenician" letters to the Greek language, but scarcely any scholars would date the Homeric epics so early: on the contrary a broad consensus dates the composition of those epics to the second half of the eighth century, while some would push the date much lower still. That, of course, means that writing down the epics can hardly have been the motivation for adopting alphabetic writing, though it may well have been an early and important use to which writing was put once knowledge of it had begun to spread.[11]

The notion that the original purpose of Greek writing was commercial was proposed by L.H. Jeffery in her foundational book on early Greek alphabets, and has much to recommend it.[12] Jeffery noted that before the fourth century, at the earliest, there was not a single uniform Greek alphabet, but rather multiple local variants that, while having most letters and letter forms in common and clearly all being derived from an adaptation of the western Semitic alphabet, showed a considerable variation in how certain letters were written, the *sigma*, the *iota*, and the *epsilon* for example; what sounds certain letters represented, for example, whether the X symbol should stand for *chi* or for the "ks" sound of modern x, and whether H should represent *eta* (long e) or the aspirate sound of English "h"; and whether or not to include certain letters, such as *digamma, san, qoppa,* and *psi*. Her analysis of these variant early local alphabets showed that they fell into two main groups (along with minor and sub-groups) with basically shared characteristics, which she conventionally named the "red" and "blue" alphabets. She also showed how the geographic distribution of the alphabetic variants belonging to these two groups showed no obvious dialectic or religio-ethnic patterning, but rather seemed to correspond to trade routes. That suggested to her that the early Greek alphabet was used and spread by traders along the routes they used in sailing across the Aegean plying their wares. The main argument that has been advanced against this hypothesis is the absence of clearly commercial texts among the surviving examples of Greek writing from the earliest period, the eighth century. Instead, we find names, groups of letters that look like the results of practicing the alphabet, apparently random letters, and what can only be classed as graffiti, including one or two literary or at least proto-literary graffiti.[13]

Before we take these earliest surviving inscriptions as evidence of a different, perhaps consciously literary origin for the Greek alphabet, however, we need to bear in mind how very few our earliest examples of Greek writing are, how uncertain and indeed obscure of purpose some of them are, and some likely or certain facts about any commercial writings that may have been produced. As to the second point, uncertainty, and obscurity, I would note that apparently random letters on broken bits of pottery may at one time and on the original complete pots have had a purpose we can no longer divine, and that it is conceivable that one such purpose could have been to record data useful to the traders in Greek pottery and/or its contents. Control marks or inventory marks, or symbols indicating ownership or batch or the like, are known to have been incised or painted on pots in the sixth century and later, and some letters on broken eighth-century pottery could very conceivably have served such a purpose.[14] As to any more elaborate commercial writing, we need to bear in mind that commercial documents—lists of goods being transported or traded, agreements of sale/purchase, and so on—on the one hand need to be portable, and on the other tend to be of only ephemeral importance to those using them. A bill of lading or any similar document would not be incised on a rock wall, or a public building, nor indeed on stone at all: something light, small, and easily portable would be chosen. And a document concerning trading activity loses interest and value once the venture or transaction is completed, and the goods have been disposed of, so that re-usable and/or perishable materials are likely to have been a medium of choice for such documents. Both points suggest that pieces of papyrus, wooden tablets, or especially wooden tablets coated with re-usable wax, would be the most commonly used surfaces for commercial documents: materials highly unlikely to survive for long except under very unusual circumstances. Those early inscriptions, thus—casual graffiti on rock walls or attempts to practice the alphabet on bits of pottery—should not be assumed to represent the earliest or most typical functions of Greek writing.

It seems probable, then, that Greek alphabetic writing did indeed have its origin in a commercial context, being used to create a record of commercial activities. Therefore, the most likely place for the borrowing to have occurred would be a trading port, and the "international" trading port at Al Mina in Syria, at the mouth of the Orontes River, with both a Greek and a Phoenician quarter archaeologically attested, would seem a plausible candidate.[15] Nevertheless, it is notable how rapidly the Greek alphabet spread, not just geographically to become used in its slightly variant forms throughout the Greek world, but also in terms of the uses to which it was put. As noted above, while it is possible that some of the earliest preserved inscriptions may have had some sort of commercial purpose, the majority of early inscriptions—that is inscriptions from the eighth and seventh centuries—served very different interests and purposes. From very early times we find names, declarations of ownership, funerary inscriptions, erotic graffiti, bits of poetry, bits of practice writing (especially abecedaria), words explaining images on pottery, and so on (see n. 13 above). The great variety of uses, many of them very personal and casual, indicate a widespread interest in and use of alphabetic writing, much of it obviously not by professional scribes, much of it not produced by members of the socio-economic elite. That is to say, from near the beginning of Greek alphabetic writing, this new technology was used by persons who had no professional interest in writing and/or no elite education, for purposes very personal to them, which suggests that some degree of literacy quickly became a widespread attainment. Before we consider the how and why of widespread literacy, there is a crucial and novel feature of Greek alphabetic writing that must be noticed.

As already mentioned, the Greek alphabet was more than a borrowing from its Phoenician antecedent: it was a creative adaptation. The western Semitic writing system used by the Phoenicians was not in fact properly an alphabet at all: instead it can be thought of as what may be called an unvoiced syllabary.[16] In a fully syllabic writing system, each syllable is represented by a discrete symbol; and since a language has many possible syllables, it requires a large number of symbols to represent even the more common range of syllables used in a language. Thus, for example, the Bronze Age Greek "Linear B" writing system had nearly 100 symbols representing common syllables, and in addition around 100 ideograms representing common items of reference like ox or horse. The western Semitic system simplified this to a more manageable twenty-two or so symbols, each of which represented a range of possible syllables: thus, the symbol *beth* stood for the possible syllables *ba, be, bo, bi, bu*, for example. The system had no symbols for pure vowel sounds, and the appropriate vowel sound needed to complete the sound of the syllable symbolized was determined by context, which worked for Semitic languages in which vowel patterns are highly predictable. Indo-European languages use vowel sounds differently, and Greek in particular is a language relatively rich in vowel sounds, including words with combinations of vowels and many words which begin with a vowel. A writing system lacking symbols for vowel sounds was thus not well suited to the Greek language, and whoever first adapted the western Semitic writing system to the Greek language remedied this by converting some symbols to represent vowel sounds.[17] Thus the Phoenician symbol *'aleph*, standing for the consonant sound called a "glottal stop" with accompanying vowel sounds, was converted to the Greek vowel symbol *alpha*, since the glottal stop sound does not occur in Greek.

In this way the "inventor(s)" of the Greek writing system created the first truly phonetic alphabet, comprising around twenty unvoiced consonant sounds (b, k, d, m, n, and so on) and seven vowel sounds: a, short e (*epsilon*), long e (*eta*), i, short o (*omikron*), u, and long o (*omega*). As a result, words could be symbolized in writing in a completely unambiguous way: the word *asphaleia*, for instance, meaning safety, would have been impossible to symbolize exactly as it sounds in the western Semitic system, but in the Greek alphabet five vowel symbols and three consonants (the "ph" sound was represented by the single consonant symbol *phi*), represented the word with clarity, enabling the initiated reader to voice the word directly from the written symbols. This made reading texts in the Greek alphabet a relatively simple matter: a person needed only to memorize some twenty-four to thirty symbols (depending on which variant of the early Greek alphabet was being used) and the sounds they represented; and to master the skill of voicing the sounds of the symbols consecutively as they appeared in the text—ancient Greek readers invariably read out loud.[18] This is a skill which, as we all know from experience, almost any child of six or seven can attain in a year or two of learning. In sum, the Greek alphabet, once it had been introduced to the Greek world in the decades around 800 BCE or so, offered the possibility of easily attained literacy to anyone ready, willing, and able to take the trouble to learn, making mass literacy theoretically possible for the first time. The question is, then, can we tell how widespread literacy became in classical Greece? Can we truly speak of a mass literate society?

Schools and the Spread of Literacy

For mass literacy to be possible in a society, three basic conditions need to be met regarding education: there must exist the opportunity to learn, in the form of teachers and schools in sufficient numbers and sufficiently widely dispersed; education must be affordable, that is people need to have disposable income and the cost of paying for schooling cannot consume too much of it; and there must be some strong motivation urging people to spend disposable income on education rather than on other wants or satisfactions.[19] To argue that the classical Greek city-states formed a literate society, it is necessary to show that these three conditions were met. Perhaps the most problematic is the first: the question of whether schools existed in sufficient numbers and sufficiently widely dispersed to make the learning of literacy a possibility for a large portion, a majority, even a substantial majority of the citizens.[20] Ancient evidence regarding schools, particularly for the archaic and classical eras, is decidedly scanty except in the case of Athens, and it therefore makes sense to examine the evidence for Athens first. Then we can see whether the more scanty evidence for the rest of Greece suggests that Athens was typical or an exception.

Discussion of schools and schooling in classical Athens inevitably begins with Aristophanes' comedy "the Clouds," in which the "new teaching" (*neos logos*) and the "right teaching" (*orthos logos*)—that is, the traditional education—compete with each other. The "right" teaching describes how things used to be:

> First it was required that no voice of a boy muttering be heard, then the neighborhood boys would march along the streets in good order to the lyre teacher *(kitharistes)*, together in a group and naked, even if it was snowing as thick as flour.
>
> Clouds 964–70

After describing the boys learning traditional hymns together, Aristophanes goes on to describe their time with the physical trainer, but though he chooses to emphasize music and physical training the key point here for our present concern is the suggestion that every neighborhood of Athens had a local school, and that it was the norm for the citizen boys to attend together their neighborhood school. Though Aristophanes' play is a comedy and there is obviously some comic exaggeration here, like the snow "thick as flour," on the whole this passage—addressed to an audience of Athenian citizens who had themselves grown up under the system Aristophanes is satirizing—must be taken seriously.[21] The suggestion that it was the norm for citizen boys to attend school is corroborated by five other sources: four roughly contemporary with Aristophanes (that is to say, late fifth and fourth century) and one much later.

In his dialogue *Krito*, beginning at 50a, Plato offers a kind of imagined discourse between Sokrates and the laws of Athens, in which the laws defend themselves against the charge of having wronged Sokrates. At 50c–e we read:

> first then did we not bring about your birth, and it was through us that your father took your mother and begot you? Say then, is it against those of us that are the laws about marriage that you find some fault as not being good? ... then is it against those concerning your rearing and the education by which you were raised? Did those of us laws established about this not set things up well, directing your father to have you taught *mousike* and *gymnastike*?[22]

Significant here is the statement that Athens had laws which required fathers to provide their sons with an education in *mousike kai gymnastike*—cultural and physical training. This, of course, fits very well with Aristophanes' picture of the boys of every neighborhood being required to march to school together, to be taught by the lyre teacher and the physical trainer; but some scholars nevertheless dismiss this statement as referring not to "statutes" but to mere customary rules, and customary rules affecting only persons of Plato's and Sokrates' social level.[23] This is clearly wrong.

In the first place, one must note the context: were the *nomoi* about marriage also mere social customs rather than "statutes"? We know they were not. In fact, we know of several laws concerning marriage and procreation: there is Perikles' law of *c.* 452 for instance, requiring that to produce legitimate citizen offspring an Athenian citizen man must marry an Athenian woman of citizen family.[24] There are also the laws regarding adultery referenced by Lysias in his speech "On the Killing of Eratosthenes," which were concerned with guarding the sanctity of marriage and the legitimacy of offspring. Why is it then obvious, as Harris claims (see n. 23), that the immediately following *nomoi* about education were not real laws? In context, in fact, they should obviously be read as being just as much real statutes as the laws on marriage. As we shall see below, the orator Aischines referenced detailed laws regarding education, established by the *nomothetes* (law-giver, a conventional way of referring to statutory law), showing that there is nothing in the least implausible about Plato's claim here regarding laws on education at Athens. It should be noted that Plato is suggesting that such laws existed already when Sokrates (born *c.* 469) was a child, so that the laws he referenced would already have existed in the time Aristophanes wrote of in his account in *The Clouds* of the "traditional education."[25] We may also note, for what it's worth, that Plato and Sokrates did not, in any case, belong to the same social class, if the ancient biographical traditions about them have any truth: Plato came from the wealthy aristocratic elite; but Sokrates' father was reputedly a craftsman who worked for a living, a stonemason.[26]

Another very interesting testimony concerning schools is found in Plato's dialogue *Protagoras* at 325d–326c. In this dialogue, as discussed in Chapter 4 above, Protagoras essentially makes the case for democracy, arguing that all men have the basic aptitude for acquiring political excellence (*politike arete*), and that all men begin to hone this aptitude from early childhood through the teaching and admonishing of parents and other adults: what we would call the socialization process. But then, he says: "they (the parents) send them to teachers, laying more emphasis on the teaching of good behavior than on letters or music; and the teachers attend to this, and when they (the children) have learned their letters and are ready to understand the written word as well as previously the spoken, they set before them on their desks poems of great poets and make them learn these poems in which are many examples and stories, eulogies, and panegyrics of the good men of old, so the boy may become eager to imitate them and be like them." Protagoras goes on to talk about the teaching practices of the music teachers and the physical trainers. He does concede that all this is done best (or most: *malista*) by those best able to do it, that is the wealthy, whose sons "begin their education at the earliest age, and continue the longest" (326c), but even in saying this he clearly implies that all Athenians sent their sons to school, though most could not afford the length of schooling that the rich could offer their sons. The point here is that Athenians sent their sons to school as a matter of course, to learn to read and to study the great poems that taught the best examples of how to behave (obviously the Homeric epics). Rich people could afford a more elaborate education for their sons; but all Athenians were expected to get a basic schooling.

In his historical work the *Hellenika* Xenophon describes the brief civil war at Athens in 403 between forces of the so-called "Thirty Tyrants" and democratic rebels led by Thrasyboulos. The fighting took place in the town square (*agora*) of the Peiraieus, and Xenophon recounts (*Hellenika* 2.4.20) how, during a lull in the fighting, a citizen on the pro-democracy side named Kleokritos addressed his fellow citizens urging them to lay down arms and come to a peaceful agreement. As part of his argument, he listed the common experiences that bound Athenians together:

> we have shared with you in the most solemn rites and sacrifices, and in festivals of the fairest: we have danced in the chorus together, gone to school together, been soldiers together. We have undergone many dangers with you both by land and by sea on behalf of the common safety and liberty of us all.

Along with shared religious observances, choral song and dance, and military service, then, going to school together is presented as a common and normal experience shared by men of the citizen class and binding them together. Along with Aristophanes and Plato, this passage clearly indicates that going to school was a normal and expected part of the Athenian citizen boy's upbringing.

In his speech *Against Timarchos* the orator Aischines had some remarks to make about proper education at Athens. What he had to say is remarkable enough to be worth quoting at length (Aischines 1.9):

> First then the *nomothetes* (lawgiver), as to the teachers to whom by necessity we entrust our own sons, whose livelihood comes from being reasonable and distress from the opposite, all the same it seems he lacks trust and he sets out explicitly, first at what hour it is proper that the free-born boy should go to school, then with how many boys he should go and at what time he should leave; and he forbids the teachers to open the schools and the physical trainers the wrestling grounds before the sun has risen, and commands them to close them before the sun goes down, having the greatest suspicion of solitude and the dark.

According to Aischines, then, Athenian law prescribed that "the free-born boy" (*ton paida ton eleutheron*) should attend school; established the hours between dawn and dusk as the proper hours for schooling; and even set limits on how many boys could attend a given school together. Now admittedly some scholars have argued that when Aischines spoke of the "necessity" of entrusting one's sons to teachers, he meant not a legal requirement but simply that, if one wished one's sons to be educated, one had no choice but to entrust them to the school teachers.[27] That is obviously wrong. Aischines was here speaking explicitly of what the law prescribed, and even had the laws in question read out in court (1.11). He was addressing a jury of hundreds of ordinary Athenian citizens and he indicated that they sent their sons to school, for they are included in the "we" who must "entrust our own sons" to the teachers. However, if no law in fact required an Athenian father to send his son to school, then there was no necessity to entrust him to school teachers, for there were other options available in that case: he could forgo schooling entirely; he could see to his son's education himself; or he could hire private tutors for his son, and thus ensure that his son was taught properly. Aischines tells us that Athenian law did establish the necessity of schooling, and one should note that this necessity affected "the free-born boy," that is in principle any and every Athenian citizen boy. All this accords well with the picture set out by Aristophanes, Plato, and Xenophon, and we can conclude that the laws referenced here by Aischines were not new laws of the fourth century, but laws that went back at least to the mid fifth century, though we cannot establish when or by whom in the mid fifth century (or earlier?) these laws were proposed and enacted.[28]

Finally, then, we come to Plutarch, writing certainly many centuries after the fact, but with sources at his disposal that are long lost to us. In his "Life of Themistokles," recounting the Athenian evacuation of Attica in the face of the advancing Persian forces after Thermopylai in 480, he tells us that many of the children of the Athenians were given refuge at Troizen, and that the Troizenians displayed their good will to the Athenians by arranging for the sons of the Athenians to continue their schooling at Troizen at no cost, the Troizenians paying the teachers' fees (Plutarch *Themistokles* 10.3). Since Plutarch names no source for this information, it's hard to know whether it is true: the fact that Plutarch names a sponsor of the Troizenian decree establishing this policy, a certain Nikagoras, speaks in favor of a possible early source, and there are potential sources one could think of—Hellanikos of Lesbos for example, or the Atthidographer Androtion, or even Theopompos of Chios in an excursus in his *Philippika*.[29] The key point for us, though, is simply the underlying assumption behind this anecdote, that Athenian citizen boys of course went to school.

Another anecdote from Plutarch, from his "Life of Alkibiades" is also relevant. Recounting the young Alkibiades' habitual arrogance and wild pranks, Plutarch tells of an occasion when Alkibiades decided to visit schools in Athens to check on the attainments of the teachers: a teacher who had no copy of Homer from which to teach received a blow of the fist; a teacher who had a copy that he had personally corrected received high praise (Plutarch *Alkibiades* 7.1). Again, while we cannot be sure how true this anecdote may be, the point is the underlying assumption that there were many schools at Athens where it was normal for boys to be taught to read.

The clear impression created by these sources, scattershot as they are, is that schools were fairly numerous and ubiquitous at Athens, and that it was normal, even required by law, that Athenian citizen boys should attend school for at least part of their childhood. Visual evidence further strengthens this impression given by the literary sources: we have school scenes depicted on a number of Attic red-figure pots. The most famous is no doubt the cup painted by the well-known red-figure artist Douris around 490, which is now in the Berlin State Museum. Both sides of the cup were decorated with school scenes which well illustrate the teaching of *mousike* at Athenian schools. On each side of the cup we see two boys being taught: on one side a boy is learning to play the lyre while another boy is shown a line of epic poetry on a scroll held open before him by a teacher (see Plate 3); on the other side a boy stands in front of a teacher playing the "flute," perhaps singing a hymn to this musical accompaniment, while another boy stands in front of a teacher who holds a writing tablet on his lap, correcting with a stylus something the boy has written.[30] This cup then, which also depicts musical instruments and writing paraphernalia (a folded tablet, an unopened scroll) hung on the wall, shows clearly that the teaching of lyre playing and *mousike* mentioned by Aristophanes and Plato included lessons in reading and writing, and a number of other vases show similar school scenes or scenes involving the learning of literacy.[31] These early fifth-century red-figure vases show school scenes as a normal part of Athenian life, and thus help to confirm what Aristophanes, Plato, Xenophon, and Aischines tell us. It has been suggested, further, that a room excavated at the *Akademia* gymnasium at Athens served as a school room: several writing tablets were found in the room, including one on which it seems a pupil had practiced writing divine names.[32] The material record thus corroborates what the literary sources tell us about schools and schooling in classical Athens, and in agreement with this is the plentiful evidence we have about reading and writing at Athens. However, before we look into that, what of the rest of Greece?

Arguably the most important single piece of evidence regarding the prevalence of schools in fifth-century Greece is a short passage in the history of Thucydides concerning the small Boiotian community of Mykalessos. Thucydides relates that in 413 a band of Thracian mercenaries arrived at Athens just too late to sail with the relief expedition to Sicily commanded by the general Demosthenes. The expense of paying these Thracians led the Athenians to decide to send them back home, but since they had to be paid during the journey, they were used to mount attacks on various enemy communities on the way. One community attacked by them was Mykalessos where, among other atrocities, the Thracians burst into a boys' school (*didaskaleion paidon*) which happened to be the largest one in the place (*hoper megiston en autothi*), and slaughtered all the boys there (Thuc. 7.29–30). We learn, thus, that in the late fifth century there were, surprisingly, several schools at Mykalessos: the phrase "the largest in the place" must mean that there were at least two schools. Properly analyzed, this evidence has major implications for the diffusion of schools around the classical Greek world, and for the proportion of citizen children, at least male citizen children, who received some schooling outside the home.

Mykalessos, it must be noted, is about as obscure a place as one can find in the Greek civic landscape, at any rate south of Thermopylai and east of Aitolia. It is mentioned a mere handful of times in our ancient sources: besides this passage in Thucydides and a couple of passing mentions in epic poetry—e.g., in Homer's "Catalogue" (*Iliad* 2.498), Statius' *Thebaid* 7.272 and 9.281, and Nonnius' *Dionysiaca* 13.77—its existence was noted only by the geographer Strabo, calling it a village (*kome*) of Tanagra, one of four villages that lay in the territory of Tanagra and were dependencies of Tanagra (9.2.11 and 14); by the travel writer Pausanias, who repeated Thucydides' account more briefly (1.23.3) and noted that the place was abandoned and in ruins in his day (9.19.4); and by such scattershot collectors of oddments as the elder Pliny (*NH* 4.12), the mythographer Apollonios, and various late antique lexicographers and encyclopedists.[33] Though Thucydides called the place a *polis*, he noted its small size twice (7.29.3 and 7.30.3), and most likely means by the word *polis* no more than "town," since as Strabo noted Mykalessos was in fact a dependency of Tanagra—itself not a very large town (see further below on Mykalessos as dependency of Tanagra). Indeed, even the word "town" may be a bit of a misnomer for Mykalessos: it was really not much more than a substantial walled village (*kome* as Strabo called it), with a population scarcely exceeding 1,500 or so, if it was even so large (see below).

It is, consequently, highly revealing to find several schools at Mykalessos. Scholars pessimistic about the degree of literacy to be found in ancient Greece, note the rarity of references to schools in our sources, interpreting that rarity to mean that attendance at schools was not very common.[34] Against this tendency it must be noted that, were it not for Thucydides' chance reference, Mykalessos' multiple schools would be unknown and certainly unsuspected. Since there were several schools at a place like Mykalessos, we can confidently assume that by the late fifth century not only every city-state of note, but even most small towns and substantial villages in the Greek world had a school or schools where the sons of the citizens could learn to read and write.[35] For there is, quite simply, not the faintest reason to regard Mykalessos as being in any way an exceptional place, the sort of place where people would place a higher importance or emphasis on education and literacy than people and communities elsewhere in classical Greece. That is an argument that can be made about Athens, to be sure; but if Mykalessos was in any way unusual, it was for its small size and obscurity, not for any great educational and cultural attainments.

Mykalessos was, in short, the sort of place where education and culture would be more likely to lag behind most city-states than to be at the forefront. Since there were multiple schools at Mykalessos, can it really be doubted that there were numerous schools throughout Boiotia in the larger and more important towns, the likes of Thebes, Plataia, Thespiai, Orchomenos, Tanagra, Lebadeia, Chaironeia, and so on? Can it really be doubted that there must have been plenty of schools in at least the larger Peloponnesian communities too: the likes of Argos, Corinth, Sikyon, Phleious, Mantinea, Tegea, Elis, Epidauros, Troizen, Hermione, Phigaleia, and so on? As it happens, we do not have to rely on probability alone. A casual anecdote in Plutarch's *Themistokles* (10.3) reveals that there were schools at Troizen in 480, as we have seen above: Athenian boys evacuated to Troizen during the Persian occupation of Attike continued their education at these schools free of charge, we are told.[36] Can we really doubt that the Cycladic island states like Naxos, Paros, Tenos, Siphnos, Melos, and the rest had schools? Again, we do not have to rely on mere probability. Another casually preserved snippet, this time from Pausanias (6.9.6–7), reveals that already in the 490s the island of Astypalaia had a large school: the boxer Kleomedes caused its roof to collapse on the approximately sixty boys in the school. Astypalaia is the remotest and rockiest of the Cyclades or Dodecanese—it lies between these two island groups—and consequently one of the poorest and least populated.[37] Like Mykalessos, it will in terms of education and culture have been a follower, not a leader. Can we doubt, finally, that the flourishing cities of Ionia would have had schools? Once more, a few oddments preserved by chance come to our aid. Herodotos 6.72.2 records a disaster that struck the island of Chios in 496, when an earthquake caused a school to collapse killing 119 of the 120 boys learning to read and write (*ta grammata*) there; and Aelian 7.15 preserves record of a school at Mitylene on Lesbos.[38]

Since none of our ancient sources, few and inadequate as they are, had any interest in discussing, let alone listing, the schools to be found in the Greek cities, these stray snippets cannot be dismissed as exceptions but must be read as evidence that schools were a common and widespread feature of Greek urban life by the fifth century: in each anecdote the existence of the school or schools is mentioned quite casually as being in no way remarkable. The cases of small and backward communities like Mykalessos and Astypalaia, and even Troizen, allow us to be quite confident about the ubiquity of schools in the Greek world by the fifth century. There may even have been legislation requiring schooling in some Greek communities outside Athens: we have evidence of a sort regarding Thourioi in Italy, and Krete. Diodoros the Sicilian tells of the foundation of the Athenian-organized panhellenic colony of Thourioi in 444 (Diodoros 12.10–11), and reports that the Thourians commissioned the "best man of those admired for learning" to write laws for the new community, the man chosen being Charondas (Diodoros 12.11.3). In fact Charondas belongs to the later seventh or very early sixth century, as we have seen above; and we learn elsewhere that the lawgiver for Thourioi was in fact the sophist Protagoras.[39] Accepting that the name of the lawgiver is an error by Diodoros does not necessary invalidate the laws mentioned, however: for what it's worth, Diodoros states that a law was established requiring all sons of citizens to learn literacy skills, the school fees to be paid by the community.[40] All readers must judge for themselves how plausible it is that Thourioi had such a law, but in light of the legislation attested at Athens by the mid fifth century it is not inconceivable. Further, the historian Ephoros apparently claimed that Kretan law required boys to be taught literacy, and Herakleides Pontikos seems to confirm this.[41] As uncertain as these two references to legislation requiring education in literacy are, the cumulative evidence for schools around the Greek world is nevertheless strong, and that such legislation could even be suggested in our sources only strengthens it.

But what proportion of citizen boys were educated at these schools? Were they just a minority? The case of Mykalessos is also revealing in this regard. While it is a pity that we do not know the population of the village, the exact number of schools there, or the number of boys attending those schools, we can nevertheless say something about the likely prevalence of school attendance among the citizen boys. I suggested above that the total free population of Mykalessos is unlikely to have exceeded 1,500. How can we determine this?

Though Thucydides casually referred to Mykalessos as a *polis*, he cannot have meant by this that it was a city-state: the evidence of the *Hellenika Oxyrhynchia* is determinative here. In section 19 of this work the author (almost certainly Theopompos of Chios) offered a rather detailed account of the organization of the Boiotian *koinon* of the late fifth and early fourth centuries (447–386 BCE).[42] Boiotia was then divided into eleven parts (*mere*), which are detailed as follows: two parts for the Thebans, and two parts for Plataia with its dependencies Skolos, Erythrai, and Skaphai, then also controlled by the Thebans; two parts for Orchomenos and Hysiai; two parts for Thespiai with Eutresis and Thisbai; one part for Tanagra; one part shared by the Haliartians, Lebedeis, and Koroneians; and one part shared by Akraiphnion, Kopai, and Chaironeia. Altogether seventeen towns are named, including three very small dependencies of Plataia, but in the region of south-eastern Boiotia in which Mykalessos lay, there was only one city to be mentioned, which provided the Boiotarch, the sixty councilors, and the 1,000 hoplites and 100 cavalry for this region: Tanagra. It is absolutely clear from this that in the time Thucydides was writing of, in the later fifth century, Mykalessos was not an independent city-state but a dependent small town or village in the territory of Tanagra.

To estimate its population, one may refer by comparison to Plataia. When the Persians at the time of their invasion of Greece confronted the combined southern Greek army in front of Plataia in 479, Herodotos tells us that 600 Plataian hoplites fought in the battle (Herod. 9.28), and we must certainly assume that some (perhaps another 400 or so?) stayed to protect the city of Plataia: based on *c.* 1,000 hoplites a free adult male population of *c.* 2,500 is a reasonable guess.[43] With women and children, perhaps an overall free population of some 10,000 is plausible for Plataia which, we should bear in mind, was one of the larger cities in Boiotia, one of the few large enough to resist successfully Theban predominance. The Boiotian federal constitution in the *Hellenika Oxyrrhynchia* states that Plataia with its dependencies made up two of the eleven sections into which Boiotia was divided, while Tanagra (with its dependencies) made up only one section, showing that Plataia was significantly larger than Tanagra, and hence a very great deal larger than Tanagra's dependency Mykalessos.[44] It is on that sort of consideration that I believe an upper limit of about 1,500 to be virtually certain for the free population of Mykalessos.

Now of a free population of *c.* 1,500, perhaps as many as 375 could be boys under eighteen.[45] Of course, boys would not be likely to go to school before reaching around seven or eight years of age, nor would most stay at school longer than the few years needed to acquire basic literacy skills—an ability to read fairly well and to write simple messages would suffice. The evidence indicates that non-elite boys would be expected to attend school, on average, for about three years (see n. 53 below), which would mean that perhaps around one sixth to one fifth of the boys would be of an age (around seven to ten) to attend school at any given time: let us say about seventy-five boys. There were several schools for these boys, indicating that many of them must have attended school; Thucydides paints the massacre of the boys in the largest of them as a major disaster for the Mykalessians: his language would be exaggerated indeed if fewer than several dozen boys were affected. All in all, these arguments (speculative as they perforce are) point to the probability that a clear majority of the free-born Mykalessian boys attended school for a few years, arguably indeed almost all of them. And what was the case in this regard at Mykalessos will have been true in all but the most backward regions of Greece. We should bear in mind here the sixty boys attending the school at Astypalaia, and the 120 boys in the school on Chios. The school at Chios was a large one but given the size of Chios there must have been other schools too, so we can't determine from it how many Chiotes would have sent their sons to school, but the Astypalaia school is more informative. Sixty boys representing three age-classes (boys aged *c.* seven or eight to nine or ten) would suggest an overall population group, of which they were the sons, of roughly 1,200 people or so. The population of Astypalaia in the 2011 census was 1,334 people, down from 1,789 in 1951; the ancient population is not likely to have been very much larger, given the aforementioned rockiness, remoteness, and poverty of the island.[46] It seems, then, that the great majority of Astypalaian boys attended school for a few years, based on this evidence.

We should also consider what sort of communities, in socio-economic terms, Mykalessos and Astypalaia formed. Harris, for example, distinguishes between urban dwellers on the one hand—the elite class, artisans, merchants, and technicians of various sorts, in his view—among whom literacy is likely to have been relatively widespread, and a country or rural population, on the other, whom he equates with farmers/peasants and day laborers, who will not have been literate. However, there is, quite simply, no reason to suppose that the vast majority of the Mykalessians were anything other than farmers of one sort or another. Nothing suggests that there was any significant manufacturing or mining or any other economic activity at Mykalessos. The distinction between urban population and farmers is in any case, though valid for the ancient Mediterranean and near eastern world generally, a false one for classical Greece: there is ample evidence to show that the normal pattern was for Greek farmers to live in large villages/towns/cities and to walk or ride out to their farmlands—

which were often small scattered plots—when needed, perhaps staying overnight for shorter or longer periods at particularly busy times, such as during the harvest.[47] That is to say, the Mykalessians who supported several schools and sent their sons to learn basic literacy skills at them were farmers. Again, the same is certainly true of Astypalaia, except that farming on that rocky island was much poorer than in Boiotia, with fishing likely playing a large role. There is no reason to believe that, in the classical Greek city-states, citizens whose livelihood depended on farming were less likely to prize literacy than citizens who lived by other economic activities: for as we shall see, the motives impelling citizens towards acquiring literacy skills were political, not economic in nature. The cases of Mykalessos and Astypalaia suggest, therefore, that by the fifth century schools were widespread throughout the Greek world, even in the smaller and more out-of-the-way towns and islands, even in places where farming and fishing were almost the only economic activities; and that a majority of the males in the citizen class attended schools and acquired at least some reasonable degree of literacy—an ability to read publicly displayed texts and write simple messages, let us say—by doing so.

To be more fully sure about the correctness of that conclusion, however, we need to be able to show that schooling was affordable to the majority of the citizen "class." To begin with, we need to know the likely or actual cost of going to school. Fortunately, this is a topic on which some reliable figures survive. We have inscriptions informing us of the salaries paid to teachers at Greek schools. Admittedly, the inscriptions in question come from a later time period than the one we are concerned with: an inscription from Miletos records the foundation of a school there about 200, and another from Teos tells of a school foundation of around 180. However, there is evidence to suggest that prices and wages had not changed significantly between the fifth and the second centuries, so that the wages paid to teachers in the inscriptions in question can be used as a good indication of likely wages teachers might expect to earn in the fifth century too. The salaries mentioned in these inscriptions are between thirty and fifty drachmas per month, depending on the "task" (that is educational level) to which the teacher is assigned.[48] The evidence that wages did not vary greatly between the fifth and the second centuries comes from a variety of scattershot pieces of data, but the information we have regarding the wages paid to mercenary soldiers is particularly noteworthy: since our sources are very much interested in military matters, and the ability to recruit and/or pay mercenary soldiers was vital to military operations, we hear a good deal about this issue of military pay. It emerges that from the fifth century through the fourth and third and into the second century BCE, there was a great deal of consistency in mercenary pay rates: pay varied between 3 obols and 1 drachma (6 obols) per day, depending on circumstances including, importantly, available finances.[49] Since the pay of mercenary soldiers, who were in a strong position to insist on being paid well, remained essentially constant, we can confidently assume that what was an acceptable salary for teachers in the late third/early second centuries would also have been so in the fifth century.

The salaries mentioned in the Miletos and Teos inscriptions, while they give a good sense of the sort of pay a teacher could hope or strive to attain, were paid from trust funds set up by wealthy benefactors; most school teachers will have been private operators, setting up a school, trying to attract pupils, and making their money by charging each pupil a fee. The question is, then, how many pupils might a school teacher be likely to have, and how much would he need to charge each pupil on a monthly basis to make a reasonable salary, in the range that is indicated by the inscriptions adduced above.[50] We have seen that the school mentioned at Astypalaia had some sixty pupils attending it on the day of the disaster, but we are not told how many teachers were present. If I am right to suggest that the number of boys who might theoretically be seeking an education at any one time at Mykalessos would be in the range of seventy-five or so, then two schools there would each likely have had between twenty-five and fifty pupils, with one of them apparently attracting more than the other according to Thucydides' testimony. A monthly fee of between 6 and 9 obols would provide a teacher with around thirty pupils a monthly salary in the 30 to 50 drachma range that the Teos and Miletos inscriptions indicate. A teacher attracting fewer than thirty students might have to get by with a somewhat lower wage; a teacher who could attract more than thirty students could do very well. If the school at Astypalaia had only one teacher, he will have done very well from his sixty pupils even if he charged a relatively low fee: just 4 obols per pupil/month would have netted him 40 drachmas per month. On the other hand, at 1 drachma per month (6 obols), the school would have provided salaries of 30 drachmas each for two teachers. We may well wonder how many pupils a teacher might have been able or likely to teach at one time. Here, comparative evidence can be of aid.

One-room schools, in which children of various ages and levels were taught together by a single teacher, were extremely common in Europe from the seventeenth century until well into the nineteenth and early twentieth centuries, mostly of course in rural areas; the same is true of the USA in the eighteenth, nineteenth, and early twentieth centuries. We have, as a result, abundant testimony as to how the one room school functioned, including how many students a teacher could handle. It was not at all unusual for a teacher to cope with forty or more students at a time, and cases of teachers having fifty or more students are not unknown. The older, more advanced students helped to maintain discipline, and to teach the younger less advanced students.[51] It is therefore entirely conceivable that the school on Astypalaia, with its *c.* sixty students (the number is obviously rounded, and probably rounded up), could have been run by a single teacher; the school on Chios with upwards of 120 boys would have needed no more than two teachers, in all likelihood. In fact, the anecdotal evidence, like Plutarch's story of Alkibiades visiting schools in Athens, seems to assume a single teacher per school as the norm. As pointed out above, any school with thirty or more students could provide a teacher with an adequate income at a cost of no more than 1 drachma per student per month, and schools of twenty or so students would still have been viable.

From all this it is clear that the cost of schooling was far from prohibitive in classical Greece. In an economic environment in which an income of 30 or more drachmas per month was readily attainable by poorer families of the so-called "working class," and enabled them to live in reasonable comfort able to have some disposable income for a few luxuries, spending about one drachma each month (in some cases less) on a son's education was perfectly feasible, if there was sufficient motivation to do so.[52] So we need to consider what sort of motivation there may have been, impelling citizens of the middling and poorer elements in the Greek city-states to spend part of their disposable income on sending their sons to school for several years: three years of schooling beginning at about age seven was standard for all but the elite, according to the literary sources, and this seems to be corroborated by the school inscription from Teos, which divides the teaching into a first, a second, and a third "task" which can be taken to represent three years of expected learning.[53] The relevant motivation is not in fact hard to pinpoint. It is to be found in the collective governance systems in the Greek city-states described in the previous chapter, systems of governance which were directly participatory.

Citizens who could be expected to participate in collective discussion and debate of proposed laws, treaties, diplomatic correspondence, policies, and so on, and to cast informed votes on these matters, needed to be able to inform themselves. The relevant information was, for the most part, publicly displayed in written form as we have seen in Chapter 4 above, and it was the need to be able to read all those public notices that provided the motivation for citizen boys to go to school and learn to read. It has sometimes been imagined that only a relatively few citizens actually needed to be able to read, and they would then read out the notices to their illiterate fellow citizens: one might imagine Greek citizens in front of public notices being like the illiterate animals of George Orwell's *Animal Farm* in front of the barn wall with their rules inscribed on it, relying on the donkey Benjamin to read out to them what was written there.[54] This notion seems to me to misunderstand ancient Greek culture in a fundamental way. The Greeks were a highly competitive people, a trait imbued in their culture by the great "teachers of the Greeks" Homer and Hesiod. Homer's Greek warriors strove to be the best, and to display their *arete* (excellence) in competitive fighting and athletic displays. Hesiod emphasized the good kind of *eris* (strife) found among the middling element of society: potter striving with potter and smith with smith to be the best, the most successful. The ideal constantly trumpeted in our Greek sources is self-sufficiency (*autarkeia*) with every man running his own life and his own affairs, standing on his own two feet, so far as possible dependent on no one. The notion that in such a society Greek citizens would have been happy to be dependent on a fellow citizen to read for them in public is frankly absurd.

To stand in front of a public notice board, needing to access the information displayed there in order to be able to participate actively in the duties and privileges of citizenship, but unable actually to read the notice and so having to call on a better prepared fellow citizen to read out the notice to him: such a situation would not have been tolerable to most Greek citizens. It would have placed the illiterate citizens in a position of dependency and inferiority, exactly the position that Greeks loathed to be in. One could retreat from active citizenship, from being a councilor, or holding a magistracy of any sort, or attending assemblies in any but the most passive way, and some poorer citizens clearly did this.[55] However, the desire to participate as a citizen was great, and so was the expectation that citizens would inform themselves and participate. As Thucydides has Perikles famously say in his Funeral Oration: "we do not say that a man who keeps out of public affairs minds his own business, we say that he has no business being here at all."[56] In sum, the social pressure on citizens to be able to read was clearly considerable and the desire not to be found to be less than one's citizen peers added a personal motivation to it. This is what impelled Greek citizens to spend some small part of their disposable income on sending their sons to school, to learn at least basic literacy skills: an ability to write simple messages, and an ability to read the public notices that informed the political process. These notices were phrased invariably in highly formulaic language, with a limited and conventional vocabulary, for a reason: they were intended to be read by average citizens. It remains, then, to consider the evidence that citizens really did read and write.

The Evidence for Reading and Writing

In the opening section of his play *The Acharnians*, Aristophanes depicts the play's protagonist Dikaiopolis sitting on the Pnyx hill, overlooking the town square (*agora*) of Athens, waiting for an assembly of the citizens to begin. Dikaiopolis describes his impatience and boredom at the delayed start of the assembly, and in the midst of a list of things he does to relieve his boredom lets drop an interesting word: *grapho*—I write. It is a seemingly innocuous, passing reference of no great importance, until one looks carefully into the context of the statement: then it begins to assume great significance. To begin with, one must note that Athenian comedy is not an elite form of entertainment, but a popular one. Performed in public for the entertainment of audiences of thousands of ordinary Athenian citizens, comedy necessarily reflected the ideas and experiences of the Athenian citizenry at large. Further, Dikaiopolis is explicitly presented not as an elite Athenian but as a rather ordinary middling sort of Athenian, a small farmer who longs for the peaceful rustic pursuits of his farm in the Attic countryside. Describing how he copes with his boredom during his lonely vigil on the Pnyx, Dikaipolis lists a series of mundane actions he engages in: "I sigh, I yawn, I stretch, I fart, I fidget, I write, I pluck hairs, I count" (*Acharnians* 30–1). The act of writing is thus placed on a level with the most mundane imaginable, almost reflexive physical actions like yawning and stretching. Aristophanes here says that to the average middling Athenian citizen, scribbling something while bored is not just a possible activity, but as natural and expected an activity as sighing or farting. Any Athenian, that is, knows how to write and does so as a matter of course.

This is not the only time Aristophanes mentions writing as something an ordinary Athenian citizen does. Another middling, not particularly cultured sort of Athenian citizen is shown writing: Mnesilochos in the play *The Thesmophoriazousai*. Captured while masquerading as a woman at the women-only festival of the *Thesmophoria*, Mnesilochos is held under arrest while the authorities are notified. Pondering a means of escape, he hits on the notion of writing messages asking for help on wooden statuettes, and casting them into the streets for passersby to find and read. It might be protested that as a relative of Euripides, Mnesilochos should be seen as coming from the more cultured and educated section of Athenian society, but not so: he is deliberately depicted as a rather rude and ignorant fellow, a middling type at best. And in any case Aristophanes was frequently at pains to suggest that Euripides himself did not come from an elite family, alleging that his mother ran a vegetable stall in the market.[57] Again, therefore, we see writing shown as something the average sort of Athenian routinely does.

But was Aristophanes here engaging in comedic fantasy? Thanks to the work of the epigraphist Merle K. Langdon we can state unequivocally that he was not. Over the course of more than forty years of study, Langdon has discovered, studied, and revealed to us a wealth of archaic rock-cut graffiti from the Attic countryside that attest an ability to write, and a habit of writing, among ordinary Athenians, many of whom were just shepherds and goatherds. For example, Langdon found about fifty graffiti inscribed into a rock face on the hill of Barako in the Vari plain, some 20 km. south of Athens. Among these graffiti was the following: "I am a memorial (*mnema*) of -sthinos the shepherd (*poimai[nontos]*)"; and at least one other graffito here also referred to shepherds.[58] Dating such inscriptions can be difficult, but among them was one that clearly belongs to the sixth century BCE: a nicely inscribed alphabet, cut retrograde and including the archaic letters digamma, qoppa, and san. Since the style of inscribing retrograde and the three letters just mentioned were not used in Attic inscriptions in the fifth century and later, that inscription must be early, and so it seems were many of the other graffiti found with it.[59] Some of these rural graffiti were erotic in inspiration: for example, Langdon found on a slope of Mt. Hymettos near Argyroupolis the words, inscribed *c.* 500 BCE, *Aithonides kalos katapugon hekon*—in English as colloquial as the Greek "Aithonides is handsome and likes it up the ass";[60] which is comparable to a graffito found in the Athenian *agora* reading "*Titas oly<m>pionikos katapugon*"—that is "Titas the olympic victor takes it up the ass," or perhaps rather "Titas is an olympic victor at taking it up the ass."[61]

What we have, in other words, is ordinary Athenians finding themselves at a loose end out in the countryside, some of them herding sheep or goats, whiling away their time and relieving their boredom by scratching words on nearby rock-faces. Often this was simply in the form of recording their names, sometimes boasting of sexual conquests or making sexual innuendos, often just practicing the alphabet. And this is just the practice Aristophanes referred to in the *Acharnians*: an ordinary Athenian relieving boredom by doing a bit of writing. It should be emphasized that with shepherds and the like we are not dealing with elite literacy or even "craftsman's literacy": we find that the ability to write extended far down the social scale. Another similar form of evidence is the practice of writing curse tablets: many Greeks, apparently from all levels of society, wrote curses against rivals and enemies, often on pieces of lead, and deposited them in wells or on graves in the hope that the underworld powers would effectuate the curse.[62] Here again we see ordinary citizens using writing for personal reasons. Further, as to Mnesilochos writing messages on wooden statuettes, we may compare a message written on a broken cup-base and found in the Athenian *agora*: "Thamneus : place : under the threshold of the garden gate: the saw."[63] There is, we can see, nothing implausible about ordinary citizens communicating by way of written messages on whatever item came to hand. And this is not limited to Athens and Attica.

One of the most common forms of ancient Greek graffiti is the so-called abecedarium, that is the writing out of all or part of the alphabet. This can be regarded in part as practice writing: at times we find two alphabets written out together, and can conjecture that one is a model written by a teacher, the other a copying out of that model. On the other hand, writing out the alphabet, or part of it, may simply be a way of relieving boredom: many modern people must have the experience, as I certainly do, of doodling the alphabet while bored at a lecture or meeting of some sort. If we try to imagine what Aristophanes' character Dikaiopolis wrote when he was bored on the Pnyx, and had finished stretching and yawning, the alphabet is the most likely answer. Graffiti alphabets are found from many locations and times, and have recently been studied by William West: examples are known from the eighth century—the very beginning of Greek writing—as well as the seventh, sixth, fifth, and fourth centuries and on into Hellenistic and Roman times. West focused on the archaic examples, and presents a tabulated list of such abecedaria from all around the Greek world.[64] And just as abecedaria are found all around the Greek world, so are graffiti recording names, and erotic graffiti.[65] These graffiti alphabets and so on make it absolutely clear that the skill and habit of writing was found throughout classical Greece, and in various strata of society, even if that skill did not go much beyond practicing the alphabet and/or writing one's name.

The best known example of writing by ordinary citizens is found in the well-known Athenian political institution of ostracism.[66] This institution was in use intermittently through the fifth century: each year in the sixth prytany (around January or early February) an assembly was asked if there was a citizen they wished to remove from Athens for a period of ten years; if the answer was in the affirmative, a special assembly was held two months later at which citizens voted for whom they wished to remove by scratching names on pieces of broken pottery (the scrap paper of the ancient world) and handing them in as votes. A minimum of 6,000 votes had to be cast for an ostracism to occur, either in total or for the candidate to be removed.[67] That is to say, this institution required thousands of Athenians to be able to write another citizen's name. Excavations in the Athenian *agora* and in the Kerameikos cemetery have uncovered some 11,000 to 12,000 actual *ostraka*, most of them with the names of men we know to have been ostracized, but many with other names, some of them completely unknown to us (see ill. 4 for some examples). Many are very well and regularly written, with good orthography and spelling; many more are very poorly written, with letters badly formed and names oddly spelled.[68] These *ostraka* provide clear evidence that thousands of Athenians were able to write at least well enough to participate in the process of ostracism: the minimum quorum of 6,000 votes would suggest that many more than that number were known or confidently expected to be able to write. Because, of course, one could not expect precisely those 6,000 Athenians who knew how to write to always show up: a quorum of 6,000 suggests that likely at least twice as many Athenians could write well enough to participate if they felt so inclined, and most likely many more.[69]

To be sure, it could be suggested that illiterate Athenians did participate, their votes being written for them by literate fellow citizens, even perhaps by scribes who made themselves available for the purpose. An anecdote from Plutarch's *Life of Aristides* (ch. 7) is often brought up: at Aristides' ostracism in 483/2, we are told, an illiterate fellow citizen got Aristides to write his own name on an *ostrakon* for him. However, before we take this to be a commonly occurring phenomenon, a few points need to be made. This is actually the only attested case of an illiterate citizen getting someone to write his vote for him, for a start; secondly, the point of Plutarch's anecdote is not to suggest that many citizens were illiterate, but that many citizens were envious of Aristides' reputation for justice, and to highlight Aristides' good nature in willingly writing his own name down and contributing thus to his own ostracism; thirdly, Plutarch explicitly reports that the citizens wrote on their *ostraka* themselves, and treats the illiterate citizen as very much an exception—an altogether rustic fellow (*tina pantelos agroikon*), as he puts it. More to the point than the unusual "rustic and unlettered fellow," then, is Plutarch's description of the procedure: "each man, taking an *ostrakon* and writing down whichever of the citizens he wished to remove, brought it (the *ostrakon*) to the marked off place in the *agora*" (*Aristides* 7.4; and see n. 66 above).

One other piece of evidence is sometimes thought to be an indication of illiterate citizens voting: archaeologists discovered in a well on the north slope of the Acropolis a deposit of some 190 inscribed *ostraka* which, on careful examination, were seen by the orthography to have been inscribed by only fourteen writers.[70] One could imagine scribes of good will making themselves available in this way—or perhaps being made available at public expense—to produce votes for illiterate citizens. One would be wrong to do so: if that were the case, the *ostraka* would have borne the names of a variety of candidates for ostracism, but in fact they all bear only one name—Themistokles. This is clearly a case of a form of electioneering. A group of citizens eager to ostracize Themistokles evidently got together in advance to produce a large number of *ostraka* with Themistokles' name, intending to persuade citizens to vote for Themistokles by handing them pre-prepared *ostraka*. It seems they overestimated Themistokles' unpopularity, since they were left with nearly 200 *ostraka* on their hands, and were reduced to dumping them in an unused well. Rather than telling us something about citizens' lack of writing skills, therefore, this find actually shows us that Athenian "electioneering" practices were already quite sophisticated in the early fifth century.[71]

The practice of ostracism, then, is strong evidence that many thousands of ordinary Athenian citizens had enough knowledge of writing to be able to scratch another citizen's name onto a piece of broken pottery, however inexpertly in some cases. Nor can we conclude that this is a proof of Athenian exceptionalism: we know that a number of other Greek city-states practiced a form of ostracism. Diodoros of Sicily reports that the Syracusans, during their democratic regime in the mid to late fifth century, conducted ostracisms using olive leaves (*petala*) to write their votes on, rather than bits of broken pottery, so that the practice was called *petalismos*.[72] Aristotle reports that the Argives conducted ostracisms (*Politika* 1302b.18–19), and we also hear of ostracisms at Megara and Miletos. Archaeologists have in fact found a few inscribed *ostraka*, very similar to those found at Athens, at Argos and Megara; and in addition such *ostraka* have been found at the Greek city of Cyrene in north Africa, and at Chersonesos Taurikos in the Crimea.[73] Clearly we are dealing here with a very widespread phenomenon: in addition to Athens we have two cities from the Peloponnesos, one from Ionia, and three far-flung colonial cities. Also, we cannot assume that these were the only cities to practice ostracism, that evidence happens to have survived from every ostracizing city; rather, inadequate as our evidence is, we must assume that many other cities did so for which no evidence has survived. This case of ostracism thus shows that the ability of thousands of citizens to write simple messages was a common attainment in the Greek cities of the classical era.

We might wonder how reformers like Kleisthenes and his associates, in establishing the system of ostracism, knew that thousands of ordinary citizens were capable of writing on *ostraka* and making the system work. Here too there is archaeological evidence that shows that such reformers had practical evidence of this ability. Pieces of broken pottery were not used only for the political purpose of ostracism, nor were they first written on when Kleisthenes instituted ostracism. In the 1930s, Carl Blegen and Rodney Young excavated a small rural sanctuary of Zeus just below the top of Mt. Hymettos. Among the finds were nearly 200 pottery fragments with writing on them. Only a relatively few were well enough preserved that the message written could be clearly understood, and Blegen and Young published these, but a full treatment of all of the inscribed fragments had to wait until 1976, when Merle Langdon published them with a commentary.[74] The pots in question here were very plain, undecorated, simply glazed, inexpensive vessels, primarily *skyphoi* (drinking cups) and one-handled cups of the so-called "Phaleron" type, belonging to the seventh century. The graffiti incised on them, sometimes on the inside surface showing the cup was already broken when inscribed, can be dated by letter forms and other indications to the seventh and very early sixth centuries: for example, about half of the readable inscriptions were written right to left, a clear indication of early date.[75] The legible graffiti are mostly either dedicatory, usually mentioning Zeus, the god of the sanctuary, or abecedaria and *egraphsen* (i.e., "So-and-so wrote me") inscriptions, or just names, though there is at least one erotic graffito preserved (no. 36 in the collection).

Dedications of writing on pieces of broken cheap drinking vessels at an out-of-the-way rural sanctuary do not at all suggest elite activity. We seem here to be dealing with ordinary rural Athenians, with obvious implications for the spread and prevalence of literacy already by the seventh century. As Langdon notes (p. 49): "it would surely be wrong to believe that they (the Hymettos graffiti) formed, when dedicated, a unique group of documents. They must instead be representative of the fairly wide extent of literacy which developed during the first century after the introduction of the alphabet." Langdon goes so far as to suggest, based on the evidence of these graffiti dedications, that as many as half of all Athenian citizens were literate by the end of the seventh century. That may be difficult to believe before the introduction of schools in the later sixth century; but we do clearly see that a great many Athenians, including non-elite rural Athenians, could read and write and used bits of broken pottery to write simple texts already during the seventh and early sixth centuries. That is to say, Kleisthenes and his associates had very good reason to believe that the institution of ostracism, requiring thousands of Athenian citizens to be able to write for it to be effective, was a perfectly feasible practice.[76]

A point well made by Harris in his book on literacy is that the active skill of writing well is likely to have been a rarer attainment than the essentially passive skill of reading well.[77] When we see that thousands of citizens in most (if not all) cities could write, even if only in a basic simple way, we can undoubtedly assume that many more thousands could read reasonably well, but what sort of reading might they engage in? Plato, in his *Apology of Sokrates* (at 26d–e), has Sokrates claim that any Athenian could go down to the *orchestra*, referring presumably to the open space in the center of the *agora*, and buy the books of Anaxagoras of Klazomenai—the noted physical philosopher—for no more than a drachma.[78] Many Athenians would have been able to afford that cost, but is it likely that anyone outside the cultural elite would have bought such a book? We can't say for sure, but it's worth noting that Plato clearly stated that it was insulting to the jurymen of Athens, who we know were mostly middling and poorer citizens, to suggest they were too illiterate to know what was in Anaxagoras' books.[79] We are told that many copies of the books of Protagoras—the famous sophist—were confiscated at Athens and publicly burned (the first recorded book burning in western history) because of Protagoras' professed skepticism about the existence of the gods. We may conjecture that most of these books will have belonged to elite Athenians, but we cannot actually know that, and if Plato was honest in suggesting that middling Athenians were reading Anaxagoras, they may have read Protagoras too.[80] The claim that books were readily purchasable in the *agora* of Athens at the relatively affordable price of "no more than a *drachma*" does hint at a reading public large enough to make some sort of "publishing" business possible, with economies of scale making the books inexpensive.

However, an interest in reading literary texts, or books, must surely have been a minority interest even at the height of classical Athens, let alone the rest of Greece. The desire to read stemmed, as I have argued, from the need of the citizen to be informed by reading public notices, and even beyond the political context, most reading will surely have focused on much shorter and simpler texts: documents related to one's business or craft; simple messages about everyday life; graffiti of various sorts; and so on. The most important evidence of reading concerns such activities, above all the reading of public notices of the sort discussed in the previous chapter. Beyond those political notices, there were other kinds of publicly displayed texts that clearly expected to be and must have been read: public dedications referencing notable achievements, and clearly aimed at spreading and perpetuating the fame of those achievements, and epitaphs on grave stones which, frequently, directly address the passerby demanding to be read. The latter phenomenon is well known and frequently commented on for the way it turns the memorial stones themselves into "speaking objects" (*ogetti parlanti*), as if the stone itself literally addresses the reader.[81] Actually, of course, it was not the stone that spoke, but the reader, voicing the text as he read it, and thereby lending his voice to the mute stone. But it remains the case that the inscribed stone "spoke" to the passerby, and demanded to be read.

The most famous example of the memorial addressing the onlooker is no doubt the epigram, perhaps composed by the great poet Simonides, that was inscribed on the memorial of the Spartans who died at Thermopylai:

> Oh stranger, report to the Lakedaimonians that here
> we lie, obeying their commands.
>
> Herodotos 7.228

The stranger (*xeinos*) who comes along and looks at the monument is thus appealed to bear witness to the obedience of the men who gave their lives; if the passerby cannot in fact read the epigram, it fails of its purpose. Why should we suppose that the Spartans were wrong to assume that most passersby would be able and willing to read what was written? The same appeal to the passerby who stops to look is made in the epitaph for the Corinthians who died in the battle of Salamis:

> Oh stranger, once we inhabited the well-watered town of Corinth,
> but now Salamis, the island of Ajax, holds us.
>
> Plutarch *de mal. Herod.* 39

Not all Greek memorial epigrams addressed the onlooker quite so directly, it's true; but the basic aim of the epigrams, that is the inscribed notices on the memorial monuments, was always to inform the onlooker about the purpose of the memorial, and to preserve in that way the memory of the memorialized and their deeds. It was their purpose, that is to say, to be read.

The same kind of addressing of the passerby/onlooker is found in private epitaphs too. For example, a very early grave epigram from Attica, dated *c.* 575–550, memorialized a certain Tettichos with the following words:

> Whether a citizen man or a stranger coming from elsewhere,
> pass by with pity for Tettichos, a good man
> who died in war, losing the flower of his youth;
> lamenting this, move on to some good deed.
>
> *CEG* 13

Notable here is that the epitaph does not just address the onlooker, it instructs him: to pass by with pity, to lament Tettichos' fate, and to take from this example the lesson to achieve some good in life. Another early epitaph from Attica, dating from *c.* 535, adorned a statue base which may well have held the famous *kouros*

Anavyssos statue, and memorialized a young Athenian aristocrat with these words:

> Stand and show pity at the memorial of dead Kroisos
> whom once raging Ares destroyed among the forefighters.
>
> CEG 27

The imperatives found here—"stand and show pity" (*stethi kai oiktiron*)—are found in other grave epitaphs too, for example in *CEG* 28 from the Kerameikos in Athens for one Thrason c. 535. In some cases, the epitaph on the stone actually assumes the voice of the onlooker speaking the words as he reads, as in *CEG* 51 from the Kerameikos (*c*. 510):

> I lament beholding this memorial of the dead youth
> Smikythos, who destroyed the good hope of his friends.

In its simplest form, the epitaph simply speaks to the onlooker without making further demands on him: "I am the *stele* of Xenwares son of Meixis, at his tomb" (*CEG* 146 from Corcyra *c*. 560). In all such cases, the words of the epitaph clearly expect to be read, and indeed lose their point if they were not read. It is no accident that such tombs and epitaphs were often located along exit roads from cities, where they would be seen, and thus potentially read, by many.[82]

We should note further the report that at Sparta, only men who died in battle and women who died in childbirth were permitted gravestones inscribed with their names.[83] Here again, the clear presumption is that persons looking at these gravestones would read the inscribed names: what else was the point of inscribing them? There would be no functional difference between an inscribed and an uninscribed gravestone if no one (or virtually no one) could read the inscribed names. The point of permitting the name on the gravestone was to preserve memory of the deceased, to guarantee him or her lasting fame because of the nature of their deaths. That aim was only achieved if onlookers read those names, and this practice thus assumes a widespread ability and willingness to read. In a similar vein, one can mention the Athenian commemoration of war dead: their names were prominently inscribed in the great public cemetery in the Kerameikos region of Athens, and again the aim to glorify those who died fighting for Athens and preserve their memory was only attained if Athenian citizens, and other visitors, could actually read the inscribed names. Even more so is this true of the men who died at the glorious battle of Marathon, in 490, fighting off the Persian invading force. Uniquely, these men were all interred together at the site of the battle and a huge mound—the *Soros,* which can still be seen prominently in the plain of Marathon today—was built up over them. On top of this mound was placed a public memorial, a prominent feature of which was an inscription listing the glorious war dead.

The most obvious case of the public dedication advertising achievement is the statue set on an inscribed base. That these statues were intended to impress and inform the viewer, and thus perpetuate the fame of the person depicted, who dedicated the statue, and his (or at times her) achievements, is obvious. In the words of the noted scholar Brunilde Ridgway "a certain consideration for the viewer must have underscored every dedication, as suggested by the many inscriptions phrased as if the statue itself were addressing the passerby."[84] Further, though not exactly common, it was by no means unknown for the sculptor to sign the statue (or rather have a stonecutter inscribe his name on it) as a means of advertising his name and skill.[85] This can be set beside the very well-known phenomenon of Greek potters and/or vase painters signing their work with the standard formula "So-and-so made me" (*epoiesen*) or "painted me" (*egrapsen*). The clearest case of the quest for perpetuation of fame by the setting up of an inscribed statue is to be found in the description of the numerous statues of victorious athletes dedicated at Olympia, as described by Pausanias. In bk. 6 of his work he reports on many of these statues, frequently referring specifically to the inscriptions on them and the information contained there. For example at 6.2.9 Pausanias wrote:

> The inscription on the Samian boxer says that his trainer Mycon dedicated the statue and that the Samians are best among the Ionians for athletes and at naval warfare; this is what the inscription says.

The intention that the inscription should be read and inform the viewer, and that it actually was read, could not be clearer, and with it is made explicit the very strong expectation of those who dedicated such inscribed statues, at considerable expense, that the passersby viewing them would read them and so be informed, and that the fame of the dedicator would thus be preserved.

Finally, one may mention again the display in the *agora* of Athens of notices on whitened boards at the monument of the tribal heroes. Attested from about 430, but surely already used earlier, these boards displayed lists of citizens being called up for military duty, laws to be debated and voted on at upcoming assembly meetings, and other notices of similar public concern. It is in this case indisputable that the boards were intended to be read and actually were read. Some scholars who are skeptical about widespread literacy do, to be sure, doubt that very many citizens could read these notices for themselves, but there is simply no good evidence to warrant such skepticism. On any day when such notices were displayed there must have been a constant stream of citizens passing through the *agora* pausing to read them. Given the ancient Greek habit of reading out loud, rather than silently to oneself, it is possible that some citizens could listen in to a fellow citizen reading, though that's not to say they read such texts out loud deliberately for the benefit of other citizens, of course (see above p. 160). However, would citizens really have stood in front of the boards patiently reading out long and rather boring texts, such as lists of hundreds or thousands of names for military/naval duty for example? That is rather hard to imagine. Surely citizens—almost any and every citizen—had to be expected to be able to find and read their own names on such lists. The whitened boards, and other such ephemeral public notices both in Attica and elsewhere in other Greek cities, are a sure indication of citizens reading, that is to say.

A very interesting literary attestation of the use of reading and writing in early fifth-century Greece is provided by a well-known anecdote in Herodotos' *Histories*, where he tells the story of the Greek fleet's retreat from Artemision in northern Euboia after the Persians had captured the pass at Thermopylai. A substantial portion of the "Persian" fleet was made up of ships and men from the Ionian Greek cities, and as Herodotos tells the story the Athenian commander Themistokles left a message for these fellow Greeks (Herodotos 8.22):

> Selecting the best sailing ships of the Athenians, Themistokles sailed around to the places where there was drinking water, cutting letters into the rocks. These the Ionians read when they arrived at Artemision the next day. The letters read as follows.

Herodotos went on to quote verbatim a rather long and detailed text that Themistokles supposedly had inscribed. There are some problems with this story: the text quoted by Herodotos seems too long and complex to have been incised into rock faces, as has been pointed out;[86] and in any case no such inscribed texts have ever been found on the rock-faces around Artemision. That need not mean that the story is entirely untrue, however: Herodotos was writing forty or so years after the event, and we are all familiar with the tendency of such stories to be "improved" in the process of telling and re-telling over time. If Themistokles really set up such texts for the Ionian sailors and rowers to read, they were more likely painted onto the rocks—a much quicker and simpler process—and the message was no doubt briefer, simpler, and more pointed than what Herodotos quotes.

However, whether this actually happened or not is almost irrelevant to what the story tells us about Greek literacy: either Themistokles himself or Herodotos' informant(s) considered it entirely likely that ordinary Ionian sailors and rowers would be willing and able to read a text left behind for them on rock faces, and Herodotos and his readers found this notion perfectly plausible too. I see no reason to doubt them: it would be rather odd for modern scholars to fancy they have a better idea of the reading skills of fifth-century Ionian Greeks than their fellow fifth-century Greeks like Herodotos, his informant(s), and his readers had. We know, as discussed above, that the mainland and island Ionian communities had schools by the beginning of the fifth century, where literacy skills were taught; we know that a large percentage of the boys on the remote and rocky island of Astypalaia, at least, attended school; and there is no reason to think Astypalaia more advanced than other Ionian communities in this regard, if anything the opposite. In sum, there really can be no good reason to doubt that Themistokles and/or Herodotos' informant(s) knew their business: this story attests to widespread literacy among the Ionian Greeks.

Altogether then, the evidence that Greeks from the seventh century on practiced reading and writing in considerable numbers, and that by the fifth century a considerable majority of the citizens in the more advanced city-states could read and write at least well enough to write simple messages and read public notices, is cumulatively very strong. I would go so far as to suggest that in fifth- and fourth-century Athens, at any rate, there was something approaching universal literacy of that sort among the adult male citizens, thanks to a network of schools that were publicly regulated, at which attendance by citizen boys was socially and perhaps legally expected, and attendance at which for some three years was affordable for all but the very poorest citizen families.[87] How similar to Athens other Greek city-states were in this regard is hard to judge, but the evidence for such things as schools, public notices, the practice of ostracism, and so on suggests that many were in fact not far behind Athens. This is to say that, as suggested at the start of this chapter, with the classical Greek city-states we are dealing with a society in which mass literacy had been attained, among citizen males at any rate: the first mass literate society we know of.

Finally, reinforcing this, we may consider a saying quoted by Plato in his *Laws* at 3.689d as a way of expressing great ignorance: "they know neither letters nor how to swim." This is introduced by Plato as a *legomenon*, that is as something commonly said; yet it has been taken as expressing merely the snobbery of the upper class. As Harris puts it in his book *Ancient Literacy*, with reference to this saying: "there was a social perspective at Athens from which illiteracy seemed disgraceful, and the arch-elitist (i.e., Plato) naturally shared it."[88] There is a modern saying that is relevant here: context is everything. Are we really to conclude that knowing how to swim was an elite attainment, and that elites expressed their snobbery by saying of poorer folk "he doesn't know how to swim"? Because literacy and swimming are placed together in this saying, as skills that everyone ought to have: one cannot just cherry-pick the literacy part of the saying and treat it in isolation. The Greek city-states were almost all at or very close to the coast, or on islands; traveling by boat or ship was the cheapest and most convenient way of going from place to place and very many city-state Greeks certainly made at least occasional sea-voyages, even if quite short ones;[89] and in city-states like Athens in particular, the obligation of rowing the fleet meant that all able-bodied poor citizens spent time at sea.[90] Spending time at sea in antiquity always carried with it the very real possibility of shipwreck, and knowing how to swim was thus a matter of life and death. We should therefore take literally the implication of this saying that almost all Greeks knew how to swim as a matter of course. The same goes, inevitably, for knowledge of reading and writing. Our ancient evidence is really clear and unequivocal: knowing how to read and write was common knowledge in classical Greece in the same way that knowing how to swim was, or as Aristophanes put it in his *Acharnians*, as we have seen, writing was much the same sort of reflexive activity to a Greek as yawning or stretching.

Conclusion: The Literate Citizen

The reality that the classical Greek city-states constituted the first mass literate society in known human history has enormous consequences for our understanding of Greek city-state culture, the culture produced by and for the literate male citizens who were the core of the Greek city-states socially and politically. This will be discussed in full in the overall conclusion to this book, but it's worth noting here that growing up literate causes humans to perceive and understand reality in a different way than do non-literate peoples, as the work of neuro-scientists like Merlin Donald and Maryanne Wolf has demonstrated.[91] What has been shown in this chapter is that city-state Greeks grew up literate, or at any rate a considerable majority of them did. The development and spread of the Greek alphabet after about 800 made this possible; the establishment of collective governing systems with their need for informed citizens made widespread literacy desirable, even necessary; the spread of schools in the sixth and fifth centuries offering an affordable education in basic literacy to children of the citizen "class," with some communities like Athens actually requiring schooling, made widespread literacy a reality; and the scattered but widespread evidence of the normality of reading and writing demonstrates that it was indeed a reality. The citizens of the Greek city-states were, that is to say, the first humans that we know of to perceive the world, *en masse*, in the new way that literacy, and its effects upon the human brain and consciousness, brought about.

One concomitant or effect of this new reality of mass literacy was no doubt precisely the further entrenchment of the collective governance system in which mass literacy had begun to develop, and indeed its further development into the radical democracy characteristic of Athens from the mid fifth century onwards. It was no accident that in the course of the fourth century, as mass literacy became more widespread, Athenian style democracy also spread throughout the Greek world, and came to be seen (though inevitably in somewhat watered down form) as the only proper and acceptable governing system for a self-respecting Greek city-state.[92] That is to say, citizenship and literacy went hand in hand, and just as every free Greek sought to be a participating citizen, so every citizen sought to be literate and to have his sons (and sometimes, by the second century, even his daughters) taught basic literacy. It was, I shall argue finally, in concluding this book, their status as literate citizens that enabled and caused the city-state Greeks to perceive and understand the world around them in a whole new way, and brought about the features of classical Greek culture that have intrigued the world ever since: rational speculation and investigation of the world, rational historical analysis, popular dramatic entertainments in which characters reasoned about their experiences, rational philosophy and communication theory, art and architecture based on rational analysis of optical laws, and so on. The classical Greeks were a remarkable people in world history, an innovative and paradigm changing people, because they were literate citizens.

Conclusion: Literate Citizen-Warriors and City-State Culture

Herodotos tells an amusing story of one of the earliest encounters between the Persians and the Greeks. When the Persian conqueror Cyrus had defeated the Lydian king Croesus in 544 BCE and taken over his kingdom, which included many Greek city-states along the Aegean coast, the Spartans reportedly sent an ambassador to Sardis to warn Cyrus not to harm the Greeks or face punishment by the Spartans. Understandably astonished, Cyrus inquired of local Greeks just who these Spartans might be, and having been informed, is said to have made the following reply: "I have never feared the sort of men who have a place set apart in the middle of their state (*polis*) where they forswear themselves and deceive each other" (Herodotos 1.153). This, says Herodotos, was in reference to the Greeks' practice of having open town squares (*agorai*) where they bought and sold goods, with much haggling, but we may surmise that Cyrus was also referring to the Greek practice of open air, collective political debate and decision making, which also tended to take place in the *agora*. These practices of the Greeks struck the great Persian king as contemptible and given the very different kind of society he belonged to, one can understand his point of view, but his judgment showed a profound lack of understanding of Greek society and politics.

Nearly 150 years later, in 401 BCE another Persian king—Artaxerxes II—had to deal with a band of Greeks. His brother Cyrus the Younger had gathered a large army to dispute his succession to their father's throne, an army that included about 10,000 Greek mercenary soldiers. At the fateful confrontation, the Battle of Kunaxa in central Mesopotamia (modern Iraq), the phalanx of Greek mercenaries defeated the royal Persian forces opposed to them, but meanwhile their commander Cyrus was killed by Artaxerxes' royal guard. That left both sides in a quandary: the Greeks were victorious, but in the middle of hostile territory with no candidate for king, no one to pay or supply them, and no allies; Artaxerxes had to find a way to deal with a hostile force that he could not defeat. The king delegated this problem to his chief subordinate and expert on Greek affairs, the former western satrap (governor) Tissaphernes who had a long history of dealing with Greeks. Tissaphernes' solution was to invite the officers of the Greek force to a feast to discuss terms: once they were at the feast he had them arrested and executed. The expectation was that, left leaderless, the Greek mercenaries would fall into chaos and be easy pickings. But the Greek warriors simply held an assembly meeting and elected new generals to command them (Xenophon *Anabasis* 2.1–3.1). Under these new leaders, they marched away still well organized and unified to make their way (not without considerable fighting and tribulation) back to Greek lands. We see that even after nearly 150 years of dealing with the Greeks the Persians still had little understanding of how Greeks thought and operated: the Greek way of life and Greek politics were just too alien.

What was so unexpected and alien to the Persians, was the ability of the Greeks, through collective debate and voting, to find agreed upon leaders, reach sensible decisions, and act in unison. The monarchical and imperial tradition of the Persians—and of other earlier near eastern powers like the Assyrians, Medes, Lydians, or Egyptians—relied on the unique and indispensable king to make decisions and enforce unified action. The Greeks in their city-states had a different way of looking at things. As the noted modern Greek poet Cavafy of Alexandria put it in his poem "When the Watchman Saw the Light":

> Of course many people will have much to say.
> We should listen. But we won't be deceived
> by words such as indispensable, unique, and great.
> Someone else indispensable and unique and great
> can always be found at a moment's notice.[1]

It has always struck me as remarkable, considering the ancient Greeks in the context of the wider eastern Mediterranean and near eastern world in which they lived, that they had this attitude towards leadership: that leaders serve the people not the other way around and that leaders are thus dispensable and replaceable. Along with this attitude to leadership went the conviction that the state belongs to the people who make it up, not the people to the state. The aim of this book has been to try to understand how and why the classical Greeks came to have such an unusual society and outlook, and how this society and outlook enabled them to develop their remarkable culture.

The basic conditions for this development are doubtless rooted in how the Greeks emerged from their long period of post Bronze Age decline, the so-called "early Iron Age" (*c.* 1050–850 BCE). During that period, as we have seen, the population of Greece was very scattered and in considerable part transhumant, and population density was very low. The emergence of the Greeks from that condition was not the result of some central, unifying and motivating power or force; instead, the development of emerging Greek agriculture, urbanization, and economic specialization happened in separate and mutually autonomous communities, affected by local conditions and happening at different paces and to different degrees according to those conditions, and involving competitive exchanges of the type that has been called "peer polity interaction."[2] A result of this process was that the urbanized communities which developed in early Greece, after about 850, were relatively small, scattered, mutually independent, and highly competitive. In these communities, the disparities of wealth and power between the elites and the rest of the society were not great, at least by the standards of, say, imperial Rome or the modern world, where some have almost incomprehensibly vast wealth while the majority live hand to mouth. This relatively small wealth disparity was crucial for the development of classical Greek society and culture: without it, the relatively egalitarian nature of classical Greek society would hardly have been possible.

For these small communities to grow sufficiently in wealth to make urbanization and the development of sophisticated material and literary culture possible, economic advances were necessary. The old notion that the classical Greek city-states were economically "primitive" and marked by a preponderance of subsistence agriculture has been fairly thoroughly debunked in recent decades, and along with it skepticism about Greek population growth.[3] In the eighth, seventh, and sixth centuries the developing city-states grew local economies based on cash-cropping, manufacturing, and the provision of services, and this economic specialization was made possible by the cultivation of short and long distance trading networks, bringing to Greece foodstuffs and raw materials from all around the Mediterranean and Black Sea basins, as well as sophisticated products from the advanced civilizations of the near east, in exchange for Greek products like wine, olive oil, and the increasingly sophisticated products of Greek manufacturing, most notably ceramic and metal wares. All of this economic growth was boosted and made possible by a burgeoning population growth that enabled key Greek communities—like Athens, Corinth, Miletos, Samos, and Aigina, for example—to become significant cities, and that enabled the Greeks to spread out around the Mediterranean and Black Seas in the great migration movement that created a host of new Greek cities, like Syracuse and Akragas (Agrigento) in Sicily, Taras (Tarentum) and Neapolis (Naples) in Italy, Massilia (Marseilles) and Nikaia (Nice) in France, and Herakleia (Eregli), Trapezous (Trabzun) and Olbia around the Black Sea.

However, all this growth and development—civic, economic, and demographic—does not explain nor offer an adequate causation for the emergence of classical Greek society and culture as we know them, though they were undoubtedly important preconditions. Other ancient peoples developed mutually independent cities in a co-operative and competitive environment and produced vibrant economies with significant generation of surplus wealth: the Sumerians in the early third millennium, for example, and the Phoenicians in the early first millennium. As impressive as these peoples were in all sorts of ways, including in terms of their cultures, they did not produce anything resembling the rational and self-reflective culture of the classical Greeks. For that to emerge, other conditions evidently needed to be met, and I have laid out in chapters 3, 4, and 5 above the reasons for seeing the relatively egalitarian citizen-militia military system the Greeks developed in the seventh and sixth centuries, the political systems based on collective debate and decision making, and the spread of schools and literacy around Greece and down the social scale, as meeting those conditions. The military system based on the self-equipped and self-motivated middling citizen, so-called hoplite warfare, emboldened and enabled the middling element of warrior-citizens to seek and claim political power in their communities. Without the self-confidence this imparted to the middling citizens the classical city-state and its culture could not have come about as we know it. Being roughly equal warriors providing for the defense of the community, and the advancement of its interests, gave the middling citizens the power and the perceived right to make themselves heard politically, and to develop the oligarchic and democratic political systems in which consensus building among a narrower or broader class of politically equal citizens was the way decisions were made. Finally, for citizens to function in this system, they needed to be well informed, and the relevant information—in the forms of laws, rules, proposals, meeting agendas, and so on—was made available by being written up and posted publicly in the town squares and civic sanctuaries. So that the citizens could read these notices and inform themselves, schools spread and an education imparting a reasonable though basic level of literacy became an expected (even in places required) part of the citizen boys' upbringing, leading to the situation in which mass literacy (meaning the ability of the great majority of citizen men, at a minimum, to read public notices and write simple messages) became a reality.

The question then is, how did this translate into the remarkable culture the classical Greeks are famous for? How did the Greeks develop what the French call their *mentalite*, inadequately rendered into English as their mind? The classical Greek mind, whatever it was that enabled them to listen to and appreciate not just emotional or religious arguments but rational ones too, to spend hours enjoyably watching plays in which the characters on stage did not engage in action but in dialogue, endlessly debating the human condition, and all the rest of Greek culture: how did it come about? It came about, clearly, not because of anything genetic or ethnic (as many nineteenth-century racialist scholars would casually assume), but because of the nature of Greek city-state society. It was because the Greeks were self-confident actors in control of their own lives and societies, and above all because they were literate actors, that they developed the world view that made possible their unique culture. It was mass literacy of the type described in Chapter 5 that was the *sine qua non* for classical Greek culture, I believe. What establishes this is the recognition by modern neuro-scientists of the effect that growing up literate has on the human brain, and thus on how the literate human perceives and interacts with the world.

As I briefly alluded to in Chapter 5, scientists like Merlin Donald and Maryanne Wolf have shown that literacy affects the architecture of the brain, and thus the way humans perceive and understand. In his book *A Mind So Rare*, Merlin Donald says the following: "The power of symbolic technology [i.e. writing] can be attributed largely to its impact on the conscious process. External symbols are revolutionary because they transform the architecture of conscious mental activity."[4] That is, the brain of the literate person functions differently to the brain of the non-literate person. He relates this specifically to the classical Greeks, furthermore, in that it was the city-state Greeks who developed the first fully phonetic alphabet and improved notational systems for geometry and mathematics. As he goes on to say: "More important, Greek society also changed the way written texts were used. They became reflective instruments, in which thought itself could be exposed to systemic analysis. As many have suggested, written symbols allow us to decontextualize ideas and abstract them from the concrete situations from which they sprang. By achieving this, the thinker can extract general principles that might otherwise remain obscure."[5] Thus, via written texts and their use, modes of thought become possible that were simply not available to humans limited by the capacity of the human memory, modes of thought that importantly include rational analysis. Written texts in societies where literacy has become a widespread attainment become a communally available and used external memory, an "external symbolic storage system" in Donald's terminology,[6] which by vastly increasing the information readily available to be thought with, changes the way in which the members of such literate societies think about themselves and the world. The written notices publicly displayed in the Greek city-states constituted such an "external symbolic storage system," a common information base via which every literate citizen could share in the process of civic debate and decision making, as we saw in Chapter 4. As Donald puts it: "Individuals connected to a cultural network can access an exterior memory bank, read its codes and content, store new contributions in permanent form, and interact with other individuals who employ the same codes and access routes."[7] This is exactly what we see happening among the literate citizens of the city-states.

Working along similar lines, Maryanne Wolf has shown how not only literacy, but different kinds of literacy directly affect how the brain works: drawing a comparison with another great culture, for example, studies have shown that learning to read Chinese, with its thousands of symbols, accesses and develops different areas of the brain than learning to read the alphabet.[8] The brain of the alphabetically literate person thus develops and works somewhat differently than the brains of other humans who are non-literate or use different systems of writing. The brain has a great plasticity in its circuit wiring and learning to read affects that circuit wiring in a way that enables us to form new thoughts. Further, what Wolf calls the "cortical efficiency" of alphabetic literacy can be seen as contributing to that ability to engage in "novel thinking."[9] As she puts it, the increased efficiency of the alphabetic system "made novel thought more possible for more people," and it can therefore "be no surprise that one of the most profound and prolific periods of writing, art, philosophy, theater, and science in all of previously recorded history accompanied the spread of the Greek alphabet."[10] This brings us to the nub of the issue here: the distinctive culture created by the city-state Greeks was, we see, a culture rooted in and made possible by the wide spread of alphabetic literacy: it was being a community of readers that enabled the Greeks to develop and appreciate their culture of reflective narrative and rational analysis.[11] Being readers is what made it possible for them to think the very thoughts that we know them for—the thoughts of Herodotos or Thucydides, of Sophokles or Euripides, of Plato or Aristotle, of Isokrates or Demosthenes—and for those thoughts to be welcomed and appreciated by large audiences of fellow Greeks. But beyond the capacity for reflection and rational analysis, there is another aspect of classical Greek culture that is notable: its interest in individuals and their stories, whether the individual be a hero, a prominent leader, or an average citizen—because, as we have seen, an average citizen like Dikaipolis had his story just as much as a Theseus or Perikles.

Modern humans are apt to think of themselves as having what psychologist Dan McAdams calls "narrative identity."[12] By this is meant the tendency to "reconstruct the past and imagine the future in order to explain how you have become the person you are becoming"; that is, narrative identity refers to the "internalized and evolving story of the self that a person constructs to provide his or her life with unity, purpose, and meaning."[13] In an interview with Matthew Sedacca in August 2019, published in the online blog *Nautilus*,[14] McAdams reflected on how narrative identity came to be developed. He raised the question of narrative identity as an evolutionary trait, and wondered whether, for example, the common man or woman in Egypt 3,000 years ago had a life story. He noted that narrative identity requires a degree of sophistication that may not have been found in most pre-modern societies, but he did find clear signs of it in Aristotle. That raises the question whether narrative identity was also a characteristic of the classical Greeks, and how it relates to the rest of their culture. I think there are very clear signs that the Greeks did have narrative identity, and not just for the heroes whose stories are told in epic poems or tragic dramas. I think again of the aforementioned Dikaiopolis, the average Athenian citizen who is the protagonist of Aristophanes' play *The Acharnians*. He has a very clear notion of who he is and what his life is, of a story arc to his life, from a happy past of living on his farm engaging in familiar rural pursuits, to a troubled present cooped up in the war-torn city of Athens, to an imagined future where peace will have been restored and he can return to his farm and its idyllic way of life. That is to say, he displays a narrative identity. But even more than poems or plays, I think of that very characteristic Greek (especially Athenian) undertaking the *apologia*, the speech in defense of oneself when accused of wrong doing. In defending themselves in formal court proceedings before large juries of fellow citizens, Greek citizens found it necessary to tell the story of their lives, of who they were, presenting that story in such a way as to put the best possible legal and moral construction on who they were, how they lived their lives, and how they had behaved in the specific context that gave rise to the court proceedings. They presented, thus, a narrative identity showing a unity and purpose to their lives that was moral, legitimate, and not blameworthy.[15]

Most noteworthy, perhaps, is Lysias 24, a speech written to be delivered by a poor Athenian citizen who was appealing against denial of the "poor relief" payment of 2 obols per day. At the beginning of his *apologia* he says:

> I am almost grateful, oh Council, to my accuser, for setting up this contest for me. Before this I had no cause to give an account (*logos*) of my life, but now thanks to this man I do; and I shall try in this speech to show that man is lying, and that I have lived my life until now in a manner worthy of praise rather than ill will.

That is to say, even the poorest Athenian citizens could think of their lives as having a narrative arc, and seek to present it in such a way as to give the story of their lives a positive spin.

When we ponder how the classical Greeks came to have the capacity for narrative identity, I think it is clear that it is a product of the reality, outlined in the above chapters, of the literate citizen-warrior. The self-confidence and sense of importance a Greek man had as a participating citizen-warrior provided the basis for thinking of his life as having a meaning and purpose, and the training in literacy (with its effect on his brain development) gave him the cognitive capacity to create that unified sense of self with a story and meaning to his life. We can thus understand much better, for example, how it came to be that the classical Greeks, led by Herodotos and Thucydides, developed analytic history writing, in which the stories of individuals and societies were not just presented as a series of events to be celebrated or deprecated, but as narrative arcs that needed to be analyzed, explained, and understood. We can understand how a Greek like Xenophon could pioneer the writing of biography, explaining the life story of an individual. When we think of thousands of Greeks spending hours sitting on stone benches, sometimes for several days in a row, watching plays (the Athenian tragedies) in which the characters discussed and analyzed their lives, their choices, the costs and consequences of their choices, how they fit into the human condition: all of that is understandable for people with narrative identities of their own, to whom the characters on the stage and their problems thus resonated. Aristophanes was able to write a play to amuse popular audiences of thousands in which he parodied the ideas of the rationalist philosophers: *The Clouds*, not his most popular and well received play it's true, but a play that shows that the Athenian man-in-the-street had at least a passing familiarity with the ideas and arguments of the philosophers. The "high culture" of the historians, the tragedians, the philosophers was a culture produced for and appreciated (on at least a basic level) by the mass audience of literate citizen-warriors. It is no accident that a widespread interest in classical Greek culture, which disappeared in late antiquity as literacy became a specialized attainment of the clergy and the elites, reappeared in western Europe at precisely the time—the sixteenth and seventeenth centuries—when widespread schooling and literacy also reappeared. It is a culture produced by and for a class of literate citizens.

Appendix 1: A Note on the Sources

The main historical sources the historian of classical Greece relies upon, the histories of Herodotos, Thucydides, Xenophon, Diodoros the Sicilian, and the like, are unfortunately overwhelmingly interested in political and military matters, and show little or no interest in such matters as the economy and education. This makes the task of the historian interested in such matters a difficult one. It is not just that the main historical sources did not research and discuss literacy rates, for instance: it is that no ancient writer of any sort thought to pay attention to how widespread literacy was and how it spread, or how the economy functioned and how it developed, or a plethora of other issues that greatly interest the modern historian of ancient Greece. Nor did city-states, despite their interest in publicly documenting an array of matters of importance to them, ever think to produce and inscribe for public notice information or statistics on things like schools, or local and international trade. To discuss such matters, therefore, the historian is obliged to cast a very wide net and look for every stray phrase, sentence, anecdote, or aside anywhere in our sources that might shed some light on these matters.

In this book, therefore, the reader will find scraps of evidence drawn from plays (especially comedies satirizing contemporary events), poems and songs, court speeches, philosophical dialogues, speeches on political issues and events, treatises on public finance or hunting or how to run one's family affairs, public documents on any matter that happen to survive inscribed on stone. Any and every surviving source must be combed for any information, however tangential, on one's topic of research.[1] Even here the historian runs into an obstacle: so much of the literary production of ancient Greece is lost, so many of the inscribed documents that once adorned the public spaces of the cities are lost or at best very fragmentarily preserved. To give a sense of the problem, the study of ancient Greece is akin to trying to reconstruct the picture shown in a 10,000-piece jigsaw puzzle of which only 3,000 pieces survive. One places the pieces in the right place, to the best of one's judgment; one connects the pieces that fit together to show a part of the picture here or there, and when one has laid out the surviving pieces as best one can, one tries to draw in at least an impression of the whole picture as the fragments seem to reveal it. The result is necessarily sketchy and subject to dispute.

For certain topics, we are fortunate in recent times to have the assistance of archaeological exploration. Urban development, demographic change, the growth of trading networks and the materials traded, the exact form of military equipment and when and how it developed, the development and spread of the Greek alphabet and of writing using it, the nature of the ancient Greek ecology: all these and others are topics that have benefited hugely in the past hundred years or so from the ongoing work of archaeological excavations of cities and sanctuaries, of underwater archaeology revealing shipwrecks and the goods being transported in them, of field studies revealing settlement patterns and density, and so on.[2]

A historian of a modern state engaging in the kind of study here undertaken would be overwhelmed by the enormous quantity and variety of evidence, documentary and other. For this book the case is the opposite: the evidence is far, far too scanty to allow us to make the kind of definitive arguments and conclusions we would like to. The reader will find, as a result, arguments being based on anecdotes and asides in our sources, ripped from context and used to reveal matters the original author was not or only barely interested in, and indeed on scraps and fragments, a few words here and a sentence there; and it may often seem like such evidence is inadequate to our purpose and/or being over-interpreted. One makes no apology for this: if such topics as the growth of the ancient Greek economy, or the spread and uses of literacy, are to be studied at all—and they are important topics that need to be studied if we are to understand the classical Greeks as best we can—then one must use the evidence that one has and make of it what one can. The point is, that the kind of sources used in this book, and the way they are used, may strike the reader as odd, but such is the nature of our source problem. The conclusions reached here are necessarily, therefore, somewhat provisional and open to dispute. One can only hope that one has cast the net widely enough, so as not to miss any stray piece of evidence that might help; and I do very much believe that the conclusions reached in this book make the best use and sense of what evidence we do have.

Appendix 2: Aristotle's *Politeiai*

In the concluding remarks to his famed work of moral philosophy, the *Nicomachean Ethics,* Aristotle transitioned from ethics to the study of politics, making it clear that his treatise the *Politika* formed part two of his philosophy of human nature, of which the *Ethika* was part one. He described the approach he followed in his study of politics in these words:

> First, then, if anything has been said well in detail by earlier thinkers, let us try to review it; then in the light of the constitutions (*politeiai*) we have collected let us study what sorts of influence preserve and destroy states, and what sorts preserve or destroy the particular kinds of constitutions, and to what causes it is due that some are well and others ill administered.[1]

He thus referred to a well-known research project he and his students carried out: the collection of historical accounts and analyses of a large number of existing *politeiai* of Greek and non-Greek states, of which the *Politeia of the Athenians* actually survives. He also made it clear that this research project furnished the evidential material for his study of "politics" in his famed treatise the *Politika*, making this research project a very important one in the history of western political thought.[2]

Though these *politeiai* are all lost except for that of the Athenians, which was recovered substantially intact on some pieces of papyrus discovered in Egypt, we do have a certain amount of information regarding them, which has been well collected and presented in Olof Gigon's great edition of Aristotle's fragmentary works.[3] Unfortunately Gigon, like almost all other commentators, regarded as settled a question which is still very much not settled, namely the number of treatises contained in Aristotle's *Politeiai*. Based on the list of Aristotle's works found in bk. 5 of Diogenes Laertios' *Lives of Eminent Philosophers*, where we find the statement "*politeiai* of cities (or states: *poleis*) two less than 160," it is widely accepted that Aristotle's project examined the constitutions of 158 states.[4] However, this assumption overlooks or ignores two things: 1. Diogenes' list of Aristotle's works gives for each work the number of "books" (i.e., papyrus scrolls) it was made up of, so that the number 158 should in context more properly be understood to say that the *Politeiai* filled 158 scrolls, the number of treatises not being specified;[5] 2. there are other sources giving a very different number for Aristotle's *Politeiai*, which seem likely to be giving the number of treatises rather than book scrolls.

In the sixth century CE there was in Alexandria a remarkable school of philosophy showing a mixture of neo-Platonist and Aristotelian ideas: among the great names associated with this school are Ammonius, Simplicius, John Philoponus, and Olympiodorus. Among the written works surviving from this school are commentaries on the works of Aristotle, which have been edited most importantly by Busse.[6] In his commentary on Aristotle's *Categories*, Ammonius wrote the following: "the *Politeiai* written by him (i.e., Aristotle) being about two hundred and fifty." This is confirmed in the work of a later teacher in the school known as Elias, who wrote "written by him are also *Politeiai*, two hundred and fifty in number."[7] These statements, by learned Aristotle commentators showing a great familiarity with Aristotle's works (more so than Diogenes) need to be taken seriously. In agreement with them, is also a late Aristotle biography known as the *Vita Graeca vulgata* which tells us at section 23: "then he researched (*historese*) the 255 politeiai."

The statements about Aristotle's *Politeiai* by the late antique commentators have been inappropriately ignored or dismissed. Ammonius, for example, was a very learned and diligent scholar, the founder of the late antique school of Aristotle commentators at Alexandria, a man who knew Aristotle's works well.[8] He and his followers had available to them a wealth of material on Aristotle now lost to us, including the editions of Aristotle's works, biographies, and lists of his writings by eminent Aristotelians like Hermippos, Andronikos, and Ptolemaios.[9] While, despite the various conjectures of scholars, it is not possible to determine which of these sources our late antique commentators and biographers relied on exactly, the information they give us must be treated seriously. So, we have two rival traditions about the scope of Aristotle's *Politeiai*: that found in Diogenes and that found in Ammonius and his followers. It is my view, as already indicated, that these two traditions are complementary rather than contradictory, Diogenes referring to the number of book scrolls filled by the *Politeiai* and Ammonius to the actual number of treatises: because not every treatise will have filled exactly one book scroll.

We can see this clearly from the case of the surviving *Athenaion Politeia*. The text was found on four papyrus rolls, which altogether amount to just about 570 cm. in width, and the surviving text is incomplete, certainly at the beginning and quite likely at the end too.[10] We know that the manufacture of papyrus was standardized, with a sheet of papyrus being about 17 cm. in width, and twenty such sheets being glued together to form a standard *tomos* (roll) of papyrus for sale, meaning that the standard roll was some 320 cm. in width.[11] This means that the surviving part of the *AthPol* comprises a bit less than two standard *tomoi*, and we need to remember that the *AthPol* is incomplete, certainly at the beginning where substantial text is missing,[12] and likely at the end too, the surviving ending being extraordinarily abrupt.[13] In its full original form, that is to say, the *AthPol* almost certainly filled significantly more than two rolls of papyrus, and would therefore probably have been divided into two "books." Further, the *AthPol* will not have been the only very long treatise: the *politeiai* of the Lakedaimonians (Spartans) and of the Syracusans are also likely to have been of substantial length.[14]

More significant though, in the present context, is the great likelihood that no small number of the *Politeiai* must have been too short to fill an entire book scroll: there will scarcely have been enough information about such communities as the Tenedians, the Aphytans, or numerous other such small and insignificant cities to produce a treatise remotely close in size to that of the Athenians. That is to say, it is highly likely that quite a few of the book scrolls making up the overall collection will have contained two or three, in some cases perhaps even four or five treatises. Thus, it was always to be expected that the number of book scrolls would be significantly fewer than the number of treatises, and that is what we find if I am right to suggest that Diogenes' number 158 refers to the number of scrolls, while the number *c.* 250 to 255 of the late antique commentators and *vitae* tells us the actual number of treatises.

Of these 250–55 *Politeiai* we know the names of some 134. The evidence, as collected and set out by Gigon, falls into three parts: there are references to and quotations from the *Politeiai* in later works;[15] there is a set of epitomes (or rather brief excerpts, seventy-six in number) put together by Herakleides Lembos in the second century BCE;[16] and there are the references to communities and their particular institutions, magistracies, and practices found in Aristotle's *Politika*, which almost certainly derive from the *Politeiai*.[17] I present here, then, a list of the known *Politeiai*, arranged by source: that is the various direct references are listed first, in alphabetical order of the names of the communities (nos. 1–44); then I list the additional communities, again in alphabetical order, known from Herakleides (nos. 45–74); and finally the communities which can be added with strong probability from mentions of them in Aristotle's *Politika* (nos. 75–134). After each community I add a letter: (P) if the community was a *polis*; (E) if the community was an *ethnos* or other non-*polis* community; (F) if the community was a foreign (non-Greek) tribe, people, or state; this all to the best of my knowledge and judgment.

1. Adramyttion (P)	46. Aphyta (P)	91. Chios (P)
2. Achaia (E)	47. Argilos (P)	92. Egypt (F)
3. Aitolia (E)	48. Athamania (E)	93. Elimea (E)
4. Akarnania (E)	49. Chalkidike (E)	94. Epidmnos (P)
5. Akragas (P)	50. Ephesos (P)	95. Erythrai (P)
6. Ambrakia (P)	51. Eretria (P)	96. Ethiopia (F)
7. Argos (P)	52. Etruria (F)	97. Hestiaia/Oreos (P)
8. Arkadia (E)	53. Herakleia Minoa (P)	98. Heraia (P)
9. Athens (P)	54. Iasos (P)	99. Herakleia Pontika (P)
10. Boiotia (E)	55. Ikaria (P)	100. Herakleia Trachis (P)
11. Bottiaia (F)	56. Keos (P)	101. Iapygia (F)
12. Delphi (P)	57. Kephallenia (P)	102. Iberia (F)
13. Delos (P)	58. Korinthos (P)	103. India (F)
14. Elis (P)	59. Krete (E)	104. Italy (F)
15. Epeiros (E)	60. Kroton (P)	105. Karchedon / Carthage (F)
16. Gela (P)	61. Kyme (P)	106. Katane (P)
17. Himera (P)	62. Kythera (P)	107. Klazomenai (P)
18. Ithaka (P)	63. Lepreon (P)	108. Knidos (P)
19. Kerkyra (P)	64. Lykia (F)	109. Kos (P)
20. Kios (P)	65. Magnesia (P)	110. Larissa (P)
21. Kolophon (P)	66. Molossia (E)	111. Leontinoi (P)
22. Kythnos (P)	67. Paros (P)	112. Lesbos (P)
23. Kypros (E)	68. Peparethos (P)	113. Libya (F)
24. Kyrene (P)	69. Phasis (P)	114. Lokroi (Italy) (P)
25. Lakedaimon (P) (Sparta)	70. Rhegion (P)	115. Lydia (F)
26. Leukas (P)	71. Rhodos (P)	116. Makedonia (E)
27. Lokrioi (E)	72. Tenedos (P)	117. Malis (E)
28. Massalia (P)	73. Thespiai (P)	118. Mantinea (P)
29. Megara (P)	74. Thrace (F)	119. Media (F)
30. Melos (P)	75. Abydos (P)	120. Messene (P)
31. Methone (P)	76. Aigina (P)	121. Miletos (P)
32. Naxos (P)	77. Ainos (P)	122. Mytilene (P)
33. Opous (E?)	78. Amphipolis (P)	123. Oinotria (F)

34. Orchomenos (P)	79. Andros (P)	124. Opikia (F)
35. Pellene (P)	80. Antissa (P)	125. Perrhaibia (E)
36. Phokaia (P)	81. Apollonia Ionian Sea (P)	126. Persia (F)
37. Samos (P)	82. Apollonia Pontika (P)	127. Pharsalos (P)
38. Samothrake (P)	83. Atarneus (P)	128. Phrygia (F)
39. Sikyon (P)	84. Ausonia (F)	129. Scythia (F)
40. Syracuse (P)	85. Babylon (F)	130. Sybaris (P)
41. Taras (P)	86. Byzantion (P)	131. Thebes (P)
42. Tegea (P)	87. Celts (F)	132. Thera (P)
43. Thessaly (E)	88. Chalkedon (P)	133. Thourioi (P)
44. Troizen (E)	89. Chalkis (P)	134. Zankle/Messana (P)
45. Amorgos (P)	90. Chaonia (E)	

Appendix 3: Overseas Settlements and *Metropoleis*

The study of archaic Greek migration generally treats the whole process of sending out settlers and founding new settlements as one uniform and undifferentiated enterprise, usually thought of as having to do with the relieving of population stress in the founding community.[1] It is my contention that this overlooks a crucial difference between two kinds of "colonizing" communities: a large number of communities founded one or a few settlements, conceivably with the aim to relieve population stress; and a small number of "colonizing" communities operated on an entirely different scale and clearly had something other than relief of population stress in mind. The easiest way to illustrate this point is simply to list the known *metropoleis* with their respective overseas settlements, beginning with the former group, and then showing the small but immensely important second group.[2] When one arranges the data in this way, I think it is immediately apparent that the "colonizers" of the second group are engaged in something different than those in the first group, and attention to geography then tells us what this is: the thirty overseas settlements of Miletos, for example, blanketed the coasts and approaches to the Black Sea, and one can hardly separate this from an interest in the immensely lucrative Black Sea trade.

1. Communities founding one or a few settlements

Achaia : Kroton, Metapontion, Skione, Sybaris
Andros : Akanthos, Argilos, Sane, Stageiros
Athens : Chersonnesos, Imbros, Lemnos, Sigeion
Chios : Maronea
Gela : Akragas
Knidos : Kerkyra Melaina, Lipara
Kolophon : Siris
Kroton : Temesa, Terina
Kyrene : Barke, Euhesperides, Taucheira
Lesbos : Madytos, Sestos
Lokris : Lokroi Epizephyrioi
Lokroi in Italy : Hipponeion, Medma, Metauros

Massalia : Agathe
Megara Hyblaia : Selinous
Methymna : Assos
Mitylene : Ainos
Pantikapaion : Tyritake
Paros : Parion (with Milesians), Thasos
Rhodes : Gela (with Kretans), Phaselis
Selinous : Heraklea Minoa
Sinope : Kerasos, Kotyora, Trapezous
Sparta : Taras
Sybaris : Laos, Poseidonia, Pyxos
Syracuse : Kamarina, Kasmenai, Heloros
Teos : Abdera, Elaios, Phanagoria
Thasos : Galepsos, Neapolis (in Thrace), Oisyme, Stryme
Thera : Apollonia in Libya, Kyrene
Zankle : Himera, Mylai

2. Communities founding multiple settlements

Miletos : Abydos, Amisos (with Phokaians), Apollonia Pontika, Berezan, Kardia (with Klazomenians), Kepoi, Kios, Kolonai, Kyzikos, Hermonassa, Istros, Limnai, Miletopolis, Myrmekion, Nymphaion, Odessos, Olbia, Paisos, Pantikapaion, Parion (with Parians), Phasis, Priapos, Prokonnesos, Skepsis, Sinope, Tanais, Theodosia, Tieon, Tomis, Tyras

Chalkis and Eretria : Assera (Ch), Katane (Ch), Kleonai (Ch), Kerkyra (E), Kymai (Ch & E), Gale (Ch), Leontinoi (Ch), Mekyberna (Ch), Mende (E), Methone (E), Naxos in Sicily (Ch), Piloros (Ch), Pithekoussai (Ch &E), Rhegion (Ch), Sarte (Ch), Sermyle (Ch), Singos (Ch), Torone (Ch), Zankle/Messana (Ch with Messenians)

Corinth : Ambrakia, Anaktorion, Apollonia in Illyria, Epidamnos, Kerkyra, Leukas, Potidaia, Syracuse

Megara : Astakos, Byzantion, Chalkedon, Heraklea Pontika, Megara Hyblaia, Mesembria, Selymbria

Phokaia : Alalia, Amisos (with Milesians), Elea, Emporiai, Lampsakos, Massalia

Samos : Bisanthe, Kelenderis, Dikaiarchia, Nagidos, Oasispolis, Perinthos, Samothrake

Notes

Introduction

1 Attic was the dialect of Greek spoken by the classical Athenians, which became very widespread around the Greek world thanks to the influence of Athenian culture and writings; the *koine* (that is, common) dialect, based on Attic Greek, was the form of Greek spoken throughout the Greek world by educated Greeks in the post-classical or Hellenistic era, from about 300 BCE onward.

2 Hansen 1997, p. 12 notes that *polis* is etymologically related to Old Indian *pur*, Lithuanian *pilis*, and Latvian *pils*, all carrying the original meaning "stronghold"; he posits the same original meaning for *polis*, noting its use in that sense in early Krete at Dreros and Anavlochos; see also Hansen 2006, ch. 8 "What is a Polis?" and cf. the articles on *polis* and *astu* by Koerner and Musiolek in Welskopf (ed.) 1981.

3 See e.g., Thucydides 2.15.6; the usage is noted by Hansen 1997, p. 16, with citations at nn. 34 and 35, and cf. the epigraphic evidence briefly surveyed by Koerner 1981, pp. 361–2. The term *akropolis* is found in Homer already (*Od.* 8.494 and 504), but only came into common use at Athens in the fifth century.

4 Musiolek 1981, p. 372 (my translation), though see Scully 1990 for a somewhat different view, especially at chapters 2 and 3. However, Davies 1997, pp. 24–38 at 27 notes the term's "epic use to denote mostly a fortified nucleated settlement seen from outside but sometimes also an unfortified nucleated settlement."

5 Cetin Sahin 1987, pp. 1–2, no. 1 is an inscription found near Priene, carved on the chest of an Egyptian basalt male statue, recording the dedication of this statue by one Pedon son of Amphinneos who had served as a mercenary under the Egyptian king Psammetichos (=most likely Psamtik II of the Saite dynasty, reigned 594–588). He boasts that in recognition for his bravery (*aristeia*) and excellence (*arete*) the king gave him a gold armband and a *polis* (*psilion te chruseon kai polin*). In my view, this surely means that he was placed in command of some fortified post by the king, the armband being no doubt the insignia of his rank as commander. The term *polis* here, then, essentially means "fort."

6 Koerner 1981.

7 Alkaios fr. 112 from *P. Berol.* 9569, line 10 "for warlike men are a city's tower"; adapted, according to Thucydides 7.77.7, by Nikias in a speech to the Athenian and allied troops under the walls of Syracuse "for men are the *polis*, not walls or ships with no men inside them"; paraphrased in Aelius Aristides *Or.* 46.207: "it is not

stones, nor wood, nor the craft of builders that make cities, but wherever are men prepared to defend themselves, there are walls and *poleis*"; and according to Aristides frequently quoted by all and sundry.

8   Another case in point would be Themistokles' famous insistence, at Salamis in 480, that not-withstanding the loss of their city and territory, the Athenians still had a *polis:* their fighting men on their ships (Herodotos 7.141–143; 8. 51 and 61).

9   Berent 2004, pp. 107–46 argued, for example, that the *polis* was what anthropologists call a "stateless society" based on the definition that the state is characterized by a government which has separated itself from the rest of society and monopolizes the use of violence. By such a definition the Greek city-state may not, indeed, have been a "state" but then if a state must have a government that monopolizes the use of violence, then we might conclude that the USA—with its Second Amendment and its gun rights advocates—does not qualify to be a state, a conclusion I take it no-one would care to accept.

10 See Solon fr. 3 "our *polis* will never be destroyed by the planning of Zeus" etc., where the word *polis* already seems to mean something more than just city; and Theognis ll. 39–52 at 39 "Kurnos, this *polis* is pregnant, and I fear it will bear a man who will punish our evil hubris" etc., where again the word *polis* is used in a way that transcends mere "city."

11 Aristotle *Politika* 6.7.1–3 (= 1321a) and cf. 4.13.10–11 (= 1297b).

12 See further Chapter 3 below for the importance of military developments, and especially the emergence of hoplite and trireme fleet warfare, for the development of the city-state.

13 See the discussion of Hansen 2006, ch. 9 "The Polis as City and as State."

14 Lists of the physical infrastructure to be expected in a developed Greek *polis* are given, for example, by Pausanias 10.4.1: gymnasium, public buildings, theater, agora, water works; by Plutarch *Adv. Col.* 31: walls, houses, theater; and by Dio Chrysostom *Or.* 48.9: gymnasia, agora, theater, stoas. Though none of the three happens to mention temples, these also obviously belong.

15 On the importance of the *chora* to the Greek city-state, and on the variety of lands and activities a city-state might encompass and its rural citizens engage in, see, for example, Osborne 1987; also Hansen 2006, ch. 16 "The Greek conception of Polis as a City with a Hinterland."

16 Examples are the so-called *hupomeiones* and *mothakes* of classical Sparta: Xenophon *Hell.* 3.3.4–11 for the former; Phylarchos in *Brill's New Jacoby* no. 81 fr. 43 and Aelian *VH* 12.43 for the latter; and cf. the discussion of Cartledge, 2002, ch. 14; and the citizens below the hoplite status at Athens during the regime of the "5,000" (Thuc. 8.97 stating quite gratuitously that under this regime Athens was better governed than ever before).

17 See e.g., Cantarella, *Pandora's Daughters* (1986), ch. 3, "Exclusion from the *polis*" for a good discussion, but see now also Blok 2017 arguing for a definition of citizenship

rooted in descent and religion, according to which women were full citizens. I would use the notions "active" and "passive" citizenship to denote the very real difference between men and women, however, see further chapters 3 and 4 below.
18 Still a very useful treatment of such communities is Gschnitzer 1958. The best-known case is that of the Spartan state, see e.g., Cartledge 2002, ch. 10 for a full treatment; Argos also reduced towns in the Argolid like Mykenai, Tiryns, Epidauros to an essentially *perioikic* status, see for instance Tomlinson 1972, pp. 96–8 discussing the evidence of Aristotle *Politika* 1303a6 and Plutarch *de mul. Virt.* 4.
19 See for example Thuc. 2.13 indicating the role metics might play in helping to defend Athens, and further Roberts 1998, pp. 28–31 for a good overview of the status; also Meyer 2010.
20 Cartledge 2002, ch. 10 for the Helots; Pollux 3.83 refers to the *Gumnetes* of Argos, cf. Tomlinson 1972, p. 68; for the Thessalian *Penestai* see Aristotle *Politika* 1269 a29, Xenophon *Hell.* 2.3.36, Theopompos in *Brill's New Jacoby* no. 115 fr. 122 and cf. *Der kleine Pauly* s.v. for other sources.
21 See, for example, Garlan 1988 for a good treatment.
22 See pp. 15–19 below; for the range of meaning of the word *ethnos* see *LSJ* s.v.: "generally any company or group of persons, more specifically a people or tribe"; unfortunately, *LSJ* overlooks the political sense of the word, roughly translatable as "tribal state," with which we are here concerned.
23 Thus, the *ethnos* is largely ignored in Aristotle's *Politika*, for example; see Giovannini 1971 for a rare modern treatment; more recently also Morgan 2003, and, for example, Bommelje and Doorn 1987 and J. Scholten 2000 on Aitolia; McInerney 1999 on Phokis.
24 For Boiotia see the discussion in Chapter 1, pp. 31–3 below; note that Aristotle in his *Politeiai* evidently treated the Arkadians as an *ethnos*, though he also treated certain Arkadian communities separately as city-states: Tegea, Mantinea, perhaps Orchomenos—though this may be the city of that name in central Greece (see App. 2 below); for Elis the key fact is that according to Diodoros the Sicilian it was not synoikized into a *polis* until 471 (Diod. 11.54.1), before which time the Elians were presumably organized along *ethnos* lines.
25 See Giovannini 1971 for a full discussion of all this.
26 Ruschenbusch 1978; revised in Ruschenbusch 1984, pp. 55–7 and 1986, pp. 171–94.
27 Ruschenbusch 1978, p. 4: he proceeded to count numerous towns and villages of *ethne* as city-states, which they were not. For example, he counted twenty-six *poleis* in Phokis, none of which was however a city-state since all of Phokis formed a single state, an *ethnos* (see McInerney 1999, and further Chapter 1 below at pp. 29–31).
28 See Hansen 1993, 1995, 1996, and especially 1997 at pp. 10–19; also now 2006, chs. 8 and 9.
29 Hansen 1997, pp. 17–19; for the finished work see Nielsen and Hansen (eds.) 2004 listing 1,029 separate *poleis*.

30 For example, of the 159 communities called *polis* by Herodotos, Hansen found that only Anthela and Alpenos near Thermopylai were not city-states (1997, p. 18). However, taking bk. 4 of Herodotos as an example, I find references to the *polis* Artake in the Kyzikene (4.14.2), to six *polias* in the region called Triphylia of the western Peloponnesos—Lepreion, Makistos, Phrixai, Pyrgos, Epeion, Noudeion—founded by Theras and in Herodotos' day taken by Elis (4.148.2), and to Taucheira a "*polis* of Barke" (4.171.1). The reference to Taucheira surely describes it as a subordinate community of the city-state Barke, and to see in the other places mentioned independent city-states confirming the "*Lex Hafniensis*" rather than subordinate communities (demes? perioikic towns?) of Kyzikos (Artake) and Elis (the six Triphylian towns)—or even in the latter case perhaps politically linked towns of a small *ethnos*-type community—is question-begging to say the least. In these cases, *polis* most likely means nothing more than town. Hansen finds only a single, partial exception to his rule among the seventy communities called *polis* by Thucydides, which means that when Thucydides called Mykalessos in Boiotia a *polis* (7.29.3 and 5, 7.30.2), he meant that this village was in his day a city-state; but I note that the *Hellenika Oxyrrhynchia* 19 (see Billows 2016 F9 with comm.), in its account of the Boiotian governing system in the period 447–387, lists ten independent cities in Boiotia besides Thebes: Orchomenos, Hysiai, Thespiai, Tanagra, Haliartos, Lebadeia, Koroneia, Akraiphnia, Kopai, and Chaironeia. Mykalessos is not mentioned, and must in this period have been a dependency of Tanagra, as Strabo 9.2.11 and 14 indicates (and see further Chapter 5 below at pp. 154–5); and cf. Fiehn in *RE* s.v. I note too that the logographer Hekataios of Miletos referred to Thorikos, a deme of Athens, as a *polis* (Pownall, "Hekataios of Miletos (1)" in *BNJ* F 126 [2013]), clearly therefore using the word *polis* to mean simply "town."

31 Day and Chambers 1967 provides a useful analysis of the *AthPol* and argues convincingly that it is indeed Aristotle's treatise; for an English translation and brief, though still useful, commentary see Moore 1983 at pp. 139–313; and see further App. 2 below at pp.186–7.

32 See App. 2 below for details.

33 Gigon 2013, pp. 561–722.

34 Gigon 2013 gives the references to known treatises, but one should add David, *Proleg. et in Porph. Eisag. Comm.* in Busse (ed.) 1895 at 74,25 to 75,2 (*Argeioi* and *Boiotoi*), and for some reason Gigon does not reckon Sopatros' brief list of treatises as true *testimonia*. He gives the reasons for treating Herakleides' summaries as referring to the Aristotelian treatises; and also for treating the references to various political and constitutional practices, institutions etc. in the *Politika* as derived from the *Politeiai* and hence providing evidence for them.

35 See the list in App. 2 below: I find thirty-four city-states from east Greece (Asia Minor) and the Aegean islands and thirty-three "colonial" city-states, as opposed to

only twenty-six mainland city-states (including the immediately off-shore Ionian Islands and Euboia). I am assuming that the preserved names do not somehow represent a geographical distortion, preserving a higher proportion of insular and "colonial" city-states than mainland ones; I can think of no reason to suppose there to be any such distortion.

36 Megara, Phleious, Sikyon and Tegea sent 3,000, 1,000, 3,000, and 1,500 hoplites respectively to the Battle of Plataia in 479 for example (Herodotos 9.28), and those figures seem likely (though to a varying degree according to local choices) to represent the larger part of their potential hoplite levies given the serious nature of the occasion. On that basis a rough estimate for total population can be arrived at as follows: if we assume 3,000 hoplites, we should double that figure to account for men below hoplite status, and multiply the result by four to account for women and children, giving an approximate citizen population of 24,000; one should probably add a few thousand for non-citizens—slaves, resident aliens—for a total population for a city of this middle rank in the 25,000 to 30,000 range. This is all very approximate, but it gives a satisfactory idea of scale for such cities. For Teos notes that the city contributed seventeen triremes to the grand fleet of the Ionians during their revolt in the early 490s (Herodotos 6.8) which—at 200 men per ship—would have required 3,400 men to crew.

37 Note for example that Aristotle's ideal *politeia* is a moderate democracy (as Athens was in the fourth century), that in it the free indigenous men are all equal and participatory citizens (as at Athens), that the citizens share in the ruling of the state (as at Athens), etc. It is true that Aristotle reduces the "working" class to slavery, but he is expressing an ideal of citizen leisure here, and one should note that Athens too had a large class of enslaved people—without doubt the largest in Greece—and that Athenians too had an ideal of leisure, however little most of them may have achieved it.

38 See on Hellenistic democracy, for example, Davies in 1984 at pp. 306–7, and in more detail Quass 1979 pp. 37–52; also O'Neil 1995, ch. 5; and note the emphasis laid on having democratic constitutions in many inscriptions, for example, *SIG* 581 line 14 (Rhodes), *OGIS* 229 lines 10–11 (Smyrna), *SIG* 398 lines 27–8 and *Staatsv.* III no. 545 line 15 (Kos), *IG* XI.4 566 lines 10–12 (Delos).

39 For this latter see MacDowell 1978, pp. 161–4 on the liturgy system in Athens; and in general see further Gauthier 1985 and Billows 1995, pp. 70–3.

40 Ehrenberg 1937, pp. 147–59; van Effenterre 1985 tried unconvincingly to find the roots of the city-state in Mycenean (Bronze Age) Greece; Snodgrass and Whitley, for example, seem to push back the origins of the city-state into the early Iron Age—the ninth or even the late tenth century—see Snodgrass 1982 and Whitley 1991, esp. in his conclusion at p. 198 para. 5, although he does not there actually use the terms *polis* or city-state.

41 We know that some women and enslaved persons could read and write, but they clearly learned to do so privately, not by attending school, and they were relatively few in number.
42 See Connelly 2007, Blok 2017.
43 A good resource for the study of women in ancient Greece is MacLachlan 2012; a foundational work of scholarship is Cantarella 1986, and see also Blundell 1995, and for excellent more specialized studies Connelly 2007 and Blok 2017; the scholarship on women in ancient Greece is vast, but these works are a good starting point. For the enslaved, an excellent starting point is Garlan 1988, and see also Fisher 1993, Thompson 2003, and Bradley and Cartledge (eds.) 2011. Extremely useful is also the work edited by Bellen, Heinen, Schaefer, and Deissler 2003.

1 The Origin and Early Development of the City-State

1 See for instance Coldstream's excellent book *Geometric Greece* (2nd ed., 2004).
2 Archaeological exploration, especially by survey archaeology, has filled out substantially our knowledge of settlements and material conditions in Geometric Greece in recent decades, but the fact remains that the evidence is far scantier than we would like: see e.g., Lemos and Kotsonas (eds.) 2020.
3 Thuc. 1.1.3 to 1.18.3, esp. at 1.5.1–6.1. See further the comments of Gomme 1945, p. 100.
4 See esp. 1.2.1–6 for the unsettled conditions of life; see further Bintliff 2006.
5 See Betant 1969 s.v. for Thucydides' use of the word *ethnos*; note that *LSJ* (9th ed.) does not give this technical sense but see Larsen 1968, pp. 3–10 for the sense and its significance, and further also the literature listed by him at p. 3 n.n. 1 and 2. Also, more recently Morgan 2003, Malkin 2001.
6 *HellOxy* 16.4 and 18.1–3. For text, translation and commentary on this intriguing work see now Billows 2016, also making the case for Theopompos as author, and see further Billows 2009, pp. 219–38; also McKechnie and Kern 1988, though unfortunately they do not comment on the term *ethnos* in these passages.
7 Note also Xenophon *Cyr* 8.8.4 (possibly an interpolation not by Xenophon, but pretty certainly early fourth century); for later usages see, for example, *IG* IV.1 68 and the sources cited at Billows 1995, p. 81 n. 1.
8 See, for example, the exposition of Giovannini in his classic treatment of the *ethnos*: 1971, esp. at 71–93 concluding that the lack of a defined urban center was the only significant difference between the *ethnos* and the city-state.
9 There is, for example, no *RE* article on the *ethnos*, or its German translation *Stammstaat*, though s.v. *koinon* in Suppl. 4 there is recognition of the early *ethnos* as an important precursor of the Hellenistic *koinon*; recently Morgan has begun to fill

in the lacuna in study of the early *ethnos* with her archaeologically based work: see Morgan 1991, pp. 131–63 and 1997, pp. 168–98, and also Morgan 2003; McInerney 1999 on Phokis; Scholten 2000 on Aitolia.

10 Note in Aristotle's final remark about monarchy here the classic opposition of *poleis* on the one hand, *ethne* on the other. The word *ethne* here is sometimes translated "foreign peoples" (e.g., in Rackham's Loeb edition and Jowett's Oxford translation), but there is no warrant at all for this intrusion of the word "foreign" when the *ethnos* was a recognized feature of Greek political life: see the passages of Thucydides, Xenophon, and the *HellOxy* cited above and the sources listed above n. 7.

11 For which see now Gigon 2013, pp. 561–722, and cf. App. 2 below.

12 Included in the 134 *Politeiai* are, besides the Epeirotes and Macedonia, also Molossians, Chaonians, and Elimea, which should perhaps be seen as sections of the former two treatises, rather than independent treatises in their own right.

13 Though one should note that Aristotle did also treat some *poleis* in Arkadia (Mantinea, Tegea), Thessaly (Larissa and Pharsalos), and Boiotia (Thebes, Thespiai).

14 The first three regions mentioned here had tribal monarchies, note Aristotle's references at *Politika* 1310b–1311b and 1342b (Macedonia), 1310a–1311a and 1313a (Molossia), and see *RE* s.v. Athamania and Amyntas for Athamania. Thessaly was in some respects an aristocracy/oligarchy, but the position of the *Tagos* or *Archon* was essentially monarchic: note particularly that in the third quarter of the fourth century Philip II and Alexander the Great held the post of *Archon* of Thessaly and ruled the region monarchically.

15 For the use of Nuristan in this way see e.g., Murray 1993, p. 68 and Whitley 1994, p. 59; for Papua/New Guinea see van Wees 1994, pp. 1–18; for the Melanesian "big man" social structure used as a model for early Greece see Qviller 1981, pp. 109–55 and Whitley 1991, pp. 184–6.

16 See e.g., Raaflaub 1991, pp. 205–56; some doubts about Homer's relevance are powerfully answered by Morris 1986; see also Crielaard (ed.) 1995, pp. 201–88, de Jong (ed.) 1999.

17 See especially Thuc. 1.3.2–3 and 1.9.3–4.

18 The main lines of the work of Parry and Lord are well summarized in Lord 1960 and 1991, and see further Morris 1986; the date of Homer, on which a consensus of *c.* 750–700 seemed to have been reached, has recently been put in play again by West 2011 arguing that he is later than Hesiod and hence mid to late seventh century. Though he presents a powerful case, West does not in the end persuade me, and I stand by the late-eighth-century date of Homer.

19 See the comments of Hope Simpson and Lazenby 1970 and Kirk 1985 *ad loc.*

20 Tribal names: the *Boiotoi*, the *Phokees*, the *Lokroi*, the *Abantes* of Euboia, the *Arkades*, the *Epeioi* of the north-west Peloponnesos, the *Kephallenes* of the Ionian Islands, the *Aitoloi*, the *Kretes*, the *Myrmidones* and *Hellenes* of Phthia and southern Thessaly, the

Enienses and *Perrhaiboi*, and the *Magnetes*. Other communities (for want of a better term) are typically described as "they who held" or "they who dwelt in" *vel sim.*; we never find the classical *polis* names—*Lakedaimonioi, Sikyonioi, Korinthioi* etc.— except in the anomalous case of the *Athenaioi* which will be discussed below.

21 For instance, the *Epeioi* have four leaders, four squadrons, and four towns, and it seems likely that these divisions go together: one town producing one squadron under one leader (see e.g., Kirk 1985, p. 219; Hope Simpson and Lazenby 1970 *ad loc.*); and note further that the *Boiotoi* have five leaders and fifty ships, which is suggestive; the three leaders of the territory of Argos, Tiryns, and the Argolid seem to be closely related; and the Minyans have two leaders (brothers) and two towns.

22 Hope Simpson and Lazenby 1970; Giovannini 1969; J. K. Anderson 1995 at 181–91; Visser 1997; also Chadwick 1976, ch. 10; Jachmann 1958; and cf. further Kirk 1985 at 168–240.

23 Hope Simpson and Lazenby 1970 argued strongly for seeing here a reminiscence of Mycenean Greece but note that many of their identifications of Homeric names with specific sites of Mycenean occupation are arbitrary and based on no more than the discovery in a particular spot, in about the right region, of a handful of Mycenean sherds; see further Kirk 1985. They did, however, make well the basic point that the geography of Homer's "Catalogue" simply accords with Greek realities of sites and names too closely to be considered fictional in any important sense.

24 Giovannini 1969; cf. Kirk 1985 at 184–5; J. K. Anderson 1995.

25 See further Kirk 1985 at 184–5, and for the rise of Olympia and Delphi in the eighth century see Morgan 1990, esp. ch. 4 on early Delphi.

26 Giovannini 1969.

27 See in the first place Thucydides 1.12; and for other sources see *RE* s.v. Boiotia and s.v. Thessalien.

28 Homer *Iliad* 2.631–36, and cf. Kirk 1985 *ad loc.* for the derivation of the name Kephallenia for the island Homer called Same or Samos.

29 The only such possible distinction of status might be the occasional listing of a town in the emphatic first place in its region, as Mycenai in the realm of Agamemnon; Athens and Salamis are exceptions in that no other settlements are listed for each realm. It should be noted that there is no reason to see the places listed in the "Catalogue" as city-states: they are presented as sub-units of larger political entities, and in the case of Phokis, Lokris, and Aitolia, for instance, we know that city-states did not develop in the Archaic and Classical periods.

30 On Archaic and Classical Sparta see e.g., W. G. Forrest 1968 and Cartledge 2002; it is true that elsewhere in Homer Sparte is given as Menelaos' home (e.g., *Od.* 1.285) but that does not seem to mean much, and in any case it is probably not Classical Sparta that is referred to—for that was formed only in the early eighth century by the synoikism of four villages (Cartledge 2002, ch. 8)—but rather the site of the classical

Menelaion on the other side of the river, which was at an important Mycenean settlement (Cartledge 2002, ch. 4).
31 It should be noted, however, that at the very time that Delphi was rising to prominence and creating its *theorodokoi* itineraries, the Spartan city-state was also rising and beginning to change the political structure and relationships in Lakedaimon.
32 This applies to the realms of Agamemnon, Nestor, Diomedes, and his associates, and various of the realms in the Thessalian region; note that Raaflaub 1993, p. 52 refers to the settlements listed in the "Catalogue" as *poleis* in a context suggesting that he means by this "city-states," but without in any way showing how these settlements are to be understood as autonomous political units, something quite at odds with the clear sense of the Homeric text.
33 For example, Raaflaub 1993 at 46–50; *contra* see e.g., Scully 1990 at 100–5.
34 Winning suitor to be king: *Od.* 1.384–401, 15.522; the suitors' provenance from the various Ionian Islands: e.g., *Od.* 1.245–47, 16.122–25 and 246–51; the suitors all attend the Ithakan assembly: *Od.* 1.50–259; the suitors own houses in Ithaka: *Od.* 1.424.
35 N.B. that Ithaka produces the smallest number of suitors: *Od.* 16.247–51: there are fifty-two from Doulichion, twenty-four from Same, twenty from Zakynthos, and twelve from Ithaka. It might, I suppose, be imagined that Ithaka was a city-state of which the other Ionian Islands formed the *chora*, only later to drop away and become city-states in their own right, but this hardly seems plausible, if for no other reason than that it conflicts with Homer's depiction of a "state" of the *Kephallenes*, that is a tribal state, both in the "Catalogue" and in the *Odyssey*.
36 Giovannini 1971.
37 See also the brief but very well put account of Austin and Vidal-Naquet 1981 at 78–81, correctly positing that the *ethnos* was the older state form out of which the *polis* developed, though unfortunately without serious argumentation.
38 E.g., Raaflaub 1993, esp. 46–59; Bowden 1993 at 45–63.
39 Hence the erroneous interpretation of Ithaka in the *Odyssey* as an early or proto city-state, see above nn. 34–35; for the institutions of the *ethnos* and their similarity to those of the city-state see Giovannini 1971.
40 So Raaflaub 1993 at 48 and n. 26, 52 and n. 38; and N.B. also Heubeck, West, Hainsworth 1988 at 293 and Graham 1983, p. 29 on Scheria; on the Achaian camp Kirk 1985/93, vol. II, pp. 276–8.
41 Scully 1990 at 23–40 and Deger-Jalkotzy 1979, pp. 25–31 point to near-eastern parallels; Raaflaub 1993 pp. 46–59 sees a Greek *polis*.
42 Cook 1958/59 at 1–34; Nicholls 1958/59 at 35–137; Akurgal 1983; and cf. Scully 1990 at 85–94.
43 On the limitations of the archaeological record when it comes to trying to discern events, institutions, and the like, see e.g., the cautionary remarks of Snodgrass 1987,

ch. 2 which concludes with the statement (p. 66): "... although classical archaeology can excel ... in revealing man the *maker* with startling clarity, man the *doer* is a different and much more elusive quarry." Cf. also Hodder 1982, esp. at p. 19.

44 On early Iron Age Athens see e.g., Morris 1987 at 63–9, Whitley 1991 at 61–4, and Snodgrass 1982 at 669: Athens in the early Iron Age was "a dispersed agglomeration of homesteads loosely grouped around the Acropolis and the Agora" (Whitley, p. 61) or at best "a cluster of villages" (Snodgrass). On Argos see Haegg 1982, pp. 297–307, detecting the beginnings of settlement nucleation in the mid ninth century but hardly any serious urban infrastructure before the eighth. More generally on the archaeology of early Iron Age Greece see Mee 2011 and Lemos and Kotsonas 2020.

45 This phenomenon led Whitley 1991 to coin the term "unstable settlement" to refer to these Iron Age sites that failed to develop into *poleis* due to abandonment: at p. 184 he lists Lefkandi, Kavousi in Krete, Zagora, Emporio on Chios, and Nichoria in Messenia with references for each; and for Koukounaries see Schilardi 1983. For Lefkandi see also Lemos 2012.

46 Archaeological remains attest to the settlements at Eleusis, Marathon and Thorikos in Attica throughout the Protogeometric and Geometric periods: see e.g., Whitley 1991, pp. 55–8, but note that his suggestion of settlement of these three sites from Athens at the end of Sub-Mycenaean is purely speculative. The archaeological evidence for settlement in Lakonia prior to the mid eighth century is vanishingly slender other than at the Menelaion (Cartledge 2002, chs. 7 and 8), but that in itself indicates the lack of any clear archaeological primacy for historic Sparta, which as we know was just a group of villages before the early eighth century. For the situation in the Argolid in this period the overview by Tomlinson 1972, ch. 6, emphasizing the independence from Argos of communities like Mycenai, Tiryns etc. in the ninth and early eighth centuries, still remains valid, but see also Jameson, Runnels, van Andel 1994.

47 For old Smyrna see n. 42 above, and on urban development in early Ionia in general see J. M. Cook 1975.

48 See Lemos 2002; also Snodgrass 1993; de Polignac 1995.

49 Two well-known exceptions are the islands of Lemnos and (before the end of the fifth century) Rhodos, the former with two cities (Hephaisteia and Myrrhine) and the latter with three (Lindos, Kameiros, and Ialysos). Both of these are of course relatively large islands, as is Lesbos with its five or so cities (Mitylene, Methymna, Eresos, Pyrrha, and Antissa). A more peculiar case is that of the tiny island of Keos, which apparently was divided into four independent "city-states"—more properly village communities: Ioulis, Karthaia, Poiessa, and Koresia. It is, nevertheless, clear that these are exceptions, and that the vast majority of Aegean islands, even such large ones as Chios and Samos for instance, formed a single state from at the latest the sixth century on.

50 On the Meliac War and the division of Melie see e.g., J. M. Cook 1975; and on Myous see R. M. Cook 1962.

51 See Graham 1982 at 109–13 for the foundations in south Italy, and p. 115 for Skione; for the Achaians as an *ethnos* see Giovannini 1971, pp. 53–5, and for the two *ethne* of the Lokrians see pp. 10 and 72.
52 Megara Hyblaia in Sicily is a well known instance: see Vallet et al. 1976, and cf. Graham 1982 pp. 149–50 making the general case and emphasizing the importance of early fortification, with relevant literature.
53 This is well brought out in Graham's summary at 1982, pp. 151–2 with references to fuller discussions.
54 Graham in 1982, pp. 144–52 for the role of the *oikistes*; Graham 1983 for the influence of metropolitan institutions. For updated discussion of the various aspects of "colonization," Tsetskhladze 2006/8.
55 See e.g., Graham 1982 for this, and cf. the list of settlements and founding communities in App. 3 below.
56 For Boiotian participation in the foundation of Herakleia Pontika see Justin 16.3.4–7; Ps.-Skymnos 975–76: Herakleia Pontika is "a foundation *(ktisis)* of Boiotians and Megareans"; and Pausanias 5.26.7: Herakleia was a colony of the Megarians with participation by "Tanagrian Boiotians"; and see further App. 3 below for a list of colonies with multiple founding communities.
57 See Chapter 4 below for these early law-givers.
58 For the important role of religious cults and temple building in developing the city-state as a community, see e.g., de Polignac 1995, and further on Sicily, Marconi 2012.
59 So e.g., Snodgrass 1991 at 10–11; Malkin 1987.
60 Morgan 1990 gives a good overview of this process.
61 Krisa and Kirrha are clearly the same name, the change being due to a simple process of metathesis of the *rho* and the *iota*, with consequent rhotacization of the *sigma*. Settlement at the site seems to have been concentrated at two main locations: an akropolis and a harbor separated from each other by only a short distance.
62 See *RE* s.v. Phokis [Schober], and cf. Pausanias' comments about Panopoeus in his own day (mid second century CE) at 10.4.1; Nielsen and Hansen 2004.
63 The coalition opposed to Krisa was led by Thessaly, Athens, and Sikyon; for sources and modern literature on this topic see e.g., Schober in *RE* s.v. Phokis and Morgan 1990. That the other Phokians joined the coalition opposed to Krisa is attested by Kallisthenes *apud* Athenaios 13.10.560 (cf. Rzepka in *BNJ* no. 124 F1), a hostility which would be explained if Krisa were trying to bring them under its control in the same way that such cities as Argos, Sparta, and Thebes were doing or attempting to do to their neighbors.
64 See Giovannini 1971 for details; also McInerney 1999.
65 For the early wars between the Phokians and the Thessalians and Boiotians, see Herodotos 7.27–28, 7.176; *FGrH* 70 F 93; Plutarch *Mor.* 244e, 558b, 1099e; Pausanias

10.1.5; Justin 16.3.4–7. For the Phokian role in the Persian War of 480–79 see Herodotos 7; for the Phokian relations with Athens and Sparta in the mid fifth century see Thucydides 2; and for the role of the Phokians in the Third Sacred War see Diodoros 16.
66 Head 1911, p. 338; R.T. Williams 1972, esp. 9–11 for the earliest coinage *c.* 510.
67 Details in Schober *RE* s.v. Phokis.
68 See e.g., Fontenrose 1978; Scott 2014.
69 See e.g., Giovannini 1971; Demand 1982; Buckler 1980.
70 Giovannini 1971; see also Larsen 1955, p. 22: Boiotia was an *ethnos* never entirely broken up by *polis* formation.
71 Justin 16.3.4–7 reports the early war against the Phokians and Boiotian participation in the foundation of Herakleia, and for the latter see also Ps.-Skymnos 975–76: Herakleia Pontika is "a foundation *(ktisis)* of Boiotians and Megareans"; Pausanias 5.26.7: Herakleia was a colony of the Megarians with participation by "Tanagrian Boiotians." For the war between the Boiotians and the Thessalians and the Battle of Keressos see Plutarch *Mor.* 866f and *Camillus* 19, Pausanias 9.14.2, and cf. Beloch *GG* 1.2 205–6. For Theban pressure on the other Boiotian towns, and especially on the Plataians, in the late sixth century see Herodotos 6.108.
72 Head 1911, pp. 343–9.
73 Head 1911, p. 346.
74 Diodoros 15.46.6 and 51.3, Xenophon *Hellenika* 6.3.1, and Pausanias 9.14 for Thespiai; for Orchomenos Diodoros 15.79.3–6, Pausanias 9.15.3, and Demosthenes 20.109; and see further Giovannini 1971, p. 50 and n. 26.
75 See e.g., Tomlinson 1972, Haegg 1982, pp. 297–307, and Whitley 1991, pp. 189–94.
76 Tomlinson 1972, pp. 75–8 and Kelly 1976, pp. 51–72 and 88–9 give fairly detailed overviews of the development of Argos' control over the Argive plain; for the brief independence of Mycenai and Tiryns after Sepeia see esp. Herodotos 6.83, 9.28 and 31, the latter two passages attesting troops from Mycenai and Tiryns fighting the Persians at Plataia, when the Argives remained neutral with pro-Persian leanings; also Diodoros 11.65 for the Argives' destruction of Mycenai in 468.
77 The fourth-century historian Ephoros seems to have discussed the "Lot of Temenos" at some length: see Parker 2011 Fs 115 and 176; Kelly 1976 already showed convincingly that the whole tradition is late.
78 See for example Kelly 1976 for a noteworthy example of this tactic applied to Argive history.
79 Below nn. 82–84 for these sources.
80 This point was well made by Kelly 1976, ch. 4.
81 Ephoros *BNJ* 70 F 176 and Pausanias 6.22.2 suggest an early date, in the eighth century; Herodotos 6.127 seems to suggest a late date of *c.* 600, accepted by Kelly 1976, ch. 6 and others; Andrewes 1949 argued very persuasively for an early-seventh-century date, which is now widely accepted.

82 Olympia: Herodotos 6.127; Ephoros *BNJ* 70 F 115; Pausanias 6.22.2; Aigina: Ephoros *BNJ* Fs 115 and 176, Strabo 8.3.33 and 8.6.16, Pollux 9.83, *Marmor Parium* 1.30, *Etymologicon Magnum* s.v. *obelos*; Corinth: Plutarch *Moralia* 772d–773b, scholiast on Apollonios 4.1212; "Lot of Temenos": Ephoros *BNJ* 70 F 176.

83 Pheidon and Corinth: Plutarch *Moralia* 772d–773b and scholiast to Apollonios 4.1212, see also Will 1955, pp. 180–7 and 344–6; on Corinth and the Peloponnesian League see e.g., Salmon 1984; for the early-fourth-century synoikism of Argos and Corinth see Xenophon *Hellenika* 4.4.1–6, 4.8.15, 5.1.34.

84 Herodotos 5.67–68 and cf. Griffin 1982, pp. 37–9 and 50–2.

85 See e.g., Tomlinson 1972, pp. 12–14.

86 See Herodotos 5.82–87; also Thucydides 5.53, and cf. Kelly 1976, pp. 119–20.

87 Herodotos 1.82; Kelly 1976, pp. 120–1.

88 Salmon 1984; Hammond 1982 at 344–54.

89 Herodotos 9.28 records 3,000 Sikyonians, 800 Epidaurians, and 1,000 from Phleious at the battle of Plataia.

90 Herodotos 1.82 and 6.76–81 records Spartan victories over Argos in the mid sixth and early fifth centuries; and see in general Cartledge 2002, chs. 8 and 9 on the expansion of Sparta in the sixth and early fifth centuries.

91 See e.g., Hope Simpson and Lazenby 1970, pp. 74–6; Kirk 1985, p. 213.

92 See e.g., Cartledge 2002, ch. 8.

93 See the description of Cartledge 2002, chs. 2 and 3.

94 Cartledge 2002, ch. 8 with references to modern discussions; also Cole 2021, ch. II.

95 Good discussion in Cartledge 2002, ch. 10 and app. 4, with references to earlier literature.

96 Sources on the Helots and the origin of their name are given in Cartledge 2002, app. 4, and cf. his discussion in ch. 7; for Helots after the loss of Messenia see e.g., Plutarch *Lykourgos* 28 and *Kleomenes* 23.

97 Cartledge 2002, ch. 10 for the annual declaration of war; for the merciless harassment see Plutarch *Lykourgos* 28, and note Thucydides 4.80 reporting the secret massacre of 2,000 Helots during the Peloponnesian War.

98 Above Intro. n. 20 for the various serf-like populations in Greece, and add Griffin 1982, p. 37 n. 13 for Sikyon's *katonakophoroi*.

99 On perioikic status see, e.g., Cartledge 2002, ch. 10.

100 Cartledge 2002, ch. 8.

101 Cartledge 2002, chs. 8 and 9 *passim*.

102 See for this constant policing effort Plato *Laws* 777b–c, Kritias in Diels and Kranz 88 B37, Thucydides 4.80.3, Aristotle *Politika* 1269b7–12, Plutarch *Lykourgos* 28; and N.B. Xenophon *Hellenika* 3.3.6 on the bitterness felt by the Helots and others of subordinate status in the Spartan state.

103 So e.g., Snodgrass 1982.

104 See Snodgrass 1982, pp. 667–9; Whitley 1991.
105 Jones 2016, F 75, already discussed in Boethius 1918, and cf. Morgan 1990 on the period when Delphi rose to pan-Hellenic importance (second half of eighth century).
106 For Thorikos see *HDem.* 126, for Eleusis *HDem. passim*. For the probable date of the hymn see Janko 1982. Note that Hekataios (*BNJ* no. 1 F126 [Pownall]) referred to Thorikos as a *polis*, but of course he may simply have meant "town." See further Hornblower 1991 with ref. to 2.15.1–2.
107 See on this passage in Herodotos and its significance e.g., Padgug 1972, but note that Herodotos' phrase *tous astugeitones en Eleusini* should most naturally be taken to mean "neighbors in Eleusis" (i.e., the Eleusinians), *contra* Padgug's supposition— based entirely on the unsupported and question-begging hypothesis that Eleusis must already have been Athenian at the time implied here—that Herodotos meant that Tellos fought at Eleusis against other, unspecified neighbors of the Athenians, whom he (Padgug) takes to have been the Megarians: Herodotos' word order would surely have been different had he meant to say what Padgug would have him say.
108 See especially Sealey 1976, chs. 4 and 5 for the regionalist disunity and disputes of sixth-century Athens; now also G. Anderson 2003.
109 Snodgrass 1982, pp. 667–9, Andrewes 1982, and Whitley 1991 have argued for an early (tenth- or ninth-century) synoikism of Attica based on the archaeological evidence showing Athenian cultural influence on the rest of the Attic settlements; but see e.g., Hornblower 1991 with ref. to 2.15 for some incisive criticisms, and on the limitations of archaeological evidence generally; also Snodgrass and Hodder at n. 43 above.
110 Instead of listing the settlements of Attica, the "Catalogue" as it stands refers to the cults of Erechtheus and Athena on the Athenian akropolis; on the oddity of this entry see e.g., Kirk 1985 at I.179. For the importance of the Peisistratid recension of Homer, see also S. West in Heubeck, West, Hainsworth (eds.) 1988 at I.36–39, esp. 38 n. 15 on the suspicious character of the Athenian "Catalogue" entry.
111 Aristotle *Rhet. A* 15.1375b30, cf. Kirk 1985 at I.207–9. Other cases are the presence of the fugitive Orestes at Athens rather than in Phokis at *Od.* 3.307; Athena's visit to Athens at *Od.* 7.80–81; the mention of Theseus and Peirithoos in the underworld at *Od.* 11.631.
112 On Peisistratid Attica and Peisistratid policies see e.g., Frost 1990, Andrewes 1982, pp. 392–416, Shapiro 1995; note also the setting up throughout Attica of *horoi* with moral exhortations by Hipparchos: see [Plato] *Hipparchos* 228d–e, and cf. Quinn 2007 at 93–5.
113 Boardman makes this argument on the basis of the scenes depicted on sixth-century Attic Black-Figure pottery: it appears that Herakles was very popular as a

subject, while Theseus was very rarely depicted, in contrast with fifth-century Red-Figure pottery on which he was a popular subject: Boardman 1972, 1975, and 1989; see also Shapiro 1995, Walker 1995, Mills 1997; and also G. Anderson 2003.

114 Note, for example, that Homer seems not to have known of participation by Theseus in the battle of the Lapiths and Centaurs.

115 For Theseus in fifth-century tragedies, note esp. Sophokles' *Oidipous at Kolonos*, Euripides' *Suppliants* and *Phoinissai*.

116 For Theseus in fourth-century political debates about the origins of democracy, see e.g., Jacoby 1949, G. Anderson 2003 at 48–51; for Theseus' role in the "synoikism" of Attica as a Kleisthenic invention, see Boardman (n. 113 above) and G. Anderson 2003 at 134–46 and 174–7.

117 There is a myth of Herakles seizing the Amazon queen, just as there is of Theseus—indeed in some versions the two are reconciled by having Theseus accompany Herakles and receive the Amazon queen from him: see Boardman 1982, pp. 1–28—and the Amazonomachy has clearly been at the very least elaborated through the prism of Athens' wars against the Persians between 490 and 479.

118 On this process of the development of Athenian citizenship, see Sealey 1983, Brook Manville 1990, and G. Anderson 2003.

119 See e.g., Ober 1985.

120 See Knoepfler 1985 on relations between Eretria and Oropos; Herodotos 1.52 for Theban control *c*. 550; Herodotos 5.77 and 6.101 suggest Athenian control by the end of the sixth century; and cf. in general *RE* s.v. Oropos [Wiesner].

121 For early conflict with Megara over Eleusis see Legon 1981 at 63 and 100–1, and note also the support of the Megarian tyrant Theagenes for Kylon's attempted tyranny at Athens, a possible source of Kylon's unpopularity with the Athenian people; for conflicts between Athens and Megara over Salamis see Herodotos 1.59 and Plut. *Solon* 8–10; for subsequent border disputes note e.g., the infamous Athenian "Megarian Decree(s)" (see e.g., the full if not always convincing discussion of de Ste. Croix 1972); and in general on early Megara see Legon 1981 and Figueira and Nagy (eds) 1985.

122 See e.g., Meyer in *RE* s.v. Megara; Legon 1981 and Figueira and Nagy 1985.

123 On Megarian colonization see above n. 36 and App. 3 below for details; on the tyranny of Theagenes see Berve 1967; for conflict with Athens over Salamis see above n. 121; and on Theognis see e.g., Figueira and Nagy (eds) 1985.

124 For Theseus' connections with Megara, including his boundary marker, see Plut. *Theseus*; for Peisistratos and Megara see Herodotos 1.59, Aristotle *AthPol* 14.1 and 17.1, and Aineias Taktikos 4.8–12; and on Athens and Megara in the fifth century see e.g., de Ste. Croix 1972; on Megara's early war with Corinth see Meyer in *RE* s.v. Megara cols. 185–6.

125 It is interesting to note the purported proposal of Thales that the Ionians of the east Aegean synoikize into one *polis* with Teos as their *astu* and the other Ionian towns as demes (Herodotos 1.170).

2 Economic Development and the City-State

1 See for example Meyer 1895 for a classic exposition of the so-called "modernist" view of the ancient economy; French 1964 for a re-statement of the "modernist" view.
2 Basing themselves on the work and ideas of the great sociologist Max Weber and the noted economic sociologist Karl Polanyi (see Polany 1944 and 1957), scholars like Hasebroek 1928 and above all Finley 1973 presented a "primitivist" view of an "embedded" Greek economy dominated by subsistence agriculture.
3 Engels 1990.
4 Note for example that when the Thebans launched a surprise attack on Plataia in spring of 431, many Plataians were out in the fields (Thucydides 2.5); Xenophon tells us that the Mantineans lived in the city and traveled out to work their farms, until the Spartans forced them in 384 to abandon the city and live in villages near their farms (*Hellenika* 5.2.7); when the Macedonian general Arrhidaios attacked Kyzikos in 318, most of the Kyzikenes, it being a time of peace, were out in the countryside (Diodorus Siculus 18.51.2–3); and cf. Osborne 1987, and on fragmented and scattered landholdings as an important survival strategy see e.g., Gallant 1991, esp. at 41–5; also Rackham 1983, pp. 291–352; Runnels and van Andel 1987.
5 This was noticed long ago already: see the discussion in Trever 1916; and cf. now Weinstein 2009, pp. 439–58.
6 Note especially the flat statement by Herodotos at 1.32: "no country is entirely self-sufficient; any given country has some things but lacks others, and the best country is the one which has the most. By the same token, no one person is self-sufficient: he has some things but lacks others" (tr. Waterfield in Oxford World's Classics ed.).
7 See for example Ps-Xenophon *Constitution of the Athenians* 1.11–12 and 19–20, and esp. 2.11–12; and note Xenophon *Poroi* on the vast income the Athenians got from the harbor dues of the Peiraieus.
8 See for further examples, Chant 1999.
9 As Hippokrates put it in his *Airs, Waters, Places* 24: "where the land is bare, waterless, rough, oppressed by winter's storms and burnt by the sun, there you will see men who are hard, lean, well-articulated, well-braced, and hairy; such natures will be found energetic, vigilant, stubborn and independent in character and in temper, wild rather than tame, of more than average sharpness and intelligence in the arts, and in

war of more than average courage." Note also the story with which Herodotos finishes his history at 9.122, noting that "soft lands tend to breed soft men" and that "it is impossible ... for one and the same country to produce remarkable crops and good fighting men," with the obvious implication that the Greeks who had defeated the Persian were the good fighting men produced by a hard country.

10 Sallares 1991 notes several times that Messenia is more fertile and has more cultivable land than Attica, for example: see esp. p. 478 nn. 70 and 72 where he notes that some 34 percent of Attica was classified as farmland, whereas between 42 and 60 percent of Messenia is cultivable. The well-watered nature of Thessaly and Macedonia did have the drawback of providing fertile breeding grounds for mosquitoes, with the consequent prevalence of malaria: see Borza 1995, ch. 3 pp. 57–84.

11 In modern times much of the population has left northwest Greece in search of better opportunities, and the heart of the region is referred to as the *agrapha*, the unwritten places: see for example the interesting travelogue by Salmon 1995.

12 On southeast Greece see e.g., the extensive discussion of Attica in Sallares 1991, pp. 295–312; and also the extensive exploration of the Argolid by Jameson, Runnels, and van Andel 1994.

13 For the predominance of barley over wheat see Sallares 1991, pp. 313–89.

14 Sallares 1991 at 1–41 and 295–308.

15 On olive cultivation see Foxhall 2007, and cf. Sallares 1991 at 30–8; for the use of intercropping see Gallant 1991, pp. 38–41.

16 Transhumant sheepherders have been a feature in Greece and the Balkans into modern times: see the classic study of the Sarakatsani people by Campbell 1964; see also e.g., Chang 1993; for sheepherding and transhumance in ancient Greece see e.g., Forbes 2013.

17 E.g., Jones 1976; Crane 1999; Anderson-Stojanovic and Jones 2002.

18 On fishing in ancient Greece see the excellent articles in Bekker-Nielsen (ed.) 2006, esp. at 21–30 on "Fish as a source of food in Antiquity" and at 83–96 on "The technology and productivity of ancient sea fishing" (by Wilkins); on garum see RE s.v. [Zahn].

19 See Ormerod 1924, de Souza 2002, Tsetskhladze 2000/1, esp. at 11–26.

20 On raiding and trading see for example the chapters by Jackson and Rihll in Rich and Shipley (eds.) 1993, chs. 4 and 5; on the Phoenicians see now Niemeyr 2006.

21 See Sallares 1991 at 390–6 on the climate and its variations; Gallant 1991 is the classic exposition of the precariousness of the farming economy.

22 Cf. Burford 1994.

23 For a good summary, including results of surveys, Snodgrass 1991; see also Tandy 1997 at 38–42, Bintliff 1997, Eder 1998, Morris 2000, Mee 2011, Lemos and Kotsonas 2020.

24 The case for significant demographic growth (which should always have been obvious) was put strongly by Sallares 1991 at 42–93; and cf. now also Scheidel 2003,

p. 120: "recovery was underway in the ninth before accelerating in the 8th [century] ... demographic and economic growth continued into the late classical period ..." At this point Scheidel still resisted the idea of "explosive" population growth in the eighth/seventh centuries but see now Scheidel 2013 accepting very substantial demographic growth based on urban growth (see Hansen 2006) and economic development (see Morris 2004) and acknowledging a likely population of some 7 to 9 million for classical Greece.

25 On resettlement and urban growth e.g., Snodgrass 1991 and Owens 1991 at 11–29; the cumulative evidence for Greek urban development is now collected in Nielsen and Hansen (eds.) 2004 and Hansen 2006, and proves demographic growth incontrovertibly, as Scheidel 2013 acknowledges.

26 Snodgrass 1977 and 1980 laid out the burial evidence and suggested a demographic underpinning; Morris 1987 and 2000 questioned the direct link between burial and demography, but while the link may not have been as straightforward as Snodgrass supposed, we must surely still acknowledge that significantly more burials on some level imply more population: see e.g., Tandy 1997.

27 See e.g., Scheidel 2003 on the necessary linkage between demographic growth and economic growth; and see also Boserup 1965 and 1981 on the relationship between population pressure and development.

28 Scheidel 2003, Boserup 1981; and cf. also Morris 2004.

29 The evidence is well summarized by Scheidel 2003, see also Bintliff 1997 for Boiotia; Jameson, Runnels, and van Andel 1994 for the Argolid; Eder 1998 for southern Peloponnesos more generally; and cf. the interesting model of urban centralization by Rihll and Wilson 1991 at 59–96.

30 For example, Laertes' farm in *Odyssey* 24.200–260, and Odysseus' own orchard at *Odyssey* 24.330–345; the *temenos* of the Lykian *basileus* in *Iliad* 12.310–314 is agricultural land; see further Donlan 1989, and note also Homer's extensive use of similes drawn from agriculture: ploughing, reaping, etc.

31 N.B. for examaple, *Iliad* 6.47–48 "in my rich father's house lie many treasures (*keimelia*), bronze is there, and gold, and hardly wrought iron" and cf. 10.330, 12. 132, etc.; also *Odyssey* 4.613–14 "loveliest of the treasures my house holds, a mixing bowl (*krater*) of wrought metal," and cf. 2.75, 11.40 etc.; note that this emphasis on *keimelia* indicates the scarcity (and so high value) of metals of all sorts.

32 Cf. Finley's discussion in 1979; for the wrestling prizes at the funeral games: *Iliad* 23.702–5; for the exchange of armor between Diomedes and Glaukos: *Iliad* 6.119–236; for Odysseus' wealth measured in livestock: *Odyssey* 14.13–20 and 96–104.

33 Snodgrass 1980, esp. 35–6 and 1982.

34 Chang 1993 at 687–703; for sheepherding and transhumance in ancient Greece see e.g., Forbes 2013.

35 On the Vlachs e.g., Koukoudis 2003, and on the Sarakatsani esp. Campbell 1964.

36 Campbell 1964 at 124–31 on Sarakatsan marriage by abduction; for Spartan abduction-marriage see Plutarch *Lycurgus* 15
37 Campbell 1964 at 36–58 on Sarakatsan kinship groups; on ancient Greece e.g., Bourriot 1976, Roussel 1976, and Lambert 1999.
38 Campbell 1964 at 117–18, 140, 300 on Sarakatsan ritual meals; on the significance of commensality in classical Greece see e.g., Murray (ed.) 1990, chs. 2, 5, 11.
39 N.B. that Aristotle here speaks of seeking the support of the *demos* (people), and the *demos* is characterized as dwelling in the fields busy at work. For some studies on Megara see Figueira and Nagy 1985, Legon 1981.
40 Figueira and Nagy 1985 on Theognis; Campbell 1964 facing p. 288 shows the goatskin cloak of the Sarakatsan sheep and goat herders.
41 Above pp.39–40 and esp n. 103.
42 See Clark and Haswell 1964 on the economics of subsistence farming, and the benefit of increased labor input; and cf. Boserup 1965.
43 Hesiod *Erga* 235–275; Homer *Iliad* 2.213–214 and 225–242
44 *Iliad* 2.217–219; compare Aristotle's attitude to work: Nederman 2008, esp. 17–31.
45 See for example Bresson 2016 at 142–56
46 See in general on this Gallant 1991 and Jameson, Runnels, and van Andel 1994 for a detailed study of the Argolid.
47 Gallant 1991 emphasizes the role of scattered landholdings as a hedge against disaster; see also Bresson 2016 at 157–60.
48 The literature on the development of the Greek economy is vast, and there are still some scholars who are inclined to be somewhat skeptical of economic development (see e.g., Horden and Purcell 2000); but see now Morris 2004 and especially Bresson 2016; also Amemiya 2007.
49 Harris 2002 lists the trades practiced in ancient Greece: 170 separate trades all told, with evidence and analysis.
50 Foxhall 2007, and cf. Sallares 1991 at 304–8.
51 On Attic pottery production and trade see now Bresson 2016 at 364–79.
52 See Bresson 2016 at 286–409, and for the archaeological evidence see also e.g., Parker 1992.
53 Diogenes Laertius 6.2.41; Aelian *VH* 12.56; Plutarch *Moralia* 526c; Xenophon *Memorabilia* 2.7.6.
54 Again, see now Bresson 2016 at 339–80.
55 See e.g., Graham 1983; and note also Graham 1982 at 157–9 summarizing his view that desire for agricultural land (on the part of colonists) and to relieve overpopulation (on the part of metropolitan elites) were the primary motivators, and that trade as a motivation is possible in a few cases but unproven and probably unprovable.
56 Note that at Kyrene deliberate provision was made for later colonists to join and receive land allotments: see Meiggs and Lewis 1969 no. 5 at lines 30–3, and compare

Herodotos 4.159; another indicator of ongoing arrival of colonists is the quick foundation of secondary colonies, e.g., by Syracuse (Akrai, Heloros, Kamarina, Kasmenai for which see *RE* s.v.), by Zankle (Mylai), by Thasos (Neapolis and others), by Massalia (Nikaia, Antipolis), etc.; it is possible that distinctions between the first settlers and later arrivals are the origin of the class differences soon to be found in the originally distinctly egalitarian colonies; see further now Tsetskhladze (ed.) 2006.

57 See Wilson 1997 at 199–207 on new settlements as *emporia;* also Hansen in Tsetskhladze (ed.) 2006, vol. 1 ch. 2.

58 See App. 3 for a list of Milesian colonies; incomplete as our knowledge is, we know that Miletos' colony at Kardia was founded with participation from Klazomenai, that Amisos included people from Phokaia, and that Parion had settlers from Paros and Erythrai; in general though, sheer demographic realities make it certain that the majority of colonists for most of Miletos' colonies must have come from elsewhere—other Ionian communities in the first place, but no doubt all around the Aegean in general.

59 See e.g., Polybios 4.38 and Strabo 9.439 for the importance of grain, salt fish, hides, and slaves as Black Sea exports. On the metal resources of the Black Sea region see most conveniently Boardman 1980 at 238–45, esp. at 241 citing an interest in "the rich mining areas of northern Asia Minor, Armenia, and the Caucasus" as a prime motivating factor in Greek interest in the Black Sea; and note also the Greek myth of "Jason and the golden fleece" for Greek knowledge of and interest in Caucasian gold. Boardman also notes the "good supplies of fine timber" (p. 244) on the south shore of the Black Sea, see in more detail Meiggs 1980. Note, too, that Olbia, at the point on the north Black Sea coast where the two rivers Bug and Dnepr both reach the sea together, is on one occasion actually called an *emporion* by Herodotos (4.17.1), and again there can be no doubt that trade in wheat and metals with the peoples living in these two great river valleys was a prime consideration in choosing this site.

60 Herodotos 2.178 and Strabo 17.801 for the Milesian involvement at Naukratis; Herodotos 6.21 for the close relationship between Miletos and Sybaris; Plutarch *Mor.* 298c for the Milesian *Aeinautai.*

61 Mele 1979 for this distinction, but see Ridgway 1992, pp. 107–9 for some cogent doubts as to the validity of the distinction; and see now Wilson 1997 and Hansen in Tsetskhladze 2006, vol. I ch. 2.

62 See Austin 1970; also Braun 1982 at 37–43.

63 Graham 1982 at 141–2; Almagro 1958.

64 So e.g., Cook 1962; Graham 1983.

65 Ridgway 1992 in fact remarks at p. 119 that one of the key advantages of the new settlement founded a generation later *c.* 750 at Kyme (Cumae) on the mainland opposite Ischia was that it "was capable, in a way that Pithekoussai was not, ... of a degree of agricultural exploitation of the surrounding territory (*chora*) comparable with that operated at the first foundations far to the south in Sicily"; and see esp. his

remarks at 33–4 on the island's agricultural characteristics—the island has always been specialized in viticulture because of the nature of terrain (hilly), climate and soil, areas of land suitable for other kinds of agriculture are few and far between, and there is a constant fight against soil erosion. See further Buchner Niola 1965.

66 See the account of Ridgway 1992 notably at 91–5 and 99–100, summing up the results of the extensive excavations carried out by the author and Giorgio Buchner.

67 See esp. Casson 1991 and 1994 for ancient seafaring; also Andreau and Virlouvet 2002; and note ancient *periplous* literature (the *periploi* of Skylax, of Ps.-Skymnos, of the Black Sea, and of the Red Sea, for example) which consisted of little more than lists of ports of call and landmarks along trade routes.

68 Herodotos 2.178; see Austin 1970; also Braun 1982 at 37–43; Hansen in Tsetskhladze 2006, vol. I ch. 2.

69 Johnston 1972.

70 Granted a maximum population density based on subsistence farming with pre-modern technology of 60 per km^2 (Boserup 1965), 86 km^2 should sustain *c.* 5,160 people, but since a third of the island is rocky, something closer to 4,000 is more plausible.

71 Cf. Beloch 1886 offering a similar estimate; contra eg., Figueira 1991: *c.* 35,000–45,000; others estimate even lower. The low estimates assume that Aigina employed thousands of mercenary rowers in its fleets, but fail to explain whence such mercenary rowers came in 480, when the manpower of the Greek states was more or less fully mobilized in each instance for self-defense; or in the 450s when again the Aegean states were mobilized on Athens' side, the states of the Saronic Gulf and Peloponnesos were mobilized in self-defense as they were involved in the war, and Athens had the island cut off and under siege.

72 Compare the even tinier island of Hydra in the late eighteenth and early nineteenth centuries which grew wealthy based on middle man trade around the Mediterranean, so that it had a population in excess of 16,000 by 1821 and boasted a fleet of 150 vessels: see e.g., Vanderpool 1980. At *c.* 50,000 km^2, much of it rocky, the island is much smaller than Aigina, and its modern population of *c.* 2,000 much more closely approximates its natural carrying capacity.

73 Ephoros of Kyme in *BNJ* no. 70 F 176 (Parker, 2011).

74 See e.g., Kroll and Waggoner 1984, esp. at 335–9, and note the table at p. 337 showing the coin hoards with Aiginetan coins, found in places as far apart as Asyut and Sakha in Egypt, Taranto and Sambiasi in Italy, and Persepolis in Iran.

75 Another example of a city that lived from manufacturing and trade seems to be Tarrha in Krete, a large city with a thriving trade in cypress wood and glass manufacture: Rackham 1990 who points out at 108–9 that though Tarrha was a place of note, it had virtually no hinterland that could be cultivated, meaning that the city relied heavily on trade.

76 Morris 2004, Amemiya 2007, Bresson, 2016, even more skeptical scholars like Horden and Purcell 2000; and note also the shipwreck evidence collected by Parker 1992.
77 For this and what follows see e.g., Seaford 2004; also Kurke 1999.
78 E.g., Aristophanes *Wasps* 684 and 691 for jurors' 3 obols; and cf. Markle 2004. Rowers in the fleet seem to have been paid between 1 drachma and 3 obols, depending on circumstances: see Jordan 1972 at 111–16 and Peck 2001, ch. 4.2.
79 Aristophanes *Wasps* 605–620.
80 Ruschenbusch 1979 at 106–10
81 The fact that, as Aristotle tells us at *AthPol* 49, citizens suffering from some infirmity that hampered them from working, and who owned property less than 3 *mnai* (i.e., 300 drachmas) in value, received a daily handout from communal funds of 2 obols, shows that an adult man (and his family?) could survive on even less than 3 obols; it's worth noting that according to Aristophanes *Wasps* 1391 a loaf of bread cost 1 obol in fifth-century Athens (and Demosthenes 34.37 states the same price in the late fourth century); and note that at *Wasps* 300–1 a juror expects to buy "barley meal (*alphita*), wood, and a relish (*opson*)" for three people with his 3 obols. Markle has calculated based on evidence for prices of foodstuffs and standard consumption that a family of four could be fed sufficiently on 2½ obols per day: Markle 2004, pp. 110–12
82 Austin and Vidal Naquet 1980, p. 266 estimate that only *c.* 5,000 Athenian citizens did not own any land in 403, out of a likely citizen body at that time of *c.* 40,000. Jameson 1977/78, p. 125 estimates that two out of every three Athenians in fact had property worth at least 2,000 drs.
83 Evidence in Markle 2004, pp 125–6; we should not (*pace* Markle) just assume that wages had doubled between about 409 and the 330s; there may have been special reasons for the difference, e.g., in the closing stages of the Peloponnesian War, after the Sicilian disaster, wages for public work at Athens may have been depressed due to shortage of finance. Note also the crucial work of Loomis 1998, a key collection of data on wages and prices.
84 Accounts of construction at Erechtheion indicate that citizens working there earned between 23 and 30 drs. per month: see Markle 2004, p. 125 reviewing the evidence from *IG I* (3rd ed.), 475 and 476.
85 This has long been known, though it's often ignored in practice: Cohen's key 1989 article, and for early acknowledgment of this e.g., Herfst 1922; Michell 1963 at 134–9.
86 Aristophanes *Wasps* 498–501 and 1388–1412; also e.g., *Thesmophoriazousai* 387–88 for Euripides' mother.
87 Aristophanes *Frogs* 549–80; *Thesmophoriazousai* 445–58.
88 Demosthenes *Against Euboulides* 31–34; note also *IG* II^2 1533 in which various freedwomen are attested making a living as wool workers (i.e., weavers), shop keepers, market sellers of vegetables, honey, and sesame seed, among other trades.

89 Xenophon *Memorabilia* 2.7.
90 Demosthenes *Against Euboulides* 35.
91 See e.g., Sallares 1991, pp. 313–16 and via index on wheat and barley in ancient Greece.
92 The word "typical" is used here to denote prices in normal times, when scarcity of some sort was not driving prices up. For 1 *choinix* of wheat as a soldier's daily ration, see e.g., Herodotos 7.187.2; and Thucydides 4.16 for 2 *choinikes* of barley meal as the daily ration of a soldier, half that for his servant; Thuc. 7.87 names 2 *kotylai* of grain daily as a punitive diet for Athenian prisoners working in the Syracusan stone quarries.
93 The Spartan soldiers trapped on Sphakteria in 424 were allowed 2 *kotylai* of wine each per day: Thuc. 4.16, their servants half that.
94 Amemiya 2007 pp. 70–1. These are garments meant for slaves, but N.B. Ps. Xenophon *ConstAth* 1.10 pointing out that poor citizens and slaves at Athens dressed the same.
95 For example, Glotz, Boeckh, Mauri, and Michell all agreed on assuming that the average Greek working man paid about 36 drachmas per year in rent: see Michell 1963 at p. 133 citing the other three authors; the figure 36 drachmas is based on an expected 12 per cent return on a house worth 300 drachmas (3 *mnai*).
96 See Pritchett and Pippin 1953, pp. 225–99 for the texts of the inscriptions; 1956 at 260–75 for commentary, and cf. Markle 2004. Note also the "cottage" valued at 300 drachmas in 360 referenced by Davies 1981, p. 50 from Isaios 2.35. Aristotle *AthPol* 49 records the payment of 2 obols per day to the infirm with property of less than 3 *mnai* (= 300 drachmas).
97 Thucydides 2.13.
98 For the percentage of the male population per age class see e.g., Coale and Demeny 1983 model West. There would be far fewer men in the over forty-five classes than in the age classes twenty to forty-five, for obvious reasons.
99 Alkibiades' estate of 300 *plethra* or 29 hectares is reported by Plato *1Alk* 123c; for 5 hectares as the amount required for the hoplite census, see Hodkinson 1988, p. 39, and note that Jameson 1977/78, p. 125 indicates that many known plots of land were in the range of 3.6 to 5.4 hectares and valued at 2–3,000 drachmas, indicating that the 2,500 drachmas required for the *eisphora* would indeed be the value of about 5 hectares; for Demosthenes' father's workshops see his speech *Against Aphobos* at 9–11, and cf. e.g., Amemiya 2007, pp. 30 and 66, giving the value of the two workshops as 190 and 230 *mnai* respectively, for a total of 420 *mnai* or 7 talents. Demosthenes' father also owned a house rented out as apartments, and his own home, bringing his total wealth up to some 50–60,000 all told, but the point being made here stands; see also MacDowell 2010 in his chapter on Demosthenes' inheritance.

100 A point made explicitly by Xenophon *Cyropaedia* 8.2.5.
101 See Harris 2002 on the wide variety of goods on sale daily in the Athenian *agora*, and the division of the market into defined areas where each variety of goods could be found.
102 Ps. Xenophon *Constitution of the Athenians* 2.11–12; see also Xenophon *Poroi* 3.
103 Harris 2002 lists 170 distinct crafts and skills practiced by ancient Greeks to make a living.
104 For Nikias' 1,000 slaves see Xenophon *Poroi* 4.14, and Xenophon also mentions Hipponikos and Philemonides having 600 and 300 slaves respectively working in the mines; N.B. Lysias' shield factory with 120 slaves (Lysias *Against Eratosthenes* 8 and 19), Demosthenes' father's workshops with thirty-two and twenty slaves respectively (Demosthenes *Against Aphobos* 27.9–11), and Timarchos' father owning "nine or ten" slaves working in a shoe-making workshop (Aischines 1.97).
105 So, Xenophon casually states at *Memorabilia* 2.3.3: "All who are able to do so buy slaves so as to have fellow workers (*synergoi*)."
106 A well-known example of this phenomenon is the evidence of masters and slaves working alongside each other on the great Athenian building projects of the 430s: see e.g., *IG* I² 374.
107 See for example the remarks on the relative "freedom" accorded slaves at Athens by the author of the Ps.-Xenophon *Constitution of the Athenians* 1.11, pointing out that "financial considerations make it necessary to be servants to their slaves, in order to collect a portion of their earnings, and eventually to let them go free"; N.B. Aischines 1.97 reporting that Timarchos' father owned "nine or ten" slaves working as shoemakers, from whom he collected a fee of 2 obols per day each; for a comprehensive discussion of manumission and its limitations in ancient Greece see now Zelnick-Abramovitz 2005.
108 Harris 2002, p. 70 estimates the number of metics in fourth-century Athens as high as 20,000.
109 It needs to be acknowledged here that the exploitative and unjust system of enslavement played a major role in making the lifestyles of the middling and upper elements in Greek city-states possible, as well as the subordination and marginalization of women.
110 Plutarch *Perikles* 12 "*naous chiliotalantous*." Stanier 1953, pp. 68–76, drawing on comparative evidence from Eleusis, Epidauros, and Delphi, as well as fragments of the Parthenon accounts, estimated the cost at under 500 talents; the Asklepieion at Epidauros cost less, and Stanier cites a figure of 330 talents for the temple of Apollo at Delphi; and see also Burford 1969.
111 See Maier 1959–61; and cf. Lawrence 1979 esp. at 82.
112 For a convenient list see List of ancient Greek theatres, Wikipedia.

113 Kienast 2005 on the Eupalinos tunnel; Owens 1982, pp. 222–5 on the "Enneakrounoi" fountain.
114 See e.g., Owens 1991, ch. 8 on urban infrastructure.

3 The Spear: Warfare and the City-State

1. Aristotle *Politika* 6.7.1-3 (=1321a): "there are four groups useful in war, cavalry, heavy-armed forces, light-armed forces, and naval forces. Where the land happens to be suited for horses, it is natural to build up a strong oligarchy ... for the rearing of horses depends on people who own large estates. Where the land is suited for heavy-armed maneuvers, the next sort of oligarchy (i.e., moderate) is natural, since a heavy-armed force is made up of the well-off rather than the needy. But light-armed and naval forces are entirely suited to popular rule" (tr. J. Sachs).
2. This was pointed out by Clausewitz in his great work *Vom Kriege* (*On War*), see also Handel 1986; and see further A. Forrest 2009.
3. See e.g., Billows 1995, ch. 1; Billows 2018, chs. 3 and 4.
4. See the classic work of Gabba 1976, chs. 1 and 2; and cf. Billows 2008, pp. 22–6.
5. For women in Greek warfare see e.g., Loman 2004 and Carney 2021; for the roles of the enslaved in war see esp. Hunt 2021.
6. Jordan 2000 argued that the rowers in Athenian fleets were predominantly slaves, but despite his best efforts the evidence does not support this view: in particular Ps. Xenophon *Const. Ath.* 1.2 makes it clear, in arguing that lower class citizens at Athens deserved to participate and be heard in the political system because they crewed the fleet, that the fleet was in fact predominantly crewed by the poorer citizens; and Aristotle in the passage cited above makes the same point. Note also Ps. Xenophon *Const.Ath.* 1.19–20 emphasizing that every man who goes to see necessarily takes an oar at some point, so that Athenians who travel a lot are good rowers already when they board a warship.
7. Andrewes 1956; Lorimer 1947: see further Snodgrass 1965; Bowden 1993.
8. Latacz 1977; see also for example Hanson 1991 at 80–1, Raaflaub 1991 at 225–30; and cf. the discussion by van Wees 1994 at 1–6.
9. For *phalanges* see *Iliad* 2.558, 3.77, 4.254, 5.93 etc.; for *stichas* see *Iliad* 2.525, 3.113, 4.90, etc.; below pp. 87–90 on the hoplite phalanx.
10. The battle over the corpse and armor of Patroklos is described at length in *Iliad* 17.1–370, and cf. the case of Sarpedon at *Iliad* 16.477–684.
11. A fuller account, analysis, and defense of the credibility of Homeric warfare is provided by van Wees 1994, and cf. van Wees 1992; see also Brouwers 2013.
12. Note that in the late sixth century, a basic hoplite panoply would still cost some 30 drachmas, about the value of six oxen: see Jackson 1991 at 229.

13 See Greenhalgh 1973, ch. 1 "The Chariot in Homer"; on Assyrian chariot warfare see e.g., de Backer 2013 at 69–78

14 Translation by author; the Latin text reads: "*Genus hoc est ex essedis pugnae. Primo per omnes partes perequitant et tela coiciunt atque ipso terrore equorum et strepitu rotarum ordines plerumque perturbant, et cum se inter equitum turmas insinuaverunt, ex essedis desiliunt et pedibus proeliantur. [2] Aurigae interim paulatim ex proelio excedunt atque ita currus conlocant ut, si illi a multitudine hostium premantur, expeditum ad suos receptum habeant.*" See also J.K. Anderson 1965, pp. 349–52.

15 Greenhalgh 1973, ch. 2, "The Chariot in Geometric Art"; Bell and Willekes 2014, pp. 478–90.

16 Aristotle *Politika* 6.7.2 (=1321a) noted that "the rearing of horses depends on people who own large estates," and at 4.3.2 (=1289b) he wrote "with respect to raising horses ... this is not easy to do without being rich." For the use of expensive bronze facing on chariots see e.g., the well preserved ancient chariot in the Metropolitan Museum, NY: Emiliozzi 2011.

17 Finley 1957, 2nd revised ed. 1979; cf. Qviller 1981 and Brouwers 2013 arguing for *c*. 700 as the time period depicted.

18 See Lord 1960 and 1991, chs. 2 and 5.

19 The earliest depictions of what appears to be hoplite phalanx warfare, dating to *c*. 650 to 640, are on the so-called Chigi vase (see my Plate 1) and the "Macmillan aryballos" (aryballos British Museum), and see also the contemporary songs of the Spartan poet Tyrtaios.

20 See Snodgrass 1999 and cf. Bardunias and Ray 2016 at 29–35 for a detailed description of the *aspis* and how it was made.

21 Bardunias and Ray 2016 at 33–4 for the *antilabe* and *porpax*.

22 See for example the full and clear description of how this worked given by Thucydides a propos of his description of the Battle of Mantinea in 418: Thuc. 5.71; and note the Spartan view that a man wore his other defensive armor for his own protection but carried his shield for the army as a whole (Plutarch *Mor.* 220).

23 See Snodgrass 1999 for the Corinthian helmet.

24 For vulnerability of small bands of hoplites to lighter more mobile opponents see Thuc 3.97–98 on Aitolian light infantry versus Athenian hoplites under Demosthenes in 427/6, and Xenophon *Hellenika* on Iphikrates' use of more mobile peltasts to destroy a small Spartan hoplite force at Lechaion in 390ish; see further Hanson 1991 esp. p. 78 n. 1 and Krentz 1985 on the weight and cumbersomeness of the panoply.

25 See e.g., Hanson 1991, ch. 3 and Bardunias and Ray 2016 on the close link between hoplite armor and the hoplite phalanx.

26 See for example Xenophon *Hellenika* 7.4.2; also Arrian *Taktika* 11.4, and cf. Diodorus Siculus 16.3.

27 An enormous amount has been written on the hoplite phalanx formation and fighting: see for example Hanson 1991, Krentz 1985, 2002, and 2010, Lendon 2005, Kagan and Viggiano 2013, esp. at 1–56, Bardunias and Ray 2016, part 3.
28 See e.g., the remarks of the lyric poet Archilochos of Paros fr. 60 on the preferred type of general; and note also how frequently Greek generals were injured or killed in battle, for example the Athenian generals Nikostratos and Laches at Mantinea in 418 (Thucydides 5.61 and 74); the Athenian Kleon and the Spartan Brasidas at Amphipolis in 422 (Thucydides 5.10); the Theban Epaminondas at Mantinea in 361 (Xenophon *Hellenika* 7.5.25, and cf. Plutarch *Epaminondas*), and many others. See also Wheeler 1991 at 121–72.
29 See e.g., the pipers depicted on the Chigi vase (Plate 1); and see further Thucydides 5.70 on the importance of pipers in the Spartan army.
30 Pritchett 1985, pp. 44–93, esp at 46; Lazenby 1991, esp at 90–2.
31 See LSJ (9th ed.) s.v. *othismos* for the term and its meaning, and see Herodotos 7.225, 9.62, Thucydides 4.96, Xenophon *Anabasis* 5.2.17 for examples of it in battle; cf. Pritchett 1985 at 65–73.
32 Thucydides 4.96, describing the Boiotians fighting the Athenians at Delion in 424, is perhaps the clearest example of the role of this shoving in battle; see on the *othismos* Luginbill 1994, and Matthew 2009.
33 Buckler 1980 at 46–69.
34 This is what happened at the Battle of Mantinea in 361, for example (Xen. *Hell.* 7.5.26–27).
35 Archilochos fr. 6 and Alkaios (according to Herodotos 5.95) flouted the convention about dropping their shields to escape a losing battle, but for the conventional view see e.g., Aristophanes' frequent taunting of Kleonymos for dropping his shield.
36 Pritchett 1985 at 94–260 on disposal of the dead, and 1975 at 246–75 on the battlefield *tropaion*.
37 See Krentz 1985, 2002, and 2010, for example. However, the precise details of hoplite battle are of less relevance here than the idea of hoplite warfare that held sway in classical Greece: of the hoplite as a self-reliant and self-motivated citizen taking his stand in the collective of the phalanx, alongside relatives, neighbors, fellow clansmen, members of his social group and community, as a matter of duty, honor, and commitment to the community.
38 Examples of this are numerous throughout the *Iliad*, see esp. the battles over the bodies of Sarpedon (*Iliad* 16.462–683) and Patroklos (*Iliad* 17.1–741).
39 See the excellent analysis of van Wees 1994 at 2–9 on this.
40 See the detailed analysis of van Wees 1992 and 1994 for all this.
41 See the account of van Wees 1994, pp. 132–3; the Argive or hoplite shield was only introduced around 700, see Snodgrass 1999.

42 Herodotos 2.152–53 and 163; cf. also the graffiti left behind by some of these Greek mercenaries at Abu Simbel: Meiggs and Lewis 1969 no. 7 at 12–13.
43 See Herodotos 1.66–68 and 1.82. At the end of the six century the Athenians, Boiotians, and Chalkidians fought two battles with evidently thousands of men on each side: Herodotos 5.77.
44 E.g., Bakhuizen 1976, and cf. Archilochos fr. 3 and Alkaios fr. 357 for the high reputation of Euboian and especially Chalkidian weapons.
45 For the cost of the panoply see Jackson 1991. Thucydides 2.13 details 13,000 citizen hoplites ready for active service, plus a reserve of 16,000 hoplites comprised the oldest and youngest year classes, who were detailed for home defense, and the *metoikoi* who were eligible for hoplite service; though he doesn't say how many of the 16,000 were metics, it is clear that in excess of 20,000 citizens were hoplites; see further the discussion at Chapter 2, pp. 74–6 above.
46 From at the latest the mid sixth century on the bronze cuirass came more and more to be replaced by the reinforced linen *thorax*, which was cheaper, lighter, and more comfortable to wear; see Brouwers 2007; Bardunias and Ray 2016 at 5–60.
47 In the ancient period, Macedonian phalanx warfare, and the warfare of the Roman imperial system, and in the modern era the regimented warfare of the era of so-called "great Captains" (sixteenth to eighteenth centuries), are examples.
48 For example, Athenian ephebes (young men in their late teen years training for hoplite service) reportedly received a shield and a spear from the community on finishing their training (Aristotle *AthPol* 42.4); cf. Vidal-Naquet 1986 at 106–28.
49 For up-to-date discussion of all aspects of Greek so-called "colonization," see Tsetskhladze 2006/8.
50 Andrewes 1956, Berve 1967, Pleket 1969, McGlew 1993, and Cawkwell 1995 on tyrants and tyranny.
51 Billows 1995, ch. 1 and 2018 chs. 4 and 5 on Philip II and the Macedonian phalanx; on the early modern revolution in military organization see e.g., the chapter by Rothenberg 1986 at 32–63.
52 Among numerous stories about the Argives in Herodotos, note especially 1.82 attesting to Argos' early power, and cf. the poem in the Palatine Anthology 14.73 praising the "linen-corseleted Argives, goads of war"; further Tomlinson 1972 at 67–101; Kelly 1976 was skeptical about traditions of early Argive power, however.
53 See Plate 1 for the Chigi vase; pp. 87–91 above on the beginnings of hoplite warfare and the phalanx.
54 Hence the critique of Andrewes' theory by scholars like Sealey 1976 at 38–59, Snodgrass 1965, and many others since.
55 I accept the date for Pheidon, between about 675 and 650, argued for by Andrewes 1949.

56 Pausanias 2.24.6 for the Battle of Hysiai; Herodotos 6.127 for Pheidon's usurpation of Olympic festival; Andrewes 1956, pp. 39–42 connected these matters.
57 E.g., Thucydides' account at 3.94–98 of Demosthenes' campaign in northwest Greece for the light infantry style of warfare there; see e.g., Herodotos 5.63–64 Thucydides 1.111 and 2.22 for Thessalian cavalry, and for Kretan archers e.g., Thucydides 6.25 and 43.
58 Hesiod *Works and Days* 235–60, and cf. *LSJ* (9th ed.) s.v. *doron* for the sense of the word as bribe, and s.v. *dorodokein*. See also *LSJ* s.v. *phagein* and its derivatives for the sense of greed associated with this term.
59 Archilochos fr. 60, "I do not like a tall general, nor long-legged, nor exulting in his curls, nor thoroughly clean shaven, but for me let him be a small man, well planted on his legs, steady on his feet, full of heart."
60 Finley 1979; cf. Scully 1990, de Jong (ed.) 1999.
61 See G. Anderson 2003.
62 Endorsing the notion of the Greek *polis* as a state, see Hansen 2002, pp. 17–47.
63 Note e.g., the prominent role played by a detachment of Athenian archers in the preliminaries to the Battle of Plataia in 479: Herodotos 9.21–22; and see also Winter 1990, Best 1969, Pritchett 1991.
64 See Rankov, Coates, Morrison 2000.
65 The dimensions are extrapolated from the excavation of fifth-century shipsheds in which the triremes were stored in the Athenian naval harbor of Zea at the Peiraieus: Loven and Schaldemose 2011.
66 Herodotos 3.39 reports that Polykrates of Samos employed 1,000 archers on his fleet, and archers are also well attested on Athenian warships: see e.g., Jordan 1972, esp. p. 83; the frequent suggestion in the sources of hoplites serving as marines is likely exaggerated, since the deck of a trireme would be a precarious place for a fully equipped hoplite, it is not clear what hoplites would do there or how they would succeed, encumbered with heavy shields and Corinthian helmets, in boarding another warship, and of course if they fell into the sea their armor would immediately drag them down and drown them.
67 Herodotos 3.39 tells that when Polykrates seized power on Samos he built a fleet of 100 *pentekonters* (fifty-oared galleys), but at 3.44 he reveals that some years later he had more than forty triremes.
68 Herodotos 6.7–8.
69 On Aigina, her fleet, and the source of her wealth, see Chapter 2 above at pp. 66–8; for the Athenian fleet building in the 480s based on the silver revenues from Laureion, see Herodotos 7.144, and for the wealth the Athenians derived from Laureion see further Xenophon *Poroi* 4.
70 Ps-Xenophon *Const.Ath.* 1.2–3; Aristotle *Politics* 6.7 (=1321a).
71 See further Hansen 2006 on all this; on the Ps.-Xenophon *Constitution of the Athenians* see further Chapter 4, pp. 121–3 below. Note particularly the author's

words at 1.2: "My first point is that it is right that the poor and the ordinary people there (i.e., at Athens) should have more power than the noble and the rich, because it is the ordinary people who man the fleet and bring the city her power ..." (tr. J. M. Moore).

72 Ps-Xenophon *Const. Ath.* 1.19: "because the Athenians own property abroad and public duties take them abroad, they and their attendants have learned how to row almost without realizing it, for it is inevitable that a man who goes on frequent voyages will take an oar ... the majority are competent rowers as soon as they board the ships because of previous practice throughout their lives" (tr. J. M. Moore). Note that the Athenians owning property abroad and traveling on public duties with attendants are clearly of the wealthy upper class.

4 The Pebble: Collective Decision Making and the City-State

1 Blok 2017 argued persuasively for an understanding of citizenship based on genealogical descent lines and religious participation, a view which helped to establish the role of women as citizens. In this chapter, however, I mean by citizenship the right to play an active role in the politics and governance of the *polis*. As is well known, women were precluded from sitting on the state council, or attending and voting at assemblies; they did not, that is, enjoy the active citizenship rights with which I am concerned here. As such, women will not form part of the discussion in this chapter.

2 The literature on Greek, especially Athenian, democracy is vast: see e.g., Robinson 2003 and 2011, Rhodes 2004; for Greek oligarchy see now the very insightful work of Simonton 2017.

3 See e.g., Finley 1979, Scully 1990, de Jong (ed.) 1999.

4 For the *boule* in Homer see *Iliad* 2.53, 194, 202; 11.195; 13.213; *Odyssey* 3.127; for the *agora* see *Iliad* 2.95, 808; 4.400; 9.2; 10.33; 16.283; 19.106; 20.34; and *Odyssey* 1.90; 2.26, 257; 3.127, 137; 4.818; 10.112.

5 See e.g., Herodotos 5.92 on Kypselos: "many Corinthians were exiled by him, many had their property confiscated, but the most by far lost their lives," and in the same passage we find the story of the Milesian tyrant Thrasyboulos advising Periander of Corinth to kill or exile the leading men of Corinth. There are many stories of the brutality of early tyrants: for full details and sources see Andrewes 1956, Berve 1967, McGlew 1993; G. Anderson 2005 takes a more moderate view; also Stein-Holkeskamp 2009.

6 Such notable tyrannies as those of Pheidon of Argos, Pittakos of Mytilene, Polykrates of Samos, and Theagenes of Megara seem to have ended with the death or retirement of the first tyrant, for example; Hippias of Athens is an example of a second-

generation tyrant being deposed; exceptions to the short-lived tyranny rule were Kypselos and his son Periander at Corinth, who together ruled for some sixty years, and Periander was even succeeded as tyrant for a few more years by his nephew; and the tyranny of the Orthagorids at Sikyon which lasted through multiple generations for some 100 years, according to report.

7 Examples of this, are e.g., Periander at Corinth and Peisistratos at Athens, see lit. cited in n. 5 above for details and sources.
8 On the Areopagos council at Athens see Wallace 1989; on the democratic boule at Athens Rhodes 1972; for the *Gerousia* at Sparta see Cartledge 2002; for the Argive *Bola* see Tomlinson 1972 at 194–5; for the *Aisymnetai* at Megara see Legon 1981, pp. 96–7 and 290–2; and for the Boiotian councils see Billows 2016 at F 9 commentary, and for Theopompos as author of this work see also Billows 2009.
9 Since apparently nine new members were introduced each year (that is, the annual "nine archons"), if we assume that each member lived for an average of twenty years after joining the council, that would make 180 members or so. But, in fact, we do not know if it was possible or common for Athenians to hold office as one or other of the "nine archons" multiple times, which would affect this calculation, nor how old most "archons" were when they held office, and how long they lived after office. Still, a number well over 100 seems almost certain.
10 Thucydides 2.39.1; on the role and functioning of the *Gerousia* see also Cartledge 2003 at 60–3.
11 The veto power of the *Gerousia* is mentioned in the "great Rhetra," a key constitutional set of rules reported by Plutarch *Lykourgos* 6; cf. Ogden 1994.
12 See Rhodes 1972.
13 The fullest available account of a Spartan assembly is by Thucydides 1.79–87 re the Spartan decision to declare war on Athens in 432.
14 See, for example, the two collections of articles by Hansen 1983 and 1989; also, Hansen 1987 and Hansen 2010; and Blackwell 2003 on "The Assembly."
15 See e.g., Plutarch *Alkibiades* 22 for the use of black and white pebbles to vote negatively or positively, in this case in a trial.
16 Hansen 1986 offers a widely accepted estimate of the number of Athenian citizens.
17 Note for example the claim of Demosthenes 18.273: "you were all present at every assembly, as the *polis* proposed a discussion of policy in which everyone might join."
18 See the words of Aischines 1.27: "the herald does not exclude from the speaker's platform ... the man who earns his bread by working at a trade." Aristotle *AthPol* 43.6 emphasizes that any Athenian could address the assembly on a matter affecting him.
19 Plato *Protagoras* 319c; the "Scythian archers" were armed public slaves who functioned as a kind of police force for the Athenians under the close direction and supervision of responsible public officials; at assembly meetings they would be directed by the *prytaneis*, that is the presiding sub-committee of state councilors.

20 For example, a barber addressed the assembly with first news of the Sicilian disaster (Plutarch *Nikias* 30); N.B. Sokrates' claim that any man whether smith, shoemaker, or merchant, whether rich or poor, of a good family or not, could speak in the assembly (Plato *Protagoras* 319d), and his emphasis that the Athenians liked to hear from builders on matters to do with construction, shipwrights on matters to do with ships, and so on (i.e., they prized expertise over social status: Plato *Protagoras* 319b–c); and note also Protagoras' claim that "every man," even a smith or a shoemaker, could speak in the assembly (Plato *Protagoras* 322e–324d).

21 See the detailed analysis of this passage by Billows 2016 *ad loc.*

22 For the non-native status of most of the enslaved see e.g., Garlan 1988, ch. 1; some metics (e.g., Lysias) were effectively natives.

23 35–40 percent for Boiotia accepts hoplite status for citizenship, and Hansen's estimate in his 1986 of *c.* 35–40 percent in average city as hoplites; for Sparta, Herodotos (9.10–11) says that 5,000 Spartiates, 5,000 *Perioikoi* and seven Helots per Spartiate were sent to Plataia in 479, which suggests Spartiates made up *c.* a ninth of male population, or *c.* 11 percent, from which one should subtract the reduced status Spartans.

24 Meier 1980.

25 158 "books": Diogenes Laertius 5.27; about 250 treatises: Ammonius *Comm. in Categ.* (ed. Busse), p. 3,20–4,4; Elias *Proleg. philosoph. et in Porph. Eisag. Comm.* (ed. Busse), p. 74,25–75,2; cf. *Vita graeca vulgata* saying 255. See further App. 2 below for full details.

26 For what remains of the so-called "pre-Soctratics" see Kirk, Raven, Schofield (eds) 2007.

27 For what remains of sophistic writing and thought, see e.g., Sprague (ed.) 2001.

28 Gorgias *Helen* and *Palamedes*; Antiphon *Tetralogies* and *On Truth*; and the *Dissoi Logoi* (author unknown).

29 Herodotos' *Historiai* was written between about 440 and 425: see e.g., Murray and Moreno (eds) 2007 introduction; Protagoras' speech is by internal evidence in the dialogue represented as having been delivered about 432: see e.g., Denyer 2008 introduction; the Ps. Xenophon treatise reflects the situation at Athens around the outbreak of the Peloponnesian War, and must have been composed in the early 420s: see e.g., Marr and Rhodes (eds.) 2008.

30 One could in fact imagine just such a debate having occurred then, with Peisistratos' relative Hipparchos arguing for monarchy, the aristocrat Isagoras for oligarchy, and the famous Kleisthenes for democracy.

31 Note that *isonomia* and allotment of public office were precisely characteristic of Athenian democracy, which shows the true Greek/Athenian context of this debate despite Herodotos' insistence on its Persian background.

32 See Aristotle *Politika* bk. 3; Dikaiarchos' views set out in Balot 2006 at 279–80, Polybios bk. 6, Cicero *de Re Publica.*

33 See Aristotle bk. 5 for an early form of the cycle; the fullest form is in Polybios bk. 6; see also Cicero *de Re Publica* adapting Polybios' version of the cycle; see further e.g., Balot 2006 at 260–1, 182–4, 209.
34 A useful discussion of Protagoras' political thought can be found in Balot 2006 at 74–8.
35 An accessible translation and commentary is provided by Marr and Rhodes (eds.) 2008.
36 The standard format of the treatise is more or less as follows: the author will say words to the effect of: "in so far as the Athenians do x, I do not approve of them because in doing x they harm the good and the noble and benefit the bad and the useless, but they are in fact right to do x because ..." and there will then follow a lengthy explanation and justification of the Athenians doing x, and how it benefits them to do so.
37 And, by the way, this indicates how wrong British scholars have been to characterize the author as an "Old Oligarch."
38 Or at least Sokrates is represented by Plato as having such views, for example in the *Protagoras* and in the *Republic*; and less forcefully by Xenophon in his *Memorabilia*.
39 If we can trust Plato (e.g., *Protagoras* and *Republic*) and Xenophon (e.g., *Memorabilia*).
40 Suzanne Said 1996 at 284–7 proposed to see in this play a critique by Aristophanes of the "effeminacy" of contemporary Athenians, but quite apart from the unlikelihood of Aristophanes thus criticizing the men who—after the disaster of the Sicilian expedition—fought on for nearly ten more years and won notable victories at Kyzikos, Byzantion, and Arginousai, and then after being obliged to surrender to Sparta still fought back and recovered their democracy within two years; there is another problem in the way of Said's interpretation, namely that Aristophanes ties the political equality of women to communalization of property and abolition of traditional marriage and family units, making it clear that he is parodying the kind of political theories debated in philosophical circles as we know from Plato's *Republic*. Aristophanes' interest in that sort of parody is attested of course by his play *The Clouds*.
41 The scholarly literature on Aristotle's *Politika* is vast, as one would expect, and this is not the place to list it: good resources for understanding this work are Simpson 1998 and Kraut 2002; the 2004 article on "Aristotle: Politics" by Edward Clayton in the *Internet Encyclopedia of Philosophy* is a very useful starting point for the non-expert reader.
42 See *Politika* 1252 a3–1253 a38, also 1281 a1 and 1332 a34; note also Aristotle's remarks at the end of the *Nicomachean Ethics*, transitioning to the *Politika*: "in the light of the constitutions (*politeiai*) we have collected let us study what sorts of influence preserve and destroy states, and what sorts preserve or destroy the

particular kinds of constitutions, and to what causes it is due that some are well and others ill administered" (*NE* 10.9 end =1181b12–20).
43 N.B. ideal kingship was not considered practical because the person of supreme virtue is unlikely to exist, cities being made up of people who are similar and roughly equal on the whole (1287b); tyranny is the opposite of a governing system, since it does harm rather than good.
44 Aristotle *Nicomachean Ethics* bk. 2.1–6, cf. Plato *Protagoras* 325b–e.
45 Aristotle *Politika* 3.3–6.
46 See e.g., Gagarin 1986 at 58–66; see also Szegedy-Maszak 1978, Hölkeskamp 1999.
47 Gagarin 1986 at 81–6; Whitley 1997; Gagarin and Perlman 2016.
48 See e.g., Stoddart and Whitley 1988, esp. at 766; Whitley 1997; Hölkeskamp 2000.
49 See e.g., Gagarin 2008; Martin Gonzalez 2014
50 Stroud 1968 and esp. 1979 at 41–4; Gagarin 1986 at 55 n. 14 and 127 n. 18.
51 Re. these lawgivers see e.g., Gagarin 1986 at 51–80, and cf. Gagarin 2008.
52 See also the discussion by Pébarthe 2006, ch. 5 on the use of inscribed and publicly displayed laws and other documents around the Greek world.
53 For example, Lambert 2011.
54 Gagarin 1986, 2008.
55 Note Gagarin's (1986) objection to unwritten law as a concept prior to the fifth century at p. 122; see further Cerri 1979.
56 See e.g., Gagarin 1986, esp. ch. 6.
57 *IG*³ 84.26; and see further on the "so that all may know" phrasing e.g., Hedrick 1999, Sickinger 2009.
58 See e.g., Harris 1989, p. 76 and n. 51; the translation above is adapted from that given by Harris here.
59 Lambert 2011, p. 194
60 Rhodes and Osborne 2007, no. 95; cf. Lambert 2011, p. 194
61 Durrbach 1921 no. 48; cf Austin 2006 no. 114
62 *Syll.* no. 493; cf. Durrbach 1921 no. 50, Austin 2006 no. 115
63 *SEG* I.336; cf. Austin 2006 no. 113
64 *Syll.* 354; cf. Austin 2006 no. 112
65 Harris 1989, p. 106 casually asserts that such formulas were intended to please the benefactor being honored rather than inform the onlooker, but (rather uncharacteristically) he offers no basis for this assumption. It is surely more reasonable to take the hortatory formula at face value than to make unsubstantiated assumptions about it.
66 Lambert 2011, p. 200, and see also his n. 18 at 208
67 Note that Aischines 3.179–80 explicitly likened the competition for honors to the competition between athletes to be crowned as victors at the Olympic games. Just as the fame of the athlete was important to him, so was the fame of the honoree

important to him, and the inscribed honorific decrees were intended to attain for him that fame.
68 See e.g., Harris 1989 at 76–7.
69 Aristotle *AthPol* 47.2–4; cf. Blok 2017, p. 76 and n. 126; see also Sickinger 1999.
70 See e.g., Thomas 1992, p. 39 at n. 78.
71 See Wilhelm1909, pp. 229–99 for a lengthy discussion of public notices in the Greek world, as attested by inscriptions; and cf. the review by Tod 1912 at 14.
72 *IG* II² 1237; cf. Jones 1999 at 208–10.
73 See notably Thomas 1992.

5 The Scroll: Literacy and the City-State

1 For public texts as mere monuments not intended to be read see e.g., Stoddart and Whitley 1988, esp. at 766, and Hölkeskamp 2000; that illiteracy was prevalent was argued famously by Harris 1989; that the written word suspect in ancient Greece was suggested by Steiner 1994.
2 Meyer 2013.
3 I shall be using in this chapter the terms "widespread literacy" and "mass literacy," so I should say something about what I mean by them. In the first place, by literacy in this context I mean the ability, at a minimum, to read public notices with reasonable fluency, and to write simple messages; by widespread literacy I mean literacy that extends beyond the social elite, craftsmen who need limited literacy for their work, and/or a class of professional scribes; by mass literacy I mean the situation in which the majority of the relevant population—in this case citizen males—have attained literacy as here defined.
4 An inscription from Crete, for example, mentions a *poinikastes*: Jeffery and Morpurgo-Davies 1970; see also Stoddart and Whitley 1988, p. 766.
5 *Phoinikeia grammata*: Herodotos 5.58; note also such usages as *Phoinikika grammata* in *ChronLind* B15 and Skamon F2; and *Phoinikeia* meaning (apparently) "letters" in SIG 38.37 (Teos fifth century); now also Kritzas 2010, pp. 1–16, ill. 1.
6 See e.g., Jeffery 1961 at 5–6; Harris 1989 at 45–6; Powell 1991 at 5–67; Tropper 2001; Wolf 2008 at 58–60.
7 For the standard dating see the works cited in n. 6 above; note however that there are strong dissident voices arguing for a significantly earlier date based on a variety of strands of evidence: see nn. 9 and 10 below.
8 See esp. Powell 1991, also Jeffery 1961/90, Harris 1989.
9 There is a strong scholarly minority positing earlier dates for the transmission of the western Semitic alphabet: the Semitic scholar Naveh (1973; 1982; 1991) has argued forcefully based on features of early Greek writing such as the lack of a standard

direction and the occasional use of rows of dots as word dividers that the borrowing must have occurred c. 1100 rather than c. 800; Ruijgh (1995; 1997; 1998) has offered linguistic reasons (such as the history of the aspirate /h/ in early Greek) for seeing a likely borrowing around 1000.

10 Some scholars have pointed to the development of Etruscan and Phrygian writing, in alphabets clearly closely akin to (borrowed/adapted from?) the early Greek alphabet: the earliest Phrygian writings seem to date to c. 800 (Brixhe 2007), and early Etruscan writings can also be dated to the early eighth century. It is possible, based on this evidence, that the first creation of the Greek alphabet should indeed be pushed back fifty to one hundred years, to c. 900–850. See now Waal 2018 for a full discussion, proposing a date before 1000 for the creation of the Greek alphabet. The issue of dating, however, does not materially affect the argument being presented here, which is based on the known surviving examples of early Greek writing from the early eighth century on.

11 Powell 1991 is the strongest voice favoring Homer as the main cause of creation of the alphabet; and cf. Powell 2003 on the relationship between writing and the development of early Greek literature; Janko 1982 for the standard dating of Homer; West 2011 for down-dating of Homer to c. 650.

12 Jeffery 1961, now to be consulted in the second edition with additions by Johnston 1990.

13 Powell 1991 at 123–86 gives a very useful list of the earliest inscriptions, grouped by category.

14 The issue of traders' marks, owner's marks and so on, on Greek vases, was taken up fully in a ground-breaking article by Johnston 1974; he notes that most such marks are found on the foot of the vase in question (over 2,000 examples known to him), but marks elsewhere on the body of the vase are also known (about fifty examples); particularly noteworthy are vases marked with the letters SO or SOS, perhaps relating to the well-known trader Sostratos of Aigina (Herodotos 4.152), discussed by Johnston in a separate article in 1972. See further e.g., Gill 1991 downplaying the importance of pottery as an item of trade, which does not affect the point about merchant's marks on pots.

15 Recent finds at Methone in northern Greece show an international trading post there as early as the eighth century and have suggested to some that Methone is a plausible candidate to be the home of the earliest Greek alphabet: Papadopoulos 2016; and cf. Janko 2015.

16 For this and what follows see for example the discussion of Donald 1991 at 286–99, basing himself particularly on the work of Gelb 1963 and Harris 1986.

17 See Donald 1991, p. 298: "Since Indo-European languages place great importance on fine distinctions in vowel sounds, the Greeks found it necessary to specify a number of vowel sounds in their alphabet... the result provided the basis for all later

Indo-European alphabets and was, in the opinion of most writers, the first truly phonetic script."

18 As Donald has put it (1991, p. 341): "Our concern here is not so much with the history of science or philosophy per se as with the cognitive framework that enabled such accelerated change. How had the *structure* of the human thought process changed? The answer appears to be at least partly that, in the ancient Greeks, all of the essential symbolic inventions were in place for the first time. The evolution of writing was complete; the Greeks had the first truly effective phonetic system of writing, so successful that it has not really been improved since."

19 Cf. the discussion of Harris 1989 at 11–13.

20 Harris 1989 at 96–102 offers a good overview of the debates and literature on Greek education and schools, and cf. now W.C. West III 2015. It should be noted that the evidence we have, as can be seen below, all pertains to boys attending schools: so far as we can tell girls did not do so, before about 200 BCE at any rate. Although we know that some women could read, the fact that they did not go to schools indicates they must have learned privately at home, and literacy skills must always have been rare among women. Women, therefore, will come in for no significant commentary in this chapter on the development of mass literacy among citizen men. Similarly, some of the enslaved could certainly read and write, but in their case, they clearly learned these skills only insofar as needed for the work they were required to do and learned the skills in the workshops where they were employed. Again, therefore, the enslaved do not form part of the discussion here.

21 Note also Aristophanes *Knights* 988 where the chorus refers to Kleon's attendance at school, as recalled by his school fellows, as a standard thing. Contra Harris 1989 at 58–9 who dismisses this passage of Aristophanes as "fantasy"; but though there are obvious comic elements, why should this be fantasy? For the comedic effect to work, I suggest the depiction of boys marching to school together in the old days had to be rooted in reality; and the corroborating evidence of other authors, adduced below, supports this view.

22 The term *mousike* here is often translated as "music," but it properly refers more broadly to "any art over which the Muses presided; generally, art or letters" *LSJ* s.v.; cf. also e.g., Harris 1989 at 99 noting that *mousike* includes reading and writing, and note also Xenophon *Const. Lak,* 2.1 associating *grammata* (letters) with *mousike*.

23 For example, Harris 1989, pp. 99–100; Harris claims, basing himself on Schmitter 1975, p. 281, that there exists no evidence of such laws, though he himself later cites Aischines 1.9 (below) attesting to such laws.

24 Aristotle *Athenaion Politeia* 26.4; Plutarch *Perikles* 37.2–5.

25 Perhaps relevant here is the reputed law of Solon that a son had no obligation to support his father (*trephein ton patera*) in old age if his father had not "taught him a trade" (*didaxamenon technen*): Plutarch *Solon* 22.1; a sign of some legislative interest in education, if true.

26 That Plato's family were of the aristocratic elite is well attested and not in doubt: besides numerous allusions to relatives in Plato's dialogues and the biographical remarks in his seventh and eighth *Letters*, see Diogenes Laertius *Life of Plato* 1–3; on Sokrates' much more humble family background see e.g., Diogenes Laertius *Eminent Philosophers* 2.5 stating that his father was a stonemason, his mother a midwife.

27 So e.g., W. V. Harris 1989, p. 99 n. 152, and cf. the lit. cited by him there. Harris suggests that the "we" of Aischines refers to "men of Aischines' kind who want our sons to be educated," but in fact Aischines is here addressing the jury of ordinary Athenian citizens.

28 It is worth noting that apparently Protagoras, as lawgiver at Thourioi c. 444, enacted laws requiring school education for citizen boys (see below p. 154). The fact that Protagoras was an associate of Perikles, and may well have been put forward precisely by Perikles to act as lawgiver for Thourioi, could suggest that the legislation requiring school education at Athens came from Perikles and his circle: see e.g., Barrett 1987, p. 10.

29 For Hellanikos see Pownall 2016; for Androtion see Jones 2015; also on Theopompos Morison 2014, and N.B. that bk. 10 of the "Philippika" dealt with Athenian "demagogues," likely including Themistokles and Aristides, in which context boys at Troizen could have been referenced.

30 Staatliche Museen Berlin, Antikensammlung 2285; cf. Sider 2010, arguing that the line of epic poetry, which has various errors, was probably written by the student, who is being shown his mistakes.

31 For similar scenes see e.g., Basel Antikenmuseum 465, a red-figure cup of c. 490; New York, Metropolitan Museum of Art 41.165.2, a red-figure vase of c. 470; and cf. Beck 1975 esp. nos. 38, 49, 59; Harris 1989, p. 97; W. C. West III 2015 pp. 53–4

32 E. Vanderpool 1959 at 279–80, no. 11; and cf. Balatsos 1991. We see on one stone tablet the names "ATHINA ARIS ARTEMIS" (note the iotacization of etas), and below the misspelled personal name "DIMOSOTHENIS" (i.e., Demosthenes).

33 See *RE* s.v. Mykalessos for full list of citations; now also Hansen in Nielsen and Hansen 2004 at 431–61 "Boiotia."

34 See e.g., Harris 1989 at 17 and 101–2, though Harris does recognize that the multiple schools at Mykalessos suggest that "almost every Greek *polis*, except in truly backward regions, possessed at least one school" (p. 101).

35 Harris 1989 is skeptical of village schools, even while citing evidence suggesting that Protagoras was once a village schoolmaster (Athenaeus 8.354c; Diogenes Laertius 9.8 citing Epicurus), but Mykalessos itself was in fact a village, see below pp. 155–7 and Strabo 9.2.11 and 14.

36 Literally, Plutarch says that the Troizenians voted to pay the fees of the Athenian pupils, one Nikagoras proposing the decree. Harris 1989, p. 58 and n. 64 doubts the reliability of this anecdote; its value, I suggest, lies not in whether it is literally true

(though the name of the Troizenian mover of the decree is suggestive of a historical basis), but that it was the sort of thing that seemed plausible.

37 Harris 1989, p. 58 n. 63 cites a 1951 population of 1,789 though without source; the Greek census figure in 2011 was 1,334 according to Astypalaia - Wikipedia citing the Hellenic Statistical Authority; note that more than sixty boys would likely be the great majority of the citizen boys of school age, see below p. 156 and n. 46.

38 Harris 1989, p. 58 n. 62 discusses the significance of the large number of boys at the Chios school, though he suggests these boys represented five age classes rather than the more plausible three: see n. 53 below.

39 Diogenes Laertius 9.8, citing Herakleides Pontikos.

40 "He established a law (*enomothetese*) that all the sons of the citizens learn to read and write (*ta grammata*), the city paying the fees of the teachers" (Diodoros 12.12.4); David Blair 2016 presented a strong argument for taking the laws presented here by Diodoros seriously, though not the connection to Charondas.

41 Ephoros *BNJ* 70 F149 makes the claim, as quoted by Strabo 10.482, though the verb has dropped out of the text; Heraklides (*FHG* II.211) says that the Kretan education *did not go beyond letters*, thereby seeming to confirm the education in literacy. See however the skeptical analysis by Harris 1989, p. 100 and n. 153.

42 For the *HellOxy* see now the edition and commentary of Billows 2016, esp. the end "biographical essay" for the identity of the author as Theopompos; and cf. Occhipinti 2016.

43 Assuming the hoplite class to be around 30–40 percent of the free male citizen population: see the discussion in Chapter 3 above; the guesstimate of 400 to guard the city is based on the 400 the Plataians left to guard the city when they abandoned it in the face of the joint Theban-Spartan attack in 429, indicating it took that number to man the walls (Thuc. 2.78)

44 See on the Boiotian constitution in the *Hellenika Oxyrhynchia* now Billows 2016 F 9 XIX.2–4 with commentary.

45 The extrapolations of numbers here are based on the model life tables of Coale and Demeny 1983, using model "West"; see for the methodology e.g., Frier 1982 at 245.

46 See for the calculations of numbers Coale and Demeny 1983, for the modern population of Astypalaia. Also of interest here is Clement, Hillson, and Michalaki-Kollia 2009, showing a high incidence of child burials.

47 Harris 1989 at 96–103 assumes a difference between urban and rural populations, but for the overlap between the two see e.g., the survey of the southern Argolid by Jameson, van Andel, and Runnels 1994 and Osborne 1987; and cf. Gallant 1991, Foxhall 2007, etc. Note the historical cases of citizens getting caught out in the countryside rather than in the city by sudden attacks (Plataians: Thucydides 2.5; Kyzikenians: Diodoros 18.51.2), or of the Mantineans being unwillingly forced by

the Spartans to abandon their city and live in villages closer to their farmlands: Xenophon *Hellenika* 5.2.2–7.
48 For the school at Miletos see *Syll.*577; for the Teos school *Syll.* 578; the salaries are given as monthly wages in the Miletos inscription at lines 50–5, as an annual sum in the Teos inscription at lines 10–16 of fr. A.
49 See e.g., O'Connor 2011, and for a thorough collection of data on wages in classical Athens see Loomis 1998; N.B. that wages of building workers on the Erechtheion in late fifth century were significantly lower than those paid at Eleusis in the mid fourth century (above Chapter 2 at n. 83), so if anything teachers in fifth-century Greece may have been paid less than those in the early second century.
50 For the necessity to pay fees for schooling see e.g., Xenophon *Mem.* 2.2.6; Demosthenes 18.265; Theophrastos *Characters* 30.14; and cf. Harris 1989 at 100–1.
51 On the one-room schools of modern Europe and America see e.g., Mydland 2011 doc. 5 (online); Zimmerman 2009.
52 See the discussion of wages, the cost of living, and living standards in Chapter 2 part 4 above. Harris 1989 at 101–2 states, without argument, that the poor simply could not afford to send their sons to school because they needed their labor. There is, in fact, little or no evidence for children aged between seven and ten or eleven doing any significant labor in ancient Greece outside of harvest times, however, as Harris himself acknowledged (p. 19); and the evidence for prices and wages (Chapter 2 part 4 above) makes it very unlikely that small children needed to contribute to family incomes.
53 Plato *Laws* 7.804c–810b for the standard three years of schooling, and N.B. Aristotle's clear implication at *Politika* 7.17.1336a–1336b that schooling should start at seven, confirmed by Ps.-Plato *Axiochos* 366d; the document regarding a school foundation at Teos (*Syll.* 578) arranges for teachers to be hired to teach three "tasks" at slightly different salaries, which must surely be understood as three year-classes (or "grades" as we would say today): lines 10–14.
54 So Whitley 1997; on the practice of reading aloud in ancient Greece see e.g., Harris 1989, p. 36 at n. 37.
55 For example, Carter 1986 studied those Athenians who opted out of political participation, emphasizing in ch. 4 that many of the poorer and rural dwelling citizens did so, but he overstated lack of participation in my view: see my Chapter 4, pp. 113–14 above.
56 Thuc 2.40.
57 For Mnesilochos writing see *Thesmophoriazousai* lines 768–84, for his character as rather ignorant and boorish see e.g., the opening scene of the play at lines 1–56; for Euripides' mother as a vegetable seller see e.g., Aristophanes *Thesm.*387, *Knights* 19, and see further Ruck 1975; of course, the tradition of Euripides' family as lower class is suspect as are almost all biographical traditions of fifth-century and earlier figures.

58 Langdon 2005, see also *SEG* 49.2; note that Langdon has reportedly a corpus of some 2,000 such archaic rock-cut graffiti, which he is in the process of preparing for publication: Pitt 2014/15 at p. 52.
59 As noted by Langdon 2005; see also Pitt 2014/15, p. 52; it is worth noting that in her article arguing for an early creation of the Greek alphabet, Waal 2018 argued that no early Greek abecedaria ever had both the letters san and sigma: this Attic example does have both showing how precarious arguments about early writing can be given the limited evidence and the constant finding of new evidence.
60 Langdon 2004.
61 Lang 1976 no. C5; cf. Sider 2010, p. 545 at n. 9.
62 See e.g., Jordan 2000 for a collection and further references.
63 The punctuation is as in the Greek text; Lang 1976, p. 8: B1 and pl. 2; cf. W.C. West III 2015 at 58.
64 W.C. West III 2015.
65 See for a few examples the famous Abu Simbel graffiti in southern Egypt left by Greek mercenary soldiers, Bernand and Masson 1957; erotic graffiti scratched on a rock face on Thera, *IG* XII.3 nos. 536–601 and *IG* XII.3 Suppl. nos. 1410–93; more erotic graffiti recently discovered on Astypalaia, reported by Vlachopoulos 2014.
66 For all details on ostracism see Brenne 2001; Forsdyke 2005; Surikov 2015; for a list of candidates for ostracism see Brenne 2002, esp. at 43–71.
67 Total of 6,000 votes required: Plutarch *Aristides* 7.5; 6,000 votes for the "loser": Philochorus *FGrH* 328 F30.
68 Forsdyke 2005; Surikov 2015; see also now Sickinger 2017 esp. at 454–5 and 457–62.
69 It should be noted that, while the ability to write one's own name is no sign of any great writing skill, writing down the name of a stranger, usually accompanied by a patronymic and/or demotic, simply from having heard it and knowing its sound, does indeed show an ability to transform sounds spoken and heard into a written text, and thus a genuine ability to write. Note that Sickinger 2017 at 443–508 argues convincingly, based on study of the orthography, that most *ostraka* were indeed written by the persons casting the votes, see esp. p. 463. For ostracism as evidence of basic literacy skills among Athenian citizens, see now also Missiou 2011 at 36–84.
70 Broneer 1938 at 228–43; and cf. the recent discussion of Sickinger 2017 at 462–3.
71 As Sickinger 2017, p. 462 notes: "the large dump of ballots aimed at a single candidate seems to testify to some form of campaign."
72 Diodoros Siculus 11.87; and see also Hesychios s.v. *Petalismos*.
73 The evidence for ostracism outside of Athens is collected by Forsdyke 2005 at App. 2 "Ostracism outside Athens" and see further Surikov 2015 at 121–2 for the evidence from Chersonesos.
74 Blegen 1934; Young 1940; Langdon 1976, esp. at 9–50.
75 Langdon 1976, pp. 10–11 and 41–6.

76 One might also note here the persuasive case made by Pébarthe 2006. ch. 2 that it was entirely common for many Athenians to make use of documents in their daily life (see esp. p. 109); and that Harris 1989 was wrong to apply his model of restricted literacy to classical Athens.

77 Harris 1989 at pp. 4–5 for example, but note that modern studies of literacy and the learning of literacy show that learning to write invariably precedes learning to read, though once a person has learned to read their reading skills may advance faster and further than their writing skills: see e.g., W.C. West III 2015, pp. 55–8, esp. notes 7, 8, 11, and 12 citing extensive modern literature on the topic.

78 Specifically, Plato has Sokrates say that the ideas Meletos (Sokrates' accuser) was attributing to him were in fact found in the books of Anaxagoras, and that if he tried to teach these ideas to young men as being his ideas they would laugh at him, since they could buy the books in question at "not much more than a *drachma* in the *orchestra*"; N.B. that the word *orchestra* here (literal meaning: dancing floor) undoubtedly refers to the open space in the middle of the *agora* where sacred dances were performed, *pace* translators like Jowett who wrongly think of the *orchestra* at the theater here.

79 Six thousand potential jurymen were empaneled annually, so it is statistically inevitable that most must have been middling if not outright poor, and one may note here the importance of the 2 or 3 obols paid to jurors; Plato's actual words—"do you despise these men so much and think them so illiterate (*apeirous grammaton*) as not to know that these ideas are found in the books of Anaxagoras of Klazomenai?"—if we can take them at all seriously, clearly imply that jurors were standardly literate.

80 Diogenes Laertius 9.52; Hesychios in *scholia ad Plato Rep. 600C*; Eusebius *Chron.* Ol.84; it perhaps needs saying that the silence of Plato and Aristotle regarding this "book burning" is not decisive against its historicity. For what it's worth, in this context, Aristophanes *Frogs* 1114 seems to suggest that it was normal for members of his audience to have a book (*biblion*) of tragic plays by Aischylos and/or Euripides, another passage casually dismissed by Harris 1989, p. 87 and n. 106 as fantastic.

81 For example, Lambert 2011, p. 200.

82 The examples illustrated here are taken from Day 1989, pp. 16–28; translations are my own.

83 See e.g., Cartledge 2007 at 81–2 for this practice and its significance. See further on the uses of writing at Sparta e.g., Pébarthe 2006, ch. 1, esp. his conclusion at p. 42.

84 Ridgway 1971, pp. 340–1.

85 See e.g., the study by Hurwit 2015, esp. at 101–44.

86 For example, Harris 1989, p. 60 n. 68.

87 See also, making much the same case, Missiou 2011.

88 Harris 1989, pp. 10–4

89 Aischines, for example, assumed that every Athenian would have crossed over to Salamis at one time or another (Aischines 1.25: "for I know well that everyone has sailed across to Salamis"; and cf. Aischines 3.158); and note that the ferry charge to cross to the Peiraieus from Aigina was just 2 obols, and the fee for passage from the Black Sea or Egypt to Peiraieus only *c.* 2 drachmas. (Plato *Gorgias* 511d–e), which is to say that sea travel was apparently cheap and affordable, no doubt because passengers were extras on ships designed to carry trade cargoes, would be expected to provide for themselves while on board, and might likely be called on for help rowing or the like now and then.

90 N.B. the same would have been true in city-states like Corinth, Corcyra, Aigina, Samos, Rhodes, Syracuse, Byzantion and many others where sea-power was important, to say nothing of trading activities. N.B. too that many of the rowers in the Athenian fleet were poor islanders and Ionians serving for pay.

91 Donald 1996 and 2002; Wolf 2008.

92 On Hellenistic democracy see e.g., Musti 1966, Quass 1979, Gauthier 1984, Billows 2003; and esp. O'Neil 1995, ch. 5.

Conclusion: Literate Citizen-Warriors and City-State Culture

1 Translation by Keeley and Sherrard: *C.P Cavafy Collected Poems*, translated by Edmund Keeley and Philip Sherrard (1975).

2 Note for example the collection of papers in Renfrew and Cherry (eds.) 1986 and see the detailed argument in Chapter 1 above.

3 See most importantly Bresson 2016 for the best up to date account of the classical Greek economy; for the current acceptance of archaic Greek demographic growth see e.g., Scheidel 2013; detailed argument on all this in Chapter 2 above.

4 M.Donald 2001, p. 308.

5 Donald 2001, p. 307.

6 Donald 1991, pp. 304–6.

7 Donald 1991, pp. 311–12.

8 Wolf 2007, pp. 61–4; further, Japanese readers use different areas of their brains when reading *kanji* (symbols derived from Chinese writing) than when reading *kana* (separate Japanese syllabic symbols).

9 Wolf 2007, pp. 64–5.

10 Wolf 2007, p. 66.

11 A similar argument was made already by Eric Havelock 1976, esp. at 49, but without the full benefit of modern neuro-science to back it up.

12 See for example McAdams 2015, esp. at 247–54.

13 McAdams 2015, p. 250; see also McAdams and McLean 2013 at 233–8.

14 https://nautil.us/blog/how-aging-shapes-narrative-identity
15 The most famous example is that of Sokrates in Plato's *Apology*; but see also e.g., Demosthenes *On the Crown* for another excellent example, and numerous other surviving Athenian court speeches by Lysias, by Isokrates, and by Demosthenes among others.

Appendix 1: A Note on the Sources

1 A good resource for the non-expert reader, giving a sense of the kind of source material available to the historian of early Greece, is Crawford and Whitehead (eds.) 1983. For the documents preserved as inscriptions, the annual volumes of the *Supplementum Epigraphicum Graecum* are a valuable starting point.
2 A useful survey of archaeological field work in Greece is Snodgrass 1991, pp. 1–24; see also Mee 2011 and Lemos and Kotsonas (eds.) 2020. For regional surveys e.g., Tandy 1997, pp. 38–42, Bintliff 1997, Eder 1998. A crucial resource for up-to-date information on archaeological work in Greece is the *Archaeological Reports* published annually by the British School at Athens.

Appendix 2: Aristotle's *Politeiai*

1 Aristotle *Nicomachean Ethics* 10.9 end (=1181b12–20); tr. by David Ross 1980.
2 For an excellent recent discussion see Thomas 2019, ch. 9.
3 Gigon 2013
4 Diogenes Laertius 5.27; he is followed by Hesychius in his biography of Aristotle, the so-called *Vita Menagiana*; see e.g., Chloe Balla 2019, p. 33 which she opens with the sentence: "According to Diogenes Laertius, Aristotle's works included 158 *politeiai*, divided to democratic, oligarchic, tyrannic, and aristocratic." Cf. also Toye 1999 at 235 where he opens with the statement "The *Athenaion Politeia* was one of 158 *Politeiai* attributed to Aristotle in antiquity."
5 Note that this is also implied by the statements about the total number of "books," meaning papyrus scrolls, filled by Aristotle's works, totals which only add up based on counting 158 scrolls for the *Politeiai*.
6 Busse 1895.
7 Ammonius *Comm. in Categ.* (ed. Busse), p. 3,20–4,4; Elias *Proleg. philosoph. et in Porph. Eisag. Comm.* (ed. Busse) p. 74,25–75,2.
8 See e.g., Blank 2010.
9 On Hermippos of Smyrna see Bollansee 1999a, and see also his critical edition of the fragments 1999b; for Andronikos see now Perkams 2019, pp. 445–68; for Ptolemaios'

work, chiefly known from Arabic *vitae* of Aristotle where he is called Ptolemy al-Gharib, see Gutas 2000, ch. 6, also Hein 1985, pp. 415–39. The sources and reliability of the late antique and Arabic biographies of Aristotle and catalogues of his works is a tangled topic with an extensive literature, and this is not the place to go into it. Suffice it to say that a variety of good sources were clearly available to late antique scholars, as indicated above.

10 For details on the surviving papyrus see the online presentation by the British Museum at Digitised Manuscripts (bl.uk), showing full photographs of the papyrus rolls and giving all information on the measurements etc.

11 See Pliny *NH* 13.23–4, and the excellent discussion of the papyrus "industry" in Roman times by Skeat 1982. In computing the length of the roll, one needs to allow for small overlapping sections of the sheets where they were glued together.

12 The surviving text begins *in medias res* with the trial of those who had killed Kylon's supporters *c*. 632; since the roll (roll 1) has a blank space wide enough for a column of text before the beginning of the surviving text, it is clear that the version being copied was already incomplete, lacking the beginning. The excerpts by Herakleides Lembos reveal that the missing text had mostly to do with Athenian mythical origins, discussing the arrival of Ion and his followers, the reign and reforms of Theseus, the end of the Kodrid monarchy, and similar matters. We should not conclude that the missing portion was short however: these mythical stories were taken very seriously as important origin stories by classical Greeks, and Plutarch's *Theseus* attests, for example, to how expansively such mythical figures could be treated.

13 In his 1891 *editio princeps* of the *AthPol* Kenyon noted that the ending of the existing text is very abrupt, which could suggest that further text is missing at the end as at the beginning. He opted against this view because the final column of text at the end of roll 4 is only a few lines long, leaving ample empty space, and there is a notable pen flourish at the end of the text suggesting that the copyist was indicating the ending. I note, however: there is also empty space left in the final columns of rolls 2 (half a column empty) and 3 (enough for several more lines); that there is also a pen flourish beneath the text at the end of roll 3 (though less elaborate than in roll 4); and that we know from the missing beginning that the text being copied was already incomplete. In sum, it seems in fact likely to me that our text is incomplete at both beginning and end, the original *AthPol* being substantially longer than our surviving text.

14 There was substantial information available about the Spartan constitution: see Xenophon *Constitution of the Lakedaimonians* and Plutarch *Life of Lykourgos*, for example; and note the numerous lost treatises on the Spartan constitution which may have informed Aristotle's work: see Thomas 2019, ch. 9, and Tober 2010. The many changes in constitution of the Syracusans will have provided ample material

for a historical section like the first half of the *AthPol*, informed by the histories of Antiochus of Syracuse and Philistos, among others (note the Syracusan history preserved in Diodoros Siculus' pages); and the mid-fourth-century constitution established by Timoleon will also have provided substantial material, see e.g., Plutarch *Life of Timoleon*.

15 For some reason, Gigon did not count two references by Sopatros as fragments, which I here do: the Achaians, and Kios. In addition, he overlooked a testimony by the sixth-century Aristotle commentator known as David: *Proleg. Philos. et in Porphyrii Eisagoge Comm.* (ed. Busse), p. 74,25–75,2: *hoi Argeioi, hoi Boiotoi*.

16 On Herakleides and his "epitome" see the key article by Bloch 1940, establishing clearly that the work did consist of excerpts from Aristotle's *Politeiai*, and that it was authored by the second-century-BCE Alexandrian writer Herakleides Lembos; and see also now Verhasselt 2019.

17 As witness Aristotle's transition remarks from the *Nic Ethics* to the *Politika* referenced above.

Appendix 3: Overseas Settlements and *Metropoleis*

1 See e.g., the survey of Graham 1982, ch. 37; and cf. Tsetskhladze 2006/8.
2 I rely for this data on the tabulation by Graham 1982, pp. 160–2.

Bibliography

Akurgal, E. (1983), *Alt-Smyrna I: Wohnschichten und Athenatenpel*, Ankara: Turk Tarih.
Almagro, M. (1958), *Ampurias. A History of the City and Guide to the Excavations*, Barcelona.
Amemiya, T. (2007), *Economy and Economics of Ancient Greece*, New York: Routledge.
Anderson, G. (2003), *The Athenian Experiment. Building an Imagined Political Community in Ancient Attica, 508–490 BCE*, Ann Arbor: University of Michigan Press.
Anderson, G. (2005), "Before Turannoi were Tyrants," *CA* 24: 190–6.
Anderson, J. K. (1965), "Homeric, British and Cyrenaic Chariots," *AJA* 69: 349–52.
Anderson, J. K. (1995), "The Geometric Catalogue of Ships," in J. B. Carter and S. P. Morris (eds.), *The Ages of Homer: A Tribute to Emily Townsend Vermeule*, Austin: University of Texas Press, 181–91.
Anderson-Stojanovic, V. R. and J. E. Jones (2002), "Ancient beehives from Isthmia," *Hesperia* 71.4: 345–76
Andreau, J. and C. Virlouvet (2002), *L'information et la mer dans le monde antique*, Rome: École française de Rome.
Andrewes, A. (1949), "The Corinthian Actaeon and Pheidon of Argos," *CQ* 43: 70–8.
Andrewes, A. (1956), *The Greek Tyrants*, London: Hutchinson.
Andrewes, A. (1982), "The Growth of the Athenian State," in *CAH* III.3 (2nd ed.), 360–91.
Austin, M. M. (1970), *Greece and Egypt in the Archaic Age*, Cambridge: Proceedings of Cambridge Philological Society, Supplement vol. 2.
Austin, M. M. (2006), *The Hellenistic World from Alexander to the Roman Conquest: A Selection of Sources in Translation* (2nd ed.), Cambridge: Cambridge University Press.
Austin, M. M. and P. Vidal-Naquet (1980), *Economic and Social History of Ancient Greece*, Berkeley, CA: University of California Pres.
Bakhuizen, S. C. (1976), *Chalcis-in-Euboea, Iron and Chalkidians Abroad*, Leiden: Brill.
Balatsos, P. (1991), "Inscriptions from the Academy," *ZPE* 86: 145–54.
Balla, C. (2019), "The Debt of Aristotle's Collection of *Politeiai* to the Sophistic Tradition," in P. Golitsis and K. Ierodiakonou (eds.), *Aristotle and his Commentators*, Berlin: de Gruyter, 33–48.
Balot, R. (2006), *Greek Political Thought*, Oxford: Blackwell.
Bardunias, P. and F. E. Ray (2016), *Hoplites at War: A Comprehensive Analysis of Heavy Infantry Combat in the Greek World, 700–150 BCE*, London: McFarland.
Barrett, H. (1987), *The Sophists: Rhetoric, Democracy, and Plato's Idea of Sophistry*, Novato, CA: Chandler and Sharp.

Beck, F. A. (1975), *Album of Greek Education: The Greeks at School and at Play*, Cheiron Press.
Bekker-Nielsen, T., ed. (2006), *Ancient Fishing and Fish Processing in the Black Sea Region*, Aarhus: Aarhus University Press.
Bell, S. and C. Willekes (2014), "Horse Racing and Chariot Racing," in G. L. Campbell (ed.), *The Oxford Handbook of Animals in Classical Thought and Life*, Oxford: Oxford University Press, 478–90.
Bellen, H. et al. eds. (2003), *Bibliographie zur antiken Sklaverei*, 2 vols., Stuttgart: Steiner.
Beloch, K. J. (1886), *Die Bevölkerung der griechisch-römischen Welt*, Leipzig: Duncker und Humblot.
Berent, M. (2004), "In search of the Greek state: a rejoinder to M.H. Hansen," *Polis* 21: 107–46
Bernand, A. and O. Masson (1957), "Les inscriptions grecs d'Abou Simbel," *REG* 70: 1–57
Berve, H. (1967), *Die Tyrannis bei den Griechen* 2 vols., Munich: C.H. Beck.
Best, J. (1969), *Thracian Peltasts and their Influence on Greek Warfare*, Leiden: Brill.
Betant, E.-A. (1969), *Lexicon Thucydideum* 2 vols., Heldesheim: Georg Olms Verlag.
Billows, R. A. (1995), *Kings and Colonists. Aspects of Macedonian Imperialism*, Leiden: Brill.
Billows, R. A. (2003), "Hellenistic Cities," in A. Erskine (ed.), *A Companion to the Hellenistic World*, Oxford: Blackwell, 196–215.
Billows, R. A. (2008), *Julius Caesar, the Colossus of Rome*, New York: Routledge.
Billows, R. A. (2009), "The Authorship of the *Hellenika Oxyrrhynchia*," in *Mouseion* 3.9, 219–38.
Billows, R. A. (2016), "Hellenika Oxyrhynchia," in I. Worthington (ed.), *Brill's New Jacoby* no. 66, Leiden: Brill
Billows, R. A. (2018), *Before and After Alexander*, New York: Overlook.
Bintliff, J. (1997), "Regional Survey, Demography, and the Rise of Complex Societies in the Ancient Aegean: Core-Periphery, Neo-Malthusian, and Other Interpretive Models," *JFA* 24: 1–38.
Bintliff, J. (2006), "Multi-ethnicity and population movement in Ancient Greece: Alternatives to a world of 'Red-Figure' people," in H. Sonnabend and E. Olshausen (eds.), *Troianer sind wir gewesen*, Stuttgart: Franz Steiner, 108–14.
Blackwell, C. W. (2003), "The Assembly," in *Demos: Classical Athenian Democracy*, The Stoa: A Consortium for Electronic Publication in the Humanities.
Blair, D. (2016), "Herodotos and the Laws of Thourioi," in *Abstracts of the 147th Annual Meeting of the Society for Classical Studies*.
Blank, D. L. (2010), "Ammonius Hermeiou and his School," in L. P. Gerson (ed.), *The Cambridge History of Philosophy in Late Antiquity*, Cambridge: Cambridge University Press, 654–66.
Blegen, C. (1934), "Inscriptions on Geometric Pottery from Hymettos," *AJA* 38: 10–28.

Bloch, H. (1940), "Herakleides Lembos and his *Epitome* of Aristotle's *politeiai*," *TAPhA* 71: 27–39.

Blok, J. (2017), *Citizenship in Classical Athens*, Cambridge: Cambridge University Press.

Blundell, S. (1995), *Women in Ancient Greece*, Boston: Harvard University Press.

Boardman, J. (1972), "Herakles, Peisistratos and Sons," *RevArch*: 57–72.

Boardman, J. (1975), "Herakles, Peisistratos and Eleusis," *JHS* 95: 1–12.

Boardman, J. (1980), *The Greeks Overseas* (3rd ed.), London: Thames and Hudson.

Boardman, J. (1982), "The material culture of Archaic Greece," in *CAH* III.3 (2nd ed.), 442–62.

Boardman, J. (1989), "Herakles, Peisistratos and the Unconvinced," *JHS* 109: 158–9.

Boethius, A. (1918), *Die Pythais: Studien zur Geschichte der Verbindungen zwischen Athen und Delphi*, Uppsala: Almquist & Wicksels.

Bollansee, J. (1999a), *Hermippos of Smyrna and his Biographical Writings. A Reappraisal*, Leuven: Peeters.

Bollansee, J. (1999b), *Hermippos of Smyrna: Critical Edition*, Leiden: Brill.

Bommelje, S. and P. K. Doorn (1987), *Aetolia and the Aetolians: Towards the Interdisciplinary Study of a Greek Region*, Utrecht: Parnassus Press.

Borza, E. (1995), "Some observations on malaria and the ecology of central Macedonia in antiquity," in *Makedonika* (ed. C. Thomas), Regina Books.

Boserup, E. (1965), *The Conditions of Agricultural Growth: The Economics of Agrarian Change Under Population Pressure*, London: Allen & Unwin.

Boserup, E. (1981), *Population and Technological Change: A Study of Long-term Trends*, Chicago: University of Chicago Press.

Bourriot, F. (1976), *Recherches sur la nature du genos*, Lille.

Bowden, H. (1993), "Hoplites and Homer: Warfare, hero cult, and the ideology of the polis," in J. Rich and G. Shipley (eds.), *War and Society in the Greek World*, London: Routledge, 45–63.

Bradley, K. and P. Cartledge eds. (2011), *The Cambridge History of World Slavery vol I: The Ancient Mediterranean World*, Cambridge: Cambridge University Press.

Braun, T. (1982), "The Greeks in the Near East and Egypt," in *CAH* III.3 (2nd ed.): 1–56.

Brenne, S. (2002), "Die Ostraka," in P. Siewert (ed.), *Ostrakismos-Testimonien I* (*Historia* Suppl. 155), 36–166.

Brenne, S. (2001), *Ostrakismos und Prominenz in Athen*, *Tyche* Suppl. 3.

Bresson, A. (2016), *The Making of the Ancient Greek Economy: Institutions, Markets, and Growth in the City-States*, Princeton, NJ: Princeton University Press.

Brixhe, C. (2007), "History of the Alphabet: some guidelines for avoiding oversimplification," in A.-F. Christidis, *A History of Ancient Greek: From the Beginnings to Late Antiquity*, Cambridge: Cambridge University Press, ch. II.8.

Broneer, O. (1938), "Excavations on the north slope of the Acropolis," *Hesperia* 7: 161–263

Brook Manville, P. (1990), *The Origins of Citizenship in Ancient Athens*, Princeton, NJ: Princeton University Press.

Brouwers, J. (2007), "From horsemen to hoplites," *BABesch* 82: 305–19.
Brouwers, J. (2013), *Henchmen of Ares: Warriors and Warfare in Early Greece*, Rotterdam: Karwansaray Publishers.
Buchner Niola, D. (1965), *L'isola d'Ischia: studio geografico*, Naples: Ist. Geografia dell'Universita.
Buckler, J. (1980), *The Theban Hegemony, 371–362 BC*, Cambridge, MA: Harvard University Press.
Burford, A. (1969), *The Greek Temple Builders at Epidaurus*, Liverpool: Liverpool University Press.
Burford, A. (1994), "Greek agriculture in the classical period," in *CAH* VI (2nd ed.), 661–77.
Busse, Ad. (1895), *Commentaria in Aristotelem Graeca IV.5 In Aristotelis Categorias Commentarius*, Berlin: de Gruyter.
Campbell, J. K. (1964), *Honor, Family, and Patronage: A Study of Institutions and Moral Values in a Greek Mountain Community*, Oxford: Oxford University Press.
Cantarella, E. (1986), *Pandora's Daughters: The Role and Status of Women in Greek and Roman Antiquity*, Baltimore: Johns Hopkins University Press.
Carney, E. (2021), "Women and war in the Greek world," in W. Heckel et al. (eds.), *A Companion to Greek Warfare*, Hoboken, NJ: Wiley Blackwell, 329–38.
Carter, L. B. (1986), *The Quiet Athenian*, Oxford: Clarendon Press.
Cartledge, P. (2002), *Sparta and Lakonia, a Regional History 1300–362 BC* (2nd ed.), London: Routledge.
Cartledge, P. (2003), *The Spartans: An Epic History*, London: Pan Books.
Cartledge, P. (2007), "Democracy, Origins of: Contribution to a Debate," in K, Raaflaub et al. (eds.), *Origins of Democracy in Ancient Greece*, Berkeley, CA: University of California Press, ch. 6.
Cartledge, P., E. Cohen, L. Foxhall eds. (2002), *Money, Labor and Land: Approaches to the Economics of Ancient Greece*, New York: Routledge.
Casson, L. (1991), *The Ancient Mariners* (2nd ed.), Princeton, NJ: Princeton University Press.
Casson, L. (1994), "Mediterranean Communications," in *CAH* VI (2nd ed.), 512–26
Cawkwell, G. (1995), "Early Greek tyranny and the people," *CQ* 45: 73–86
Cerri, G. (1979), *Legislazione orale e tragedia greca*, Napoles: Liguori Editore.
Cetin Sahin, M. (1987), "Zwei inschriften aus den sudwestlichen Kleinasien," *EA* 10: 1–2
Chadwick, J. (1976), *The Mycenean World*, Cambridge: Cambridge University Press.
Chang, C. (1993), "Pastoral transhumance in the southern Balkans as a social ideology: Ethonoarchaeological research in northern Greece," *American Anthropologist* 95.3: 687–703.
Chant, C. (1999), *Pre-Industrial Cities and Technology*, London: Routledge.
Clark, C. and M. R. Haswell (1964), *The Economics of Subsistence Agriculture*, London: Macmillan.
Clayton, E. (2004), "Aristotle: Politics," in the *Internet Encyclopedia of Philosophy*.

Clement, A., S. Hillson, and M. Michalaki-Kollia (2009), "The ancient cemeteries of Astypalaia, Greece," *Archaeology International* 12: 17–21.

Coale, A. J. and P. Demeny (1983), *Regional Model Life Tables and Stable Populations* (2nd ed. with additions by B. Vaughn), Amsterdam: Elsevier.

Cohen, D. (1989), "Seclusion, Separation, and the Status of Women in Classical Athens," *G&R* 36: 3–15.

Coldstream, J. N. (2004), *Geometric Greece, 900–700 BC* (2nd ed.), London: Routledge

Cole, M. (2021), *The Bronze Lie: Shattering the Myth of Spartan Warrior Supremacy*, Oxford: Osprey Publishing.

Connelly, J. B. (2007), *Portrait of a Priestess: Women and Ritual in Ancient Greece*, Princeton, NJ: Princeton University Press.

Cook, J. M. (1962), *The Greeks in Ionia and the East*, London: Thames and Hudson.

Cook, J. M. (1975), "Greek settlement in the eastern Aegean and Asia Minor," in *CAH* II.2 (3rd ed.), 773–804.

Cook, R. M. (1958/59), "Old Smyrna," *BSA* 53-54: 1–34

Cook, R. M (1962), "Reasons for the foundation of Ischia and Cumae," *Historia* 11: 113–14.

Crane, E. (1999), *The World History of Beekeeping and Honey Hunting*, London: Routledge.

Crawford, M. and D. Whitehead (1983), *Archaic and Classical Greece: A Selection of Ancient Sources in Translation*, Cambridge: Cambridge University Press.

Crielaard, J. P. ed. (1995), *Homeric Questions: Essays in Philology, Ancient History, and Archaeology*, Leiden: Brill.

Davies, J. K. (1981), *Wealth and the Power of Wealth in Classical Athens*, London: Beaufort Books.

Davies, J. K. (1984), "Cultural, social, and economic features of the Hellenistic world," in *CAH* VII.1 (2nd ed.), 257–320.

Davies, J. K. (1997), "The Origins of the Greek Polis," in L. G. Mitchell and P. J. Rhodes (eds.), *The Development of the Polis in Archaic Greece*, London: Routledge.

Day, J. and M. Chambers (1967), *Aristotle's History of Athenian Democracy*, Berkeley, CA: University of California Press.

Day, J. W. (1989), "Early Greek Grave Epigrams and Monuments," in *JHS* 109: 16–28.

de Backer, F. (2013), "Notes on the Neo-Assyrian Siege-Shield and Chariot," in Feliu et al. (eds.), *Time and History in the Ancient Near East*, University Park, PA: Penn State University Press, 69–78.

de Jong, I. ed. (1999), *Homer, Critical Assessments II: the Homeric World*, London: Routledge:

de Polignac, F. (1995), *Cults, Territory and the Origins of the Greek City-State* (tr. J. Lloyd), Chicago: University of Chicago Press.

de Souza, P. (2002), *Piracy in the Greco-Roman World*, Cambridge: Cambridge University Press.

de Ste. Croix, G. E. M. (1972), *The Origins of the Peloponnesian War*, London: Duckworth.
Deger-Jalkotzy, S. (1979), "Homer und der Orient: das Koenigtum des Priamos," *WJA* n.s. 5: 25–31.
Demand, N. H. (1982), *Thebes in the Fifth Century: Heracles Resurgent*, London: Routledge.
Denyer, N. (2008), *Plato. Protagoras*, Cambridge: Cambridge University Press.
Dijksterhuis, E. J. (1969), *The Mechanization of the World Picture*, New York: Oxford University Press.
Donald, M. (1991), *Origins of the Modern Mind: Three Stages in the Evolution of Culture and Cognition*, Cambridge, MA: Harvard University Press.
Donald, M. (2002), *A Mind So Rare: The Evolution of Human Consciousness*, New York: W. W. Norton.
Donlan W. (1989), "Homeric temenos and the land economy of the Dark Age," *Museum Helveticum* 46.3: 129–45.
Durrbach, F. (1921), *Choix d'inscriptions de Delos* (repr. 1973), Hildesheim: Georg Olms Verlag.
Eder, B. (1998), *Argolis, Lakonien, Messenien*, Vienna: Austrian Academy of Sciences.
Ehrenberg, V. (1937), "When did the polis rise?" *JHS* 57: 147–59
Emiliozzi, A. (2011), "The Etruscan Chariot from Monteleone di Spoleto," *MMJ* 46: 9–132
Engels, D. (1990), *Roman Corinth: An Alternative Model for the Classical City*, Chicago: University of Chicago Press.
Figueira, T. J. (1991), *Athens and Aigina in the Age of Imperial Colonization*, London: Johns Hopkins University Press.
Figueira, T. J. and G. Nagy eds. (1985), *Theognis of Megara: Poetry and the Polis*, London: Johns Hopkins University Press.
Finley, M. I. (1973), *The Ancient Economy*, Berkeley, CA: University of California Press.
Finley, M. I. (1979), *The World of Odysseus* (2nd ed.), London: Penguin.
Fisher, N. (1993), *Slavery in Classical Greece*, New York: Bloomsbury Academic.
Foley, A. (1988), *The Argolid 800 to 600 BC: An Archaeological Survey*, Gothenburg: P. Astrom.
Fontenrose, J. (1978), *The Delphic Oracle*, Berkeley, CA: University of California Press.
Forbes, H. (2013), "The identification of pastoralist sites within the context of estate-based agriculture in ancient Greece: beyond the 'transhumance versus agro-pastoralism' debate," *ABSA* 90: 325–38.
Forrest, A. (2009), *The Legacy of the French Revolutionary Wars: The Nation-in-Arms in French Revolutionary Memory*, Cambridge: Cambridge University Press.
Forrest, W. G. (1968), *History of Sparta, 900–192 BC*, London: Hutchinson.
Forsdyke, S. (2005), *Exile, Ostracism, and Democracy: The Politics of Expulsion in Ancient Greece*, Princeton, NJ: Princeton University Press.

Foxhall, L. (2007), *Olive Cultivation in Ancient Greece: Seeking The Ancient Economy*, Oxford: Oxford University Press.
French, A. (1964), *The Growth of the Athenian Economy*, London: Routledge.
Frier, B. (1982), "Roman life expectancy: Ulpian's evidence," *HSCPh* 86: 213–51.
Frost, F. (1990), "Peisistratos, the cults, and the unification of Attica," *AW* 21: 3–9.
Gabba, E. (1976), *Republican Rome, the Army and the Allies*, Oxford: Blackwell.
Gagarin, M. (1986), *Early Greek Law*, Berkeley, CA: University of California Press.
Gagarin, M. (2008), *Writing Greek Law*, Cambridge: Cambridge University Press.
Gagarin, M. and P. Perlman (2016), *The Laws of Ancient Crete, ca. 650–400 BCE*, Oxford: Oxford University Press.
Gallant, T. W. (1991), *Risk and Survival in Ancient Greece: Reconstructing the Domestic Rural Economy*, Stanford: Stanford University Press.
Garlan, Y. (1988), *Slavery in Ancient Greece* (tr. J. Lloyd), Ithaca, NY: Cornell University Press.
Gauthier, P. (1984), "Le programme de Xenophon dans les *Poroi*," repr. in *Etudes d'Histoire et des Institutions Grecs: Choix d'Ecrits* (D. Rousset, ed.), Geneva: Librairie Droz, 221–44.
Gauthier, P. (1985), *Les cites grecs et leurs bienfaiteurs*, Paris: de Boccard.
Gelb, I. J. (1963), *A Study of Writing* (2nd ed.), Chicago: University of Chicago Press.
Gigon, O. (2013), *Aristotelis Opera* vol. III, Berlin: De Gruyter.
Gill, D. W. (1991), "Pots and Trade: Space-fillers or Objets d'Art?" *JHS* 111: 29–47.
Giovannini, A. (1969), *Etude historique sur les origines du Catalogue des Vaisseaux*, Bern: Francke.
Giovannini, A. (1971), *Untersuchungen zu den bundesstaatlichen Sympolitie*, *Hypomnemata* 33.
Gomme, A. W. (1945), *A Historical Commentary on Thucydides* vol. I, Oxford: Clarendon Press.
Graham, A. J. (1982), "The colonial expansion of Greece" and "The western Greeks," in *CAH* III.3 (2nd ed.), Cambridge: Cambridge University Press, 83–195.
Graham, A. J. (1983), *Colony and Mother City in Ancient Greece* (2nd ed.), Chicago: Ares.
Greenhalgh, P. (1973), *Early Greek Warfare: Horsemen and Chariots in the Homeric and Archaic Ages*, Cambridge: Cambridge University Press.
Griffin, A. (1982), *Sikyon*, New York: Oxford University Press.
Gschnitzer, F. (1958), *Abhaengige Orte im griechischen Altertum*, Zetemata 17, Munich.
Gutas, D. (2000), *Greek Philosophers in the Arabic Tradition*, New York: Routledge.
Haegg, R. (1982), "Zur Stadtwerdung des dorischen Argos," in Papenfuss and von Strocka (eds.) *Palaest und Huette*, 297–307.
Haegg, R. ed. (1983), *The Greek Renaissance of the Eighth Century BC. Tradition and Innovation*, Stockholm.
Hammond, N. G. L. (1982), "The Peloponnese," in *CAH* III.3 (2nd ed.), 321–59.
Handel, M. I. (1986), *Clausewitz and Modern Strategy*, Abingdon: Frank Cass.

Hansen, M. H. (1983), *The Athenian Ecclesia: A Collection of Articles, 1976–83*, Copenhagen: Museum Tusculanum Press.
Hansen, M. H. (1986), *Demography and Democracy: The Number of Athenian Citizens in the 4th Century BC*, Athens: Systime.
Hansen, M. H. (1987), *The Athenian Assembly*, Oxford: Blackwell.
Hansen, M. H. (1989), *The Athenian Ecclesia II: A Collection of Articles, 1983–89*, Copenhagen: Museum Tusculanum Press.
Hansen, M. H. ed. (1993), *The Ancient Greek City-State: Symposium* Munksgaard: Commissioner.
Hansen, M. H. (1995), *Studies in the Ancient Greek Polis* vol. 1, Berlin: Franz Steiner Verlag.
Hansen, M. H. (1996), *More Studies in the Ancient Greek "Polis"* (with K. Raaflaub), Berlin: Steiner Verlag.
Hansen, M. H. (1997), "The Copenhagen inventory of Poleis," in L. G. Mitchell and P. J. Rhodes (eds.), *The Development of the Polis in Archaic Greece*, London: Routledge.
Hansen, M. H. (2002), *A Comparative Study of Six City-State Cultures*, Copenhagen: Danske Videnskabernes.
Hansen, M. H. (2004), "Boiotia," in T. Nielsen and M. Hansen, *An Inventory of Archaic and Classical Poleis*, Oxford: Oxford University Press.
Hansen, M. H. (2006), *Polis: An Introduction to the Ancient Greek City-State*, Oxford: Oxford University Press.
Hansen, M. H. (2010), "Was Sparta a normal or an exceptional *polis*?" in S. Hodkinson (ed.), *Sparta: Comparative Approaches*, Swansea: University of Wales Press, 385–416.
Hanson, V. D. (1991), *Hoplites: the Classical Greek Battle Experience*, New York: Routledge.
Harris, E. (2002), "Workshop, marketplace and household: the nature of technical specialization in classical Athens and its influence on economy and society," in Cartledge, Cohen, and Foxhall (eds.), *Money, Labour, and Land*, New York: Routledge.
Harris, R. (1986), *The Origin of Writing*, New York: Open Court Publishing.
Harris, W. V. (1989), *Ancient Literacy*, Cambridge, MA: Harvard University Press.
Hasebroek, J. (1928), *Staat und Handel im alten Griechenland*, Tubingen: J. C. B. Mohr.
Havelock, E. (1976), *The Origins of Western Literacy*, Princeton, NJ: Princeton Univeristy Press.
Head, B. V. (1911), *Historia Nummorum: a Manual of Greek Numismatics* (2nd ed.), Oxford: Oxford University Press.
Hedrick, C. (1999), "Democracy and the Athenian Epigraphical Habit," *Hesperia* 68.3: 387–439.
Hein, C. (1985), *Definition und Einteilung der Philosophie. Von der spätantiken Einleitungsliteratur zur arabischen Enzyklopädie*, Frankfurt am Main: P. Lang.
Herfst, P. (1922), *Le travail de la femme dans la Grèce ancienne*, Utrecht: A. Oosterhoek.

Heubeck, A., S. West, and J. B. Hainsworth (1988), *A Commentary on Homer's Odyssey, Vol. I Introduction and Books I–VIII*, Oxford: Clarendon Press.

Hodder, I. (1982), *The Present Past. An Introduction to Anthropology for Archaeologists*, London: B. T. Batsford.

Hodkinson, S. (1988), "Animal Husbandry in the Greek *Polis*" in C. R. Whitaker (ed.), *Pastoral Economies in Classical Antiquity*, Cambridge: Cambridge Philological Society, 35–74.

Hölkeskamp, K.-J. (1999), *Schiedsrichter, Gesetzgeber, und Gesetzgebung im archaischen Griechenland, Historia Einzelschriften* 131, Stuttgart: Franz Steiner Verlag.

Hölkeskamp, K.-J. (2000), "(In-)Schrift und Monument. Zum Begriff des Gesetzes im archaischen und klassischen Griechenland," *ZPE* 132: 73–96.

Hope Simpson, R. and J. F. Lazenby (1970), *The Catalogue of the Ships in Homer's Iliad*, Oxford: Clarendon Press.

Horden, P. and N. Purcell (2000), *The Corrupting Sea: A Study of Mediterranean History*, Oxford: Blackwell.

Hornblower, S. (1991), *A Commentary on Thucydides* 3 vols., Oxford: Oxford University Press.

Hunt, P. (2021), "War and Slavery in the Greek World," in W. Heckel et al. (eds.), *A Companion to Greek Warfare*, Hoboken, NJ: Wiley Blackwell, 271–85.

Hurwit, J. (2015), *Artists and Signatures in Ancient Greece*, Cambridge: Cambridge University Press.

Jachmann, G. (1958), *Der homerische Schiffskatalog und die "Ilias,"* Cologne-Opladen: Westdeutscher Verlag.

Jacoby, F. (1949), *Atthis: The Local Chronicles of Ancient Athens*, Oxford: Clarendon Press.

Jackson, A. H. (1991), "Hoplites and the Gods: the dedication of captured arms and armor," in V. D. Hanson (ed.), *Hoplites: The Classical Greek Battle Experience*, London: Routledge.

Jackson, A. H. (1993), "War and raids for booty in the world of Odysseus," in J. Rich and G. Shipley (eds.), *War and Society in the Greek World*, London: Routledge, 64–76.

Jameson, M. (1977/78), "Agriculture and slavery in classical Athens," *CJ* 73: 122–45.

Jameson, M., C. Runnels and Tj. van Andel (1994), *A Greek Countryside: The Southern Argolid from Prehistory to the Present Day*, Stanford: Stanford University Press.

Janko, R. (1982), *Homer, Hesiod, and the Hymn*, Cambridge: Cambridge University Press.

Janko, R. (2015), "From Gabii and Gordion to Eretria and Methone: the rise of the Greek alphabet," *BICS* 58.1: 1–32.

Jeffery, L. and A. Morpurgo-Davies (1970), "Poinikastas and poinikazein: BM 1969:42.1 a new archaic inscription from Crete," *Kadmos* 9: 118–54.

Jeffery, L. (1961/90), *The Local Scripts of Archaic Greece: A Study of the Origin of the Greek Alphabet and its Development from the 8th to the 5th Centuries BC* (2nd expanded ed. with additions by A. W. Johnston), Oxford: Clarendon Press.

Johnston, A. W. (1972), "The rehabilitation of Sostratos," *Parola del Passato* 27: 316–23
Johnston, A. W. (1974), "Trademarks on Greek Vases," *Greece and Rome* 21: 138–52.
Jones, J. E. (1976), "Hives and honey of Hymettus: Beekeeping in ancient Greece," *Archaeology* 29: 80ff.
Jones, N. F. (1999), *The Associations of Classical Athens: the Response to Democracy*, Oxford: Oxford University Press.
Jones, N. F. (2015), "Androtion of Athens (324)," in *Brill's New Jacoby*, Brill: Leiden.
Jones, N. F. (2016), "Philochoros of Athens (328)," in *Brill's New Jacoby*, Brill: Leiden.
Jordan, B. (1972), "The Administration and Military Organization of the Athenian Navy in the 5th and 4th Centuries BC," PhD diss., Berkeley, CA: University of California.
Jordan, B. (2000), "The Crews of Athenian triremes," *L'Antiquite Classique* 69, 81–101.
Jordan, D. R. (2000), "New Greek curse tablets (1985–2000)," *GRBS* 41: 5–46.
Kagan, D. and G. F. Viggiano (2013), *Men of Bronze: Hoplite Warfare in Ancient Greece*, Princeton, NJ: Princeton University Press.
Kelly, T. (1976), *A History of Argos*, Minneapolis: University of Minnesota Press.
Kenyon, F. G. (1891), *Aristotle on the Constitution of Athens*, London: British Museum.
Kienast, H. J. (2005), *The Aqueduct of Eupalinos on Samos*, Athens: Archaeological Receipts Fund.
Kirk, G. S. et al. (1985/93), *The Iliad: A Commentary* 6 vols., Cambridge: Cambridge University Press.
Kirk, G. S., J. E. Raven, and M. Schofield, eds. (2007), *The Presocratic Philosophers: A Critical History with a Selection of Texts* (revised & expanded edition), Cambridge: Cambridge University Press.
Knoepfler, D. (1985), "Oropos, colonie d'Eretrie," in P. Ducrey and A. Altherr-Charon (eds.), *Eretrie, cite de la Grece antique* (Les Dossiers d'Archeologie 94).
Koerner, R. (1981), entry on "astu" in E. Welskopf (ed.), *Soziale Typenbegriffe im alten Griechenland und ihr Fortleben in den Sprachen der Welt* vol. 3, Berlin.
Koukoudis, A. I. (2003), *The Vlachs: Metropolis and Diaspora*, Athens: Zitros Publications.
Kraut, R. (2002), *Aristotle: Political Philosophy*, Oxford: Oxford University Press.
Krentz, P. (1985), "The Nature of Hoplite Battle," *CA* 4.1: 50–61.
Krentz, P. (2002), "Fighting by the Rules: The Invention of the Hoplite *Agon*," *Hesperia* 71: 23–39.
Krentz, P. (2010), *The Battle of Marathon*, New Haven: Yale University Press.
Kritzas, Ch. (2010), "Phoinikeia grammata. Nea archaiki epigraphe apo ten Eltyna," in G. Rethemiotakis and M. Egglezou, *To Geometriko Nekrotapheio tes Eltynas*, Herakleion, 1–16.
Kroll, J. and N. Waggoner (1984), "Dating the earliest coins of Athens, Corinth, and Aegina," *AJA* 88: 325–40.
Kurke, L. (1999), *Coins, Bodies, Games, and Gold: The Politics of Meaning in Archaic Greece*, Princeton, NJ: Princeton University Press.
Lambert, S. D. (1999), "The Attic *genos*," *CQ* 49.2: 484–9.

Lambert, S. D. (2011), "What was the point of inscribed honorific decrees in classical Athens?" in S. D. Lambert (ed.), *Sociable Man. Studies in Ancient Greek Social Behaviour in Honour of Nick Fisher*, Swansea: Classical Press of Wales, 193–214.

Lang, M. (1976), *The Athenian Agora: vol. XXI Graffiti and Dipinti*, Princeton, NJ: American School of Classical Studies.

Langdon, M. K. (1976), *A Sanctuary of Zeus on Mt. Hymettos*, Hesperia Suppl. 16, Princeton, NJ.

Langdon, M. K. (2004), "Hymettiana V: A willing katapugon," *ZPE* 184: 201–6.

Langdon, M. K. (2005), "A new Greek abecedarium," *Kadmos* 44: 175–82.

Larsen, J. O. A. (1955), *Representative Government in Greek and Roman History*, Berkeley, CA: University of California Press.

Larsen, J. O. A. (1968), *Greek Federal States: their Institutions and History*, Oxford: Clarendon Press.

Latacz, J. (1977), *Kampfparänese, Kampfdarstellung und Kampfwirklichkeit in der Ilias, bei Kallinos und Tyrtaios*, Munich: Beck.

Lawrence, A. W. (1979), *Greek Aims in Fortification*, Oxford: Clarendon Press.

Lazenby, J. (1991), "The Killing Zone," in V. D. Hanson (ed.), *Hoplites: The Classical Greek Battle Experience*, London: Routledge, 87–109.

Legon, R. P. (1981), *Megara: The Political History of a Greek City-State to 336 BC*, Ithaca, NY: Cornell University Press.

Lemos, I. S. (2002), *The Protogeometric Aegean: the Archaeology of the Late 11th and 10th Centuries BC*, Oxford: Oxford University Press.

Lemos, I. S. (2012), "Euboia and Central Greece in the Post Palatial and Early Greek Periods," *AR* 58: 19–27.

Lemos, I. S. and A. Kotsonas eds. (2020), *A Companion to the Archaeology of Early Greece and the Mediterranean* 2 vols., Oxford: Wiley Blackwell.

Lendon, J. E. (2005), *Soldiers and Ghosts: A History of Battle in Classical Antiquity*, New Haven: Yale University Press.

Loman, P. (2004), "No woman, no war: Women's participation in ancient Greek warfare," *G&R* 51: 34–54.

Loomis, W. T. (1998), *Wages, Welfare Costs, and Inflation in Classical Athens*, Ann Arbor: University of Michigan Press.

Lord, A. B. (1960), *The Singer of Tales*, Cambridge, MA: Harvard University Press.

Lord, A. B. (1991), *Epic Singers and Oral Tradition*, Ithaca, NY: Cornell University Press.

Lorimer, H. L. (1947), "The Hoplite Phalanx," *BSA* 42: 76–138.

Loven, B. and M. Schaldemose (2011), *The Ancient Harbors of the Piraeus: The Zea Shipsheds and Slipways* 2 vols., Athens: Danish Institute at Athens.

Luginbill, R. D. (1994), "Othismos: the importance of the mass-shove in hoplite warfare," *Phoenix* 48.1: 51–61.

MacDowell, D. M. (1978), *The Law in Classical Athens*, Ithaca, NY: Cornell University Press.

MacDowell, D. M (2010), *Demosthenes the Orator*, Oxford: Oxford University Press.

MacLachlan, B. (2012), *Women in Ancient Greece: A Sourcebook*, London: Bloomsbury Academic.
Maier, F. G. (1959/61), *Griechische Mauerbauinschriften* 2 vols., Heidelberg: Quelle und Meyer.
Malkin, I. (1987), *Religion and Colonization in Ancient Greece*, Leiden: Brill.
Malkin, I. (1998), *The Returns of Odysseus: Colonization and Ethnicity*, Berkeley, CA: University of California Press.
Malkin, I. ed. (2001), *Ancient Perceptions of Greek Ethnicity*, Washington, DC: Center for Hellenic Studies.
Marconi, C. (2012), "Sicily and South Italy," in T. J. Smith and D. Plantzos (eds.), *A Companion to Greek Art* vol. 1, Oxford: Wiley-Blackwell, 369–96.
Markle, M. M. (2004), "Jury pay and assembly pay at Athens," in P. J. Rhodes (ed.), *Athenian Democracy*, New York: Oxford University Press, 95–131.
Marr, J. L. and P. J. Rhodes (2008), *The "Old Oligarch": The Constitution of the Athenians Attributed to Xenophon*, Oxford: Oxbow Books.
Martin Gonzalez, E. (2014), "Reading archaic Greek inscriptions," in W. Eck and P. Funke et al. (eds.), *Offentlichkeit-Monument-Text: Akten XIV Congressus Internationalis Epigraphiae Graecae et Latinae*, Berlin: de Gruyter, 683–5
Matthew, C. A. (2009), "When push comes to shove: What was the *othismos* of hoplite combat?" *Historia* 58: 395–415.
McAdams, D. P. (2015), *The Art and Science of Personality Development*, New York: Guilford Press.
McAdams, D. P. and K. C. McLean (2013), "Narrative identity," *Current Directions in Psychological Science* 22: 233–8.
McGlew, J. F. (1993), *Tyranny and Political Culture in Ancient Greece*, Ithaca, NY: Cornell University Press.
McInerney, J. (1999), *The Folds of Parnassus: Land and Ethnicity in Ancient Phokis*, Austin: University of Texas Press.
McKechnie, P. R and S. J. Kern (1988), *Hellenica Oxyrhynchia*, Warminster: Aris and Philips.
Mee, C. (2011), *Greek Archaeology: A Thematic Approach*, Oxford: Wiley-Blackell.
Meier, Ch. (1980), *Die Entstehung des Politischen bei den Griechen*, Munich: Suhrkamp Verlag.
Meiggs, R. (1980), *Trees and Timber in the Ancient Mediterranean World*, Oxford: Clarendon Press.
Meiggs, R. and Lewis, D. (1969), *A Selection of Greek Historical Inscriptions to the End of the 5th Century BC*, Oxford: Oxford University Press.
Mele, A. (1979), *Il commercio Greco arcaico: prexis ed emporia*, Naples: Institut Français de Naples.
Meyer, Ed. (1895), *Die wirtschaftliche Entwicklung des Altertums*, Frankfurt am Main: Fischer.
Meyer, E. (2010), *Metics and the Athenian Phialai-Inscriptions: A Study in Athenian Epigraphy and Law*, Stuttgart: F. Steiner.

Meyer, E. (2013), "Inscriptions as Honors and the Athenian Epigraphic Habit," *Historia* 62.4: 453–505.

Michell, H. (1963), *The Economics of Ancient Greece*, Cambridge: Cambridge University Press.

Mitchell, L. G. and P. J. Rhodes eds. (1997), *The Development of the Polis in Archaic Greece*, London: Routledge.

Mills, S. (1997), *Theseus, Tragedy, and the Athenian Empire*, Oxford: Clarendon Press.

Missiou, A. (2011), *Literacy and Democracy in 5th century Athens*, Cambridge: Cambridge University Press.

Moore, J. M. (1983), *Aristotle and Xenophon on Democracy and Oligarchy*, Berkeley: University California Press.

Morgan, C. (1990), *Athletes and Oracles: the Transformation of Olympia and Delphi in the 8th Century BC*, Cambridge: Cambridge University Press.

Morgan, C. (1991), "Ethnicity and early Greek states: historical and material perspectives," *PCPS* 37: 131–63.

Morgan, C. (1997), "The archaeology of sanctuaries in early Iron Age and Archaic *ethne*: a preliminary view," in L. G. Mitchell and P. J. Rhodes (eds.), *The Development of the Polis in Archaic Greece*, London: Routledge, 168–98.

Morgan, C. (2003), *Early Greek States Beyond the Polis*, London: Routledge.

Morison, W. S. (2014), "Theopompos of Chios (115)," in *Brill's New Jacoby*, Leiden: Brill.

Morris, I. (1986), "The Use and Abuse of Homer," *CA* 5: 81–138.

Morris, I. (1987), *Burial and Ancient Society: The Rise of the Greek City-State*, Cambridge: Cambridge University Press.

Morris, I. (2000), *Archaeology as Cultural History: Words and Things in Iron Age Greece*, Malden, MA: Blackwell.

Morris, I. (2004), "Economic growth in ancient Greece," *JITE* 160.4: 709–42.

Murray, O. ed. (1990), *Sympotica: A Symposium on the Symposium*, Oxford: Clarendon Press.

Murray, O. (1993), *Early Greece* (2nd ed.), Cambridge, MA: Harvard University Press.

Murray, O. and A. Moreno, eds. (2007), *Commentary on Herodotus Books I–IV*, Oxford: Oxford University Press.

Murray, O. and S. Price eds. (1990), *The Greek City from Homer to Alexander*, Oxford: Clarendon Press.

Musti, D. (1966) *Lo stato dei Seleucidi: dinastia, popoli, citta da Seleuco I ad Antioco III*, Studi Classici e Orientali 15.

Musiolek, P. (1981), entry on *"polis,"* in E. Welskopf (ed.), *Soziale Typenbegriffe im alten Griechenland und ihr Fortleben in den Sprachen der Welt* vol. 3, Berlin.

Mydland, L. (2011), "The legacy of one-room schoolhouses: A comparative study of the American Mid-West and Norway," *EJAS* 6.1: 1–23.

Naveh, J. (1973), "Some Semitic epigraphical considerations on the antiquity of the Greek alphabet," *AJA* 77: 1–8.

Naveh, J. (1982), *Early History of the Alphabet*, Leiden: Brill.

Naveh, J. (1991), "Semitic Epigraphy and the Antiquity of the Greek Alphabet," *Kadmos* 30: 143–52.

Nederman, C. J. (2008), "Men at Work: Poesis, Politics and Labor in Aristotle and Some Aristotelians," *Analyse&Kritik* 30: 17–31.

Nicholls, R. V. (1958/59), "Old Smyrna," *BSA* 53-4, 35–137.

Nielsen, T. and M. H. Hansen eds. (2004), *An Inventory of Archaic and Classical Poleis*, Oxford: Oxford University Press.

Niemeyr, H. G. (2006), "The Phoenicians in the Mediterranean," in G. Tsetskhladze (ed.), *Greek Colonisation* vol. I, ch. 5.

Ober, J. (1985), *Fortress Attica: Defense of the Athenian Land Frontier, 404–322 BC*, Leiden: Brill.

Occhipinti, E. (2016), *The Hellenica Oxyrhynchia and Hostoriography*, Leiden: Brill.

O'Connor, S. (2011), *Armies, Navies, and Economies in the Greek World in the 5th and 4th Centuries BC*, PhD diss, New York: Columbia University.

Ogden, D. (1994), "Crooked speech: the genesis of the Spartan rhetra," *JHS* 114: 85–102.

O'Neil, J. L. (1995), *The Origins and Development of Ancient Greek Democracy*, Lanham, MD: Rowman and Littlefield.

Ormerod, H. A. (1924), *Piracy in the Ancient World*, Liverpool: University of Liverpool Press.

Osborne, R. (1987), *Classical Landscape with Figures: The Ancient Greek City and its Countryside*, London: George Philip.

Owens, E. J. (1982), "The Enneakrounos Fountain-House," *JHS* 102: 222–5.

Owens, E. J. (1991), *The City in the Greek and Roman World*, London: Routledge.

Padgug, R. A. (1972), "Eleusis and the Union of Attica," *GRBS* 13: 135–50.

Papadopoulos, J. (2016), "The early history of the Greek alphabet: new evidence from Eretria and Methone," *Antiquity* 90: 1–32.

Parker, A. J. (1992), *Ancient Shipwrecks of the Mediterranean*, Oxford: British Archaeological Reports.

Parker, V. (2011), "Ephoros of Kyme (70)" in *Brill's New Jacoby*, Leiden: Brill.

Pébarthe, C. (2006), *Cité, démocratie et écriture: histoire de l'alphabétisation d'Athènes à l'époque Classique*, Paris: de Broccard.

Peck, R. (2001), *Athenian Naval Finance in the Classical Period. The trierarchy, its place in Athenian society, and how much did a trieres cost?* (http://www-atm.physics.ox.ac.uk/rowing/trireme/thesis.html)

Perkams, M. (2019), "The date and place of Andronicus' edition of Aristotle's works according to a neglected Arabic source," *Archiv fur Geschichte der Philosophie* 101.3: 445–68.

Pitt, R. K. (2014/15), "Archaeology in Greece: 2014–2015," in *AR* 61, 50–2.

Pleket, H. W. (1969), "The Archaic Tyrannis," *Talanta* 1, 19–61.

Polanyi, K. (1944), *The Great Transformation*, New York: Farrar & Rinehart.

Polanyi, K. ed. (1957), *Trade and Markets in the Early Empires: Economies in History and Theory*, Glencoe, IL: Falcon's Wing Press.

Popper, K. (1945), *The Open Society and Its Enemies*, London: Routledge.
Powell, B. (1991), *Homer and the Origin of the Greek Alphabet*, Cambridge: Cambridge University Press.
Powell, B. (2003), *Writing and the Origins of Greek Literature*, Cambridge: Cambridge University Press.
Pownall, F. (2016), "Hellanikos of Lesbos (323a)," in *Brill's New Jacoby*, Leiden: Brill.
Pritchett, W. K. (1975), *The Greek State at War* vol. II, Berkeley, CA: University California Press.
Pritchett, W. K. (1985), *The Greek State at War* vol. IV, Berkeley, CA: University of California Press.
Pritchett, W. K. (1991), "Stone throwers and slingers in ancient Greek warfare," in *The Greek State at War* vol. V, Berkeley, CA: University of California Press, 1–67.
Pritchett, W. K and A. Pippin (1953), "The Attic Stelai, part I," *Hesperia* 22: 225–99.
Pritchett, W. K. and A. Pippin (1956), "The Attic Stelai, part II," *Hesperia* 25: 260–75.
Quass, F. (1979), "Zur Verfassung der griechischen staedte im Hellenismus," *Chiron* 9: 37–52.
Qviller, B. (1981), "The dynamics of Homeric society," *Symbolae Osloenses* 56: 109–55.
Quinn, J. C. (2007), "Herms, Kouroi, and the Political Anatomy of Athens," *G&R* 54: 82–105.
Raaflaub, K. (1991), "Homer und die Geschichte des 8. Jh. v. Chr.," in J. Latacz (ed.), *200 Jahre moderne Homerforschung: Rückblick und Ausblick*, Stuttgart: Coll. Rauricum 2, 205–56.
Raaflaub, K. (1993), "Homer to Solon: The Rise of the Polis (The Written Sources)," in M. H. Hansen (ed.), *The Ancient Greek City-State*, Copenhagen: Royal Danish Academy, 41–105.
Rackham, O. (1983), "Observations on the historical ecology of Boiotia," *ABSA* 78: 291–351
Rackham, O. (1990), "Ancient Landscapes," in O. Murray and S. Price (eds.), *The Greek City from Homer to Alexander*, Oxford: Clarendon Press, 85–111.
Rankov, N. B., J. F. Coates, and J. S. Morrison (2000), *The Athenian Trireme: The History and Reconstruction of an Ancient Greek Warship*, Cambridge: Cambridge University Press.
Renfrew, C. and J. Cherry eds. (1986), *Peer Polity Interaction and Socio-Political Change*, Cambridge: Cambridge University Press.
Rhodes, P. J. (1972), *The Athenian Boule*, Oxford: Clarendon Press.
Rhodes, P. J. ed. (2004), *Athenian Democracy*, Edinburgh: Edinburgh University Press.
Rhodes, P. J. and R. Osborne eds. (2007), *Greek Historical Inscriptions, 478–404 BC*, Oxford: Oxford University Press.
Rich, J. and G. Shipley eds. (1993), *War and Society in the Greek World*, London: Routledge.
Ridgway, B. S. (1971), "The setting of Greek sculpture," *Hesperia* 40: 340–1
Ridgway, D. (1992), *The First Western Greeks*, Cambridge: Cambridge University Press.

Rihll, T. (1993), "War slavery and settlement in early Greece," in J. Rich and G. Shipley (eds.), *War and Society in the Greek World*, London: Routledge 77–107.

Rihll, T. and A. Wilson (1991), "Modelling settlement structures in ancient Greece: new approaches to the *polis*," in J. Rich and A. Wallace-Hadrill (eds.), *City and Country in the Ancient World*, London: Routledge, 59–96.

Roberts, J. W. (1998), *City of Sokrates: An Introduction to Classical Athens* (2nd ed.), London: Routledge.

Robinson, E. W. (2003), *Ancient Greek Democracy: Readings and Sources*, London: Wiley & Sons.

Robinson, E. W. (2011), *Democracy Beyond Athens: Popular Government in the Greek Classical Age*, Cambridge: Cambridge University Press.

Rothenberg, G. (1986), "Maurice of Nassau, Gustavus Adolphus, Raimondo Montecuccoli, and the 'Military Revolution' of the 17th century," in P. Paret (ed.), *Makers of Modern Strategy, from Machiavelli to the Nuclear Age*, Princeton, NJ: Princeton University Press, 32–63.

Roussel, D. (1976), *Tribu et cite*, Paris: Les Belles Lettres.

Ruck, C. (1975), "Euripides' mother: vegetables and the phallos in Aristophanes," *Arion* 2.1: 13–57

Ruijgh, C. J. (1995), "D'Homère aux origines proto-mycéniennes de la tradition épique: analyse dialectologique du langage homérique, avec un 'excursus' sur la création de l'alphabet grec," in J. P Crielaard (ed.), *Homeric Questions: Essays in Philology, Ancient History and Grchaeology*, Amsterdam: J. P Gieben.

Ruijgh, C. J. (1997), "La date de la creation de l'alphabet grec et celle de l'epopee homerique," *Bibliotheca Orientalis* 54: cols. 533–603.

Ruijgh, C. J. (1998), "Sur la date de la creation de l'alphabet grec," *Mnemosyne* 51: 658–87.

Runnels, C. and Tj. van Andel (1987), *Beyond the Acropolis: A Rural Greek Past*, Stanford, CA: Stanford University Press.

Ruschenbusch, E. (1978), *Untersuchungen zu Staat und Politik in Griechenland vom 7.–5. Jh. v. Chr.*, Bamberg.

Ruschenbusch, E. (1979), "Zur Besatzung athenischer Trieren," *Historia* 28: 106–10.

Ruschenbusch, E. (1984), "Die Bevölkerungszahl Griechenlands im 5. und 4. Jh. v. Chr.," *ZPE* 56: 55–7.

Ruschenbusch, E. (1986), "Zur Wirtschafts- und Sozialstruktur der Normalpolis," *ASNSP* 3rd ser. 13: 171–94.

Sallares, R. (1991), *The Ecology of the Ancient Greek World*, Ithaca, NY: Cornell University Press.

Said, S. (1996), "*The Assemblywomen:* Women, Economy, and Politics," in E. Segal (ed.), *Oxford Readings in Aristophanes*, Oxford: Oxford University Press, 282–313.

Salmon, J. B. (1984), *Wealthy Corinth: A History of the City to 338 BC*, Oxford: Clarendon Press.

Salmon, T. (1995), *The Unwritten Places*, Athens: Lykabettos Press.

Scheidel, W. (2003), "The Greek demographic expansion: models and comparisons," *JHS* 123: 120–40.
Scheidel, W. (2013), "Population and Demography," in A. Erskine (ed.), *A Companion to Ancient History*, Oxford: Wiley Blackwell, 134–45.
Schilardi, D. U. (1983), "The Decline of the Geometric settlement of Koukounaries on Paros," in R. Haegg (ed.), *The Greek Renaissance of the Eighth Century BC*, Stockholm.
Schmitter, P. (1975), "Compulsory schooling at Athens and Rome?" *AJP* 96: 276–89.
Scholten, J. (2000), *The Politics of Plunder: The Aitolians and their Koinon*, Berkeley, CA: University of California Press.
Scott, M. (2014), *Delphi: A History of the Center of the Ancient World*, Princeton NJ: Princeton University Press.
Scully, S. (1990), *Homer and the Sacred City*, Ithaca NY: Cornell University Press.
Sealey, R. (1976), *A History of the Greek City-States 700–338 BC*, Berkeley, CA: University of California Press.
Sealey, R. (1983), "How citizenship and the city began in Athens," *AJAH* 8, 97–129.
Seaford, R. (2004), *Money and the Early Greek Mind: Homer, Philosophy, Tragedy*, Cambridge: Cambridge University Press.
Segal, E. ed. (1996), *Oxford Readings in Aristophanes*, Oxford: Oxford University Press.
Shapiro, H. A. (1995), *Art and Cult under the Tyrants in Athens*, Mainz: Zabern.
Sickinger, J. P. (1999), "Literacy, Documents, and Archives in the Ancient Athenian Democracy," *American Archivist* 62: 229–46.
Sickinger, J. P (2009), "Nothing to do with democracy: 'formulae of disclosure' and the Athenian epigraphical habit," in L. Mitchell and L. Rubinstein (eds.), *Greek History and Epigraphy. Essays in Honour of P. J. Rhodes*, Swansea: Classical Press of Wales, 87–102.
Sickinger, J. P. (2017), "New *ostraka* from the Athenian *agora*," *Hesperia* 86.3: 443–508.
Sider, D. (2010), "Greek verse on a vase by Douris," *Hesperia* 79, 541–54.
Simonton, M. (2017), *Classical Greek Oligarchy: A Political History*, Princeton, NJ: Princeton University Press.
Simpson, P. (1998), *A Philosophical Commentary on the Politics of Aristotle*, Chapel Hill: University of North Carolina Press.
Skeat, T. C. (1982), "The length of the standard papyrus roll and the cost advantage of the codex," *ZPE* 45: 169–76.
Snodgrass, A. (1965), "The Hoplite Reform and History," *JHS* 85: 110–22.
Snodgrass, A. (1977), *Archaeology and the Rise of the Greek State*, Cambridge: Cambridge University Press.
Snodgrass, A. (1980), *Archaic Greece: The Age of Experiment*, Berkeley, CA: University of California Press.
Snodgrass, A. (1982), "Central Greece and Thessaly," in *CAH* III.1 (2nd ed.), Cambridge: Cambridge University Press, 657–95.
Snodgrass, A. (1987), *An Archaeology of Greece: The Present State and Future Scope of a Discipline*, Berkeley, CA: University of California Press.

Snodgrass, A. (1991), "Archaeology and the study of the Greek city," in J. Rich and A. Wallace-Hadrill (eds.), *City and Country in the Ancient World*, London: Routledge, 1–24.

Snodgrass, A. (1993), "The rise of the polis: the archaeological evidence," in M. H. Hansen (ed.), *The Ancient Greek City-State: Symposium*, Munksgaard: Commissioner.

Snodgrass, A. (1999), *Arms and Armour of the Greeks* (2nd ed.), Baltimore: Johns Hopkins University Press.

Sprague, R. K. ed. (2001), *The Older Sophists*, Indianapolis: Hackett Publishing.

Stanier, R. S. (1953), "The cost of the Parthenon," *JHS* 73: 68–76.

Stein-Holkeskamp, E. (2009), "The Tyrants," in K. Raaflaub and H. van Wees (eds.), *A Companion to Ancient Greece*, Oxford: Wiley Blackwell, 100–16.

Steiner, D. (1994), *The Tyrant's Writ: Myths and Images of Writing in Ancient Greece*, Princeton, NJ: Princeton University Press.

Stoddart, S. and J. Whitley (1988), "The social context of literacy in archaic Greece and Etruria," *Antiquity* 62: 761–72.

Stroud, R. S. (1968), *Drakon's Law on Homicide*, Berkeley, CA: University of California Press.

Stroud, R. S. (1979), *The Axones and Kyrbeis of Drakon and Solon*, Berkeley, CA: University of California Press.

Surikov, I. E. (2015), *Ostracism in Athens*, Moscow.

Szegedy-Maszak, A. (1978), "Legends of the Greek Lawgivers," *GRBS* 19.3: 199–209.

Tandy, D. W. (1997), *Warriors into Traders: the Power of the Market in Early Greece*, Berkeley, CA: University of California Press.

Thomas, R. (1992), *Oral Tradition and Written Record in Classical Athens*, Cambridge: Cambridge University Press.

Thomas, R. (2019), *Polis Histories, Collective Memory and the Greek World*, Cambridge: Cambridge University Press.

Thompson, F. H. (2003), *The Archaeology of Greek and Roman Slavery*, London: Duckworth.

Tober, D. (2010), "Politeiai and Spartan Local History," *Historia* 59.4: 412–31.

Tod, M. N. (1912), "Review of Ad. Wilhelm *Beitraege zur griechischen Inschriftenkunde*," *CR* 26–7: 14

Tomlinson, R. A. (1972), *Argos and the Argolid*, Ithaca, NY: Cornell University Press.

Tomlinson, R. A. (1976), *Greek Sanctuaries*, New York: St Martin's Press.

Toye, D. (1999), "Aristotle's Other Politeiai: Was the Athenaion Politeia Atypical?" *CJ* 94.3: 235–53

Trever, A. A. (1916), *A History of Greek Economic Thought*, Chicago: University of Chicago Press.

Tropper, J. (2001), "Entstehung und Fruhgeschichte des Alphabets," *Antike Welt* 32: 353–8.

Tsetskhladze, G. R. (2000/1), "Black Sea Piracy," *Talanta* 32–3: 11–26.

Tsetskhladze, G. R. ed. (2006/8), *Greek Colonisation* 2 vols., Leiden: Brill.

Vallet, G. et al. (1976), *Megara Hyblaea 1: le quartier de l'agora archaique*, Rome: Ecole Française de Rome.
van Effenterre, H. (1985), *Le cité grec, des origines à la défaite de Marathon*, Paris: Hachette.
van Wees, H. (1992), *Status Warriors: War, Violence, and Society in Homer and History*, Amsterdam: Gieben.
van Wees, H. (1994), "The Homeric Way of War," *G&R* 41: 1–18 and 131–55.
Vanderpool, E. (1959), "Newsletter from Greece," *AJA* 63: 279–83.
Vanderpool, C. (1980), *Hydra*, Athens: Lycabettus Press.
Verhasselt, G. (2019), "Herclides' Epitome of Aristotle's *Constitutions* and *Barbarian Customs*: Two Neglected Fragments," *CQ* 69: 672–83.
Vidal-Naquet, P. (1986), *The Black Hunter*, Baltimore: Johns Hopkins University Press.
Visser, E. (1997), *Homers Katalog der Schiffe*, Leipzig: Teubner.
Vlachopoulos, A. (2014), "New erotic graffiti from Astypalaia," in online journal *Ancient Origins*.
Waal, W. (2018), "On the 'Phoenician Letters': the case for an early transmission of the Greek alphabet from an archaeological, epigraphic, and linguistic perspective," *Aegean Studies* 1: 83–125.
Walker, H. J. (1995), *Theseus and Athens*, New York: Oxford University Press.
Wallace, R. W. (1989), *The Areopagos Council, to 307 B.C.*, Baltimore: Johns Hopkins University Press.
Weinstein, J. (2009), "The Market in Plato's Republic," *CP* 104.4: 439–58.
Welskopf, E. ed. (1981), *Soziale Typenbegriffe im alten Griechenland und ihr Fortleben in den Sprachen der Welt* vol. 3, Berlin.
West, M. L. (2011), "The Homeric Question Today," *PAPS* 155: 383–93.
West III, W. C. (2015), "Learning the Alphabet: Abecedaria and the Early Schools in Greece," *GRBS* 55: 52–71.
Wheeler, E. (1991), "The general as hoplite," in V. D. Hanson (ed.) *Hoplites: The Classical Greek Battle Experience*, London: Routledge, 121–72.
Whitley, J. (1991), *Style and Society in Dark Age Greece*, Cambridge: Cambridge University Press.
Whitley, J. (1994), "Proto-Attic pottery: a contextual approach," in I. Morris (ed.), *Classical Greece: Ancient Histories and Modern Archaeologies*, Cambridge: Cambridge University Press.
Whitley, J. (1997), "Cretan Laws and Cretan Literacy," *AJA* 101: 635–61.
Wilhelm, Ad. (1909), *Beitraege zur griechischen Inschriftenkunde*, Vienna: Alfred Holder.
Wilkins, J. (2006), "The technology and productivity of ancient sea fishing," in T. Bekker-Nielsen (ed.), *Ancient Fishing and Fish Processing in the Black Sea Region*, Aarhus: Aarhus University Press, 83–96.
Will, E. (1955), *Korinthiaka. Recherches sur L'Histoire et la Civilisation de Corinthe des Origines aux Guerres Médiques*, Paris: E. de Boccard.

Williams, R. T. (1972), *The Silver Coinage of the Phokians*, London: Royal Numismatic Society.
Wilson, J.-P. (1997), "The nature of Greek overseas settlements in the archaic period: *emporion* or *apoikia*?" in L. G. Mitchell and P. J. Rhodes (eds.), *The Development of the Polis in Archaic Greece*, London, Routledge.
Winter, T. N. (1990), "The place of archery in Greek warfare," *The Longbow* 7.3: 12–16.
Wolf, M. (2008), *Proust and the Squid: The Story and Science of the Reading Brain*, New York: Harper Perennial.
Young, R. S. (1940), "Excavation on Mt. Hymettos, 1939," *AJA* 44: 1–9.
Zelnick-Abramovitz, R. (2005), *Not Wholly Free: The Concept of Manumission and the Status of Manumitted Slaves in the Ancient Greek World*, Leiden: Brill.
Zimmerman, J. (2009), *Small Wonder: The Little Red Schoolhouse in History and Memory*, New Haven: Yale University Press.

Index

A Mind So Rare (Donald) 179
Abantes of Euboia 21
abecedarium 163
The Acharnians (Aristophanes) 60, 161–2, 181
Achilles 55
Aeinautai (perpetual sailors) 63
Aelian 154
Against Euboulides (Demosthenes) 72
Against Timarchos (Aischines) 149
Agamemnon 20, 22, 34
agora (public meeting/market) 60, 77, 108, 135, 175
agriculture 47–65, 68–9, 72–3, 77, 95, 208n.4, 209n.11, 210n.30, 211–2nn.39, 56
Aigina/Aiginetans 35–6, 66–8, 104, 213nn.70–2
Aiginetika 66
Aineias Taktikos 80
Aischines 148–51, 230n.27
Aitolia/Aitolians 15–16, 49, 152
Ajax 41
Akademia gymnasium, Athens 151
Akarnania/Akarnanians 15–16, 49
Akraiphia 32
Al Mina, Syria 144
Alkaios 2, 95, 193–4n.7
Alkibiades 159
Amphiktyonic League 31
Amyklai 37–8
Anabasis (Xenophon) 16
Anaxagoras of Klazomenai 167
Ancient Literacy (Harris) 172
Anderson, G. 20
andrapoda see slavery
Andrewes, Anthony 82, 100
Andromadas of Rhegion 130
Androtion 150
Anemoreia 30
Animal Farm (Orwell) 160
animal husbandry 51–2, 55–7

Antigone (Sophokles) 131
Antikyra 30
Antiphon 124
apoikiai (new settlements) 27–9, 62–4
Apollo 29, 79, 152
Apollonios (mythographer) 152
apologia 181
Apology of Sokrates (Plato) 167
"Archaeology" (Thucydides) 15
Archaic Age
 abandoned settlements 25
 and Argos 33
 blood feuds/guest-friendships 56
 communities not highly centralized 97
 description 18, 21
 populations during 53–4, 57
 and state development 45
 use of short swords 96
 and western *apoikiai* 28–9
Archilochos 101, 221n.59
archontes (magistrate) 41
Areopagos Council, Athens 109–10
arete (excellence/virtue) 119, 126, 160
Argolid 31–7, 52
Argos/Argives
 Aiginetan links with 67–8
 assembly of 115–16
 battle of Hysiai 100
 development of 45–6, 204n.76
 early Iron Age 25–6
 and hoplite phalanxes 94, 98
 and population movements 57
 prominence of 33–7
 size compared to Athens 43
Aristoboulos of Thessalonika 134
Aristophanes
 and the act of writing 161–3
 dialogues of 80
 and Dikaiopolis (*The Acharnians*) 60, 181
 and Philokleon (*The Wasps*) 70–2

schools and schooling 146–51, 229n.21
skills of 182
and *The Ekklesiazousai* 124, 225n.40
Aristotle
class structure 75, 79–80
democracy 122
homo politicus 141
introduction 3–4, 6, 8–10, 12, 197n.37
narrative identity 181
and origins of the *polis* 17–19, 23, 25, 199nn.10, 13
and ostracisms 165
and Plato's political theory 125–6
Politeiai 185–9
political theory of 126–8
research project 116–17
on warfare 81, 217n.1
Arms and Armour of the Greeks (Snodgrass) 96
Artaxerxes II, king 175
Artemision 171
Aspis (Argive shields) 87, 96–8
Assyrians 176
astu 2, 48
Astypalaia 153–4, 156–9, 172
Athena 25
Athenaion Politeia (Aristotle) 110, 117
Athenodoros 134
Athens
and agriculture 60–1
and Aiginetans 67–8
Areopagos Council 109–11
and Attica 36
and Boiotia 32–3
comedy in 161
commemoration of war dead 169
constitution of 121, 125
Council of the 500 110, 223n.9
deme system 39–46
democracy in 117–18, 121, 224n.31
display of *axones* 130
economic development in 47
education/literacy 146–51, 153–4, 159, 162–6, 172, 233n.71, 234n.76
and the *ekklesia* 113–16, 233nn.17–20
governing system of 104–5
introduction 1, 4, 6, 8–10
laws, decision making in 131, 136–7

major city-state 25–6, 28, 30, 202n.44
and marriage 148
and men of "hoplite status" 95, 220n.45
a model to Greek cities 80, 112
pay of the poor 71, 214nn.81–3
pay of rowers 70
and population movements 57
public opinion in 102
regime of the "Five Thousand" 101
travel 173, 235nn.89–90
and the trireme 103–5, 221–2n.71
Attica
and agriculture 60–1
Athenian evacuation of 150
and the Athenians 32, 39–44, 46, 193n.1, 206n.109
city state development 26
honey of 52
introduction 1
medimnos 73
Persian occupation of 153
public notices in 171
and trade 66
autarkeia (self-sufficiency) 49, 136, 160, 208n.6
axones 130

barbaroi (foreigners) 6
barley 51, 72–3
basileis (aristocrats) 58, 101–1, 108–9, 111
beekeeping 51–2
"bell" cuirasses 96, 220n.46
Beyond Good and Evil (Nietzsche) 125
Blegen, Carl 166
Boardman, J. 42, 206–7n.113
Boiotia/Boiotians 31–7, 43–6, 115–16, 152–3, 155, 157, 224n.23
Boiotian shield 31
Boiotoi 16, 20–2, 30
Boulagoras 134
boule (council) 108, 111
Bronze Age 33, 39–41, 53, 145, 176
burials 54, 210–11n.26
Byzantion 65

Caesar, Julius 85–6
Campbell, J. K. 56

"Catalogue of Ships" (Homer) 19–23, 29–32, 34, 37, 41–4, 152, 200n.29, 201n.32, 206n.110
cattle 51, 55
Cavafy of Alexandria 176
centrifugal polis model 31–7
centripetal polis model (1) 37–9
centripetal polis model (2) 39–45
Chalkedon 65
Chalkidians of Euboia 95
chariots 85–6
Charondas of Katane 28, 129–30, 154
"Chigi vase" 99–100
Chios 104, 156, 159
chora 5, 47
chorta (wild greens) 73
Christianity 1
Cicero 119
Classical period 53
classification of constitutions 127
The Clouds (Aristophanes) 146–8, 182
collective decision making
    conclusions 136–7
    introduction 107–8, 222n.1
    political theory 116–28
    public information 128–36, 226–7nn.65, 67
    varieties of 108–16, 222n.15
Constitution of the Athenians (Xenophon) 77
control marks 144, 228n.4
Corinth Canal 52
Corinth/Corinthians
    assembly of 115–16
    battle of Salamis 168
    and centrifugal polis model 32, 35–6
    economic development in 47
    helmets of 88, 96–7
    and Megara 44
    settlements of 63
"cortical efficiency" 180
Crimea 63
Croesus, Lydian king 175
curse tablets 162–3
Cyclades 27–8, 153
Cyprus 26
Cyrus 175
Cyrus the Younger 175

Darius, king of Persia 118, 130
"Dark Age" 11, 25, 40, 43
De Bello Gallico (Caesar) 85–6
Delian League 67–8, 104, 134
Delphi 21, 29–31, 40
Delphic Oracle 40
deme system 39–45
Demetrios II, king 134
democratic Council of the 500 109
demography 53–4, 63, 209–10n.24
Demonax of Mantinea 130
demos (common people) 105, 123
Demosthenes 30, 72, 75–6, 152, 214n.88
Dijksterhuis, Eduard Jan 125
Dikaiopolis 60, 161, 163, 180–1
dike (justice) 126
Diodoros 154, 165, 231n.40
Diogenes Laertios 8
Diomedes 55, 84
Dionysiaca (Nonnius) 152
Dionysos 79–80
Dodecanese *see* Cyclades
Donald, Merlin 173, 179
doron (gift) 101
Doulichion 23
Douris (artist) 151
drachma 70–6, 104, 157–9, 167
Drakon's laws 130
Dreros, Krete 129
Dymaines tribe 44

education *see* literacy
Egypt 176, 181
Ehrenberg, Victor 11, 197n.40
eisphora (occasional property tax) 75
Ekklesiazousai (Aristophanes) 124, 225n.40
Elateia 30
Elba 65
Eleusinian Mysteries 41–2
Eleusis/Eleusinians 26, 40, 42, 44–5, 71, 206n.107
Elis 50, 115–16
emporia/emporion (trading settlement) 64
Emporiai, Spain 64
Engels, Donald 47
Enneakrounos (nine source) fountain 80
Epaminondas 90
Epeioi 20, 21, 200n.21

Ephesos 134
Ephialtes 10, 111
Ephoros 35, 67, 154
Epidauros 36
epigrams 168
epitaphs 169
Eratosthenes 148
Erechtheion, Athens 71, 214n.84
Eretria 44
eris (strife) 160
Etesian wind see *meltemi*
ethne 9, 16–19, 21–5, 27, 29, 101
ethnos 7, 16, 30–1, 33, 36–7, 43, 45–6, 195n.23
ethnos model 29–31
Etruria/Etruscans 65–6
Euboia 26, 64–5
Euboian Channel 43–4
Eumaios 55
Eupalinos tunnel 80
Euripides 71, 132, 161–2
Eurotas valley 37–8
Euxitheos 72

farming *see* agriculture
Figueira, T. J. 67
Finley, Moses 19, 69, 86–7, 102
First Sacred War (590) 30, 46
fish 52, 63, 68, 74, 77–8, 157
food 72–4, 215n.92
France 81
French Revolution 81
Frogs (Aristophanes) 72

galleys 98, 103
Genealogy of Morals (Nietzsche) 122
Geometric Age *see* Iron Age
Gerousia (council) 109–10
Gigon, Olof 8, 196n.34
Giovannini, Adalberto 20, 23, 31
Glaukos 84
goats 12, 51, 55–6, 162
graffiti 163, 233n.65
grapho 161
gravestones 169
Graviscae 66
Greek alphabet 141–6, 227–9nn.9–11, 17, 229n.18

The Greek Tyrants (Andrewes) 100
Gustavus Adolphus of Sweden 99

Hagnous 41
Hammurabi's "code" 130
Hansen, Mogens H. 1, 7, 193n.2, 196n.30
Harris, W. V. 147–8, 153, 166, 172, 229n.23, 230nn.34–5, 231n.37–8, 234n.77
Hasebroek, J. 69
Hekataios of Miletos 18
Helen 37
Hellanikos of Lesbos 18, 150
Hellenika Oxyrhynchia (Thucydides) 16, 115, 155
the Hellenika (Xenophon) 149
Helos plain 38
Helots 38
Heraion 33, 35
Herakleia Pontika 31, 204n.71
Herakleides of Salamis 133
Herakleides/Heraklidai 8, 34
Herakles 42, 207n.117
Heraklides Pontikos 154, 231n.41
Herodotos
    and the Argive *aspis* 99
    Battle of Plataia 155
    "bronze men" 94
    Chios disaster (496) 153–4
    classification of constitutions 127
    and democracy 107, 118–19
    and *ethne* 16
    extension of Argive influence 36
    and Greek alphabet 141
    naval fighting 104
    Persian and Greek encounters 175
    reading/writing 171–2
    skills development 182
    and Tellos of Athens 40
    Thebes and Plataia 32
    towns destroyed by Persians 30
    and trade 61, 66–7
Hesiod 11–12, 19, 57–9, 97, 101, 160
hetairoi (companions) 82–3, 85, 93
Hippias of Elis 18
Hippokrates 50, 208–9n.9
Histiaia on Euboia 134
Histories (Herodotos) 171

Homer
    and agriculture 55, 57–8
    and Athens 41
    and Attica 43–4
    city-state development 19–25, 34–7
    and education 152, 160
    and ethnos model 29–32
    and Greek language 142–3
    Hymn to Demeter 40
    and piracy 52
    and "ritual meals" 56
    rule of aristocratic leaders 108–9
    and warfare 82–7, 91–4, 102
homo lector 141
Honor, Family and Patronage (Campbell) 56
hoplite panoply 95–6
hoplites
    census 115
    class description 78–9
    democracy comparison 121–2
    description 75–6, 215nn.98–9
    warfare 82–4, 87–93, 109, 178, 217n.12, 218n.22, 219nn.28, 37
hoplon (shield) 96
horses 86, 218n.16
"hortatory formula" 135
Hylleis tribe 44
Hymettos graffiti 166
Hymn to Demeter (Homer) 40
Hyrie 32

Iliad (Homer) 19–21, 24, 57–8, 82–4, 91, 94
inventory marks *see* control marks
Ionia 2, 44, 94, 172, 193n.5
Ionian Revolt (490s) 104
Iraq *see* Mesopotamia
Iron Age
    and Argos 33
    and the Boiotians 31
    communities not highly centralized 97
    control of territory 26
    early communities 15–26, 198n.2, 202nn.45–6
    and *ethnos* 45
    introduction 15
    population during 53, 57
    settlements evidence 55–6

Ischia 64–5, 212–13n.65
Ithaka 23, 201nn.35, 39

Jeffery, L. H. 143

kaloi k'agathoi (aristocrats) 101
Kardia 28
Kephallenes 22–3
Kerameikos cemetery 164
Khalkidian apoikia 27–8
Kirk, G. S. 20
Kirrha *see* Krisa
Kleisthenes of Sikyon 10, 36, 42, 113, 165–6
Kleisthenic Athens 42
Kleokritos 149
Kleomedes (boxer) 153
Kleonai 36
Kodros sanctuary, Athens 132
koine 1, 5, 193n.1
Koiratadas of Thebes 16
Kolophon 62
kome (village) 17
Koukounaries 25
kouros Anavyssos statue 168–9
Krete 26, 154
Krisa 29–30, 46, 203nn.61, 63
Krisaian plain 30–1
Kroisos, king 40
Kronos 84
Kunaxa, Battle of 175
Kynosoura 37
Kyparissos 29–30
Kypselid tyranny 36
Kyrene 62
Kyzikos 61

"Labors of Herakles" 42
Lakedaimon/Lakedaimonians 18, 22, 32, 36–9, 56, 201n.31
Lambert, Stephen 134
Langdon, Merle K. 162, 166, 233nn.58–9
Latacz, Joachim 82
Laureion, southern Attica 104
"law code of Hammurabi" 130
laws 129–32
Laws (Plato) 61, 172
Lefkandi/Xeropolis settlement 25
legomenon (ignorance) 172

Lex Hafniensis de civitate 7
liberalism 81
Life of Alkibiades (Plutarch) 151
Life of Aristides (Plutarch) 164
Life of Themistokles (Plutarch) 150
Limnai 37
literacy
   citizen-warriors 175–82
   and the city-state 141–4, 227n.3, 229n.20, 230n.28, 231–2nn.47, 52–3, 55
   conclusions 173–4
   evidence 161–73, 233n.69
   spread of 146–60
Lokrian Aias 83
Lokris/Lokrians 27, 49, 84
Lord, A. B. 19, 199n.18
Lorimer, H. L. 82
"Lot of Temenos" 34–35, 204–5nn.77, 81
Lydia/Lydians 40, 176
Lysias 148, 181

McAdams, Dan 180–1
Macedonia 50, 81
machaira (short-sword) 96
Macmillan *aryballos* 100
Marathon 26, 40, 66–7, 169–70
marriage 56, 58, 148
Massilia 68
Maurice of Nassau 99
The Mechanization of the World Picture (Dijksterhuis) 125
Medes 176
"Mediterranean triad" 72
Megara/Megarians 41, 44–5, 56
Megarid 42–4, 207n.121
Meier, Christian 116
Meliac War 26
Melie 26
meltemi 53
Memorabilia (Xenophon) 72
Menelaos 20, 22, 37
Menestheus son of Peteos 42
mentalite 178
mercenary soldiers 157–8
Mesoa 37
mesoi (middlemen) 79
Mesopotamia 130, 175

Messenia/Messenians 36, 39, 45, 50, 65, 209n.10
metal goods 94–5
metoikoi (registered aliens) 6, 78–9
metretes 73
Metroon, the 135
migration 52, 54, 61–2, 66, 79, 98, 177
Milesian settlers 28
Miletos 62–3, 66, 104, 157–8, 212n.58
Mills, S. 42
Mitylene, Lesbos 154
Mnesilochos 161, 163, 232–3n.57
monarchy 107–8, 127, 226n.43
mousike 147, 151, 229n.22
Mycenai 20, 25, 33–4, 200n.23
Mykalessos 152–8, 230n.34
Myous 26

narrative identity 180–2
nationalism 81
Naukratis, Egypt 64, 66
Nauplion 33
Nautilus (online blog) 180–1
Nemea 36
Nicomachean Ethics (Aristotle) 126, 225–6n.42
Nietzsche, Friedrich 122, 125
Nikagoras 150
Nikias 78
Nisaia harbor 44–5
nomoi (laws) 131
nomothetes (lawgiver) 130, 148–9
Nonnius 152
"Normalpolis" 7

Odysseus 22, 55, 102
Odyssey (Homer) 23, 102
oikistes (founder) 27–8, 98
oikoi 55, 100, 102, 108
Oikonomika (Xenophon) 12, 71
oikos (family) 108
"The Old Oligarch" *see* Ps-Xenophon
oligarchy 4, 81, 107–8, 110, 116, 119–20, 123, 127
Olympia 35, 170
Olympic games 100
The Open Society (Popper) 125
Orchomenos 31–3, 45–6
Oropos 44

Orwell, George 160
ostracism 163, 165-6
ostraka 164-5
othismos (pushing/shoving) 89-91
overseas settlements 26-9
oxen 55, 84-5, 94
Ozolian Lokrians 15-16

Paian (hymn) 89
Pallene 41
Pamphylloi tribe 44
Panathenaic Games 41-2, 61
Pandora myth 11-12
Parnes mountain 43
Paros 62, 68
pastoralism *see* animal husbandry
Patroklos 55, 83
Pausanias 30, 153, 170
"peer polity interaction" 177
Peiraieus 67
Peisistratid Athens 41-2, 80
Peisistratid tyranny 118, 224n.30
Peisistratos 44-5
Peloponnesian League 33
Peloponnesian War 32, 72
Peloponnesos 34-7, 39, 44-6, 50, 52, 153
Peneios river 50
pentekonters (fifty-oared vessels) 98
Perikles 10, 109, 131, 148
perioikic system 37-9
Perioikoi 38-9
Persia/Persians 104, 118, 153, 155, 169, 171, 175-6
petala (olive leaves) 165
petalismos 165
Peteon 32
phalanges (lines) 82-3
phalanxes 11-12, 88-92, 98-102, 106-7, 137
"Phaleron" cups 166
Pheidon of Argos 35-6, 100
Philippika (Theopompos of Chios) 150-1
Philokleon 71-2
Philolaos of Corinth 130
Phoenicians 52, 65, 141-5, 228n.15
Phokaia 64
Phokis/Phokians 16, 21, 29-31, 31, 45-6
phratry 135

Pindar 12
piracy 15, 52
Pitana 37
Pithekoussai 64-5
Pittakos of Mitylene 130-1
Plataia 45-6, 155
Plataia, battle of (479) 36, 231n.43
Plataians/Plataia 31-3
Plato
    and economic specialization 48-9, 61, 76, 78, 80
    education 149-51, 167, 172, 234nn.78-80
    introduction 3
    law and justice 132, 148
    political equality for all 124-5
    and *Protagoras* 115, 118
    and social status 122-3, 147-8, 230n.26
Pliny the Elder 152
Plutarch 41, 79, 150-1, 153, 159, 164, 230-1n.36
Pnyx hill 161
polis
    centrifugal model 31-7
    description 1-4, 116, 194nn.8-10
    development of 26-7, 30, 202n.49
    economic development in 48
    formation of 17-20, 23-4, 199-200nn.12, 18, 20
    inconsistent with monarchy 127
    and the laws 132
    nature of 4-13, 194-5nn.17-18, 196n.30, 197-8nn.35-6
    "reciprocal equality" 126
    and Tanagra village 152
    and trade 64
Politeia see Republic (Plato)
politeia (governing system) 104-5, 117, 127-8
Politeiai (Aristotle) 185-9
Politika (Aristotle) 4, 8, 10, 12, 17, 25, 75, 81, 117-19, 122, 125-7
politike arete 120
politike techne 119-20
politikon zoon 126
Polybios 119
Polykrates of Samos 104
Popper, Karl 125

"Pre-Socratics" 117
probouleumata (proposals) 111
Protagoras 117–21, 124, 127, 154, 167
Protagoras (Plato) 115, 132, 148
prytaneia (town hall) 41
Ps-Xenophon *Constitution of the Athenians* 80, 105–6, 118, 121–2, 127, 222n.72, 224n.29
public notices 139
public opinion 102
Pythian festival, Delphi 40
Pytho 29

Republic (Plato) 3–4, 10, 48, 123–5
Rhegion 65
Ridgway, Brunilde 170
"ritual meals" (Homer) 56
Rome 82, 177
rowers 13, 70–1, 82, 103–4, 106, 114, 171–2, 178, 217n.6
Ruschenbusch, E. 7, 195n.27

Saite dynasty 94
Salamis 44–5
Salamis, battle of 67, 104, 168
Samos 64, 66, 104
Sarakatsan/Sarakatsani 56–7
sarissa (Macedonian pike) 99
Saronic Gulf 43–4
Scheidel, Walter 53
Scheria of the Phaeacians 24
Schoinos 32
schools 11, 146–60
    see also literacy
Scythians 63
sea warfare 103
Sedacca, Matthew 180–1
Shapiro, H. A. 42
sheep 51, 61
Shield of Achilles 24
Sikyon 36
Simonides 168
Siphnos 68
skepticism 167, 171, 177
slavery 11–12, 63, 75, 78–9, 82, 123, 198n.41, 216nn.107, 109
Smith, Adam 80, 94
Snodgrass, Anthony 43, 55, 96
social structure 75–80, 216n.104

socialization process 120
Sokrates 72, 78, 115, 122, 124–5, 147
Solon 3, 40, 84, 130–1
"Sophistic movement" 117
Sophists 118
Sophokles 131
Soros mound 169–70
Sostratos of Aigina 66
Sparta/Spartans
    battle of Hysiai 100
    battle superiority of 90
    and Boiotia 33
    citizen rights in 137
    and Corinth 35–6
    economic development in 47
    encounter with Cyrus 175
    the *Gerousia* (council) 109–10, 112–13, 116
    gravestone policy of 169
    and hoplite phalanxes 94
    incursions into Athens 60
    and Lakedaimonian city-state 22, 26, 200–1n.30
    major city-state 28, 30, 32, 43, 46
    the perioikic system 37–9, 205n.90
    and traditional *nomoi* 131
    unusual community 78
"Spartan basin" 38
stichas (files) 82–3, 91
Strabo 30, 152
Sumeria/Sumerians 178
sunaspismos (shields together) 88–91
Suppliants (Euripides) 132
swimming 172–3
synedrion (royal councils) 111
synoikeia 37, 39–43
Syracuse/Syracusans 165

Tanagra (village) 152, 155
Tarrha 69, 213n.75
Tegea 94
telamon (neck-strap) 91
Telamonian Aias 83
Tellos of Athens 40
Temenos 34
Teos 157–8
Tettichos 168
Teukros 83
Thasos 68

Theagenes 44, 56
Thebans/Thebes 30–3, 43–4, 46, 155
Themistokles 165, 171–2
Themistokles (Plutarch) 153
Theognis (poet) 3, 44, 56
Theogony (Hesiod) 12, 57
Theophrastos 53
Theopompos of Chios 16, 109, 150–1, 155
theorodokoi (sacred representatives) 21
theoroi (sacred representatives) 40
Thera 62
Thermopylai 150, 152, 171
Thersites 58
Theseus 39–40, 42, 44, 207n.114
Thesmophoriazousai (Aristophanes) 72, 161
Thespiai 31–3, 45–6
Thessaly/Thessalians 22, 30–1, 50
Third Sacred War (347/6) 30
"Thirty Tyrants" 149
thorax 95
Thorikos 26, 40
Thourio/Thourians 154
Thracia/Thracians 63, 152
Thrasymachos of Chalkedon 117, 121, 123–4, 127
Thucydides
　and Athenian obedience to laws 131
　and Attica as city-state of Athenians 39–43
　development of city-state 15–19, 23–5
　and education 152–3, 155–6, 158, 160
　introduction 6
　and Perikles 12
　and regime of "Five Thousand" 101
　and skills development 182
　and Sparta 37
Thyreatis 36, 39
Tiryns 33–4
Tissaphernes 175–6
trade 61–9, 211n.55, 212n.59
transhumant pastoralism 51, 56, 209n.16
trieres see trireme warships
trireme fleets 103–7, 221nn.65–6

"the trireme project" 103
Troizen/Troizenians 150, 153–4, 230–1n.36
Trojan War 82
tropaion (trophy) 90–1
Troy 20, 24–5
tyranneia 107
tyrants 102, 108–9, 222–3nn.5–6

unvoiced syllabary 145

Vlachs 56

Walker, H. J. 42
warfare
　demise of the citizen-militia 81–2
　early Greek 82–7
　hoplite 82–4, 87–93, 217n.12, 218n.22, 219nn.28, 37
　hoplite origins 103–4
　hoplite revolution 93–102, 220nn. 47–8
　part played by the poor 103–6
The Wasps (Aristophanes) 70–2
The Wealth of Nations (Smith) 94
West, William 163
wheat 72–3
"When the Watchman Saw the Light" (Cavafy) 176
whitened boards 135, 139–40, 170–1
Whitley, J. 43
Wilhelm, Adolf 135
Wolf, Maryanne 173, 179–80
women 11–12, 71–2, 74, 82, 124, 198n.41
Works and Days (Hesiod) 12, 97
The World of Odysseus (Finley) 19, 86

Xenophon 12, 16, 48–9, 71–2, 77, 80, 105, 149–51, 182

Young, Rodney 166

Zagora 25
Zaleukos of Lokroi 28, 129–31
Zankle 65
zeugitai (middle property class) 84
Zeus 66, 84, 166